D0936398

To Independence
and
Beyond

With Mum, Dad and brother Ken, *c.* 1948.

TO INDEPENDENCE AND BEYOND

Memoirs of a colonial and Commonwealth civil servant

Peter Snelson

The Radcliffe Press
London · New York

To Nicholas, Andrew and Ann

Published in 1993 by the Radcliffe Press
45 Bloomsbury Square
London WC1A 2HY

An imprint of I.B. Tauris & Co Ltd

In the United States of America
and Canada distributed by
St Martin's Press
175 Fifth Avenue
New York
NY 10010

A CIP record for this book is available from the British Library

Library of Congress Catalog card number is available
A full CIP record is available from the Library of Congress

ISBN 1–85043–572–3

Typeset by Cambridge Composing (UK) Ltd, Cambridge
Printed and bound in Great Britain by
WBC Print Ltd, Bridgend, Mid Glamorgan

Contents

General Foreword to the Series

A. H. M. KIRK-GREENE
Lecturer in the Modern History of Africa, University of Oxford,
and formerly of the Colonial Administrative Service, Nigeria.

A whole generation has passed, nearer two in the case of the Asian sub-continent, since Britain's colonial territories in South-East Asia, Africa and the Caribbean, achieved independence. In the Pacific the transfer of power came about a decade later. There was little interest in recording the official or the personal experience of empire either in the inter-war years – viewed by some, often among those personally involved, as the apogee of the British empire – or in the immediate aftermath of empire. And in this latter period attitudes were critical, largely condemnatory and even purposively hostile. This is not surprising: such a reaction is usual at the end of a remarkable period of history.

With the passing of time and with longer historical perspective it was possible to see events in a better and more objective light and the trend was gradually reversed. In due course there came about a more sympathetic interest in the colonial period, both by those in Britain or in the countries of the former empire who were intrigued to know how colonial government operated – in local, everyday practice, as well as at the policy level of the Colonial Office and Government House. Furthermore, those who had themselves been an integral part of the process wanted to record the experience before, in the nature of things, it was too late. Here was a potentially rich vein of knowledge and personal experience for specialist academic historians as well as the general reader.

Leaving aside the extensive academic analysis of the end of empire, the revival of interest in the colonial period in this country may be said to have been stimulated by creative literature. In the late 1960s there were novels, films, radio and TV programmes now and again tinged with a touch of nineteenth-century romance and with just a whiff of nostalgia to soften the sharp realism of the colonial encounter. The focus was primarily on India and the post-1947 imagery of the 'Raj': there were outstanding novels by Paul Scott — surely destined to be one of the greatest twentieth-century novelists — J. G. Farrell and John Masters; epic films like *A Passage to India*, and *Gandhi*, or the charming and moving vignette of *Staying On*, and, for Africa, *Out of Africa* and *Mister Johnson*.

In the second half of the 1970s there emerged a highly successful genre of collective 'colonial' memoirs in the *Tales of . . .* format: Charles Allen's splendid trilogy *Plain Tales from the Raj* (1975), *Tales from the Dark Continent* (1979) and *Tales from the South China Seas* (1983), followed by others like *Tales of Paradise: Memories of the British in the South Pacific* (1986) and *Tales of Empire: the British in the Middle East* (1989) all good history and good reading.

Throughout the period from India's independence until that of the last crown colony there had, of course, been those splendid works which combined both academic history and creative literature: for example, Philip Woodruff's *The Men Who Ruled India: The Founders* (1953) and *The Guardians* (1954); and Jan Morris's *Heaven's Command*, *Pax Britannica* and *Farewell the Trumpets* (1973–8).

Finally as the 1970s gave way to the 1980s, those voices which had remained largely silent since the end of empire now wanted to be heard. The one-time colonial officials, be they district officers, agriculturists, veterinary, medical or forestry officers, policemen or magistrates, and just as often their wives, began to write about their experiences. They wrote with relish and enthusiasm, with a touch of adventure and few personal regrets. There was a common feeling of a practical and useful task well done, although some thought that more could have been achieved had independence come about more slowly.

These memoirs often began as little more than a private record for the family, children and grandchildren, some of whom had never seen a colonial governor in full fig, shaken hands with an emir or paramount chief, discussed plans with a peasant or local politician, or known at first hand the difference between an *askari* and *alkali*, an *amah* and an *ayah*. By 1990, the colonial memoir had begun to establish itself as a literary genre in its own right.

The initiative of the Radcliffe Press in harnessing and promoting this talent, primarily autobiographical but also biographical, promises to be a positive addition to both the historical and literary scenes. Here is a voice from the last Colonial Service generation, relating from personal experience the lives and careers involved in the exercise of latter-day empire. They were part of what was arguably the most influential and far-reaching international event of the second half of the twentieth century, namely the end of empire and the consequent emergence of the independent nations of the Third World. It could perhaps also be argued that this is part of an even greater process – decolonisation 'writ large', a sea-change in world affairs affecting greater and lesser powers into the late twentieth century.

It may well be that by 2066, the centenary of the closing down of the Colonial Office, great-great-grandchildren will find the most telling image of Britain's third and final empire in these authentic memoirs and biographical studies, rather than in the weightier imperial archives at the Public Record Office at Kew or in Rhodes House Library, Oxford.

Foreword

T he transition from Empire to Commonwealth brought about radical changes in the lives of millions of people. It started in 1947 with the emergence of India and Pakistan as free and independent nation states, and the decisions of their governments to join the Commonwealth of Nations. Their lead was followed by nearly all the British possessions which achieved independence during the next 35 years. In that period, Britain's colonial empire virtually disappeared. In its place developed the modern Commonwealth, an association of independent states, a power for good in a troubled world, although little understood by outsiders.

My career, first as a colonial and then as a Commonwealth civil servant, covered the period 1954–87. Fourteen of those years were spent in Northern Rhodesia/Zambia, ten before independence and four after. For the next 19 years, I worked in the Commonwealth Secretariat which came into being, as the headquarters of the Commonwealth, in 1965. I was thus a member of the last Colonial Service generation and the first Commonwealth generation. Few contemporaries enjoyed a similar dual career. Since the process of decolonization is now over, no-one in future can have a career like mine. This account of my working life will, I hope, have some interest as a grass-roots contribution to the story of the end of Empire and the growth of the Commonwealth.

Both the colonial system and the Commonwealth have come in for a good deal of criticism, much of it due to ignorance or misunderstanding. My story contains no breast-beating, no whitewashing and, I hope, no trumpet-blowing. I have tried to tell it 'as it was', without excuses and without frills. Two impressions, I hope, will come through. First, despite its imperfections, the *Pax Britannica* and the Colonial Service were a form of outreach from Britain that brought benefits in health, education, agriculture and general well-being to millions in Africa and other less well-endowed areas of the world. Second, the Commonwealth, which provides a bridge between the races and religions, the rich and the poor, and which is committed to international co-operation in the pursuit of freedom, peace, justice and sustainable economic growth, deserves the strong support of its member governments and peoples. I feel no blush of shame for having worked both for the Empire and the Commonwealth. Indeed, I am proud to have served both.

I want to record my thanks to the many people with whom I worked in Northern Rhodesia/Zambia and the Commonwealth at large. They include clerks, messengers and drivers as well as permanent secretaries, ministers, vice-chancellors and secretaries-general.

My special thanks, in this and everything else, go to Evelyn, my wife. She encouraged me to write this book and prepared the index. We met and married in Northern Rhodesia where she was first a teacher and then a teacher-trainer. She discontinued her career in order to provide a secure and loving home for the children. This was all the more important because of my frequent and sometimes lengthy absences from home on official duties. She gave up a lot so that I could pursue my career. When I retired it was a joy to be able to work together for two years as mature volunteers with Voluntary Service Overseas. That adventure, though, is another story.

I should also like to thank Dr Lester Crook of The Radcliffe Press for his encouragement and helpful suggestions. Thanks are also gratefully extended to those who helped with the illustrations: R. Krag-Olsen (number 3), Claude Slater (9), University of the South Pacific (18), Jim Houston (19), Commonwealth Secretariat (20, 25), Barbados Government Information Office (21), Kenya Information Service (22), and Rhodesia Information Service (23).

Peter Snelson
Welwyn Garden City
September 1992

1

'Start with Livingstone and Rhodes'

'We come now,' I said, 'to one of the most disastrous events in Britain's imperial history.' Thirty pairs of eyes were raised from the notebooks in which Form 3B were recording the history of India in the nineteenth century, and fixed on me. It was the last period of the day. All the classroom windows and the door were open, but the temperature was well into the upper 80s. Black clouds were piling up over Lusaka and the heavens would soon open. The final of the inter-house football competition might have to be postponed. Phiri, on the front row near the window, was centre-forward for Maybin, and Ngulube, just behind him, was a solid right-half. At the back, under the portrait of the Queen, were Ndhlovu and Mwamba, goal-keeper and left-back for Aggrey. You could hardly wonder if they found the lesson dull. The story of British rule and misrule in India seemed to have little relevance to young Northern Rhodesians in 1954. But this was the history syllabus prescribed for overseas students by the Cambridge Syndicate and 3B knew only too well that they would have to sit the examination within the next year. Discipline, therefore, was no problem in 3B or, indeed, in any of the other classes. Pens poised, they waited to fill the next page of their notebooks.

As succinctly as I could, I explained that Lord Palmerston, Foreign Secretary in Lord Melbourne's Government, feared that Russia would invade India via Afghanistan. Palmerston decided to place Shah Shuja, a friend of Britain, on the Afghan throne, protected by a British Resident and a British army. I could see eyes glazing over and one or two heads beginning to nod. 'Take this

1

down,' I instructed. 'At the end of 1841, the Resident was murdered and the British had to retreat from Kabul to Jallalabad via the Khyber Pass.' I wrote the names on the blackboard. 'In January 1842, they were ambushed by Afghan tribesmen and annihilated. This was the worst defeat ever suffered by a British army in India.' I concluded: 'Of the two thousand troops who entered the Khyber Pass, only one survived.'

There was a half-suppressed cry. Kasonde's hand was waving. 'Excuse me, sir, do you mean one thousand survived?' 'No,' I replied, 'not one thousand; only one man, named Brydon, reached Jallalabad. The rest were all killed by the Afghans or froze to death in the mountains.'

The effect on 3B was electrifying. There was a moment's silence and then pandemonium broke loose. They stamped their feet, they clapped their hands, they shouted with joy that Britain had suffered such a disaster. Some leaped from their seats and embraced their friends with a mixture of astonishment and delight. 'Sit down, Phiri,' I shouted. 'All of you, stop that noise at once.' The bell rang to mark the end of afternoon school. Quickly they gathered up their books. 'Good afternoon, sir,' they called as, still whooping with excitement, they disappeared in the direction of their dormitories.

A little shaken, I started towards the staff room. On the way, the principal stopped me. 'Was it your class making that hullabaloo?' he demanded. I briefly explained what had happened. 'Their behaviour, of course, was quite inexcusable,' he said, 'and I shall gate them next weekend. But, you know,' he continued, 'you can't really blame them, can you?' At that moment, lightning forked the leaden sky; thunder crashed about our ears. You could first hear and then smell the oncoming rain. There would be no football match. 'Come and have some tea.' As the first drops fell, we ran to the principal's bungalow which stood just inside the school boundary. From his study window, he could keep an eye on the comings and goings through the main gate. Not much went on at Munali Secondary School that Clifford Little did not know about.

As a principal, Clifford was both knowledgeable and wise. He had first come to Northern Rhodesia before the 1939–45 war as a young education officer not long down from Oxford. He was

2

appointed Principal of Munali in 1947 and was to hold the post until 1955 when he was promoted to the top job of Director of African Education. He ran Munali on the lines of a British public school: academic standards were high; the house system flourished; service to others was encouraged; discipline was strict; a muscular form of Christianity prevailed. Clifford would cheerfully cane offenders and then pray for the miscreants. He was held in high esteem by the boys. They knew him as 'he who never sleeps' because of his habit of walking his dog around the dormitory area late at night and again at first light. He knew each boy by name, knew how to make them work and how to make them laugh. A bachelor, he gave all his time and energy to the school.

In his study, where books on all manner of subjects overflowed the bookcases and lay in heaps on the floor, he poured some tea and offered me a biscuit. 'I'm not trying to tell you your job,' he said gently, 'but you mustn't be surprised if 3B draw parallels between what happened in Afghanistan a hundred years ago and what is happening in Northern Rhodesia at present. You know, the British really had no right to be in Afghanistan in the 1840s. Those chaps in 3B would say that the British have no right to be here in NR in the 1950s. Oh, yes, some of Rhodes' agents signed treaties with Lewanika and other chiefs, gave them guns, money and liquor in exchange for mineral rights and so on. But you can't be surprised if these lads want us out of the country, that they want independence and an African government. Don't take it personally. They probably quite like and respect you as a person. But they also see you as a representative of an occupying power which denies them what they consider to be their rights and treats them as seond or third class citizens in their own country.'

He poured some more tea. 'I think we're going to see important changes here in the next decade or so. I only hope that they come about peacefully and without bloodshed. You'll know of the independence movement in the Gold Coast and of the Mau Mau emergency in Kenya. The experts would have us believe that it's only a small minority of hotheads who support Nkrumah and Kenyatta, but I think you'll find that they've got a lot of popular backing.'

'But there's no sign of anything like that happening here,' I said.

3

'Not on the surface,' Clifford agreed, 'but there's much more going on than meets the eye. Have a chat with some of the African members of staff; perhaps they'll brief you on the political scene.' He consulted a notebook. 'Let me see,' he said, 'I haven't seen any of 3B's written work recently. I'd like to have a dozen of their history essay books on my desk tomorrow morning, please.' The meeting was over.

There were 30 or so of us on the Munali staff, giving a generous staffing ratio for the 400 boys in the school. Most of us were from Britain, there being very few African graduates in the country. Wesley Matsie was headmaster and worked very closely with Clifford Little in running the school. Next to him in seniority were John Mwanakatwe, the first African from Northern Rhodesia to obtain a university degree, and Joseph Mwemba. Both were friendly and helped me, a newcomer, to settle in, but they would say little about African hopes for political advancement. They made no secret, however, that they strongly resented the imposition, as they saw it, of the Central African Federation which had come into operation in October 1953, despite the bitter opposition of African political opinion. The federation, bringing together Northern Rhodesia, Southern Rhodesia and Nyasaland, was intended to strengthen the three territories and to create a viable economic entity which, in course of time, would be given its independence by Britain. In common with nearly all Africans, John and Joe were totally opposed to the federation; they were sure it would entrench the power of the European settlers, particularly those in Southern Rhodesia, and would wreck any chance there might have been for Northern Rhodesia to achieve its own independence under black majority rule.

As they gave me their views in the staff room, none of us could guess that within ten years the federation would have been dismantled, Zambia would be an independent republic, John Mwanakatwe would be Minister of Education in President Kaunda's government and Joe Mwemba would be Zambia's permanent representative at the United Nations. Clifford Little lived to see that day, although he did not, alas, survive for long after independence. Even he was surprised at the speed at which the changes he accurately predicted actually took place. As a civil servant, I was under orders not to get involved in politics. Nevertheless, the rapidly changing political scene was going to impinge increasingly on my life and work for the next 14 years. The incident with 3B was but a gentle foretaste of exciting things to come.

I had arrived in Northern Rhodesia in January 1954. When the Colonial Office informed me of my posting to Munali Secondary School as a teacher of history and English, I was naive enough to assume that I would be required to teach, among other things, the history of Northern Rhodesia. How to prepare myself? The Colonial Office were vague: 'Start with Livingstone and Rhodes,' they said. 'For the later stuff, you'll find the reports of Legislative Council in the library.' But did Northern Rhodesia's history really begin with Livingstone? What had happened of significance in the centuries, the millenia, before the Europeans arrived on the scene? I soon found that very little was known about the country before the middle of the nineteenth century. Some writers made vague and highly speculative references to the migration of Bantu tribes from the south and from the north, but because there were no written records, and no archaeological remains of significance, the early history of the country was virtually a blank.

Everyman's Encyclopaedia, hot from the press in 1953, put it this way: 'On the early history, or even late history of NR there exists little but travellers' tales, and these are less than a century and a half old. In the early nineteenth century, Portuguese traders brought back stories of a great interior kingdom of the Lunda people, extending from Lake Mweru to Barotseland. Very few historical facts are known concerning it.'[1] For a teacher searching for material, this was depressing. *Everyman* went on: 'The first expedition of any geographical value was that of Livingstone's famous missionary journey of 1851 and his subsequent discovery of the Victoria Falls.' How on earth, I wondered, could Livingstone be given the credit for discovering the Victoria Falls when he was led to them by members of the tribe which had lived within sight and sound of them for some hundreds of years?

Anyway, the Colonial Office was clearly right: 'Start with Livingstone.' Of course, I knew something of Livingstone already. He had been a boyhood hero. But hearing the story of his extraordinary life as a ten-year-old, I had never imagined that I

5

would see, let alone live in, the country which he had opened up. To his companions, Livingstone had been known as Munali (perhaps a corruption of *mijnheer*, the Boer word for 'mister'.) Since this was the name of the school to which I was going, it was all the more appropriate to read his diaries and his life story.

What an extraordinary man David Livingstone was! Born of poor parents at Blantyre in Lanarkshire, Scotland, he went to work at the age of ten in a cotton mill. Despite these humble origins, he made up his mind to train as a doctor and to become a missionary. With determination and a lot of hard work, he qualified as a doctor in 1840 and was accepted by the London Missionary Society. In July 1841 he arrived at Kuruman, missionary headquarters of Robert Moffat. Kuruman, 200 miles beyond the borders of Cape Colony, was the most northerly and most remote of the mission stations in southern Africa. Beyond it, Moffat wrote, lay 'the vast plain to the north where I had sometimes seen, in the morning sun, the smoke of a thousand villages, where no missionary had ever been.'[2] The challenge to Livingstone proved irresistible. Moffat and his wife had made no converts in the last five years. Rather than spend time at Kuruman on what seemed to be a hopeless task, and to escape the acrimonious atmosphere of the place, Livingstone resolved to take the Gospel to the unknown territory to the north.

Within two years, he had established a new mission station 250 miles north of Kuruman. There he set about the task of mastering the languages of several tribes, studying their ways and learning how to treat their diseases. In 1845 he married Mary, a daughter of the Moffats. For some years, Livingstone and his wife ran a typical mission station, preaching the Gospel (with a dismal lack of success), treating the sick and providing a rudimentary education for the children of the area. But Livingstone was not satisfied. God, he felt, was calling him to explore the land to the north which the map makers of the so-called 'dark continent' left blank or filled in with strange beasts and even stranger and quite fictitious peoples, towns and natural features.

In 1851, accompanied by his wife and three small children, he journeyed for the first time to Sesheke on the upper Zambesi and made known in Europe the existence of this huge river in the heart of Africa where it had been thought that there was only desert.

Gaining in confidence he began, the following year, the first of his three great journeys. Having reached Sesheke again, he continued northwards and then turned westwards until he reached the Portuguese settlement of Loanda on the Atlantic coast in May 1854. From here, he retraced his steps and having reached the Zambesi again, followed the river downstream. In November 1855, members of the Makololo tribe took him to see what he named the Victoria Falls. Continuing along the left bank of the Zambesi, Livingstone completed the first coast-to-coast crossing of Africa by a European in May 1856 when he reached the Indian Ocean at Quelimane. He described his incredible journey in his book *Missionary travels and research in South Africa*, which became an immediate bestseller. Home on leave, Livingstone was astonished to find himself the best-known man in Britain, received by Queen Victoria and lionized at meetings up and down the country. It was to be the high point of his career.

Within two years, Livingstone was back on the Zambesi, leading an expedition to which the British Foreign Office contributed £5,000. The purpose of the expedition was to see if the Zambesi could be opened up to 'trade with the natives' and, more important in Livingstone's eyes, to look for ways of ending the slave trade in central Africa. Most of the period 1858–64 was spent in 'discovering' Lake Nyasa and the Shire highlands, which were suitable for European settlement. Mary Livingstone died in 1862 and, to add to Livingstone's sadness, there was little he could do to halt the traffic of slaves in which a number of African chiefs had vested interests. Frequently he and his party came across groups of African men, women and children, chained together, being marched down to the coast by Arab traders, thence to be shipped as slaves to Arabia and Persia. The Zambesi expedition produced no trade and no converts to Christianity. It was recalled by a disappointed British Government. Livingstone's sense of failure was acute.

After visiting Britain, where he was coolly received, Livingstone set out on his third great expedition in 1866. He had two main objectives – to carry on the fight against the slave trade and to explore the country between Lake Nyasa and Lake Tanganyika where he believed the Nile must rise. The death of his pack animals, theft and desertion by his porters and damage to his chronometers created serious difficulties. Nevertheless, he reached the southern end of Lake Tanganyika, travelled extensively around it, and 'discovered' Lake Bangweulu in July 1868. In Europe, when no news was forthcoming of his whereabouts it was assumed that he was lost or dead. An expedition under Henry Stanley, journalist turned explorer, found him at Ujiji on the eastern shore of Lake Tanganyika in November 1871. Stanley provided Livingstone with fresh supplies and encouragement and he continued his journey of exploration. But everything was against him. In the fever-ridden swamps around Lake Bangweulu he suffered from malaria, pneumonia, dysentery, internal bleeding and agonizing haemorrhoids. On 1 May 1873, at Chief Chitambo's village in Ilala district, Livingstone's faithful servants found him dead, kneeling beside his bed where he had been praying. His heart and viscera were removed from his body and buried in a tin box under a large mpundu tree. The body was roughly but effectively embalmed and wrapped in calico and the bark of a tree. It was lashed to a pole and hoisted on to the shoulders of his few remaining followers, led by Susi and Chuma, for the long 1,500 mile journey to the coast at Bagamoyo. Nine months later, the weary party reached their destination. Livingstone's remains were taken by sea to Southampton. It was a tragic tale of heroic proportions which captured the hearts of the nation. On 18 April 1874, David Livingstone was buried in Westminster Abbey on a day of national mourning.

Livingstone saw his life as a failure: he had failed to find the sources of the Nile; he had failed to end the slave trade; he had failed as an evangelist; he had failed as a husband and as a father.[3] Recent biographers have diagnosed that Livingstone suffered from a form of manic depression known as cyclothymia.[4] This, it is said, was responsible for his behaviour which was frequently bizarre and offensive and sometimes bordered on the psychotic. A cyclothymic temperament would certainly account for the violent swings in Livingstone's behaviour – from energetic activity, extravagant optimism and utter disregard for the feelings of others, to moods of intense gloom, lethargy, sullenness and general misanthropy. If we now know that Livingstone was not the saintly figure portrayed by his early biographers, he remains one of the great men of the nineteenth century. His influence was enormous. His writings, his epic journeys, his indomitable spirit and his poignantly tragic death far from his home country and his loved ones made a huge impact on public opinion, not only in Britain but throughout the Western world. Within a comparatively few years of his death, other explorers capitalized on his pioneering geographical work to complete the mapping of central Africa, the vile slave trade was wiped out, and Christian churches in their dozens sprang up in the vast areas of forest, lake and desert where he had travelled.

Livingstone provided both an example and a challenge. While home on leave in 1857, he addressed a series of public meetings in an effort to inspire young men to devote their lives to missionary work in central Africa. At the most famous of these meetings, held at the Senate House, Cambridge, Livingstone told a packed and enthusiastic audience:

> I beg to direct your attention to Africa. I know that in a few years I shall be cut off in that country, which is now open. Do not let it be shut again. I go back to Africa to try to make an open path for commerce and Christianity.[5]

As a direct response to his appeal, a new missionary society, the Universities Mission to Central Africa, was founded and the work of older-established societies took on a new lease of life.

No one read Livingstone's diaries more avidly than Cecil John Rhodes, the second white colossus in Northern Rhodesia's history. Born in Bishop's Stortford in 1853, the son of a parson, Rhodes first went to Cape Province in 1869 in the hope that the African sun would improve his poor health. Within a few years he had made a huge fortune in diamonds, becoming head of the immensely wealthy De Beers mine at Kimberley. He also founded what later became Consolidated Gold Fields of South Africa Limited. He was convinced that further mineral wealth awaited discovery and exploitation in the lands beyond the Limpopo river. Here, he believed, lay the Biblical Ophir, the land of King Solomon's mines, comparable to, if not more prodigiously rich than, the golden reef of the Transvaal. It was not simply the desire for personal gain which motivated Rhodes to plan to gain control over the northern lands. As a young man he had dreamed of the British taking over and settling the entire continent of Africa, the whole of South America, the islands of the Pacific, the seaboard of China and Japan, the whole process to be completed by 'the ultimate recovery of the United States of America as an integral part of the British Empire.'[6] In this way, the youthful Rhodes argued, further wars would be rendered impossible.

Maturity brought a scaling down of this early vision, but he remained convinced that the best hope of peace and justice for the world lay in its being brought under the leadership of the English-speaking peoples, preferably the British. 'We happen to be,' he said, 'the best people in the world, with the highest ideals of decency and justice and liberty and peace, and the more of the world we inhabit, the better for humanity.'[7] Rhodes had no doubt that Africa should be British. He dreamed of the construction of a railway which would extend British influence from the Cape to Cairo. The spread of British rule, he was convinced, was in the best interests of the African people whose living conditions could be improved only if their resources were developed with the help of capital and expertise from Britain.

If the creation of a new empire which would rival the British Raj in India was necessary in Rhodes' view, to bring about the agricultural and economic development of Africa, it was no less important for Britain itself. Rhodes argued that unless Britain could continue to expand its commercial and industrial markets, large-scale unemployment and civil unrest were inevitable. He wrote:

> In order to save the 40 million inhabitants of the United Kingdom from a bloody civil war, we colonial statesmen must acquire new lands to settle the surplus population, to provide new markets for the goods produced by them in the factories and mines. The Empire is a bread and butter question. If you want to avoid civil war, you must become imperialists.[8]

In order to achieve his ambitions, Rhodes needed political power as well as his colossal financial strength. He entered public political life in 1881 when he was elected a member of the Cape parliament.

He rapidly established himself as the dominant figure and became Prime Minister of the Cape in 1890. We are not concerned here with Rhodes' activities in South Africa, his increasingly bitter relations with the Afrikaners, the disastrous Jameson raid, Rhodes' disgrace and enforced resignation, and the outbreak of the Boer war. These events caused Rhodes, on his deathbed in 1902, to conclude that his life had been a failure. Beyond South Africa's borders, however, he could claim a considerable measure of success in his efforts to open up 'the road to the north'.

It was Rhodes' influence which persuaded a reluctant British Government to proclaim a protectorate over Bechuanaland in 1885. Bechuanaland's significance lay first in the fact that it separated the Transvaal from German settlements in South West Africa, and secondly in that it provided a springboard, as Livingstone had found, for expeditions to the territories of the Zambesi valley and beyond. But Rhodes could not plant the Union flag in these lands without the active support of the British Government. Rhodes and his agents lobbied intensively the members of Lord Salisbury's administration which came to power in 1886. The attitude of the Salisbury Government was cautious. There was little evidence that the possession of colonies brought clear-cut advantages to colonial powers; the case for the expansion of Britain's colonial empire was unproven. Nevertheless, Britain needed new markets and must not be left behind in the scramble for Africa in which other European powers, particularly Belgium, France, Germany and Portugal, were engaged.

In 1889, Rhodes won a major victory. Salisbury's Government was prepared to see an extension of British influence in southern Africa provided it could be achieved without cost to the British taxpayers. It therefore acceded to Rhodes' suggestion that a chartered company should be set up to develop the Bechuanaland protectorate and the countries lying to the north. In July 1889, a formal petition was made to Queen Victoria. The petitioners made glowing promises:

> Your Majesty's petitioners believe . . . that the condition of the natives inhabiting the said territories will be materially improved and their civilisation advanced, and an organisation

11

established which would tend to the suppression of the slave trade in the said territories, and to their being opened to the immigration of Europeans and to the lawful trade of Your Majesty's subjects and other nations.[9]

The charter was granted in October 1889, giving Rhodes' British South Africa Company (BSAC) the necessary authority to open up a vast and ill-defined territory extending from the northern boundaries of the Transvaal to Lake Tanganyika. Rhodes wasted no time in despatching a column of settlers and soldiers across the Limpopo, through the country of Lobengula, Paramount Chief of the Matabele, into the territory of the weaker Mashona tribe. There, at what they named Salisbury in honour of the British Prime Minister, the Pioneers raised the Union flag. The Matabele, who traditionally raided the Mashona for cattle and women, soon proved a thorn in the company's flesh. War broke out and resulted in the rapid overthrow of the Matabele warriors whose bravery and spears were no match for the modern weapons, including machine guns, of the European settlers. Victory over the Matabele firmly secured the company's position in what now became southern Rhodesia.

Across the Zambesi, the company established itself not by force of arms but by negotiation. During the 1890s, a series of treaties were signed between the company and the chiefs of many of the main tribes. In return for the right to prospect for and to exploit mineral resources, the company undertook to provide protection against enemies, annual subsidies for the chiefs, and to assist with social development through the provision of schools. In what came to be called North-eastern Rhodesia, for instance, the company bound itself in treaties with several chiefs, who ceded full mineral rights 'to promote Christian missions and education, to stamp out slavery, and generally to advance the civilisation of the native tribes.'[10] In North-western Rhodesia, the key figure was Lewanika, Paramount Chief or king of the Barotse tribe. Rhodes' representatives signed a number of treaties with Lewanika, culminating in what was known as the Lewanika Concession of 1900. This gave the mineral rights of Lewanika's kingdom to the company. In return, the company undertook to protect the king and his nation from all outside interference or attack and to pay Lewanika and his successors an annual sum of £850, or the equivalent in trading goods. The treaty went on: 'The British South Africa Company further agrees that it will aid and assist in the education and civilisation of the native subjects of the King by the establishment, maintenance and endowment of schools and industrial establishments.'[11]

As a teacher, I was particularly interested to read of the company's promise to establish schools. Here, surely, was a wise and humane provision, an important step in the development of the country. I was anxious to discover how the undertaking had been honoured. Alas, as further reading made all too apparent, the company reneged on its promises. In the period in which the company ruled the country, from 1890 to 1924, it established precisely one school. This was the Barotse National School, founded in 1907, which was funded from part of the native tax collected from the Barotse people. The provision of elementary education was left in the hands of the numerous missionary societies which soon spread themselves across the country. Their schools were run at the expense of the societies' supporters overseas; the company contributed nothing to their costs.

The company achieved considerable success in ending the cruel and degrading slave trade, in which some African chiefs, as well as Arab traders, had played a shameful part. It also put a stop to inter-tribal wars, brought a measure of law and order to the country and created a skeletal administrative system. Why did it fail so lamentably and disgracefully to implement the explicit promises on education which had been made in the treaties with Lewanika, Kazembe and other chiefs? Why did it evade its responsibility for furthering the social and economic development of the people who had been entrusted to its care and protection? The answer, briefly, is that Northern Rhodesia (the two territories of North-eastern Rhodesia and North-western Rhodesia were merged in 1911) was a source of great disappointment to the company and its shareholders. It was the dream of a second Witwatersrand gold field or another Kimberley diamond mine that had led the company to cross first the Limpopo and then the Zambesi in its quest for quick returns. *Zambezia, England's El*

13

Dorado,[12] a book published in 1892, reflected the optimism of the day. The country was envisaged as a land teeming with easily-extracted minerals which could be cheaply and rapidly exploited to the great advantage of the shareholders in the company which gained control over the mineral rights. In reality, of course, the position was very different. The commercial revenue of the BSAC, derived from mining royalties, from sales of land, and from dividends on investments, was inadequate to provide any return to its shareholders throughout the period of company rule. The development of the Copperbelt did not take place until after the company had handed over the country to the British Government in 1924. In the meantime, since the company's affairs north of the Zambesi were run at a loss, it was company policy to keep administrative expenditure to the minimum consistent with the maintenance of law and order.

For more than three decades, the country was run on a shoestring budget; there was no question of embarking on a programme of human resource development of even the most modest nature. Thus, in the 34 years of company rule, 'these somnolent years',[13] as Richard Hall has dubbed them, such educational development as took place depended almost entirely on the efforts of missionary societies, which received no financial support from the company.

Some years later, I was able to make a detailed study of the contribution made by missionary societies to Northern Rhodesia's educational development; and a fascinating story it turned out to be.[14] In 1953, however, the component parts of the story lay scattered in the histories of the societies, in the archives of numerous mission stations, in the records of the General Missionary Conference and in the reports of the Department of African Education. I read some of the last-named in the library of London University's Institute of Education. The missionary societies, it was clear, were still making an immense contribution to education. Indeed, the whole system of education in the country was based on co-operation between government and the missionary societies. Mission educationists were members of the district and provincial education authorities and sat on the department's advisory boards and committees. The number of schools run directly by the local education authorities was increasing but the greater proportion of the schools, although heavily subsidized by government, were managed by the missionary societies. The societies trained many of the teachers and were also active in writing textbooks and producing other learning materials.

From the arrival of the first missionaries in the country in the 1880s it had been the aim of the missionary societies to encourage the spread of literacy so that people could read the Scriptures. Education was seen as an essential tool in proselytizing. It was also considered to be a civilizing force which would help overcome pagan belief in witchcraft and sorcery. One of the most influential of the mission educationists, the Rev. John Fell of the Primitive Methodists, told the General Missionary Conference held in 1914: 'As a civilising force, education has no equal. It will make rational, thinking men who perceive cause and effect instead of those believing silly notions arising from generations of paganism. It is a valuable adjunct in Christianising. Indeed, the spread of Christianity is largely dependent on education.'[15]

Government supported the missionaries' desire to provide an elementary education for as many children as possible. For decades, this was the over-riding priority of the Department of African Education. Robert Caldwell, director of the department, set out his objectives in his annual report for 1934: 'It is the advance of a great multitude of villagers, rather than the higher education of a select minority, that must be our aim.'[16] Conrad Opper, another senior officer in the department, wrote: 'The policy of this Government has always been to build a sound foundation of village education, to improve and develop the primary school and diffuse education as widely as possible among the people, rather than to concentrate attention and expenditure on the higher education of a select few.'[17]

When I arrived in Lusaka in 1954, the development of primary education remained the principal aim of the department. The annual report for that year reaffirmed that the long-term goal was 'to extend facilities towards a system of universal primary education by providing, in the first instance, a minimum 4 year elementary course for all children between the ages of 8 and 12 years.'[18] This course was designed to provide permanent literacy in the vernacular language and minimum social adjustment. The

15

curriculum emphasized the three Rs but also included health and hygiene, some geography, handwork, gardening, physical education, singing, and moral and religious instruction. A further two years of primary education, in 'middle' schools, was provided for most of the children living in the larger towns and for about one-third of those in the rural areas. About a quarter of those who completed the middle school course could go on to upper primary schools. Here the chief aim, as spelt out by the director, was 'to help the pupils become more useful members of economic society and to recognise their duty as members of the community.' The course allocated one-third of the time to practical subjects such as agriculture, building, carpentry, craftwork, homecraft and community service training. 'It is of great importance to the Territory's ordered development,' wrote the director, 'that the practical side of education should receive full emphasis in order that those who leave school should have received an all-round training in preparation for the increased economic and civic responsibilities ahead of them.'[19]

The 1954 report of the department showed that there were 175,000 African children enrolled in primary schools that year. Of these, 148,000 were in the first four elementary or lower primary classes. The estimated number of children in the country in the 8–12 age group was 160,000. Therefore, the director concluded, 92.5 per cent of the age cohort was receiving an elementary education. If true, this would have been quite remarkable; in most African countries in 1954, much less than half the age cohort received any education at all. Northern Rhodesia was certainly providing its children with considerably greater primary education opportunities than almost any other country on the African continent, but the figure of 92.5 per cent was greatly exaggerated. The statistics were based on an estimate of the country's population which was false. In 1954, the African population of the country was thought to be 1.8 million. Later, in 1963, a census showed this to have been an underestimate of at least a million.

What of post-primary education? There was very little of it. Twelve hundred students were following courses in building, carpentry and plumbing at trades schools, and a further 300 were taking more advanced technical training courses at the Hodgson

Technical College in Lusaka. Nearly 1,000 were being trained as primary school teachers. In addition 722 youngsters, of whom only 45 were girls, were enrolled in secondary schools. Of these, more than half were at Munali. Only Munali provided teaching above the junior secondary level. Munali was thus the only school in the country where African pupils could prepare for the Cambridge School Certificate examination. Only boys were admitted to Munali. Of the seven junior secondary schools in the country, girls were admitted to Chikuni and Mapanza, run by the Jesuits and Anglicans respectively as co-educational schools, and to the Methodists' secondary school for girls at Chipembi. They were excluded from the Local Education Authority schools at Kasama and Mongu and from the White Fathers' school at Malole and their junior seminary at Lubushi, where African priests received their preliminary training.[20]

When President Kaunda was installed as Chancellor of the University of Zambia in 1966, he condemned Britain's colonial record in Northern Rhodesia in the field of education as 'most criminal. This country has been left by her as the most uneducated and most unprepared of Britain's dependencies on the African continent.'[21] Insofar as this accusation applied to elementary education, it cannot be sustained. Elementary education, as we have seen, was more widely spread in Northern Rhodesia than in almost every other African country. But Dr Kaunda's charge that post-primary education was seriously neglected cannot be denied. As a result of decades of painfully slow development in secondary education, Zambia entered its independence in 1964 with a pathetically and dangerously small stock of educated manpower and womanpower. At that time, there were only 100 Zambian university graduates, a bare 1,500 Zambians with a School Certificate and no more than 6,000 who had received as much as two years of secondary education. These were totally inadequate numbers from which to draw the leadership, professional, managerial, technical and entrepreneurial skills which the new country needed.

Why was the development of post-primary education so late in Northern Rhodesia? The Colonial Office, through its Advisory Committee on Education in the Colonies, and a constant flow of despatches to Government House, made it clear that Northern

Rhodesia was lagging behind other territories in the provision of post-primary facilities for Africans. The message from London to Lusaka was that advanced and elementary schooling were not antagonistic but complementary, and that there was a moral obligation on the government to open as widely as possible the doors of knowledge to those who could profit from an advanced education. But until Clement Attlee's administration came to power in 1945, Britain was not prepared to help open those doors of knowledge. Even then, the contribution which Britain made to the development of social services, including education, in her colonial dependencies was quite small. Educational development in Northern Rhodesia had to be funded by the government from its own resources.

Northern Rhodesia's wealth lay almost entirely in copper. Production of copper was cut back severely during the great depression of the 1930s. When copper boomed during the 1939–45 war and copper prices remained high for several years, government revenues increased. They would have increased even more if the mineral royalties due from the mining companies had been paid to the Northern Rhodesia Government. But these royalties were the property of the British South Africa Company. The company continued to enjoy the royalties, which were running at a figure of £10 million a year by 1964 when the indefensible situation was ended by Dr Kaunda's Government on the very eve of independence.[22] Had those royalties accrued to Northern Rhodesia rather than to the BSAC, they could have been used to finance a radical programme of economic and social development.

But a shortage of resources alone cannot explain Northern Rhodesia's failure to promote the development of secondary and higher education for Africans. With its rich copper mines, Northern Rhodesia was better off than many other colonial territories in Africa. Yet several of these managed to provide a greater range of post-primary education opportunities for a bigger number of their people than did Northern Rhodesia.

I think it has to be acknowledged that the Northern Rhodesia Government in general and the education planners in particular lacked both vision and foresight. Senior government officers in the 1930s, 1940s and much of the 1950s simply could not envisage a society where Africans would carry out tasks involving the creative use of intelligence, imagination, initiative and responsibility. For far too long, it was assumed that Africans would continue to occupy junior posts in the economy, whether in the public service or the private sector. What was the point in providing people with education which they would never need and which would only unsettle them? In this context, the influence of the white settlers was important. Some of the settlers, particularly those working in the mines and running commercial farms, were indispensable to the country's development. But some Europeans had no special skills, qualifications or experience. They owed their jobs to the colour of their skins. They received salaries out of proportion to the value of their work for filling posts such as shop assistants, clerical workers, road foremen, railway workers and mine opera- tives. Africans could quite easily have been trained for these positions as was quickly proved after independence. The presence of unqualified and semi-skilled Europeans, fearful of losing their jobs, militated against any proposals to prepare Africans for positions of increased responsibility, whether in the public service, in commerce or in industry. For years, fear of alienating the white settlers contributed to the government's failure to provide substan- tial numbers of African students with secondary education and technical training which would have enabled them to compete with Europeans.

Another very genuine fear was that of producing a class of educated unemployed. India, Pakistan and Sri Lanka were held up as examples of what could happen when education facilities were rapidly expanded. These countries could not provide employment for all their university graduates, let alone for their millions of secondary school leavers. Those who could not find employment, it was said, were potential trouble-makers. The lessons to be learned, it was argued, were two-fold. First, the output from post- secondary education must be closely geared to the known man- power requirements of the economy. Second, emphasis should be given to practical and character-building education rather than to purely academic subjects.

With the benefit of hindsight, of course, it is easy to see that the Northern Rhodesian Government should have given much higher

19

priority, particularly after 1945, to the expansion of post-primary education facilities. Africans should have been prepared for an increasingly wide range of middle-level occupations; those who could benefit thereby should have been given the opportunity of higher education and for advancement to senior positions of responsibility and authority.

Unbeknown to the education planners in 1954 or, indeed, to anyone, independence would come to Zambia in 1964. Then, the demand for high-level African manpower would be insatiable. As the decade before independence progressed, the need to expand post-primary education facilities would become unmistakable and strenuous efforts would be belatedly made to increase the number of secondary school students. In 1954, however, the mood in the Department of African Education was one of complacency rather than of anxiety about the future. In his report for that year the director wrote: 'An expansion in education facilities during the ten year period 1937–46, which was perhaps unparalleled – at least in quantity – in the history of Colonial education had, by 1954, been consolidated by improving the quality of education to a degree seldom attained in African education.'[23] It was an extraordinary claim. It did not take me long to realize that the director's sense of self-satisfaction was misplaced. For the time being, however, I was concerned not with the magisterial pronouncements of headquarters but with learning my job as a young and very inexperienced teacher at Munali secondary school.

The school was well established on an attractive site just off the Great East Road, some three miles from the centre of Lusaka. Members of staff all lived on the site. We paid a modest rent for our bungalows. The boys were all boarders; they were accommodated in dormitories. They wore uniforms of khaki shorts and shirts. Many came from rural areas where children did not start school until they were seven or eight, or even older. By the time they were ready to enter form one at the start of the secondary cycle, they were 15. Some of the boys at the top of the school were well into their twenties, only a year or two younger than I was.

My task was to teach English and history to the first and third years, to be an assistant housemaster and to keep an eye on the school Scout troop. For a young man, it was a good life, full of interest. The boys were very receptive, provided you kept to the syllabus. If, however, you pursued a red herring, or digressed from the subject in hand for more than a minute or two, a hand would go up and a plaintive voice would ask: 'If this part of the syllabus, sir?' If it was not, the class would be inattentive until the end of your digression. Such was the effect of the intensely competitive education system. For these lads, education was not a matter of broadening and extending the mind. Its purpose was to enable them to pass examinations, to gain certificates and thus to qualify for what, to them, was well-paid employment, the rewards from which would be used to support other members of the family. Too much depended on success in the School Certificate examinations to waste time on frivolities. A good pass was essential; failure was unthinkable.

It was only one boy out of several hundred of the age cohort who reached Munali each year. Each had been clever and fortunate enough to overcome several hurdles which had ended the scholastic careers of his contemporaries: entry to primary school in the first place, then the selection procedures at the end of four years (standard two), six years (standard 4) and nine years (standard six upper.) Those who survived this obstacle course were certainly bright. Their understanding might be limited but their memories were prodigious. They positively relished note-taking and hand-outs; they were capable of memorizing large amounts of material and of reproducing it accurately in tests and examinations. They were much less proficient at analysis and at drawing conclusions from events. While 3B could accurately reel off the dates and names of Clive's battles, they floundered over identifying the reasons for his success.

The staff was multi-national. It is tempting to look back on Munali in the mid-1950s as a little island of non-racism in the midst of a sea of racial bigotry and discord; but it was not like that. In Northern Rhodesia at that time, the colour bar was firmly entrenched. In terms of their salaries, housing, schooling, social and entertainment amenities, whites enjoyed privileges not because of their superior abilities but simply because of the colour of their skin. One of the worst examples of the colour bar was the practice of some Lusaka shops of serving African customers through a

21

window, and not allowing them into the shop. Hotels, clubs and cinemas in Lusaka did not admit Africans. I knew this was wrong, but I have to say that I did nothing about it. While I did not, as far as I know, ever treat or regard Africans as in any way inferior to me, I have to confess that I did not raise my voice in protest against the injustice and humiliation to which they were subjected. The reason, I suppose, was partly cowardice and partly an unwillingness to 'rock the boat.' As a young teacher there was, in fact, little one could do to influence the social customs and racial attitudes of the time. If you had wanted to complain about the inhumanity and injustice of a way of life, it would have been difficult to know where to begin. *Mea culpa, mea maxima culpa.* But let the self-righteous acknowledge that each country and age has its own share of injustice, bigotry and discrimination in which most people acquiesce with a shrug of the shoulders as if to say 'There's nothing I can do about it.'

On the surface, at least, relations between black and white members of the Munali staff were cordial. There was no racial discrimination but there was a recognition that there were profound differences in culture, background, tastes and political opinions between the African teachers on the one hand and the Europeans – the British – on the other. At mid-morning break, the Africans formed a circle at one end of the staff room, the whites at the other. The Africans declined to take part in the play-readings with which we occasionally entertained ourselves in the evenings and did not join in the picnics which were sometimes arranged at local beauty spots. They rarely accepted invitations to dinner, perhaps because they felt unable to reciprocate the hospitality. On professional matters we worked happily together. Socially, we were all conscious of an embarrassing divide.

Many of the boys enjoyed performing in public and there was no shortage of volunteers when the head of English decided to put on *Toad of Toad Hall*. The play was written by A. A. Milne and is based on Kenneth's Grahame's *The Wind in the Willows*. Finding a play where the story would be suitable for African schoolboys, where the language would not be too difficult, and which would provide opportunities for a large cast, was not easy. *Toad* proved to be an excellent choice. Soon most of the staff, myself included,

22

were busy with preparations for the play – helping with stage management, lighting, scenery, speech training, costumes. Much of the success or otherwise depended, of course, on the principal actors. A first-former, Edward Cresta Ngebe, made a splendid Toad. Schoolboy actors are frequently wooden and painfully shy; they have to be carefully coaxed into projecting themselves in their roles. Not so Ngebe. A likeable lad, with lots of personality, he threw himself into the part. I am sure that A. A. Milne, whom I had met when he visited his son, Christopher Robin (who had rooms below mine in Trinity) would have approved of him. The episode which Ngebe enjoyed most was the court scene where Toad, irrepressibly and exuberantly defiant, declaims to an astonished judge and jury:

> The world has held great heroes,
> As history books have showed,
> But never a name to go down to fame
> Compared with that of Toad.

I came to know Ngebe quite well in the weeks leading up to the performances. He never showed any sign of anti-European feeling. We lost touch after I left Munali. I heard no more of him until May 1960, a time of wide-spread political disturbance, when he suddenly became headline news. The country was horrified to learn that a European woman, Mrs Lilian Burton, had been seriously burned when a gang of men stopped her car on the road between Ndola and Mufulira, threw petrol over her while her children watched, helpless, and set her alight. She soon died from her terrible burns. Edward Ngebe was one of four men who were charged with her murder, were tried, sentenced to death and subsequently hanged. Many Africans regarded Ngebe and his colleagues as heroes and freedom fighters, such was the political climate of the time. To his great credit, Kenneth Kaunda would have none of that. His policy was one of non-violence. He condemned the killing of Mrs Burton as 'a shameful act . . . I will regret it as long as I live.'[24] I had assumed that Ngebe, whom I knew as a gentle and kindly lad, would bitterly regret his part in the murder. According to the 'Voice of UNIP', however, he

23

remained defiant to the end. Just before his execution, he wrote a farewell message telling people to 'bear in their minds that we shall not die in spirit but be with them wherever they are carrying on the national work.'[25]

The part of Water Rat was played very well by Edward Shamwana. He subsequently became a lawyer. In 1980, he was accused of attempting to overthrow President Kaunda; he was convicted of treason and sentenced to hang. After protracted appeals, the president commuted the sentence to life imprisonment. Shamwana was released in 1990.

Most of the Munali alumni, of course, had much less sensational careers than Ngebe and Shamwana. Many achieved positions of responsibility and, after independence, rose rapidly. Godfrey Muwo, for example, who had played Badger, became the first African magistrate and subsequently a respected judge of the Supreme Court. Kirkwood Achiume, a delightful Mole, achieved distinction as a surgeon. Since Munali at this time was the only school in the country where African boys could gain as much as the Cambridge School Certificate, it was not surprising that many of the senior positions in the country were held by ex-Munali boys. Returning to Zambia 20 years after I had left Munali, I found that many of the permanent secretaries, under-secretaries and directors whom I met were former students from Munali. They were kind enough to remember me although I could not always put names to their faces.

The boys were curious about the staff, especially those from Britain. 'How old are you?' they would ask. 'Did you have a big house in England? How many servants did you have? Why are you not married? Why have you come here?' Why, indeed, had I come to Munali? It was then, and remains now, a fair question. I shall try to answer it in the next chapter.

Notes

1 A. Ridgway (ed.), *Everyman's Encyclopaedia*, Vol. 11, 3rd edn (London: Readers Union, J. M. Dent & Sons, 1953), p. 146.
2 Quoted in Elspeth Huxley, *Livingstone and his African journeys* (London: Weidenfeld & Nicolson, 1974), p. 22.
3 *Ibid.*, pp. 213–17.

'Start with Livingstone and Rhodes'

4 See Oliver Ransford, *David Livingstone, the dark interior* (London: John Murray, 1978).
5 W. Monk (ed.), *Dr Livingstone's Cambridge lectures* (Cambridge: Deighton Bell, 1860).
6 J. G. Lockhart and C. M. Woodhouse, *Rhodes* (London: Hodder & Stoughton, 1963), p. 70.
7 From R. Faber, *The vision and the need – late Victorian imperialist aims* (London: Faber, 1966), quoted in Bernard Porter, *The lion's share, a short history of British imperialism, 1850–1970* (New York: Longman, 1975), p. 134.
8 From B. Semmel, *Imperialism and social reform* (London: Allen & Unwin, 1960), quoted in Porter, *The lion's share*, p. 132.
9 Quoted in Richard Hall, *Zambia* (London: Pall Mall Press, 1965), p. 59.
10 Quoted in L. H. Gann, *The birth of a plural society* (Manchester: Manchester University Press, 1958).
11 *Ibid.*, p. 217.
12 E. P. Mathers, *Zambezia, England's Eldorado in Africa* (London: King, Sell & Railton, 1892).
13 Hall, *Zambia*, p. 96.
14 P. D. Snelson, *Educational development in Northern Rhodesia, 1883–1945*, 2nd edn (Lusaka: Kenneth Kaunda Foundation, 1990).
15 Minutes of the General Missionary Conference, Livingstone, 29 June–1 July 1914.
16 *Native Education Department Annual Report* (1935).
17 *Native Education Department Annual Report* (1936)
18 *African Education Department Annual Report* (1954)
19 *Ibid.*
20 *Ibid.*
21 *Addresses at the installation of His Excellency the President as first Chancellor of the University of Zambia, July 12 and 13, 1966*, (Lusaka: Zambia Information Services, 1966).
22 Hall, *Zambia*, pp. 230–4.
23 *African Education Department Annual Report* (1954).
24 Fergus Macpherson, *Kenneth Kaunda of Zambia* (Nairobi: Oxford University Press, 1974), p. 372.
25 *Ibid.*, p. 378.

2

Early days – Cambridge and the Royal Air Force

M y father's family were from Cheshire. Family legend had it that one or more Snelsons were among the knights who landed at Hastings with William of Normandy in 1066. Recently, however, a distant kinsman in Australia with a flair for genealogy has proved beyond reasonable doubt that we are descended not from the Normans but from the Vikings. In the Domesday Book, the Senelstune family are recorded as landholders at Peover in Cheshire. The Cheshire county records of the thirteenth century mention an Adam de Sneleston and William, Lord of Snelleston. Other Snellestons, Snelstons, Snellsones and Snelsons occur in the records of Tudor and Stuart times but the line of succession down the centuries has not been established. Thanks, however, to the research carried out by my niece, Nicola, and our far-removed cousin John, of Tarramurra, New South Wales, we can now trace our forbears over the last 250 years.

My great, great, great, great grandfather, John Snelson, was born in 1725. A yeoman, he lived for much of his life at Manley Hall, Cheshire. We do not know the surname of his wife, Catherine. Their son, Peter, one of four children, was born at Manley in 1761. Peter's grandson, another Peter, was born in 1830. The family must have been reasonably well off. We have a photograph of a large oil painting, done in 1852, of a family group in the drawing room of Manley Hall. Peter, my great grandfather, is shown as a tall, smartly dressed young man of 22; he holds a copy

26

of the Cheshire Courier. On the wall behind is an oil painting of a greyhound, Major, which had a successful career in coursing.

Peter had seven children, the second of whom, Joseph Wainwright Snelson, was my grandfather. He was working in Birkenhead or Chester in about 1885 when he saw a notice in the Pawnbrokers Gazette about a vacancy in Norman Bradley's shop in Cambridge. The young Joseph cycled the 200 miles to Cambridge. There, he got the job at Norman Bradley's and, soon afterwards, met and married Annie Alsop. My father, Briscoe, was born in 1890, the first of ten children of the union.

My grandfather must have been an astute businessman. Soon he was manager of the three Norman Bradley pawnshops in Cambridge. The main shop was in Bridge Street, opposite St John's College, where it was well placed to receive the watches, cufflinks, signet rings, cigarette cases, gramophones, hockey sticks and other valuable items of university students who had run into financial difficulties. You see few pawnshops nowadays, but before the welfare state developed they were an important part of the social scene. Many suits, for instance, which were worn in Cambridge churches on Sundays, spent most of the week in the wardrobes of grandfather's shops. A suit would be brought to a side door on Monday morning and be pledged for a pound or so. On Saturday, when the weekly wages had been paid, the pledge would be redeemed with a shilling or two of interest, and the suit would be restored to its owner, ready to be worn again on the morrow. In addition to the pawnbroking side of the business, grandfather dealt in men's clothing, jewellery, sports gear and travelware such as cabin trunks and Gladstone bags.

Business flourished and my father, who did well at school, had hopes that he would be able to go to university and qualify as an architect. Grandfather, however, decreed that Dad should leave school at the age of 15 and join him in the business. This was a decision for which Dad, as mild-mannered a person as you could ever hope to meet, never forgave his father; even when he was an old man, he still spoke with great bitterness of how his father had robbed him of the opportunity of achieving his life's ambition.

When war came in 1914, Dad joined the Suffolk Yeomanry and, after training at Halton, went to France. Shortly before a big

27

offensive planned for the Spring of 1917, he was badly wounded when a German shell landed in *la grande place* at Arras. His right foot was almost completely severed by a piece of shrapnel. For many months he lay in hospital. He limped heavily for the rest of his life. Ironically, being wounded almost certainly saved his life. In the offensive which was launched soon after he was hit, all his young brother officers in his regiment were killed.

Among those who helped his convalescence in Cambridge and pushed him around in a wheelchair was May Nicholas, three years his junior who worked as a secretary with the Great Ouse Catchment Board. May's mother had died some years earlier. Her father, John Nicholas, was one of four brothers who ran a wood yard in Carlyle Road. He was looked after by a housekeeper, Maud, a diminutive, hard-working and kindly soul, who was like an older sister to May. John Nicholas owned the house next door to his own and two small cottages at the bottom of his garden. The Smith family, who lived next door, always referred to him as Uncle Jack and it was by this name that I knew my grandfather. He must have fallen out with his brothers. In any case, he rarely went to the wood yard. He had considerable skills in technical drawing and my most vivid memories of Uncle Jack are of him leaning over the kitchen table, pipe firmly clenched between his teeth, steel-rimmed spectacles on the end of his nose, executing beautiful drawings of architects' plans. In the evenings, he would continue his work on the sitting room table, often drawing into the early hours. He was an obstinate and awkward man in many ways. He considered electricity to be dangerous and, although he lived until 1945, would never have electricity installed in his house. He would not go near a doctor nor allow one into his house until he was on his deathbed. When he needed new spectacles he would send the faithful Maud to Woolworths to buy him a pair for sixpence.

Nevertheless, he could be generous. When May and Briscoe married in 1923, he gave them £100 so that they could furnish a small terraced house in Victoria Road which Briscoe's mother had helped them to buy. The house faced the parish church of St Luke's and its adjoining infants and primary schools. Ken, my brother, was born in 1924. I arrived on the scene three years later, weighing in at the unusual size of 12 pounds.

Of my first decade, I have few specific memories but no shortage of general impressions. Mine was a happy childhood which, in retrospect, seems to have been much more structured than it actually was. Each season had its own pastime and amusement. In September we threw sticks into the horse chestnut trees on Mid-summer Common, bored holes in the conkers which fell, and challenged each other to contests. In November we played marbles in the gutters of the street, often by the light of the gaslamps. After the excitement of Christmas, there was always snow in January; the meadows at Grantchester were flooded and froze, providing wonderful skating. Even now, the arrival of Spring reminds me of the games we played with cigarette cards. I would wait outside a corner shop at the top of Searle Street. If anyone came out with a packet of cigarettes I would ask: 'Will you give me the card, please, mister?' We stuck the cards – of film stars, footballers, aeroplanes, animals – into albums. The spares we flicked against a wall in a game with fair but complicated rules that only eight year olds could devise. Summers, of course, were invariably hot and sunny. They brought swimming, tennis (which Mum taught me), cricket on Alexandra Gardens and long cycle rides into the country along roads which, by modern standards, were virtually empty.

There was no television, of course. In the evenings, we read and played family games. On Saturdays, after a bath and hairwash, I was usually allowed to stay up until nine o'clock to listen to 'In town tonight' and 'Music hall' on the family wireless. There must have been ten cinemas in prewar Cambridge. Very occasionally, I would be given threepence over and above my penny a week pocket money, to go to 'the pictures'. On Sunday afternoons, Ken and I were packed off to the Primitive Methodist Sunday School, where Maud was a teacher. This supplemented the Anglican teaching we got at school in the week.

Because of his war wound, Dad could not run. He shared with me, however, many of his interests and pastimes. He taught me to fish and, until I was old enough to go on my own, would cycle with me to his favourite reaches along the Cam and the Ouse. He was an excellent photographer and became first an associate and then a fellow of the Royal Photographic Society. His forte was landscape photography. Having chosen his subject, he would spend

29

hours waiting for the sun to move to a favourable position and for clouds to arrange themselves in an agreeable pattern. He was a great admirer of John Constable's oil paintings and tried to capture some of that artist's mastery of light and shade and the atmosphere of serenity which his pictures convey. Of course, he did his own processing. He built up several lectures, illustrated by lantern slides, on East Anglia and the Thames and would deliver these to photographic clubs up and down the country. He taught me to use a camera, how to compose a picture, how to develop films and make my own black and white prints. Many of Dad's prints and slides now form part of the Cambridgeshire Collection which is held by the Cambridge City Library.

Dad's other major interest was rowing. Before the war, he had been an oarsman. Because of his wound, he could not row after the war but he agreed to become secretary of the Cambridgeshire Rowing Association, a position he held for some 40 years. The highlights of the rowing year were an eight-oared time race and, two weeks later, the bumping races. As a small boy, there was not much I could do to help Dad with the organization of these events but he would take me with him when he cycled along the towpath, watching the crews. When he went into a pub for a beer, I had to wait outside; he would always bring me a glass of lemonade. I think he was proud when I was a member of the Rob Roy crew which rowed head of the river in 1946.

School was just across the road. I did well enough at my lessons. At the age of 11, we sat an examination to determine which secondary school we would go to. Ken was already at the Cambridge and County High School for Boys and this was my first choice. I did sufficiently well in the 11+ examination to win a County minor scholarship and in September 1938, wearing my new outfit of short grey trousers, grey shirt, school blazer, tie and cap, I started at the 'County'.

Suddenly, life became serious. Our headmaster, Arthur Mayne, irreverently known as Tish (after a racehorse which had an unusual gait), had two objectives for the school. The first was to obtain the best possible results in external examinations. The second was to beat the Perse, our rival school, at rugby and cricket. Of these, the first aim, of course, was by far the more important. It was pursued with relentless determination. Preparation for the School Certificate examination which we would take four or five years later, began in the first year. After every three weeks' period, a mark list was drawn up showing the marks we had gained in each subject. From these marks a form order was deduced. This was the invariable pattern of school life; everything was subordinated to the three-weekly mark list. On the list, good marks were underlined; bad marks were starred. When the new mark list was posted, the head would conduct a post-mortem with each form. From our first year classroom, we could see him approaching across the courtyard, gown billowing behind him, mortar-board firmly in the centre of his huge head. Since then, I have met a great many headmasters, vice-chancellors of universities, ministers of education and other notables of the world of education; they hold no fear for me. But even at this distance of time, I cannot recall the approach of Tish to our classroom half a century ago without an acute feeling of apprehension. The fact is, he terrified us. He would say very little. Those who had done well were told to stand. He would survey them over the top of his spectacles; the frown which permanently creased his brow would lift momentarily. Then it was the turn of those who had met with academic disaster. As they stood in their places, Tish's expression would become thunderous. He would rock backwards and forwards on the soles of the boots he always wore and his complexion would become puce. Those with one star against their names would be ordered to attend Saturday morning detention. Those with two or more stars were despatched immediately to Tish's study. They would return, chastened, later, clasping their backsides and endeavouring to hold back the tears. Since all the teachers were under constant pressure to produce marks for the three-weekly lists, teaching was of a traditional and unadventurous variety. All of us, masters and boys alike were engaged in a routine of orthodox teaching and learning and an unending struggle for existence in the marks jungle.

My father had a small car and we always managed to have a family holiday in the summer. In 1939 we were staying in Cornwall when Hitler invaded Poland. We returned to Cambridge immediately and sat together round the wireless to hear Neville Chamberlain tell the nation on the morning of Sunday, 3 September that a

31

state of war existed between Britain and Germany. That night, in the early hours, the air raid sirens sounded. Convinced that Cambridge was about to be subjected to the kind of aerial bombardment which Warsaw and other Polish cities had recently suffered, we were very frightened. In darkness, we crowded into the little cupboard under the stairs, our gas masks (which had been issued a few weeks earlier) at the ready. Mum put a saucepan on her head. Within an hour, the 'all clear' sounded and we returned to our beds. Dad decided that the dining room should be turned into the family bedroom; so we all moved downstairs. A blast-proof contraption was fixed to the window of our new bedroom and stayed there for the rest of the war. Arrangements were made to black out all the other windows in the house. You could not show any lights for fear, it was said, that the crews of German bombers would see them. In the event, Cambridge received little attention from the Luftwaffe. Bombers on their way to the Midlands and other industrial towns frequently passed over Cambridge and there were numerous air raid alarms. After a time, however, we became blasé and would simply turn over in bed when the sirens sounded.

Gradually, we settled down to life in wartime Britain. Food rationing was introduced and the nation tightened its belt, especially when the German U-boats achieved temporary superiority in the Atlantic and sank many ships bringing food to the country. There were many shortages but we were never in danger of starvation. We became used to eating dried eggs, reconstituted potatoes, snoek and other unusual fish instead of meat, and saccharin instead of sugar. Reduced to a simple diet, and deprived of the rich food to which they were accustomed, most people's health improved.

At school, air-raid shelters zig-zagged their way across the playground and we would adjourn to the shelters when the sirens sounded during school time. Once we reached the third year, we were all expected to join the Junior Training Corps. Every Wednesday there was a parade. Dressed in our khaki battle dress, black boots, gaiters and side caps, and with old .303 Lee Enfield rifles on our shoulders, we would march up and down the playground. There were also lessons in weaponry, field tactics, signals, aircraft recognition and other military subjects. Every so often, we had a field day. Buses took us into the country. 'Blue' company, faces smeared with mud and camouflaged with small branches, would crawl across ploughed fields and through ditches to attack 'Red' company, firing blank ammunition and hurling thunderflashes as they made their assault. We larked about, of course, but we knew there was a serious side to our military manoeuvres. If the war continued, there was every likelihood that we would be engaged in real fighting.

Tish rarely showed any of the gentler human emotions. Periodically, however, at morning assembly he would read out the latest casualty list. I remember his voice breaking as he informed us that the boy who, only a few months previously, had been company sergeant major in the Corps, and a brilliant wing three-quarter, had been killed leading an assault on a German machine gun position.

I liked the Scouts better than the Corps. We had a flourishing troop with some outstanding leaders. I passed my first class badge and became a patrol leader. Apart from the regular Scouting activities, which had barely changed since Baden-Powell's day, we made our little contribution to the war effort. It is many years since I last saw a trek cart in use but a cart was an essential part of Scouting life in those days. We used the trek cart, pulled by two boys on their bikes, to transport all our gear to camp. We also used it every week to collect waste paper from the houses in the streets around the school. Some of us trained to pull 50 gallon drums of water, mounted on small carts. The idea was that we would deliver water to homes which had had their supply cut off by German bombing. Fortunately, we never had to go into action.

The summer term ended in mid July. Then, with a few friends, I would sign on as an agricultural labourer on a farm at Horningsea, a village just outside Cambridge. Following the reaper, drawn by a tractor, we would put the sheaves of wheat, barley or oats into 'stooks'. When they were dry, we loaded them on to carts with pitchforks and took them to the threshing machine. We all tried to avoid the task of collecting the chaff from the thresher, a filthy job. It was hungry work; as a supplement to the weekly ration, we received half a pound of margarine and a few slices of corned beef with which to make sandwiches. When the weather was fine, we would work a 12-hour day. At seven (old) pence an hour, we could earn £2 in a good week.

At Christmas, we worked at the Post Office, sorting the mail and then delivering it. The money we earned was enough to finance occasional holidays. Dennis Jude (a very good friend) and I thought nothing of cycling 200 or more miles to Devon or North Wales, touring from one youth hostel to another then, when our money ran out, cycling back to Cambridge.

Academically, the school was highly successful. School Certificate and Higher School Certificate results were always good and each year a large proportion of the sixth form went on to university. I found myself in a fast stream. At the end of my second year I was asked whether I would like to do Greek. The headmaster's son was in our form and his parents wished him to go to Rugby. To secure admission he needed some Greek. The head's wife was available to teach but it would have looked bad if she had been employed to teach a class of only one. Four of us joined him. The snag was that I had to drop chemistry in order to find time for the Greek. Effectively, therefore, a career on the science side was thereafter closed to me. I think none of us had any regrets. Roger, the head's son, duly won a place at Rugby; two of the little group won classics scholarships to Christ's College, Cambridge and the remaining two, who included myself, also gained admission to Cambridge.

I tried for a scholarship to Trinity College in March 1945 but did not do well enough to win one. However, as my tutor, George Kitson Clark, subsequently told me, some of my papers had 'a whiff of alpha' about them and I was given admission to read history. Victory in Europe was celebrated on 8 May 1945; VJ day followed on 15 August. Mercifully, the war was over. Cambridgeshire County Council gave me a County major scholarship of £120 p.a. and thus it was that in October 1945, I went 'up' to Cambridge.

Ken, my brother, had already spent two years at the university, taken a wartime degree in mechanical engineering and then gone into the Royal Navy. Somehow, I hope without arrogance, I had assumed that I would follow in his footsteps in this, as in so many other things. Until I walked across Trinity Great Court in my undergraduate gown, it did not really hit me how fortunate and privileged I was to be a member of one of the most prestigious of all the Cambridge colleges, the alma mater of Isaac Newton, Francis Bacon, Edward Coke, Byron, Macaulay, Tennyson, Lawrence Bragg, Bertrand Russell, G. M. Trevelyan et al. My parents, neither of whom had been able to stay at school beyond the age of 15, were immensely proud that their two sons had got to Trinity.

In 1945, Cambridge was a very different university from what it is today. Men whose education had been interrupted by the war made up a sizeable part of the student body; they brought with them a maturity and breadth of experience which made us 18-year-olds feel very inadequate. Colleges were single sex. Women undergraduates were concentrated in Girton, Newnham and New Hall. If you invited one to your rooms, she had to be off the premises before 10 p.m. Far fewer grammar schoolboys found their way to Cambridge then than do so now. For the first time in my life, I found myself rubbing shoulders with the products of some of the most prestigious public schools in the country such as Westminster, Eton, Harrow, Winchester and St Paul's. Many were the sons of very wealthy families. Class distinctions were much more evident then than they are now and I learned to avoid contact with those who were at all snobbish or cliquish.

Trinity was a large enough college to enable you to find friends easily. Most of mine I met through rowing. The boat club, known as First and Third, was very lively and the standard of rowing was high. Most of my afternoons for three years were spent on the Cam, paddling down to Baitsbite Lock and then rowing back in bursts round First Post Corner, through the Gut, round Grassy Corner, down the Plough Reach, Ditton Corner and then the exhausting haul down the Long Reach, under the railway bridge and thus back to the boathouse for a shower. The best crew I rowed in was the 1st Lent boat in 1949. We bumped Clare, Pembroke and Trinity Hall and finished second on the river. Footballers dream of playing at Wembley, cricketers at Lords and rugby players at Twickenham. For oarsmen, of course, their Mecca is Henley and one of my most enduring memories is of taking part in the famous regatta there. As we went to the start in our heat of the Thames Cup, our coach, Michael Warriner, a former 'blue' and Olympic gold medallist, said: 'Whether you win or lose, this is a day you'll remember for the rest of your lives.' We lost, by two lengths or more, but he was right. It is a great pity that commercial pressures nowadays are threatening to spoil the traditional delights of the royal regatta.

For a year I was rowing correspondent of *Varsity*, the undergraduate newspaper. I gathered material for my weekly column by observing the other college crews as we passed them in practice outings. Disaster struck when I described one crew as looking as if they were rowing through treacle. The next week, they won the inter-college time race. I had stuck my neck out too far; my judgement was shown to be faulty. I hastily retired from the journalistic scene.

Throughout my time at the university, I kept in touch with the County School Scout troop. I had passed my Wood Badge course at Gilwell Park and thus qualified as an assistant scoutmaster. Northrepps, near Cromer on the Norfolk coast was our favourite campsite and I was glad to be able to help with the organization of summer camps there. While at the County, I had been introduced to the delights of hill-walking by the senior history master who each year led parties of 5th and 6th formers to the Lake District. I took groups of senior scouts both to the Lakes and to North Wales. On balance, I preferred North Wales. In the Lakes we stayed at youth hostels but in North Wales we used a hut in the Nant Gwynant, at the foot of the Watkyn path that leads to the summit of Snowdon. It was primitive, strenuous but idyllic living and we usually succeeded in our aim of climbing all 14 mountains of 3,000 feet or more in the Snowdon range, the Carneddau and the Glydrs during our holidays.

Not being a scholar or exhibitioner of the college I lived at home for my first year. For the next two years, I had rooms in New Court. I shared with an economist. We would read our weekly essays to each other and in this way I learned most of the economics I have ever managed to grasp. He was keen on classical music. Unfortunately, he had only two records and these he played several times a day. Forty and more years later, I cannot hear Ravel's *Bolero* without thinking of Peter Muir sitting at his desk waiting for that dreadful cacophony which brings the piece to an end. Eventually, after a particularly riotous bump supper, I broke the record over his head. He bore me no ill will and we remained the best of friends. We usually went together to the weekly debates at the Union Society where there was an opportunity to hear some of the leading politicians and personalities of the day. On our way back to Trinity we frequently met the University Proctor, a don with policeman-like duties, whose lot it was to patrol the streets of Cambridge, accompanied by his 'bulldogs', to ensure that members of the university wore their gowns and behaved themselves. The college gates were closed at 10 p.m. If you returned between 10 and 11 o'clock, you were fined one penny, between 11 and 12, two pence. Return after midnight meant that you were reported to your tutor; you needed a good excuse if you were to avoid being gated, that is, being confined to the college after 10 p.m. for a week or a month, or longer. For more serious offences, you ran the risk of being rusticated, suspended for a period. Heinous offences carried a penalty of being sent down, or expelled.

History and politics had been my main interests in the sixth form and I revelled in most of the subjects I took for the history tripos. I was fortunate in both my lecturers and supervisors. Each supervisor was brilliant in his own way. Perhaps the most brilliant, and certainly the most eccentric, was Kitson Clark. Kitson, as everyone knew him, intimidated me. He was a large man in every sense. He specialized in the Stuarts but was extraordinarily well versed in a wide range of historical periods. Each Monday morning I was required to leave my weekly essay in a basket placed on the third step of the staircase leading to his magnificient rooms above the Great Gate, the main entrance to Trinity. On Wednesdays at noon, I would climb the staircase and knock at his door. A great voice would boom: 'Enter.' Kitson would be there, larger than life amidst numerous piles of books. He would hand me my essay and bid me read it. This done, from the depths of his armchair he would address me as though I was a public meeting. Pausing occasionally to relight his pipe, he would tear the essay to shreds, making it clear that my reading had been totally inadequate, that my reasoning was specious and that my findings were superficial. Some weeks elapsed before I realized that he expected me to answer back, to

37

defend my opinions, to criticize his views and to point out weaknesses or inconsistencies in his arguments.

Thereafter, we got on famously until one evening when the history students at Trinity were invited to Kitson's rooms to meet Arnold Toynbee who had recently written a six-volume history of civilization. The room was crowded; most of us sat on the floor but I had one of Kitson's dining chairs. As the great man was speaking, I was suddenly conscious of a cracking, splintering sound. The next I knew I was on the floor covered in confusion and the remains of Kitson's chair. There I remained, in a state of acute embarrassment, for the rest of the evening. Of course, I offered to have the chair repaired. Kitson refused: 'It would cost far more than you could afford,' he said. This was probably true but did not make me feel any better. But Kitson was not a man to bear a grudge. The next Wednesday, he went out of his way to greet me graciously. He heard my essay without a single interruption and then offered virtually no criticism. He puffed furiously at his pipe. 'That chair must have been getting weak,' he muttered as if to himself. It was the closest he could get to apologizing. 'Let's have some sherry,' and he poured two generous measures of the college's amontillado. 'Tell me, which boat are you rowing in this term?' It was Kitson's way of signalling that the incident was forgotten.

I have very little recollection of the details of the history or the political theory which I studied. Recently, I came across a long-forgotten box of essays which I wrote at the time. The titles both intrigue and baffle me. 'What reflections does examination of Sorel's doctrines provoke on the popular appeal of communism and fascism?' 'Do you agree with Sir William Temple's explanation of the rise of the United Provinces and their subsequent prosperity?' 'Without Mohammed, Charlemagne would have been impossible: comment.' 'The relevance of Kant's essay on Perpetual Peace to the fundamental contemporary problems of international organisations.' Nowadays, I would have difficulty in writing two sentences on any of these topics. What were Sorel's doctrines? Who was Sir William Temple? What on earth is the link between Mohammed and Charlemagne? The fact that I do not know the answer to any of these questions, and that the thrust of Kant's essay has long since left my mind, in no way detracts from the value of reading history. Detailed studies are means to an end. Clio, the muse of history, teaches us not to remember facts, dates or even ideas. Rather, she teaches us to handle large amounts of material, to question, to sift evidence, to present a balanced and coherent case and, hopefully, to reach impartial, valid and reasonable conclusions. Through the study of history, we also learn something of the extraordinary diversity of the human race, of the need for tolerance, of the heights to which the human spirit may aspire and the depths to which it so often sinks.

In my third year, my supervisor of studies was Jim Butler (later knighted for his editorship of the official history of the war). It was he who suggested that I might think of staying on at Cambridge and reading for a doctorate. Had I done so I would have done some research on the representation in the House of Commons of the City of Westminster. But it was not to be. To be considered for a research grant I needed to get a first class degree. A bad morning on European history put paid to these hopes. I had no reason to complain about an upper second but reading for a doctorate was now out of the question. Instead, I opted for a postgraduate Certificate in Education.

This meant following a year's course at the university Department of Education. At that time, the course was very theoretical, although we each spent either the first or second term on teaching practice. I spent the Michaelmas term of 1948 at St Paul's, a very good public school in London. Since this was the first term of the academic year, I had barely set foot in the Department of Education and had certainly not attended any lectures. There were two other student teachers at St Paul's, one from London and the other from Oxford. We were each given a 75 per cent teaching timetable. This gave us far more opportunities for teaching practice than we could possibly have expected. It was fine for us but hard lines on the parents who paid high fees for their sons' education and were entitled to expect that they would be taught by experienced teachers. The student from London was visited each week by a tutor from the Institute of Education; the man from Oxford received monthly visits. The Department at Cambridge took no interest in me whatsoever; certainly no-one ventured up to Hammersmith to see how I was getting on.

I returned to Cambridge for the second and third terms. Lectures covered the principles of education, the practice of education and the history of education. Principles included psychology. Our lecturer in educational psychology, R. H. Thouless, was brilliant; he had many publications to his credit. Unfortunately, I could not follow him and soon gave up attending his lectures. As the time for examinations approached, I began to panic. While the class of pass you obtained in the examination was of little importance, it would be disastrous to fail. Hastily, I read a book on psychology written for the American businessman on topics such as how to get the most out of your employees, how to impress your customers. It gave me some familiarity with the jargon of psychology and helped me to make a reasonable stab at answering the questions on the exam paper. When the results were published, I found to my astonishment that I had a first class pass, with a distinction in psychology! Ever since, I have regarded examination results with considerable scepticism.

By June 1949, when I emerged from Cambridge as a qualified graduate teacher, the war had been over almost four years. Conscription, however, was still in force. My call-up had been deferred until I had finished at Cambridge but now I was due to spend two years in one or other of the services. The Royal Air Force had a scheme which appealed to me: by taking a short-service commission for three years, you would qualify for a gratuity of £300 on completion. At that time, £300 seemed a lot of money. I applied, was accepted and in August 1949 I reported to RAF Spitalgate in Lincolnshire for initial training. This consisted mainly of square-bashing, weapon training, assault courses and King's Regulations. We were also taught some of the social graces expected of young officers. Initial training was followed by a course at the RAF School of Education. While there I volunteered for an overseas posting, a decision, taken lightly one lunchtime, which was to have a decisive effect on my life. Within a week or so, I learned that I had been posted to the Rhodesian Air Training Group.

After spending Christmas at home I said my goodbyes and set

off for Africa. The Union Castle shipping company ran a regular weekly service to South Africa. Each Thursday afternoon one of their liners left Southampton bound for Cape Town, 6,000 miles away. I was fortunate in that the ship in which I travelled, the *Pretoria Castle*, was one of the newest in the Union Castle fleet. With a displacement of 26,000 tons, it was much more stable in the water than some of the older, smaller ships. Nevertheless, it pitched and rolled, creaked and groaned as it made its way down a stormy English channel and into the Atlantic. For two days I lay in my bunk, not caring whether I lived or died, and wondering how a burial at sea was conducted. Once we were clear of the Bay of Biscay, the wind dropped, the sea calmed and the sun came out. We stopped briefly at Madeira and then sailed on, the ship a tiny speck on the immensity of the ocean, a little world of its own. Nowadays, when those travelling between Britain and Africa invariably fly, it is pleasant to recall those more leisurely and relaxed days when the time was filled with nothing more taxing than deck tennis, bucket quoits, table tennis, bridge, a daily flutter on the number of miles travelled by the ship in the previous 24 hours, a fancy dress competition, and the genuinely difficult task of selecting from the lengthy menus which were presented at breakfast, lunch and dinner.

On the last morning, the fourteenth, I got up in good time and watched first Table Mountain and then Cape Town, nestling at its foot, emerge from the early morning mist. Landfall! Soon I was setting foot on the continent of Africa for the first time in the unromantic setting of the customs shed at Cape Town docks. A RAF liaison officer met us. There was time to see something of the streets of Cape Town and to take the cable car up Table Mountain before reporting to the railway station and starting on the next stage of our journey.

It is some 1,200 miles from Cape Town to Bulawayo. The journey took us two and a half days. The line led first through the beautiful rolling countryside of Cape Province, with glimpses of vineyards in the lush valleys; then across the seemingly endless plains to Kimberley and Mafeking, and a long dusty haul through scrub country between Gaborone, Mahalapye and Francistown. At the last-named, customs and immigration officers joined the train and accompanied us to Bulawayo where, weary, dirty and dishev-elled, we thankfully left the train. The headquarters of the Rhode-sian Air Training Group were at Kumalo. Here I reported to the Group Education Officer and was told that I had been posted to RAF Thornhill, outside Gwelo, some 120 miles beyond Bulawayo. An Avro-Anson was going to Thornhill the next day and it was in this that I had my first flight and completed the long journey from England.

During the war, most RAF aircrew were trained overseas where the skies were safer than those in Britain. Many thousands of pilots, navigators and observers won their wings in Southern Rhodesia where there were a dozen or so RAF stations. Most of the stations closed at the end of the war but three remained open. These were Kumalo, the Group headquarters, Heany, 20 miles north of Bulawayo, and Thornhill. At Thornhill navigators were trained in groups of 30 or so. Each group stayed about a year and there were usually three or four groups on the station at a time. My task was to conduct classes in current affairs for the trainee navigators and to help with the general education, chiefly in English and mathematics, of the airmen – fitters, clerks, cooks, drivers and so on – who serviced the planes and provided support services for the navigators.

Life at Thornhill was good. As a young, bachelor junior officer, I had a small room to myself. For most of the year, the working day began at 7 o'clock and ended at half past one. After a late lunch in the mess and a short rest, one was ready for tennis, riding, hockey, squash, swimming or a host of other sporting and recrea-tional activities. I bought myself a small, second hand Vauxhall car, did it up with the help of a sergeant in the station workshops, and was then able easily to get to Gwelo, our nearest town, to go down to Bulawayo, up to Salisbury, or to explore places like the Great Zimbabwe ruins. With friends, I spent a marvellous leave in the eastern highlands of Rhodesia, surely one of the most beautiful regions in the whole of Africa, and reached as far as Beira in what was then Portuguese East Africa, now the unhappy country of Mozambique.

The last exercise for the trainee navigators was a trip to Durban. I went with them a couple of times. The hospitality, arranged by members of the RAF Association, many of whom had served in the RAF during the war, was superb, but I was appalled by what I saw of the treatment of black South Africans. In Southern Rhodesia an obnoxious colour bar was in operation but it had not been developed into a philosophy. In South Africa, however, the National Party had come to power for the first time in 1948 on a programme of rigid apartheid; the separate development of the races. In those two weekends in Durban, I saw just enough of apartheid in action to realize that here was an unjust and evil system which discriminated between people solely on the basis of the colour of their skins. It was bound to be a source not only of bitterness, humiliation and misery but also, in due course, of bloodshed.

Shattering news reached me a year or so after I reached Thornhill. Dad wrote to say that mother was dying of breast cancer. On the strength of a letter from Mum's doctor, I was given a month's compassionate leave and a seat was found for me on a Hastings flying to England. It was a leisurely journey. We flew only by day, spending the nights on the ground at RAF stations at Nairobi, Aden, El Hamra (Egypt) and Malta. The last leg, between Malta and Lyneham, in Wiltshire, proved to be quite exciting. As we crossed France, the starboard outer engine failed. Slowly we descended to about 1,000 feet. Then for varying periods the starboard inner engine had to be feathered because of overheating, making the plane very difficult to manoeuvre. We lost height steadily as we crossed the Channel, wearing our Mae Wests. A cheer went up as we saw the Needles off the Isle of Wight and crossed the English coast. I stayed at home for two months, doing what I could to help Mum in her last weeks. I had the impression that she was hanging on to life simply to spare me the pain of seeing her die. When the doctor gently suggested that I should go, I had to agree that this was the kindest thing for me to do. It was agonizing leaving her, knowing that this was for the last time. She died two weeks later.

Back at Thornhill, the last of the trainee navigators were leaving and the first of the trainee pilots had arrived. In the hangars, Ansons gave way to Tiger Moths (subsequently Chipmunks) and Harvards. Once the pilots began to go solo, the accident rate rose sharply. I was appointed a section leader in the ground rescue team. Our role was to locate the wreckage of any planes which crashed and to bring back the survivors, if any; it was not a job for the squeamish.

Other jobs also landed in my lap. When a monthly magazine was started, I became business manager and deputy editor. When the station entertainments officer left, I took over. This meant that I was henceforth the manager of the station cinema. We were open six evenings a week and there was a change of programme each evening. My job was to bank the takings and go to Gwelo railway station each evening to send off the film we had just screened and collect the film which would be shown the next evening. Fortunately, I did not have to sit through all the programmes. Occasionally, we put on a variety show. On a station with several hundred men there was a lot of dramatic, comic and musical talent, and no shortage of those who were prepared to make fools of themselves. My task was to audition, draw up a programme, write topical lyrics about station life and personalities, beg, borrow or steal the props and costumes, and produce the show. In a pre-television age, when people were used to entertaining each other, they did not demand a professional standard. Most of the shows went down well and did something, I think, to keep morale high.

My best friend at this time was Chris Hoyte, who was the station medical officer. Chris came from a long-established Northern Rhodesian family. His grandfather, Dr Walter Fisher, was an outstanding pioneer medical missionary in Northern Rhodesia's history. In 1889, he had been one of a band of Brethren missionaries who sailed to Lobito Bay in the hope of establishing a number of mission stations in Angola. Within a few months, three of the party were dead; two from malaria and the other from yellow fever. Dr Fisher survived numerous attacks of malaria while he and his wife worked for 17 years at mission stations in Angola. The continued poor health of his family and colleagues was a constant source of worry and he decided to set up a sanatorium for missionaries, located on high ground. He chose Kalene Hill, near Mwinilunga, in the far north-west of Northern Rhodesia, as the site for his hospital. Apart from caring for his fellow missionaries, Walter Fisher was also anxious to treat the sick among the local population. Initially, he was regarded with fear and suspicion by the people living around the mission station; they assumed he was a slave trader. Gradually he won their confidence and became a much-loved figure in the community until his death in 1935. In addition to his medical work, Dr Fisher and his colleagues ran a number of schools for the villagers around the mission. They also opened a school for the children of missionaries working in Angola, the Rhodesias and the Congo. Chris had received some of his early education there at Sakeji. His sister, Joan, was matron of the school. We decided to visit her and, while we were about it, to see something of Katanga Province in the Belgian Congo. This involved a round trip of 3,300 miles.

We made it in my little 1940 model Vauxhall, which had a maximum speed of 45 m.p.h., used vast amounts of oil and had a very uncertain suspension. Quite definitely, this was not the ideal vehicle in which to tackle the strip roads of Southern Rhodesia and the severely corrugated surfaces of Northern Rhodesia's earth roads. Nevertheless, we reached Sakeji unscathed and were warmly received by Joan and her colleagues. I marvelled at the sturdy faith, perseverance, ingenuity, dogged determination and Christian love displayed by the missionaries, living and working in very difficult conditions among a people who did not appear to be very receptive of the Gospel message. Within a few miles of Sakeji is the source of the river Zambesi. A few days earlier we had gazed spellbound at the mighty, raging Victoria Falls where the mile-wide Zambesi plunged, roaring, over a 350 feet drop in an enormous cloud of spray. Here, at the very beginning of its long and tortuous journey to the Indian Ocean, the river consisted of no more than a few puddles in a forest clearing. From this remote spot, we made our way to Elizabethville, now Lumumbashi, which dazzled us with its bright lights and sophistication. Africa frequently astonishes with its contrasts and infinite variety. The Belgians had done their best to create a European-style city in the middle of Katanga. As we sat drinking wine in the cafés of the tree-lined boulevards, it was difficult to imagine that we were in the heart of so-called darkest Africa.

Encouraged by the success of this first trip to the north, Chris and I began to think of further expeditions. He was keen on hunting; I wanted to do some game photography; Eric, a mutual friend, was weary of the sometimes claustrophobic atmosphere of Thornhill and wanted to get away from it. Where to go? Chris spoke longingly of the Luangwa river. Game of all shapes and sizes, he assured us, teemed in the valley of this great river which rose near Northern Rhodesia's border with Tanganyika, slashed its way across the eastern part of the country and then joined the Zambesi at Feira. But how to get there? Game reserves covered much of the Luangwa valley. In those parts which were open, hunting was very strictly controlled. Very few hunting licences were issued; mostly they were bought by wealthy Americans, not by impecunious RAF officers. Quite by chance, Chris discovered that the Provincial Commissioner of the Eastern Province, through which the Luangwa flowed, had been a young district officer at Mwinilunga when Chris was a schoolboy at Sakeji. He knew him quite well. There was a rapid exchange of letters and, as a great concession, the Provincial Commissioner ensured that the last of the 1952 hunting licences was allotted to Chris.

It was another 3,000-mile journey. We made it longer than it need have been by going first to the Copperbelt, where Chris's uncle, Charles Fisher, was a surgeon, and his wife, Monica, was also in medical practice. None of us could guess, of course, that when Monica and I next met she would be the Schools Medical Officer for the Copperbelt and I would be the Provincial Education Officer.

From Luanshya, we crossed the Congo pedicle, as it is called, and re-entered Northern Rhodesia when we crossed another great river, the Luapula, by pontoon. We spent a night at Johnston Falls, a long-established Brethren mission station, run by Willie Lammond, who knew Chris of old. One of the educational activities of the mission was a school for the blind. I found it a moving experience to sit among a group of blind African children who were struggling to learn Cibisa, their mother tongue, in braille. I told Mr Lammond that I was interested in returning to Northern Rhodesia as a teacher. 'I shall pray for you, my boy,' he said, then added, with a twinkle in his eye, 'I've been here 52 years. You'll find the first 40 years are the worst.'

Five hundred miles on at Fort Jameson (now Chipata), head-

46

quarters of the Eastern Province, the Provincial Commissioner, Norman Price, was kindness itself. We stayed with him and his wife while we laid in stocks of food, drink and petrol for our two-week *ulendo* to the Luangwa Valley. Through his good offices, and the co-operation of the Provincial Game Officer, we acquired the services of Chepasani, a game scout. Chepasani was a gem; he knew the valley well, he was an expert and fearless hunter and he spoke some English. He sat with his rifle between his knees as we left Fort Jameson and headed for the Luangwa, 50 miles away. It was late October, the hottest time of the year. As we negotiated the escarpment, dotted with curious, grotesquely shaped baobab trees, and descended into the river valley, the heat was overpowering. An earth road of sorts ran the length of the valley, a mile or two from the river. In glades among the mopane trees, we saw the first signs of animal life, waterbuck, zebra and puku startled into immobility by the sudden appearance of Chris's old Ford V8; impala which leapt gracefully over bushes as they fled from our approach.

We made our camp just outside Katopeka's village. Katopeka, the headman, greeted us gravely and soon organized the villagers into building us a rondavel, or small hut, of branches, grass and leaves and this became 'home' for the next two weeks. A new daily pattern quickly emerged. We would wake with the dawn, dress hastily, take up our rifles, ammunition and cameras, and would eat a handful of raisins as we followed Chepasani and a local guide away from the village and into the bush. As we had been promised, game teemed on the dried-up flood plain of the river. Frequently, we shot nothing, content to revel in the beauty of the scene and the peace that comes from being close to nature. On the way back to camp, dripping with perspiration, we often stopped at a pool in the Luangwa where the water was deep enough to cover us when we lay down, but not deep enough to enable a crocodile to approach us unawares. Just to make sure that none of us became a crocodile's breakfast, Chepasani stood guard with his rifle and kept a wary eye on the ugly twelve-foot brutes which lay motionless for hours on end on the sandbanks a little way upstream. Back at the camp in mid-morning, we would have a late breakfast and would then flake out until mid-afternoon when a cup of tea would revive us in readiness for the second expedition of the day, when many of the animals went to the river to drink.

As dusk fell, we returned to camp and took our paludrine (a prophylactic against malaria) with a swig or two of brandy which made the local water more drinkable. Our cook, hired locally, would then produce dinner – impala steak, warthog liver or roasted guinea fowl – after which we turned in, lulled to sleep by the grunts of hippo, the eerie whooping call of hyena and the distant roar of lions.

It was Chepasani who taught us how to walk in the bush without making a noise, how to 'freeze' when an animal was sighted, and how to keep down-wind of an animal when getting into position for a shot, with either gun or camera. At these skills we became reasonably proficient, but remained quite hopeless at tracking. From insignificant marks on the ground here, a bent twig on a bush there, or a flattened blade of grass, Chepasani and the local hunters who accompanied us could follow an animal for miles. All their tracking skills were put to the test when I foolishly accepted Chris's invitation to shoot one of the two buffaloes on his licence, using his .475 magnum. My vision was partly obscured by some grass and my shot hit the big bull too high in the shoulder. He and the others in the small herd crashed away into the thick bush. We had no choice but to follow, fingers on the triggers of our rifles, since a wounded buffalo will frequently lie in wait for its pursuers and charge them. The trackers were superb, and we followed quickly in the wake of the fleeing herd. Chepasani pointed out to me a minute speck of blood on some tall grass and, soon afterwards, a pool of blood where the wounded buffalo had obviously rested. The trail now led across bone-hard ground – there had been no rain in the valley for six months – but 'my' animal was limping and this enabled the trackers to distinguish his spoor from the tracks of other animals. We followed up for three hours in stifling heat, not knowing when the beast might suddenly appear and charge us. Anticlimax followed. The tracks clearly showed that the herd, including 'my' unfortunate beast, had crossed the Luangwa into a game reserve on the far side where we were not allowed to go. Our backs, arms and legs stinging and swollen from the bites of tsetse flies, and physically and mentally exhausted, we returned to camp. Chepasani consoled me by saying that the buffalo could not have been badly wounded; otherwise, he would have charged us. In the seclusion of the game reserve, he would in all likelihood recover.

After this episode our stock with the villagers needed a boost. They made us very welcome but on the understanding that we would keep them well supplied with meat. Our reputation rose significantly when Chris shot a buffalo and soared to great heights when he killed an elephant within a few hundred yards of the village. We marvelled at the speed and skill with which the huge beast was dismembered under Katopeka's direction. The whole population moved to the site of the kill. While the men used their axes to pierce the thick grey hide and to hack enormous, bloody steaks from the limbs, women and children made fires, roasted titbits for immediate consumption and began the long task of smoking the bulk of the meat for eating later. According to Chepasani, the dried meat would provide relish for the village for the next 6–8 weeks. We contented ourselves with eating the last few inches of the elephant's trunk. Someone had said it tasted like ox tongue. We concluded it must be an acquired taste; or perhaps we cooked it wrongly.

I would certainly not dream of taking part in the shooting of an elephant in the Luangwa valley nowadays, when ruthless poachers, using automatic weapons, have dramatically reduced the herds. In 1952, however, there were far too many elephants in the valley; they were destroying their environment. Moreover, they caused immense damage to crops, often ruining in a single night the fruits of months of toil. Each year, the Game Department culled several hundred beasts in order to keep the numbers down. The bull which Chris shot, and whose dismemberment we observed in such ghoulish fashion, might well have been one of the Game Department's future victims.

Be that as it may, this second visit to Northern Rhodesia convinced me that I wanted to live and work there. As we made our way back to Fort Jameson, a buffalo's head tied to the front bumper of the car, the elephant's tusks, stuffed with grass, and Chepasani's bundle of dried meat on the roof rack, I decided not to accept the offer I had received of a permanent commission in the RAF. Rather, having finished my time in the RAF (which had been extended to four years because of the war in Korea), I would try to get a place in the Colonial Education Service and would opt for a posting to Northern Rhodesia. Norman Price encouraged me. He introduced me to the Provincial Education Officer who arranged for me to visit a couple of African primary schools. Already I knew that I liked the people of Northern Rhodesia and that the country was fascinating. Now instinct told me that I could make a small contribution to its educational development.

I returned to England on the *Carnarvon Castle* in March 1953, and served my remaining few months in the RAF at the School of Apprentices at Halton, Buckinghamshire. Before I left the RAF in August 1953, I had already written to the Colonial Office and had filled in the application form they sent me. In due course I was called for interview and eventually received a letter informing me that Mr Secretary Lyttleton had pleasure in offering me probationary appointment in the Colonial Education Service in the African Education Department in Northern Rhodesia. It was just what I had hoped for. The Colonial Office clearly expected that its education officers would be versatile for their letter went on: 'You may be required to perform general administrative or inspection duties or to teach African students in secondary school, teacher training institute or development area school.' In other words I might be an administrator, a teacher, a teacher's college lecturer, or an inspector of schools. A tall order for a young man of 26 with very limited experience. In return for the efficient discharge of these responsibilities, I would receive an annual salary of £765. The offer seemed generous and I wrote at once to accept it. Thereupon, information and advice was showered upon me: Colonial Regulations, the special regulations of the Colonial Education Service, the provisions of the East Africa Widows and Orphans Pension Scheme (which was rather discouraging and certainly premature since I had no immediate plans for matrimony or parenthood), and an impressive, not to say daunting volume in a special insecticidal binding. This last graphically described a selection of tropical diseases which were prevalent in Central Africa and which could well prove fatal, and gave detailed illustrations of a range of helminth and other parasites to which one might easily become a reluctant host. I read this with mounting apprehension and could not help but wonder if the 'obedient servant' in the Colonial Office had had his tongue in his cheek when, in a covering letter he wrote: 'The Secretary of State desires me to take this opportunity of wishing you all success and happiness in your new appointment.'

I was to leave in the New Year. I filled in the intervening weeks by teaching for a term in a secondary modern school in Cambridge. Dad was sorry that I was returning to Africa again so soon. Ken, now married, was in the southern Sudan, working on an irrigation scheme. But Dad would not be left on his own; he had married again and I was sure that Kathleen, his new wife and an old family friend, would look after him well. I felt I could leave with a clear conscience.

January 1954 saw me sailing again from Southampton, bound for Cape Town and then Lusaka. In a strange, exciting way, I felt I was going home.

3

Colonial Education Officer

I had been only a few months at Munali when I had to pack up and move. Clifford called me to his office to explain that the wife of the education officer in Fort Jameson, 350 miles up the Great East Road, was expecting a baby. There was a rhesus negative complication and the baby would require a blood transfusion shortly after birth. The necessary specialist care was available in Lusaka hospital but not in Fort Jameson. 'It's only a temporary transfer, of course,' said Clifford. 'I'm sure you'll be back here long before Christmas.'

Having not long got my house fitted out with curtains and cushions, and having spent a fair amount of time, not to mention money, knocking the garden into shape, I was not looking for a transfer. However, as a bachelor and with no children's education requirements to consider, I was the obvious staff member to uproot for a few months. The move would have its compensations: it would take me much closer to the Luangwa valley and to what I regarded as the 'real' Africa.

Thus it was that in June 1954, having said *au revoir* to friends and colleagues at Munali, and consigned my heavy baggage via Thatcher & Hobson, the carriers, I set off in my Hillman Minx and headed east. I had bought the Minx second hand in the expectation that I would use it in and around Lusaka where the roads were good. It was not a suitable car for the bush or for protracted driving on earth roads. These were apt to degenerate into seas of slippery mud in the rains and to become badly corrugated in the dry season. My Hillman, however, never let me down. For six years it carried me faithfully and reliably over all

52

manner of roads and in every kind of weather. It had only two weaknesses. When the engine was hot and idling, it was apt to cut out completely, creating an airlock in the petrol system. The answer was to get out, open the bonnet and manually to actuate the petrol pump until the flow of petrol to the carburrettor was resumed. This was a simple operation which even an engineering simpleton like me could successfully perform in two or three minutes. Twice, however, it was to cause me acute anxiety. On each occasion I was in the Luangwa valley. Once the engine stalled as I found myself in the middle of a herd of alarmed and trumpeting elephants at dusk. On the other occasion, when we had stopped to watch a pride of lions at their kill, I had to get out of the car and go through my pump-priming operations while, from a distance of 30 yards, eight pairs of smouldering amber eyes watched my every movement over the dismembered and bloody carcase of a wildebeest.

The other drawback of the car was that, in heavy rain, water would run down the windows and accumulate in the bottom of the doors. I solved this problem by drilling holes in the bottom of the doors so that the water could drain away. Thinking this was a good idea, I wrote to Rootes, the manufacturers, in Coventry. In course of time, I received a reply thanking me for my suggestion but saying that a drain was unnecessary because rain could not possibly get into the doors! Since this was their attitude, I shed no tears when they were taken over by another company.

A one-way traffic system operated over the middle section of the Great East Road where it traversed the escarpment of the Luangwa river. I had to wait at Rufunsa for a couple of hours until the Lusaka-bound traffic had passed. The road snaked its way over the escarpment, affording splendid views as it ran close to some pretty terrifying drops. Passengers regularly closed their eyes and sang hymns as buses lumbered their way up the hills, negotiated numerous hairpin bends and then thundered down the other side.

Arriving in Fort Jameson, or Fort Jimmie as it was nearly always called, (now Chipata), I drove straight to the *boma*, the cluster of offices from which the Eastern Province was administered. The Department of African Education occupied a single storey block of six brick-built offices, painted white, with green corrugated iron roofs. The Provincial Education Officer had the far office, shaded by two blue-gum or eucalyptus trees. The door was open; I knocked tentatively. The figure at the desk looked up and surveyed me over gold-rimmed, half-moon spectacles. 'Come in, man,' he said as we shook hands, 'you look as if you could do with a cup of tea.' He called to the messenger seated outside his office, 'Godile, you old reprobate, tengani chai tsopano lino'.

My new boss was a shrewd and dynamic Welshman named Evan G. Goddard, usually referred to as Glyn. He was very experienced, very intelligent, very wise and had a delicious sense of humour. It was he who taught me most of what I ever knew about education administration, and much more besides. A week in his company was worth more than a year in an institute of education. He wore a long-sleeved shirt and a tie above a pair of knee-length khaki shorts, khaki stockings and brown shoes. I was covered in red dust from the journey. 'You're booked into the rest house,' said Glyn, 'but you'll spend the evening with the wife and me. Rita will be there, too.' Rita was the attractive young woman education officer.

Win, Glyn's wife, greeted me warmly when, having bathed and changed at the rest house, I arrived for dinner. While Glyn was every inch a professional, with a hard cutting edge, Win was very maternal. Their three children were at school in England; their twice-yearly visits to Fort Jimmie were clearly the highlights of the year. In between times like many other colonial wives, Win worried about them and lavished her motherly instincts on young education officers like me. It was Win who helped me settle into the two-bedroomed house which was allocated to me, who gave me tips about the local shops (not that there was very much choice), who introduced me to the unattached ladies of the town (again, the choice was very limited) and provided a sympathetic ear when I had twinges of home-sickness. I owed a lot to her.

The Eastern Province was like a reversed L. To the east, it was bounded by Nyasaland (now Malawi), to the south by Portuguese East Africa (which became Mozambique at its independence). The river Luangwa sliced its way roughly through the middle of the province. Its valley was at a much lower altitude than the plateaux on either side. Fort Jimmie was a district headquarters as well as the provincial capital. The other districts were Lundazi to the north and Petauke to the west. The main tribes were the Chewa, the

Ngoni, the Senga, the Nsenga, the Kunda and the Tumbuka. The official language of the province, along with English, was Chinyanja (the language of the lake), although each tribe had its own language. Civil servants in the administrative and professional grades, such as myself, had to pass a lower standard language examination, written and oral, within three years and a higher standard examination within five years. Otherwise, you received no salary increments.

Most of the African population were peasant farmers, growing just enough maize, beans and pumpkins to feed their families, with perhaps a little to spare in a good season. In Petauke District, where the soil was more productive, and in the area around Katete, agricultural development schemes had been successfully launched by government and had led to the growth of co-operative unions of farmers who regularly produced cash crops such as tobacco and groundnuts. In the Luangwa valley, by contrast, maize was difficult to grow and the staple diet of most villagers was cassava, often eaten with barbel and other fish from the river, supplemented, when they were lucky, with game meat.

Fort Jimmie was at the junction of the horizontal and vertical limbs of the L shape. As both district and provincial headquarters, it was the biggest settlement for hundreds of miles around. About 5,000 blacks lived in the African township; most were junior civil servants and their families, small traders, shop assistants, domestic servants and general labourers. The whites, nearly all Europeans, numbered about 500. Most were civil servants, living in pleasant, detached bungalows along roads lined with jacaranda, frangipani and flame trees. Working in the private sector were the bank manager, the owners or managers of the main stores and the hotel, some Catholic missionaries, known as White Fathers, and Father Rogers, vicar of the Anglican church. Some of the early European settlers in and around Fort Jimmie had married African wives and this accounted for the small community of people of mixed race, known as coloureds, at Katapola, just outside the town. To complete the community, there were several families of Indians. They dominated trade in the African township. They worked long hours; some, reputedly, were very rich.

Social life for the Europeans centred on the club. This gloried in the name of the Victoria Memorial Institute, or VMI for short. It was much less stuffy than the name implied. It was at the VMI that you met your friends, swam, played tennis, golf, squash and billiards, drank your 'sundowner', danced, read the newspapers from Britain and generally made yourself at home. Wherever they have gone in the world, whether it be Asia, Africa, the Caribbean or the Pacific, the British have created clubs, little oases of Britishness in the midst of alien environments. Perhaps it was the desire to keep them British which led them to exclude other races from membership. More likely, alas, it was simply a question of the colour bar. The fact remains, in any case, that the Fort Jameson club at that time was for whites only.

Fort Jameson owed its name to Leander Starr Jameson, Cecil Rhodes' lieutenant, who led the raid which resulted in Rhodes' downfall. It was first occupied by the British South Africa Company in the early 1890s. Reputedly, the last slave caravan in the British Empire was liberated there in 1896. At that time, Fort Jimmie was at the back of beyond. It was 350 miles east of Lusaka and a similar distance west of Blantyre in Nyasaland. There was only one way of getting there in those early days and that was on foot. Riding was out of the question because the tsetse fly killed all horses. Because of its remoteness, it attracted a certain type of individual seeking solitude. Land was made available by the company at three pence an acre, later increased to six pence. This attracted a trickle of white settlers who took up blocks of 5,000 acres each. Some were birds of passage; they lived rough, shot the elephant and other animals on their land and moved on. Others cleared the land, built homesteads, worked very hard and created successful farms which their descendants were still working in the 1950s.

The early administrators and settlers believed that only firm treatment could 'keep the natives in their place'. Before more enlightened practices were adopted, life must have been very brutish. On the inside cover of the District Notebook, which recorded the history of the district and was passed from one district commissioner to the next were pasted instructions on 'The use of the chikoti', a whip made of rhinoceros hide which was used to maintain discipline in the prison. The instructions required that, after use, the whip must be scraped and washed in permanganate of potash in order to destroy injurious bacteria which might infect the next man to be flogged. Other instructions covered the procedure to be followed for 'the hanging of natives'.

Those days of rough and ready, brutal 'justice' were, of course, long over. Fort Jameson, beautifully situated in a ring of hills, a bit sleepy and with more than its fair share of tittle-tattle and rumour (for everyone knew everyone else) was a very pleasant place in which to spend two and a half years.

Glyn gave me a week to settle in, to read the files and to get to know the staff. The staff numbered about 15. Rita, already mentioned, was the Woman Education Officer. Vivacious and attractive, she was nearing the end of her three-year tour of duty. She was responsible for developing what was known as girls' work in schools throughout the province. In the main, this meant running short courses for women teachers and helpers, many of whom had a very low academic standard, and showing them how to teach needlework, knitting and simple cookery. Rita had a degree in English and found 'girls' work' tedious and unrewarding. She had decided not to return after her leave. Malcolm, a burly, open-faced South African, looked after the accounts, paid the teachers, organized the office and was Glyn's general factotum. He was conscientious to a fault and worked long hours, a fact which worried his delightful wife, Pat, who was afraid that his health would suffer. Another South African, Kevin, assisted Malcolm. Single, he was an habitué of the club and could be found propping up the bar every weekend, engaged in marathon drinking sessions; he always wore dark glasses on Mondays. The senior African member of staff was Safeli; he was manager of the Local Education Authority schools in Fort Jameson District. A former primary school headmaster, with a family of six, a lay preacher, always impeccably dressed, Safeli was a pillar of rectitude, highly respected in the community. He was a fund of information and displayed great patience with my faltering attempts to learn Chinyanja.

Glyn had his own secretary, a European, wife of the Superintendent of Police. There were four others who typed, all men. Gilly was the senior. His education had unfortunately stopped at Standard 6, the top class of primary school, and he had some difficulties with

57

his English. Fortunately, he never raised objections when I corrected his spelling and had to tell him to retype a letter or report. Sometimes, he had to make three attempts, but he persisted until he got it right. The typist who handled most of my work was Charles. Poor Charles, he was always in trouble. Not long out of primary school and about 20 years of age, he went through a succession of girlfriends at remarkable speed. According to Charles, they all had expensive tastes and this accounted for his state of permanent indebtedness. Unwisely, I lent him a pound or two to tide him over a particularly bad period. I then discovered that he owed money to every member of staff, black and white. He found it difficult to concentrate on his work and would have been sacked had this not meant that his creditors would never be repaid. Thus Charles remained with us, looking permanently sad and worried, his face a startling contrast, so Gilly informed me, to the animated expression it bore when, with his latest girlfriend, he gyrated to 'high life' music in the African township on Saturday evenings.

The senior messenger was Godile, one of the Ngoni tribe, with a fine head of grizzled, grey hair. He did not know his age but was clearly approaching retirement. Each morning he took up his position outside Glyn's office and was required to do little more than salute smartly and smile cheerfully whenever Glyn entered or left the office. But if Godile, bless him, was not much more than a friendly status symbol, Benjamin, the second messenger, was a tower of strength. Able and intelligent, Benjamin was capable of more demanding work than that of a messenger. His education, however, had stopped at Standard 4 and this prevented him from obtaining more skilled employment in the civil service. With Glyn's encouragement, he was attending evening classes and hoped to take his Standard 6 examination eventually.

Benjamin was a great friend of William, the senior driver. William was in charge of our little fleet of vehicles. This comprised a five-ton lorry (for carrying bags of maize, beans and to transfer teachers, their furniture and their luggage), a one-ton vanette (for delivering items of school equipment), two Land-Rovers (for touring purposes) and a Chevrolet Impala, which was used exclusively by Glyn. William was good at organizing the other drivers, making sure that they serviced their vehicles regularly and did not use them for private purposes. He could be very harsh and one would often hear him bawling out a driver whose vehicle was dirty or whose petrol tank was empty. Towards the European members of staff, however, he was always most courteous and gentle. He spoke no English and would grin delightedly when my language studies progressed to the point that we could carry on a fairly lengthy conversation.

This, then, was the staff. Between us, we were responsible for the planning and administration of virtually all education in the province. Within the Federation of Rhodesia and Nyasaland, African education was a responsibility of each of the three territories. Non-African education, however (the education of Europeans, Asians and coloureds), was a responsibility of the Federal Government in Salisbury. We had nothing to do, therefore, with the small school for European children in Fort Jimmie, one for Asian children, and a boarding school for coloured children at nearby Katapola. There was plenty to keep us busy in the schools for African children. About 250 of these were scattered over an area about the size of Wales. There was one junior secondary school, just outside Fort Jimmie, two trades schools, where Standard 4 leavers could learn carpentry, and building; the remainder were primary schools. Of these, a dozen offered education up to Standard 6, about 40 went up to Standard 4, and the rest, about 200 and the vast majority, provided four years of education, ending at Standard 2. Completion of the four-year lower primary course, which began in sub-standard A at the age of seven or eight, progressed through sub-Standard B, Standard 1 and Standard 2, was supposed to make a child permanently literate. In fact, of course, many of those whose education stopped at Standard 2 at the age of 12 or so soon lapsed into illiteracy. Those who dropped out along the way – and they were legion – were educationally doomed, unless they were lucky enough, later in life, to be able to join an adult education class.

About a third of the schools were run by the Local Education Authority.[1] This meant that they were managed on a day-to-day basis by members of Glyn's staff, that is, Rita, another education officer who lived in the west of the province at Katete, and myself. The other schools were run by mission agencies – the Dutch

Reformed Church Mission, the Universities Mission to Central
Africa, the White Fathers Mission and the Seventh Day Adventist
Church. Government subsidized the mission schools by paying
grants to cover the costs of teachers' salaries, books and equipment.
Quite a lot of Glyn's time was spent in scrutinizing the grant
applications of the mission educationists. They never made fraud-
ulent claims but some certainly sailed very close to the wind and
regarded government as fair game. Glyn would take great pleasure
in cutting back their claims and pointing out errors in computation
which, by extraordinary coincidence, were nearly always to the
benefit of the mission and to the detriment of government. To
ensure that the grants were being properly spent, that the mission
schools were being well run, that the curriculum was being
followed, and so on, Glyn was responsible for inspecting the
schools.

'I want you to take on Lundazi District,' he told me.

'What does that entail?' I asked.

'Quite a lot,' he explained. 'You'll be my representative on the
District Education Authority and you'll be manager of the 40 or so
LEA schools in the district. You'll need to work closely with the
White Fathers, who manage about 20 schools on the plateau, and
you'll have to inspect those at least once a year. You'll attend the
estimates meetings of the main native authorities, the Chewa,
Senga and Tumbuka.' I must have looked bemused. 'You'll soon
get the hang of it,' he said encouragingly, 'so don't let it worry
you.'

Worry or not, the fact remained that I had never managed a
school in my life, had never inspected a school, knew nothing of
the work of local education authorities or native authorities. Now,
suddenly, I was to be a manager of schools, an inspector and an
education planner. The training course I had followed at Cambridge seemed both remote and irrelevant. I could only hope that I
would soon learn what was required.

The one thing that I did know a little about were the White
Fathers. Chris, Eric and I had visited one of their mission stations
during our hunting expedition three years earlier. It was a roughly
similar station that Glyn took me to at Lumezi, a hundred miles
north of Fort Jameson and ten miles south of Lundazi, when he

decided to show me something of the district. 'Your patch,' he called it. The White Fathers or, to give them their proper name, La société des missionaires de Notre Dame d'Afrique, were founded in 1868 by Cardinal Charles Lavigerie, Archbishop of Algiers and Primate of Africa in the Catholic church. The original aim of the society was to work among the Moslem population of north Africa. As other regions of the African continent were opened up, Cardinal Lavigerie sought to enlarge the scope of the White Fathers' work. In 1878, he was given permission by Pope Leo XIII to send missionaries to east and central Africa, not only to spread the Gospel message but also to work in education, agriculture and health.

It was not until 1895 that the White Fathers succeeded in opening their first mission station in Northern Rhodesia. This was at Kayambi in the Northern Province. Thereafter, expansion was quite rapid and a network of stations was established across the Northern and Luapula Provinces. Progress in the Eastern Province was much slower. A group of Fathers from Kachebere mission in Nyasaland eventually opened a station at Naviruli, near Fort Jameson, in 1914. A second, at Minga in Petauke District was established some ten years later. Lumezi, the first White Fathers station in Lundazi District was not opened until 1939.[2]

Father Rykers, the Dutch priest in charge, met us as William brought the Chev to a dusty halt in front of the Fathers' house. It was Cardinal Lavigerie's inflexible rule that each station should be manned by three Fathers. Sure enough, two other Fathers, each clad, like Father Rykers, in the distinctive dress of an Arab gondoura (a full-length, loose-fitting white robe) and wearing round his neck a large rosary of white and black beads, came bustling down the steps to meet us. 'Mr Goddard, you do us much honour,' said Father Rykers. Glyn introduced me. 'You will be the replacement for poor Richard?' Father Rykers asked. There was a burst of laughter from his two colleagues. I was puzzled by Rykers' reference to my predecessor. 'I'll explain later,' growled Glyn as we followed Father Rykers into the refectory. We sat at a well-scrubbed table to eat a simple meal of soup made from vegetables grown in the mission garden and a stew with the unmistakable flavour of impala. One of the Fathers had shot it on a visit to the

Luangwa valley a few days earlier. To the evident delight of the Fathers, we washed it down with a bottle of German wine. Normally, the Fathers drank no alcohol but their rules allowed them to open a bottle when they had visitors.

The Fathers were a fund of information on Lundazi District. They had each undergone a rigorous selection process and lengthy training before being appointed as missionaries. The society took language training very seriously and all the Fathers were fluent in the language of the area to which they were posted. Their tour of duty lasted ten years. They were, of course, celibate and hence had no family responsibilities to distract them. They had every opportunity, therefore, to immerse themselves in the affairs of the mission and to get to know and understand the people among whom they were working. At Lumezi, as at all the other White Father mission stations, the dominant building was the church. A lay brother had designed the church and had supervised its building. It was here that the Fathers heard confession and conducted public worship. Their own devotions took place in a small, dimly-lit chapel adjacent to their sleeping quarters.

All Christian missionary activity is inspired by Jesus's exhortation to his disciples, as recorded in St Matthew's Gospel, to spread the Good News to others. 'All authority in heaven and on earth has been given to me,' he told them. 'Go, therefore, make disciples of all the nations; baptize them in the name of the Father and of the Son and of the Holy Spirit, and teach them to observe all the commands I gave you. And know that I am with you always, even to the end of time.' An important new impetus to missionary endeavour was given by David Livingstone's epic journeyings, the publication of his journals and his lonely death at Chitambo's village. The White Fathers were just one of several missionary societies which entered Northern Rhodesia during a great burst of evangelistic outreach which began in the 1880s. Misssionaries converged on the country from north, south, east and west.

Among the earliest arrivals was Frederick Arnot. Born in 1858, he had played with Livingstone's children when the two families were neighbours in Hamilton, Scotland. Landing in Durban in 1882, not quite 24 years old, he made his way after a series of adventures to the upper reaches of the Zambesi river. It was there, at Limulunga, the summer capital of Lewanika, king of the Barotse people, that Arnot opened the country's first school. It did not last long for Arnot was forced to withdraw because of persistent sickness. Nevertheless, his pioneer work had broken down the first barriers of resistance and eased the task of the next group of missionaries who would try to bring the Gospel and education to the Barotse.

Within a short time of Arnot's departure, Francois Coillard of the Paris Evangelical Misssion had established mission stations at Sesheke in 1885 and at Sefula in 1887 with Lewanika's full approval. Life was hard and dangerous. Coillard, his wife and colleagues, had to contend with the indifference and sometimes hostility of the people. They suffered many privations and battled against a difficult and enervating climate. They were regularly incapacitated by diseases such as malaria, amoebic dysentery and yellow fever against which the medicines of the time were largely ineffective.

The price paid in bringing the Gospel to Northern Rhodesia was high. Coillard suffered a grievous blow when, in October 1891, his wife died. Broken-hearted, he wrote in his diary: 'When we were married she spoke these words to me: "I have come to do the work of God with you, whatever it may be and wherever it may be. Remember this, wherever God may call you, you will never find me crossing your path of duty." '³ Coillard's wife was but one of many who died in the early years of the mission's work. 'We have not only stations,' said Coillard, 'we have graves.' Of 24 Paris mission workers who reached the country in the last years of the century, eight died and eleven were sent home as invalids or as widows. By 1902, 36 mission graves (16 of children) were mute reminders of the cost of attempting to convert the Lozi people to Christianity. When, in 1967, I accompanied Arthur Wina, then Minister of Education and himself a Lozi, on a visit to Sefula, I found it a moving experience to make a pilgrimage to the mission cemetery. Standing among so many graves, I could but marvel at the faith, fortitude and spirit of self-sacrifice which enabled this cloud of witnesses to seek to serve the Lord in this remote spot far from their home country, from family, friends and creature comforts. I think Arthur Wina shared my feelings of awe and gratitude.

'For My sake and the Gospel's, go
And tell redemption's story';
His heralds answer, 'Be it so,
And thine, Lord, all the glory!'

Thus ran one of the popular hymns of the period. There was no shortage of those willing to take up the challenge. At the same time as Coillard and his colleagues were making their way northwards from Basutoland, the London Misssionary Society were settling in the north-east of the country around the southern end of Lake Tanganyika. Others followed swiftly. By the time war broke out in Europe in 1914 and temporarily halted the inflow of missionaries, the Primitive Methodists, the Church of Scotland, the Dutch Reformed Church, the Brethren, the Jesuit Fathers, the Seventh Day Adventist Church, the Brethren in Christ, the South African Baptists, the South Africa General Misssion, the Universities Mission to Central Africa (UMCA), and the Wesleyan Methodist Misssionary Society had all established themselves in various parts of the country. Of the three which were working in the Eastern Province, the Dutch Reformed Church Misssion (DRCM) was by far the largest. It was with resources provided by the Dutch Reformed Church in the Orange Free State, South Africa, that a mission station was opened at Magwero, some 12 miles from Fort Jameson, in 1899. Soon a chain of strategically-sited stations covered Fort Jameson and Petauke Districts, providing the bases for a very large number of outposts which reached nearly every village.

The Dutch, like all the other missionary bodies, placed great emphasis on education as an essential element in the work of evangelization, or saving souls. The reasoning was simple: in order that the people might receive and understand the Gospel message, they must be able to read the Bible. And to ensure that the Good News might spread to those whom the missionaries were unable to reach, African teachers must be trained who could teach others to read and who could preach the Word. The Dutch therefore trained teacher-evangelists on their mission stations and then sent them to set up outposts among a group of villages. The outpost system (Buiteposstel) was so successful that by 1925 the DRCM were running nearly 450 schools attended by adults as well as by children. By 1954, a process of rationalization and the need to economize had reduced the number to just under a hundred of which approximately half satisfied Glyn's standards and were grant-aided. The other half were unaided; they were run entirely at the expense of the mission.

I was never entirely comfortable in the presence of DRCM missionaries although I knew many of them to be tremendously conscientious and caring. I could not forget that their church maintained that the hateful policy of apartheid, practised in their home country of South Africa, had a sound biblical basis. Fortunately, our contacts with the DRCM were mainly with their Education Secretary, a burly Afrikaner, but one who seemed to have little sympathy with the extreme views of the divines of his church. (The Dutch Reformed Church abandoned its support of apartheid in the 1980s.)

Earlier in the century, the Dutch had engaged in bitter competition with the Roman Catholics (represented by the White Fathers) and the Anglicans (in the person of the Universities Misssion to Central Africa). These inter-denominational rivalries, which consumed a great deal of time, money and energy, bewildered the people, presented a sorry picture of a divided church, and rendered even simple education planning, which depended on co-operation between the missions, quite out of the question. By 1954, however, the battles for territory and for souls were largely a thing of the past. Each missionary society was usually content to operate in its own area and not to encroach on that of others.

Some societies found it difficult to hold on to what they had; the UMCA was a case in point. The mission had been launched on a great wave of enthusiasm in the wake of David Livingstone's address to a packed audience in the Senate House of Cambridge University. For the first 50 years, work had centred on Zanzibar and Nyasaland. In 1907, on the 50th anniversary of Livingstone's lecture, another great meeting in the Senate House vociferously approved a resolution proposed by the Archbishop of Canterbury to establish a third diocese of the mission in what was to become Northern Rhodesia. The mission claimed the whole country as its sphere of evangelism. Time was to show that the mission had neither the human nor the material resources to make any real impact over so vast an area. The UMCA, representing the Anglo-Catholic side of the Church of England, was never to make a major contribution to the Northern Rhodesian education scene as their low church colleagues of the Church Misssionary Society did in Uganda and Kenya for instance. Shortages of staff and money were a permanent feature of the UMCA's work in Northern Rhodesia. They had to be content with a thin scattering of mission stations, separated by great distances. One of the stations, Msoro, served the Akunda people in Fort Jameson District. Father Mudford was the priest-in-charge. Dedicated to his work, dressed always in knee-length khaki shorts, khaki shirt and open-toe sandals, he toiled long hours to keep the mission station going, to minister to his flock, to preach the Word, to visit his schools and to keep up with the paper work with which we bombarded him. The cares of the world seemed to hang heavily about his shoulders and he rarely smiled. I found it sad that serving the Lord could result in so much apparent gloom and despondency. I shared the delight of many when, years later, in his 70s, the good father married one of the lady workers at Msoro and lived happily to a ripe old age.

Lundazi District was divided fairly amicably between the White Fathers and the Church of Scotland. Most missionary societies faced severe difficulties in establishing themselves in central Africa; the Church of Scotland proved no exception. In April, 1874, the embalmed remains of David Livingstone were laid to rest in Westminster Abbey. Within a month, the General Assembly of the Church of Scotland resolved to establish in central Africa, as a memorial to Livingstone, at a place to be named Livingstonia, an institution 'at once industrial and educational, to teach the truths of the Gospel and the arts of civilised life to the natives of the country.'[5]

In less than a year, the necessary money had been raised, preparations made, and a party of eight men, including a carpenter, an agriculturalist, a blacksmith, an engineer and a seaman, sailed for Cape Town in May 1875. They were led by Captain Young from the Royal Navy and Dr Robert Laws, a medical missionary. The party reached the mouth of the Zambesi river and proceeded to assemble the sections of a small steamer they had brought with them in packing cases from Edinburgh. The wood-burning steamer, named *Ilala* from the place where Livingstone died, was 15 metres long and built of steel plates which were fastened together with bolts. In the *Ilala*, the party steamed up the Zambesi and Shire rivers as far as the Murchison Rapids. Here, they disembarked, dismantled the boat and distributed its sections among 1,000 carriers who transported their loads over more than 60 miles of difficult country. At the head of the cataract, the boat was reassembled, the carriers were paid off, and Young piloted his way the remaining 100 miles up the Shire. The party entered Lake Nyasa on 12 October 1875, less than five months after sailing from London, a truly remarkable feat of organization, enterprise and endurance.

Progress in opening mission stations was slow; difficulties were numerous; hopes were raised only to be dashed. It was not until 1894, at Kondowe, nearly 3,000 feet above Lake Nyasa, that the Livingstonia Institution was finally set up. It rapidly grew into one of the leading education establishments in central Africa, providing a full primary school course, teacher training, craft and secretarial training. Livingstonia's reputation was such that young boys from Northern Rhodesia would trek very long distances in order to obtain there the education and training opportunities which were not available to them in their own country.

Once they were firmly based in Nyasaland, the Church of Scotland missionaries began to look westwards, particularly into the Northern and Eastern Provinces of Northern Rhodesia. In 1894, a mission station was opened at Mwenzo among the Winamwanga people in the far northeast corner of the country. In 1907 an attempt was made to establish a station at Chitambo village where Livingstone had died. The area proved unhealthy, however, and scantily populated. Within three years the station was closed and shifted to a new site northeast of the present Serenje. Soon after, Lubwa mission station was opened near Chinsali, among the Bemba people. I recall these names with particular pleasure. I met my wife at Mwenzo mission, we became engaged at Serenje, and we were married at Lubwa.

In Lundazi District, a mission station was opened in 1903 at Kazembe, west of Lundazi towards the Luangwa valley, but it had to be abandoned in 1906. It was not until 1922 that the Church of Scotland made another attempt to get a footing in the district. This time, Chasefu mission station was set up some 25 miles north of Lundazi *boma*. The church's schools, which covered most of the district and which had previously been run from Nyasaland, now came under the control of Chasefu. For 30 years, Chasefu was the hub of educational activity as successive groups of missionaries endeavoured to impart something of Scotland's rigorous and disciplined approach to schooling. Gradually, however, the church's policy changed. The efficient management of the schools took up a great deal of time; the number of ministers offering for service in the mission field was declining. Scarce human resources could not be spared to run the schools; other requirements merited higher priority. Accordingly, after much heart-searching, the Church of Scotland approached the African Education Department and it was agreed that the Church would hand over to the Local Education Authority its 40 or so schools in Lundazi District. The missionaries withdrew from Chasefu.

These were the schools that I was to manage. Glyn took me to Chasefu. En route, we called at Lundazi *boma* and collected Laban Ndlovu, the Assistant Manager of Schools. Laban and I hit it off at once. A man of 45 or so, Laban had passed Standard 6 at a time when this was as high a qualification as Africans could obtain. He had trained as a teacher and served in several schools before successfully taking a Higher Teacher Certificate course. With good experience as a headmaster behind him, an excellent record in the church, wide respect in the district, a more than adequate command of English and a keen sense of humour, he had been selected by the missionaries to help manage their schools. Now he would be helping me. I knew instinctively that he would teach me a lot. He showed me round the school and the deserted mission house with its wide verandahs and high ceilings. Where once missionary families had made their homes, termites were attacking the woodwork, the garden was overgrown, and droppings on the living-room floor indicated that either rats or bats had taken up residence in considerable numbers.

Back at Lundazi, Philip Farwell, the District Commissioner, had just finished hearing cases in his court. Maintenance of law and order was just one of his responsibilities. As DC he was the Governor's chief representative in the district and was responsible, in theory at least, for all government activity in a 'parish' of some 10,000 square miles. In education, for instance, I was the Education Officer but he was chairman of the Local Education Authority. Living on the *boma* were a small number of Europeans – an agricultural supervisor, a road foreman, a building foreman and two policemen. As long as they got on with their jobs, Philip supported them. But he was on to them, or to their superiors in Fort Jimmie, like a ton of bricks if they stepped out of line. The DC and his district officer were the link men between the government and the chiefs. A fair amount of their time was spent in checking the accounts of the chiefs' treasuries, reviewing judgements given in the chiefs' courts, and generally trying to improve the efficiency of the native authorities through which, under the policy of indirect rule, much of the business of government was supposed to be conducted.

Philip sniffed disparagingly at Glyn's Chevrolet but invited us into his office for tea. It was clear that he took a poor view of civil servants who lived in Fort Jameson although their main responsibilities were in his district. He wanted to build up his district team. 'If you can't live here,' he told me, 'I hope at least that we shall see you up here often and that you won't try to run Lundazi's schools from your office in Fort Jimmie.'

'There's no danger of that,' said Glyn. 'He'll spend at least half his time in the district and will visit all your schools regularly.'

'Including Lundu and Mulilo?' asked Farwell.

'Why not?' Glyn was cautious.

'You can reach them only by using carriers,' replied the DC, getting up from his chair and pointing to two small dots on the large map which covered much of one wall of his office. 'Apart from my district officers, no European ever goes there. I don't suppose you'd like to go?' he looked directly at me.

'If you can help me to get some carriers, I'll go next month.' Glyn looked doubtful but Philip was clearly pleased.

'I'll get you carriers,' he promised, 'and I'll lay on a game guard as well. Have some more tea.'

Returning to Fort Jimmie that evening, we had first one and then a second puncture. The tyres were tubeless and we had no means of mending them. Traffic on the road, never very heavy, had stopped for the night. William lit a fire and we sat around it. There was not a village within miles. 'You didn't tell me what Father Rykers meant when he mentioned Richard,' I said.

Glyn laughed. 'I sent him off on tour,' he explained, 'to visit some schools north of Fort Jimmie. For several miles the road runs in and out of Nyasaland; of course, there are no boundaries marked. Richard came back after a week or so. I asked him how he had got on. He told me that the trip had gone well but that two of the schools he visited were so awful he had closed them. Of course, I told him that he had no right to close a school; that was a responsibility of the Provincial Education Authority. Anyway, I asked him which were the two schools involved. When he told me their names I couldn't place them. Then I looked at the map and found that they were both in Nyasaland.'

I could imagine the scene in Glyn's office as the truth dawned on Richard. Not only had he grossly exceeded his authority by shutting down two schools, the schools were in the wrong country. Glyn's anger must have been something to behold.

Glyn resumed: 'I had to go at once to Lilongwe, the provincial headquarters in Nyasaland, and apologise to the Provincial Commissioner as well as to the PEO. Very embarrassing.'

'When is Richard due back?' I ventured.

'He'll come back only over my dead body,' said Glyn. 'I've told the director that. You won't be going back to Munali. You're here for good. Or ill,' he added mischievously.

'Suits me,' I said.

Soon after dawn, a worried Win Goddard, accompanied by the faithful Godile, drove up in Glyn's private car. On the way back to Fort Jimmie, Glyn insisted on stopping to visit a school. It was typical of hundreds which I subsequently visited. A lower primary school, it consisted of four classes, sub-Standard A, sub-B, Standard 1 and Standard 2, each of 40 pupils. A double-session, or hot-seat, system was in operation. This meant that two classes attended in the morning and the other two in the afternoon. Thus, two classrooms, with a small office cum storeroom in between, sufficed. The two teachers, both men, lived on the school site. The wife of one of the teachers was on the payroll as a woman helper. Many of the children lived within walking distance of the school but about 50 came from villages farther afield; they were weekly boarders. Parents had erected a compound of half a dozen pole and mud huts with thatched roofs; these served as dormitories. The children would arrive each Sunday afternoon with a small bag of mealie meal and perhaps a little relish. They cooked their own food and looked after themselves until Friday afternoon when they would return to their villages.

It was a hard life for the youngsters, whose ages ranged between 7 and 13. It was difficult for the teachers, too. They were required to teach for six–seven hours a day with no free periods, with not much equipment and with very little professional stimulation. I found the visit discouraging. The teaching was listless, the children were inattentive, the classroom floor was dirty, the office was untidy, one of the pit latrines was on the point of collapse. If the director, from his office in Lusaka, thought that the quality of education in the country's schools had reached 'a degree seldom attained in African education', it was time he got off his chair and went to see what the schools were actually like. Glyn agreed. 'But don't worry about the director,' he said. 'It's what you do that matters.' He was right, of course. It did not need much imagination to see that, despite my unfamiliarity with primary education, a very restricted budget with which to work, and a language problem – since many of the people in Lundazi District spoke Chitumbuka, not Chinyanja – there were many ways in which Laban and I could help the teachers to raise their standards.

Preparations for the *ulendo* (expedition) to Lundu, Chiwale and Mulilo took a little longer than expected. This gave me time to settle into the pleasant two-bedroomed thatched bungalow which had been allocated to me and to Peter Greening, an agricultural officer. Both of us spent much of our time on tour and we each, therefore, needed a cook. Temani had accompanied me from Munali. He was a Ngoni and was glad to be back in his home district. The delay also enabled me to tackle an outbreak of bigamy among a group of teachers. Now that their schools were managed by the Local Education Authority rather than by the Church of Scotland, some teachers thought they were free from the discipline imposed by the church. Six took second wives. The members of the Provincial Teaching Service Committee, who included Dutch Reformed, UMCA and White Father missionaries, decided to take a firm line. I had to write to the teachers and tell them that unless they divorced their second wives by such and such a date, they would be suspended from duty and would probably be dismissed for bringing the Teaching Service into disrepute. Four of the teachers did as they were told. The other two refused to send away the wives they had so recently married; they were suspended and eventually dismissed. (Subsequently, fate took a hand in this unhappy affair. The second wife of one who remained a bigamist died in childbirth. The remaining teacher, taking this as evidence of divine retribution, promptly resumed the monogamous state. Both were reinstated.) I did not claim then, and neither do I claim now, to know the rights and wrongs of all this. At the time, it was a very worrying business and I was very relieved when the time came to leave these troubles in the office and to head up the road to Lundazi again.

The vanette was piled high with equipment to be distributed to schools, food and drink to last a month, bicycles, a tent, poles and fly sheet, a camp table, camp bed, collapsible chairs, sleeping bags, spare clothes, rifle and shotgun. Somehow, Temani and Benjamin found room for themselves among all the *katundu*. Like me, they seemed glad to get away from Fort Jimmie.

We camped for a week just outside the *musumba*, or head-quarters, of Senior Chief Mwase Lundazi, an important leader of the Chewa people, while I visited schools in the area. The Chief was courtesy itself. Each day he ensured that wood and fresh water were brought to the camp, and that gifts of chickens were provided regularly. Laban had been at school with him years before. He suggested that we should invite the Chief and leading members of his entourage to tea. Temani made scones, we opened a jar of strawberry jam, borrowed some cups and some chairs from the headmaster's wife, and had an enjoyable teaparty. The Native Authority, of which the Chief was head, had an important part to play in maintaining school buildings and encouraging parents to send their children to school, so it was useful to get to know the Chief and his leading counsellors. Mwase kept them all on their

72

toes and was reckoned to be one of the most progressive chiefs in the province.

After a week under canvas, I was glad to enjoy the comparative luxury of a night in the rest house at Lundazi. Every district headquarters, or *boma*, had a rest house which was primarily intended for use by touring government officers and passing holiday-makers. Most of them were of simple design, consisting of two or three bedrooms, a sitting room, a bathroom, toilet and a kitchen where a resident cook would prepare meals using ingredients provided by the client. Lundazi rest house was completely different. An imaginative and enterprising DC had decided to build a castle. The prisoners in his gaol provided the labour. It was said that carpenters and bricklayers who appeared in the DC's court were certain to be found guilty and sentenced to long terms of imprisonment since he needed them to help build his castle. Be that as it may, the castle, complete with battlements, towers, turrets, arrow slits and drawbridge, stood by a delightful lake, inhabited by hippo, on the outskirts of the *boma*. Seeing it for the first time came as a surprise to everyone. It was particularly appreciated by American big game hunters who used the castle as a base before descending into the Luangwa valley. It was much less popular with the Public Works Department foreman who had to maintain it.

Philip Farwell assured me that he had arranged for 20 carriers to meet us at Tembwe in the Luangwa valley. I could not imagine why as many as 20 carriers would be necessary. Philip said that the number of carriers to which each grade of officer was entitled was laid down in General Orders. My entitlement was 20, neither more nor less. The Governor, apparently, enjoyed an entitlement of 150 carriers but it was a long time since a governor had travelled in this way. On Philip's advice, I bought 60 lbs of salt to be used for bartering and for giving as presents in the valley, where salt was highly prized and difficult to obtain. Benjamin, on behalf of Temani, William and himself, came to ask for an advance of ten shillings. He shortly reappeared, holding a pack of 800 Tom Tom cigarettes. I shuddered at the thought of the state of their lungs when they had puffed their way through that lot.

We spent a week visiting and inspecting schools on the eastern side of the Luangwa river, being joined by Hezekiah Kumwenda, a former headmaster and now a Jeanes Supervisor, or adviser.[6] By now it was October, the hottest month of the year. At midday, the heat was intense. For the first time in my life I found the heat affecting my breathing. This proved to be a good introduction to the next two weeks when, with bicycles and carriers, we were to cross the Luangwa, climb the escarpment on the western side, make managerial and inspection visits to four schools before being picked up again by William in the headwaters of the Luangwa, 150 miles or more later.

The carriers assembled at Tembwe. They had been recruited by one of Philip's *boma* messengers, White Zulu. Second in command was a messenger, or *kapasu*, of the Chief. The party would need meat to eat during the next fortnight. Philip had arranged for a game guard to meet us and authorized him to shoot a buffalo. I gave the game guard five rounds of .404 ammunition and told him to return to me the spent cartridge cases and the unused ones after he had done his stuff.

From my diary, I can recall some of the flavour of the next two weeks.

Sunday, 3 October 1954

Today was one of preparing and waiting, chiefly waiting. I wrote up some school inspection reports and will send these to the PEO with William when he returns to Fort Jimmie tomorrow. The game guard went out soon after 5a.m. If he returned by 10.00, there was a good chance of drying the meat today and leaving tomorrow. But the hours went by and I began to wonder if he had killed the buffalo or the buffalo had done for him. Eventually, he returned at 4p.m., saluted smartly, placed two empty cases and three unused rounds on my table, and announced that he had shot two buffalo. It appears that he came on a herd of about 40. He fired at one but did not think he had killed it. So he fired again at what he thought was the same beast. In fact, it was a different one. Result: two dead buffalo. I hadn't the heart to question him too closely. In any case, there is no means of proving whether he intended to kill one or two.

It was after 7.00 by the time all the meat was in. I allotted the whole of one animal and part of the other to the *ulendo*, a leg to the Chief, part of the remains to the game guard and the rest to the school. Everyone seemed happy, or perhaps they just pretended to be, as I made it clear that anyone quarrelling about the distribution would be sent away empty-handed.

Earlier in the day, the carriers had constructed a great rack for drying the meat. Now they lost no time in starting this operation which will last all day tomorrow, I fear.

Monday, 4 October

The carriers spent the whole day drying the meat. I kept well to windward. In fact, Laban and I used the time to have a closer look at the school. Having checked the stock book, I sat in on several English lessons with Standards 3 and 4, and gave the teachers some ideas on how they might enliven their lessons. The *boma* messenger and Benjamin have been mentally dividing up the *katundu* into loads, and seem to be satisfied that nothing will have to be discarded. When I look at the mountain of meat which has to be carried, I have my doubts, but am happy to leave it in their hands. I do quite well for food. Lunch today was green mealie, cold chicken and buffalo tongue. For supper, Temani produced a mixed grill or buff. liver and steak, and eggs.

Tuesday, 5 October

I was up by 5.00 and shaved and packed hurriedly before the critical gaze of the carriers who wanted to take down the tent and be on their way before the sun got too hot. I left the loading operations to White and Benjamin and made an early morning visit to the school to watch, and even join in, the PE lesson. By the time I returned to camp, the last of the carriers had gone. The day's ride was an easy one, not more than about 12 miles. We crossed the Luangwa by paddling across a shallow pool and reached Mpyanak-unda soon after 9.00. Here the Native Authority itinerant dresser and his carrier were waiting. The dresser is allegedly lazy and the DC thought it would be a good thing if he came with the *ulendo*.

His presence will spare me the necessity of treating blisters on unwashed feet.

Our party is now thus:

myself – *der Fuehrer*
Laban and his orderly, Absalom
Benjamin (orderly) and Temani (cook)
Hezekiah Kumwenda, Jeanes Supervisor
White Zulu, *boma* messenger
20 carriers and the *kapasu*
dresser and his carrier

Total: 30

It seems scarcely credible that it requires a party of 30 to enable four schools, one of which is closed, to be visited.

Mpyanakunda is a small village memorable for two things – the large number of tsetse flies and the wind that blows so persistently. Laban and I took a stroll with our guns. I shot a wart hog which the villagers were glad to exchange for meal. None of them has a shotgun and the only time they get meat is when they are able to chase a lion from its kill. Only one person here can read and write. When he is away, letters have to be taken to Tembwe to be read.

Wednesday, 6 October

The *ulendo* is only two days old but already a pattern is emerging. We wake up at 5.00. I hurriedly drink my tea, wash, shave, pack and vacate the tent by 5.30. The tent is then taken down by the carriers. Meanwhile, I eat some breakfast and no sooner have I finished than plates, cup, pots, chair and table are whisked away, stowed on someone's back and the carriers are on their way by 6.00a.m., shepherded by the *kapasu* (whose name, I have discovered, is Enoch). The 'O' group, i.e. Laban, Kumwenda, messengers, cook and dresser, prepare for the journey in more leisurely style but we are in pursuit of the carriers by 7.00. We catch them up within the hour. A few words of encouragement and abuse are exchanged as we overtake them. Another hour and a half's pedalling brings us to our next resting place. We go to the camping area which is traditionally used by the DC and other visiting government officers (if any) and sit in the simple shelters. The village headman and the other males come to greet us. My halting Chinyanja is of no use since the people here speak Chitumbuka. It is Laban who explains who we are and what we are doing. We are told that we are welcome. The men depart and soon the women appear. They go down on their knees, clap their hands and ululate. Shortly, the headman returns with a fowl for me and a basket of meal for the carriers. A few shillings change hands, the amount depending on the size of the offerings, and the rituals are over. Within an hour, the long-suffering women are back, bringing water and wood. We sit in the shelters and kill tsetse flies.

By 11.00, the carriers have started to arrive, hot and perspiring, (the temperature is well into the 80s) and complaining, but glad that their day's stint is over. Within half an hour they have all arrived. They drink some water and some erect the tent. The table and chairs are placed on the verandah. Temani brings mugs for Laban and me, the water bag and a bottle of lemon squash. At noon we all have something to eat and then enjoy a siesta. The camp wakes up at 4.00p.m. The carriers go to the stream to wash. Laban and I take our shotguns and take a stroll, hoping to find an unwary guinea fowl. By the time we return to the camp, it is dusk. The lamps are lit and water is heated. Having endured the purgatory of a canvas bath, I am ready for supper which I wash down with a bottle of 'Castle'. That over, I read or write a little while the camp gradually quietens, the 'O' group divided between two shelters, the carriers stretched out round their fires. By 9.00, I, too, turn in, to be ready to repeat the whole performance tomorrow.

Today's journey was about 18 miles. We are camped at Sikalinga, a tiny spot of 30 souls. The water is very muddy. There used to be an unaided mission school here but attendance must have been shocking. There is no village for miles around and we passed none between Mpyanakunda and here. No-one in the village can read or write. Outside the headman's house is what looks like a model of a church. Laban says that the people gather at this *kavua*, as it is called, at important times such as death, harvest, drought, etc., to ask their ancestors to intercede with God on their behalf. A few of the carriers are complaining of tummy trouble. I suspect they have eaten too much of the buffalo meat. It's not serious but keeps the dresser busy.

Thursday, 7 October

Today began very early. Last evening, I told Temani that I wanted tea at 4.45. I heard preparations for tea taking place in the kitchen. Looking at my watch, I discovered it was 2a.m. I told Temani this and he crept shame-facedly back to bed. But some of the carriers had heard me tell him the time and today they have pulled his leg unmercifully. Poor Temani, he has been none too well for the last day or two, but he took the bantering well and doubtless gave as good as he got. An Ngoni, he has a pretty low opinion of the Senga. I enjoyed today's two and a half hours' ride. There were incidents en route. First Benjamin fell off his bike and broke the carrier. This was repaired with strips of bark, known as *mtambo*. We crossed a stream, which was actually flowing. Then Laban shot a plump guinea fowl; his aim seems to be improving! We reached our stopping place before 9.00. It is called Mwakana, a pleasant spot with good, running water, a welcome change after the muddy mess at Sikalinga.

I have made a fairly close study of latrines. At each camp stands a grass shelter in which is concealed a pit. So far, so good. Over this pit, however, there is invariably erected a rustic seat with a hole cut in the middle. It is the size and shape of that hole that calls for comment. It always shows a profound disregard for the most elementary facts of human anatomy. Further, its minute dimensions call for the highest degree of marksmanship at a time when it is frequently not possible to see in which direction matters are heading. It is another example, I fear, of the unbounded but often totally misplaced, confidence which the African seems to have in the European. For these latrines and their extraordinary thrones are used only by Europeans; no self-respecting African would go near them. Here at Mwakana, I thought things had changed for the better; there was no seat. But White, the *boma* messenger, who makes a careful inspection of the usual offices at each site, soon spotted the deficiency. He constructed a magnificent affair on to which one clambers with difficulty only to find an aperture of

six–eight sq. ins. awaiting one's deliberations. I have abandoned
the whole structure in favour of the open bush.

On our way here, we met a group of cyclists heading for
Tembwe. They had been seeking fame and fortune on the Copperbelt and now were on their way home to help with the hoeing, to
display their bicycles and other symbols of their wealth and to tell,
doubtless, fantastic stories of Kitwe and Luanshya. It is a pity they
have to go so far to find employment. The effect on family life here
in the valley must be devastating. Tonight the carriers seem
happier. A number of them were troubled with diarrhoea at
Sikalinga but that has cleared up. One of them was asking who
would like to go with him to the Mwakana bioscope. This sally
has had them rolling in the aisles for the last couple of hours. They
are simple and likeable souls and as strong as lions. They average
a good three miles an hour for five or more hours carrying loads
which would have me staggering after a couple of hundred yards.

Friday, 8 October

The day's journey began very pleasantly. The women of Mwakana
escorted us out of the village for nearly a mile, singing a song
which meant: 'We are glad the *bwana* has come because he is a
good man. But we do not like the *capitao* (the *boma* messenger) as
he makes us work hard.' We were soon climbing the Muchinga
hills. A man from Mwakana insisted on carrying my bike to the
top, a kind thought. We emerged on to an attractive, wooded
plateau, with just a few ups and downs where we crossed streams.
The drop in temperature was very noticeable. The sultry heat of
the valley is behind us; here it is just pleasantly warm. After a ride
of ten miles, we reached Lundu. The camp was filthy and I made
my displeasure known to the Chief. Feeling much better, I went to
inspect the school. It was depressing. The school is made of poles
and mud: the children attend only on compulsion from the Native
Authority; the people are not merely apathetic but positively hostile
to education. One's reaction is to say that the school should be
closed. But as the school is the only 'service' the people receive in
return for their taxes it is difficult to do this. The effect of
compulsion can be clearly seen. In Standard 2 there are children

who can neither read nor write. Since entering the school three years ago, they have followed a policy of passive resistance and have resolutely refused to learn anything. In such circumstances, the teachers' lot is not a happy one. Laban and I spoke to each class, trying to instil some motivation. We also spent time with the teachers. It is easy to criticize their low standards but they are terribly isolated here and very frustrated. What they need is encouragement, some new ideas and regular visits.

Saturday, 9 October

Last night, there was dancing in the village until midnight. The village gave a party for the carriers. Benjamin and White came to me soon after 10.00 to ask if they might go into the village 'to make sure that the carriers are behaving.' They both had sleepy heads this morning. I had a session with the Chief before we left Lundu at 8.30. We left to a musical accompaniment. The women lined the path and sang as we passed. We heard the same tune at each of the villages we passed through. Each time, we were met about half a mile from the village by a group of women. My bicycle was taken from me. As I walked, the women sang their song of greeting and 'washed' me with cloths. Laban said this was a great honour. I must confess that I found it rather embarrassing but couldn't help wishing someone had a camera to record it. A three-hour ride through pleasantly undulating country brought us to Mulumika. This is a small village, miles from anywhere. It seems that only the men ever stray from the immediate surroundings. The women just stay here all their lives, producing and bringing up children, growing and cooking the food, becoming old and dying. This evening I wrote a fairly long report on Lundu school, a depressing affair.

Sunday, 10 October

I forgot to mention yesterday that one of the problems at Lundu school is that of early marriage. Recently, a boy and a girl in Standard 2 left school when they got married. She was only 13 and he was but two or three years older. As soon as the 'flower age', as

80

it is called, is reached, little time is wasted before defloration. Early marriage is probably preferable to the kind of situation I read about at Fulaza school recently. The head recorded in the log book that a boy in Standard 2 and a girl in Standard 1 'had the mating instinct'. Another entry, a few days later, gave the dismal news that the girl had died while attempting an abortion.

Today we went first to Mwenso, a pleasant hour's ride from Mulumika. There was a White Fathers' school here until June when it was handed over to the Local Education Authority. It has not opened this year for lack of a teacher. I promised to send a teacher next year if the village will look after the school in the meantime. The headman promised to see to it. Headman Mwenso was a dear old chap. I asked him about the *kavua* in front of his house and reminded him that the children would be brought up in the school to be Christians. He said that he quite understood that but, for himself, the old ways of worship were good enough.

Our stopping place today is Nganjo, one of several villages by that name. It means a kiln. Iron ore used to be smelted here and made into axe-heads, spears, hoes, etc. There is no sign of that nowadays. Indeed, the village is very run-down. It seems they have very little food and I was reluctant to take any of it. However, the carriers have to be fed. I eased my conscience by giving a very generous measure of salt in exchange for the meal which was brought. Temani was able to do some washing today. This will ease my wardrobe problems considerably. The fact that I wished to wear clean clothes while travelling clearly surprised the Nganjo women who had to bring the water. They shrugged it off, as they do so many things, with 'Ah! those Europeans. You never know what they will do next!'

In return for food, water and wood, the *ulendo* provides medical attention through the dresser. At nearly every village, the entire population lines up for treatment. The dresser's diagnoses do not take long. No-one can have anything wrong with them other than coughing, sore eyes, malaria, diarrhoea, constipation, headache or cuts as these are the only things he can treat. The names of all the patients are written in a book. What happens to these records is not clear. The people here have no doctor within reasonable reach. Their lot is a hard one. It is an area of scattered population and very poor communication. Little progress has been made, educational, medical or agricultural. I doubt if things will change much in the next 20 years.

About the most entertaining time of each day is sunset when the chickens received as presents are rounded up. Mine, now six in number, rival in their perverseness those of Kenneth Bradley as he described them in his *Diary of a district officer*. They seem to sense when their freedom is about to be ended and run hither and thither, squawking loudly. The carriers adopt exaggeratedly casual poses, feigning indifference, and then make sudden swoops on the fowls, usually missing them completely. When captured, the birds are put into a 'cage', made by splitting a branch and making a bark net between the strands. Tonight, two of the chickens had been captured and the chase was getting hot against the others, when the first two escaped and the whole procedure had to begin anew. I think the carriers quite enjoy this daily sport. Soon only one bird remained free. They formed a circle around it and slowly closed in. Just as capture was imminent there was a flurry of feathers and a terrified squawk and the chicken flew over their heads and disappeared into my tent. Great laughter. Enoch, who was in disgrace for losing my water bag, retrieved part of his shattered reputation by effecting a neat capture.

Monday, 11 October

Today's journey, about 20 miles, ran through country that reminded me very much of the New Forest, round about Lyndhurst. It was really lovely, with only a few elephant droppings to remind one that this is Africa. Where we are staying, at Samson Kamamwamba, the view is splendid. Through a gap in the trees, you can look down into the Luangwa valley, across the river and as far as Indunda hill on the other side. It raised my spirits considerably to see the end of the journey in sight. Not that I am, or have been, at all unhappy. On the contrary, I am enjoying the trip very much. But I shall be glad to see a European again. Then I shall cease to wonder whether I am really as curious a spectacle as the stares of the African villagers would make me believe. Enoch, the *kapasu*, had disappeared by the time I got up this morning at

5.00. He turned up again just after 2p.m., triumphantly carrying my 'lost' water bag. He had had to retrace his steps as far as Mulumika before he found it. A stout effort. During the afternoon there were some distant rumbles of thunder. A few drops of rain fell, the first since March. But the rains proper will not begin for another few weeks.

Tuesday, 12 October

Today began early and we were on our way by 6.00. We passed through a gap in the Muchingas and then descended, mostly on foot, to the valley floor. From there, it was an easy run to Chiwale. The other members of the party were glad to be on the flat again, in spite of the heat and the tsetse fly. Chiwale school has some magnificent shade trees but they are about its only positive feature. Early marriages keep the numbers down; the teachers have lost heart; and their relations with the Chief (particularly important in a place like this), are poor. Their lessons were badly prepared and their teaching lacks life. Many of the written exercises in the children's books were unmarked. The latrines were dirty and the school vegetable garden was a mass of weeds. It was difficult to find anything to praise. Laban, Kumwenda and I tried to stir up some life in the teachers. The equipment we brought will certainly help.

The Chief is not a very impressive figure. He was one of several who were imprisoned in 1947 for dealing in poached ivory and is the only one who has been restored to his stool. Several of the carriers live in the village or nearby, and they have been asking for leave of absence to visit their wives. I would have been happy for them to sleep at their homes as long as they returned by 5.30 tomorrow. But White, the *boma* messenger, who probably knows best, had them all back here by dusk. I was interested to see one of the carriers conducting a little service this evening. According to Laban, he is one of the Jehovah's Witness sect, known as Watch-towers. At the start of the *ulendo* there were only two or three who took part. Now, nearly the whole group of 20 gathered in a circle for Bible reading and prayers.

Wednesday, 13 October

Chief Chiwale arrived during breakfast to speed us on our way. We didn't exactly speed, but an hour and a half's easy riding brought us to Mulilo. En route we crossed the Luangwa, not a very impressive river this far upstream. The headman carried my bike across the river bed which was dry apart from a few pools. We are thus now back on the Lundazi side of the river. This camp at Mulilo is the most pleasant I have met. It's really lovely and is dominated by an enormous and quite magnificent tree. The shelters are on a slope and my tent is pitched at the top. From here, I look down on the huge fire which the carriers have built to scare away the lions that are supposed to be numerous about here.

Mulilo school could have been worse and two arithmetic lessons I sat in on were good. The teachers deserve stronger support from the Chief. I told him so and he promised to assist with the repair of the thatch on the school roof and to encourage more girls to come to the school. The Chief has certainly done his stuff with regard to hospitality. He conducted me to the camp and within a short time of my arrival headmen were coming in ones and twos to pay respects and to bring meal and chickens. As many of them had come several miles, it would have been rude not to accept their gifts and to offer salt in exchange. I now have too much food and will give the unneeded balance to the school. As for the chickens, they have been rolling in during the last two days. White tells me that 'enrolment' is now 17. I suppose that somehow we shall get them back to Fort Jimmie where I can dispose of them.

The carriers' pay has been arranged:

Sept 28–October 2: 5 days @ 1s 4d		6s 8d
Oct 3–14: 12 days @ 1s 0d		12 0
Oct 15: 1 day @ 1s 4d		1 4
	Total	20 0 or £1

The extra fourpences, it seems, are for the days when they were travelling to and from the *ulendo* and had to find their own food. In all conscience, 20 shillings seems pitifully small reward for all the work they have done. Laban, however, tells me that they are quite happy at the thought of receiving this sum when we reach Chunga tomorrow. They have fed well, received medical attention, and had to work only about six hours a day. So Laban says. I can't help but feel, however, that the carriers have earned their shilling a day much more than I have justified the seventeen shillings and sixpence a night which is my subsistence allowance entitlement. And on top of that, my salary works out at about two pounds and ten shillings a day.

Thursday, 14 October

Despite the confident forecasts of the carriers, no lions came to disturb the peace of the night. We were all anxious to complete the last leg of the journey. The carriers were away in good time; the rest of us, after I had made a final call at the school, were on the road by 6.00. We reached Chunga within a couple of hours. Chunga is accessible by a road, of sorts, from Lundazi, and it is here that William will come to pick us up in the vanette. The carriers made very good time. They erected the tent, collected firewood for the night and then lined up to collect their pay. As Laban had predicted, there were no complaints. All wanted to shake hands; several said that they would like to travel with me again. They wished us a safe journey back to Fort Jimmie and then set off for their villages.

The departure of the carriers, in a sense, marked the end of the *ulendo*, although, because of a broken water pump in the vanette. It was another three days before we got back to Fort Jimmie. I have recorded the *ulendo* in some detail because this was, in fact, the only time that I went on such a journey with a full complement of carriers. I preferred to travel light. As Glyn had promised, about half my time was spent in Lundazi District although I continued to live in Fort Jimmie.

A tent became my second home. It was a good life for a young, single man. By our frequent visits to schools, holding meetings with chiefs, headmen and parents, running refresher courses for the teachers, and by ensuring that each school received a fair share of the textbooks, exercise books, pencils, chalk, and any other materials that were available, Laban and I felt that we were gradually helping to raise educational standards in the district. As an experiment, we decided to run a community service camp for boys from the upper primary schools. We looked around for a worthwhile project which could be tackled by 100 boys in two weeks. It was a colleague in the Health Department who suggetsed the answer – to construct a pole and dagga village for people suffering from leprosy. There were at that time, and still are, very considerable numbers of leprosy victims in Northern Rhodesia. Nowadays, by the careful use of multi-drug therapy, the spread of the disease can be halted. Surgeons can sometimes operate to put right some of the damage which leprosy has caused. Physiotherapy helps sufferers to use deformed hands and limbs. Modern treatment, in other words, brings new hope and new life to leprosy sufferers. Unfortunately, in many parts of Africa, Asia and South America, such treatment is not available and millions of people suffer unnecessarily as a result. In the middle 1950s in Northern Rhodesia, little was provided by way of treatment. Sufferers gradually lost all sense of feeling in their hands and feet; their faces became ulcerated; their inability to use muscles in the eyelids to blink sometimes caused early and permanent blindness. Misconception, fear and superstition about the disease were rife. People who contracted leprosy were treated with suspicion and were rejected by their communities. To the pain inflicted by the disease was added the anguish of rejection by friends and family. The village which the boys constructed provided a haven for sufferers who could no longer live in their home villages. The camp was a great success, full of fun and good spirit. For the boys, it gave them an opportunity to help those who were less well off than themselves and perhaps broke down some of their irrational feelings about leprosy. For me, it aroused an interest (which was to be lifelong) in this cruel and hateful disease.

We managed to get some extra facilities for upper primary education. It was sad and unjust that only about one in four of the children who completed Standard 2 were able to go on to the middle schools, which covered Standards 3 and 4, and only a third of those who passed Standard 4 were selected for the three-year upper primary course. This meant, of course, that the education of many youngsters was cut short at a very early age. Late developers were particularly hard hit as they were excluded from school before they even showed their potential. Each district was anxious to expand its provision of middle and upper primary schools. Unfortunately, shortages of funds for new buildings and the lack of suitably qualified teachers meant that the waiting time was often lengthy. With the help of Philip Farwell and other members of the District Education Authority, we worked on Glyn and got him to give priority to a new upper primary school at Msuzi, some five miles south of Lundazi. I had a hand in the siting and layout of the school, the design of the buildings, and the supervision of its construction. It was a proud and happy day when the school was opened. Jock Cottrell, the Director of the African Education Department, agreed to perform the opening ceremony. Glyn was cynical enough to say that Cottrell came only because he wanted an excuse to go and catch butterflies on the Nyika Plateau in neighbouring Nyasaland. Certainly, he disappeared in that direction very soon after he had opened the school. He was around long enough, however, to ask me where I would like to go on my next tour of duty. I told him that I would be happy to return to Fort Jimmie. By this time I had passed both the lower and higher examinations in Chinyanja, the language of the province. I knew my way around, had many friends, and was a frequent and, I think, welcome visitor to the nurses' home. Another three years in Fort Jimmie would suit me very well. 'Don't bank on it,' said the Director, 'we might have something more challenging for you. But first, go and enjoy your leave.'

Glyn nurtured a healthy scepticism towards the department's headquarters and all who worked there. 'Don't read anything into what Jock said,' he advised, when I told him of our conversation. 'He'll have forgotten all about it before he's caught a couple of butterflies. He gets a bit out of touch. You know, we all have to call on Jock when we go on long leave and when we come back six months later. Last time I did so, he told me that I had earned my leave, that I would be missed and that he hoped I would be able to relax.'

'Sounds reasonable,' I said.

'But I wasn't going on leave,' snorted Glyn, 'I'd just come back.'

Despite what he said about headquarters, Glyn never seriously questioned the conscientiousness and integrity of the Director and his senior colleagues. He knew they had a difficult task to perform

– to meet the legitimate aspirations of the African population, to balance the requirements of the Colonial Office with those of the white settlers, to raise educational standards in thousands of schools scattered over huge areas, and to do all this with a small staff and limited financial resources. It was hardly surprising if the Director was glad to get away from Lusaka every so often and to enjoy the peace and solitude of the beautiful Nyika Plateau.

Notes
1 Local education authorities, at provincial and district levels, were composed of representatives of government, native authorities, and mission agencies. They were responsible for the planning of education in their areas, the registration of schools, for financial management, the maintenance of standards and the management of LEA schools.
2 For a more detailed account of missionary penetration, see Snelson, *Educational development*, especially chapters 2, 3 and 6.
3 *Ibid.*, p. 43.
4 Hymn by E. H. Bickersteth (1825–1906), in the *Church Hymnary* (London: Oxford University Press n.d.).
5 Quoted in J. W. Jack, *Daybreak at Livingstonia* (Edinburgh: Oliphant, Anderson & Ferrier, 1901).
6 Jeanes Supervisors owed their name to Misss Anna T. Jeanes, an American Quaker philanthropist who believed in the value of the little schools for negroes in the southern states of the USA. She gave her fortune for their improvement and endowed a fund to be used in training itinerant supervisors, or senior teachers, who would demonstrate new methods in the schools they visited, discuss difficulties sympathetically with the teachers and inspire them to greater efforts. The concept was copied in several British territories. In Northern Rhodesia a Jeanes training school was opened in 1929.

4

Education and the struggle
for independence

How to spend six months' leave? It was an intriguing question to try to resolve during the long evenings. There was so much I wanted to do, so many countries I wanted to see. It was Ken who solved the problem. He and his wife, Moyna, had spent a month with me in Fort Jameson. Now they were in Denver, Colorado, where Ken was doing postgraduate studies at the Federal Bureau of Reclamation and would be going on to the Berkeley campus of the University of California while I was on leave. Ken suggested a number of possible rendezvous points. 'Stay as long as you like,' he wrote, 'and we'll help out with the dollars,' (a reference to the fact that, because of strict exchange control regulations, you could take a maximum of £100 holiday money out of Britain.)

The USA was already on my short list of countries to visit. Ken's letter clinched it. Apart from having a natural curiosity about the United States I had two special reasons for wanting to go. First, it would give me an opportunity to meet my two nieces, Debbie and Niki, who had been born since Ken and Moyna visited me. Second, I wanted to see how the process of desegregation of schools in America was progressing. No-one could forecast the likely pattern of political development in Northern Rhodesia but instinct told me that the present situation could not continue for much longer; conscience told me that Africans must be given an increasing share in the government of the country. At the same time, I was sure that the enormous disparities between education facilities for Africans

89

on the one hand, and those for Europeans, Asians and coloured children on the other, must be removed. Most of my colleagues thought it premature even to consider such possibilities; others accused me of wanting to rock the boat, but I was confident that it would not be long before the country's schools would be open to children of all races.

In the southern states of the USA, the school system had developed on a segregated basis. Not only were there separate schools for whites and for blacks, but the whites enjoyed a much higher standard of education than negro children. In 1954, the Supreme Court declared that segregated schools were unconstitutional, and ordered that segregation in education on grounds of colours should be ended. Some of the southern states, notably Alabama and Louisiana, refused to implement the Supreme Court's ruling; others, such as Georgia, adopted delaying tactics. The fight for integration was spearheaded by the National Association for the Advancement of Coloured Peoples. Soon, the Reverend Martin Luther King, minister of a Baptist church in Montgomery, Alabama, would emerge as the leader of the movement for negro emancipation. I thought there might be lessons to be learned from the American experience which, in course of time, could be applied in the Northern Rhodesian context. Accordingly, I planned an itinerary which would enable me to do a fair amount of sightseeing and also to visit the States where opposition to schools integration was strongest.

Thus it was that March 1957, found me crossing the Atlantic for the first time in the *Queen Elizabeth*, the 83,000 ton flagship of the Cunard line. No tourist can fail to be impressed by the vastness of the United States, the rich diversity of its peoples and institutions, the stunning beauty of many of its national parks, and the excellence of its transportation systems. Equally, one cannot fail to note the squalor, violence and ugliness of the downtown areas of its cities and the superficiality of much of its culture. As a tourist, I had a magnificent holiday: sightseeing in New York and Washington, then down through Virginia, the Carolinas, Georgia, Alabama and Mississippi to Louisiana where I made the planned rendezvous with Ken and his family. In Ken's station wagon, we travelled across Texas, along the Rio Grande into New Mexico and thence via Arizona, the Grand Canyon and Las Vegas into California, meeting the Pacific coast at San Francisco.

I left Ken and Moyna there. With very few dollars but a long Greyound bus ticket in my pocket, I went north to Portland (Oregon) and thence to Salt Lake City, across Wyoming, Nebraska, Iowa and Wisconsin to Chicago, then to Detroit, Buffalo, Niagara Falls (only half as high and half as wide as the Victoria Falls), Boston and hence back to New York. The *Queen Mary*, older sister of the *Queen Elizabeth*, brought me back to Southampton. A glance at the map will show that I covered a good deal of ground, travelling from east to west and back again, and from the Mexican border in the south to Canada in the north. A memorable experience, and one that I would recommend to anyone to do at least once in their life.

As an introduction, however, to successful methods of integrating school systems which had grown from different origins and which served people from very different cultural and economic backgrounds, the trip was a failure. Despite the Supreme Court's ruling, the vast majority of schools, colleges and universities in the southern states were still rigidly segregated. It would take many court cases, spread over several years, and an unrelenting campaign of peaceful demonstrations, boycotts and passive resistance before significant inroads would be made into the problem. Although no-one could have forecast it at the time, the black and white education systems of Northern Rhodesia would be fully integrated before those of the southern states of the USA. If I learned little about schools integration, other than the strength of the opposition likely to be encountered, there was a positive side to the fact-finding part of the trip. By visiting several elementary and high schools and a wide variety of higher education institutions for negroes, including Howard University in Washington, Tuskegee Institute (founded by Booker T. Washington in Alabama in 1881), and Grambling College in Louisiana, I had the opportunity to see institutions which, by any standards, were first-rate in terms both of their physical resources and their staffs. I wondered if the racial attitudes of some whites in Northern Rhodesia would change if they were to see black people holding positions of academic distinction and high-level financial responsibility.

As the Greyound coach sped south from Washington, evidence of discrimination on the basis of colour, similar to that in South Africa, became increasingly apparent. When we left the Washington terminal, all the passengers were at liberty to sit where they liked in the coach. When we stopped for a short break at Richmond, Virginia, I was astounded to see that there were separate waiting rooms, toilets and cafés for white and for coloureds. I noted in my diary: 'A coloured girl of about seven or eight came into the "white" soda fountain and asked for a coke. The person behind the bar said: "I can't serve you." The little girl asked: "Why not?" There was no answer. The little girl slowly turned and looked around her. Slowly it dawned on her that everyone else in the room had a different-coloured skin from hers; she ran out, crying. A pretty sick-making introduction to the southern branch of American democracy.' In fact, worse was to follow. When we boarded the coach again, the first ten rows were reserved for whites. The blacks had to wait until the whites had sat down before taking their seats in the rear of the coach.

In Atlanta, Georgia, I was to meet an ex-Munali student, Nalumino Mundia. He was studying at the local university and had asked the department in Lusaka to send him some material for the thesis on which he was working. The Director had asked me to take it to him and to see how he was getting on. Because the rooms were cheap, I was staying at the hostel run by the YMCA. I managed to telephone Nalumino and invited him to come to the hostel for a chat. Just before he was due, I thought I should mention it to the hostel manager. 'Excuse me, but I'm expecting a friend of mine in a few minutes. Is it all right if I take him into the common room?'

'Sure thing. No problem.'

'He's from Northern Rhodesia.'

'Where's that?'

'It's in Africa.'

'Uh, uh.'

'He's an African.'

A long pause. Then, in tones of incredulity, 'You mean he's black?'

'Yes.'

'A nigger! A flaming nigger! Are you nuts? You must know you can't bring a nigger in here.'

In vain did I point out that racial discrimination was totally contrary to Christian principles and that I could not believe that a person would be turned away from a YMCA hostel because of the colour of his skin. The manager was adamant; he neither knew nor cared what happened anywhere else. This YMCA was for whites. Coloureds were not allowed in, except as servants.

With my visitor due at any moment, I was desperate and pleaded for understanding. Eventually, with much ill-grace, he relented. He agreed that Nalumino could be allowed on to the premises as long as he was not seen by anyone other than myself. The upshot was that I met Nalumino at the front door and explained the situation to him. We then walked round the block to the rear entrance to the hostel, sneaked in and sat, out of sight, in a cupboard under the stairs, for two hours. Fortunately, Nalumino merely laughed at my embarrassment. He was used to the colour bar, with all its cruelty and absurdities. He preferred to sit among the brooms under the stairs rather than to look for a café or drug store where we would both be allowed in and would feel comfortable. He was only a year or so younger than I and we got on well. In 1982, 25 years later, in Lusaka, I had the opportunity to remind Nalumino Mundia of this bizarre incident. He laughed uproariously. By that time, he was Prime Minister of Zambia. Subsequently, he was appointed Zambia's Ambassador to the United States, the country in which he had suffered many indignities. He bore no ill-will. Tragically, he died in 1988 at the age of 60, just as he was about to present his credentials as Ambassador to Bolivia.

I was surprised to find considerable unemployment among negro graduates in the southern states. These included large numbers of trained teachers. At a meeting with staff members at Grambling College I tentatively asked whether it was likely that any of these teachers might be interested in working in Northern Rhodesia. The response was enthusiastically positive. I wrote to the Director in Lusaka, suggesting that American negro teachers might be taken on to fill some of the vacancies in the department's establishment. Jock Cottrell's response reached me c/o Thomas Cook in New York. My suggestion had been carefully considered, he assured me, but the staff recruitment position was improving and it was not necessary to recruit from America at considerable extra cost.

The Director's letter went on: 'You will wish to know where you have been posted on your return from leave. I know you hoped it would be Petauke. [the thought had never crossed my mind!]. We cannot open an office there just yet and, in any case, Chinsali, with its 45 former Church of Scotland schools, is presenting a big challenge. After your success in the Lundazi area, I felt you would be just the man to tackle the situation at Chinsali.'

I had not expected a posting to the Northern Province but I had no reason to protest. Glyn Goddard had been transferred to Kasama, the Provincial headquarters, and I wondered whether he had had a hand in my posting. In any case, September 1958 saw me bowling 500 miles from Lusaka up the Great North Road and arriving at Chinsali *boma*, covered in dust from the earth roads. Although I did not know it at the time, I was to spend more than six years in the Northern Province. During that period, the province was to be periodically convulsed by disturbances arising partly from political unrest and partly from religious fanaticism. Chinsali, one of the seven districts into which the province was divided, was to be at the centre of these disturbances. It was a fascinating place to be at one of the most critical periods in Northern Rhodesia's evolution to the Republic of Zambia.

But it was not immediately apparent that life in the north would be very different from what it had been in the Eastern Province. True, I was now much more my own boss; provincial headquarters in Kasama were 120 miles away and Glyn's visits were infrequent. Another difference was that I was responsible for two districts instead of one; in addition to Chinsali, I was also to look after education in Isoka District which had international boundaries with Tanganyika and Nyasaland. The tribal set-up was also different. In Isoka District, there were several small tribes, the largest of whom were the Inamwanga. Chinsali District, on the other hand, was mostly populated by the Bemba, one of the largest and formerly most warlike tribes in the country. While Chitimu-kulu, the Paramount Chief, had his headquarters in Kasama District, the burial ground of Bemba royal chiefs was located at Mwalule in Chinsali District. Europeans were not allowed into the sacred grove. It was said that those few Europeans who had defied the restriction had come to a sudden and unpleasant end. During my time in the district, I never heard of any white person trying to see Mwalule although I used to visit Shimwalule school, a mile or so away, quite frequently. There were six Bemba chiefs in the district, the most important of whom was Senior Chief Nkula. When Africans greeted an ordinary chief, they would crouch or drop to one knee and clap their hands. When they greeted Nkula, it was customary to lie down on their backs on the ground, avert the eyes and clap hands softly. Europeans were not expected to prostrate themselves but I always made a point of showing respect to chiefs, both the good and the bad.

Membership of their tribe is of enormous significance to African people. A chief embodies much of the history of the tribe, the spirits of the ancestors, the collective ethos. Loyalty to the tribe has, of course, its disadvantages as well as its positive aspects. Tribalism is one of the curses of African political life. It leads to nepotism and corruption on an enormous scale. Inter-tribal conflict leads frequently to bloodshed and sometimes erupts into full-scale war. African leaders may challenge this; certainly they are reluctant to admit it. But I have no doubt that tribalism and a belief in witchcraft (to which I will turn later) are the dominant and most destructive influences in life in Zambia even today.

Chinsali was a very much smaller station than Fort Jameson. The African population numbered about 250, mostly government employees and their families. None had advanced very far in the civil service; the most senior were a district assistant in the DC's office, and two managers of schools who worked closely with me. The Europeans did not muster more than 16. They were the DC and his wife, the DO and his wife, two young learner district assistants (bachelors), three policemen (only one of whom was married), a Public Works Department (PWD) building supervisor, his wife and baby daughter, Joe, a road foreman (a huge South African, very much a bachelor), Claude, an agricultural supervisor from Lancashire (also single) and myself. The unmarried policemen and the learner district assistants shared houses. The rest of us had our own bungalows. Water came from a stream, pumped up by a hydram. It was usually plentiful but had to be boiled. Prisoners

95

from the little gaol looked after the *boma* vegetable garden, the produce of which was distributed daily by the DC's wife. There was no electricity; we used pressure lamps and hurricane lanterns for lights and cooked on wood-burning stoves. Hot water for the bath was heated by what was known as a Rhodesian boiler, consisting of a 44-gallon drum, filled with water, under which the garden 'boy' lit a fire.

There were a couple of Indian-run shops on the *boma* but usually we got our supplies from Kasama. We could fish for bream and barbel in the *boma* fish ponds. Meat came from Shiwa Ng'andu, some 60 miles away, the home of Sir Stewart Gore-Browne. Sir Stewart had first come to the country in 1912 as a member of a boundary commission. He had returned after the First World War and had built himself a large house, in the style of a Scottish baronial castle on a large tract of land which he bought between Chinsali and Mpika. Here he cleared the land and pursued a number of agricultural schemes, including one to grow essential oils needed in the perfume industry. For 15 years, he represented African interests in the Northern Rhodesian Legislative Council, leaving the running of his estate to his daughter, Lorna, and her husband, John Harvey. There was a rest house at Shiwa and I frequently made use of it when touring in the area. If Sir Stewart knew I was there, he would send for me to come for drinks or a meal at 'the big house'. He was happy to sit for hours in the castle library, overlooking a large lake, his reminiscences occasionally interrupted by the grunts of hippo in the water below us. His political life was by no means over. As a friend and trusted confidant, he was regularly consulted by Kenneth Kaunda. In 1962, he was to accompany a United National Independence Party [UNIP] delegation to the United Nations; he also stood as a UNIP candidate in a general election.

The only other Europeans living in Chinsali District were missionaries. Just five miles from the *boma* was Lubwa mission station. It was opened in 1913 but its origins go back several years earlier. In 1904, the Reverend James Henderson of the Church of Scotland mission station at Livingstonia in Nyasaland took a group of trainee teachers on an evangelistic tour of Chinsali District. One of this group was a young man of the Tonga tribe named David

Julizga Kaunda. In 1906, having completed his teachers' course, he volunteered for work in the Chinsali area. He made his way on foot to the *boma* and introduced himself to the Native Commissioner, 'Bobo' Young, who encouraged him to start schools. In 1907, David Kaunda could report as follows:

> Chinsali is growing and is now quite changed since the time that Mr Henderson, the great hunter of villages, hunted it. Many are coming searching school. They do not wish me to go away but make Chinsali as my home. They are very much willing to hear the words of God preached among them. Many are crossing Chambeshi river in search of school. There are many people and many villages – over 100 villages, east, west, south and north just in deep sleep. A European missionary should quickly take place at Chinsali.

Another six years, however, were to elapse before the Church of Scotland could send a European missionary to the Chinsali area. During that period it was David Kaunda who preached the Gospel, opened schools, gave a preliminary training to the teacher–evangelists and supervised their work. In 1913, when the Reverend R. D. McMinn arrived, to set up Lubwa mission station, there were 20 village schools in operation, attended by some 1,500 children. David Kaunda's record is unique in the history of the country's educational development. A member of the Tonga tribe from Nyasaland, working as a teacher and evangelist among the Bemba people of Chinsali District, he was as much a missionary as those who came to Northern Rhodesia from Europe and America.

After McMinn's arrival at Lubwa and the opening of the mission station, David Kaunda remained a major influence in the life and work of the church, as well as of the schools he loved so much. He worked with McMinn in effecting a big expansion of education both on the mission station and in the villages. Together, they ran a primary school at Lubwa and selected new teachers from those who passed Standard 4. Twice each year, teachers were called to Lubwa from their village schools for refresher courses conducted by McMinn and Kaunda. Their wives went with them and were instructed by Mrs McMinn and Mrs Kaunda in sewing, housewifery, oil and soap-making, starch-making and gardening, as well as in literacy and simple arithmetic. The emphasis placed on education at Lubwa, and the combined efforts of the Kaundas and McMinns, led to Chinsali becoming one of the best-developed districts in the country as far as education was concerned. Thanks to the later work of people like Maxwell Robertson and John Nelson, Chinsali District held this position for many years.

One of Maxwell Robertson's pupils was the second son of David and Helen Kaunda, who had been born in 1924 and christened Kenneth David Kaunda. In due course, after primary schooling at Lubwa and two years at the newly opened Munali secondary school, the young Kaunda trained as a teacher. He taught at Lubwa and then elsewhere, before embarking on the political career which, in 1964, would lead to his election as the first president of the Republic of Zambia. In the late 1950s, of course, this lay in the future. During my time at Chinsali, Kenneth Kaunda was a highly controversial figure, a hero to many Africans, hated and feared by most whites. In Chinsali, we knew him as a frequent visitor to his ageing mother who still lived near the mission station.

As in the Eastern Province, the Church of Scotland had decided to divest itself of responsibility for running schools and to concentrate its resources on evangelism and medical work. I was to be responsible for managing the schools in Chinsali District which had formerly been under the control of Lubwa mission, and the church's schools in Isoka District which had been run from Mwenzo mission. A further 30 or so schools in the two districts were managed by the White Fathers. They had first arrived in Chinsali District in 1934. Dr Brown, then missionary in charge at Lubwa, reported to Church headquarters in Edinburgh:

> The Romanists have arrived. We do not propose giving way to Rome but shall, with God's help, go on. It is a tremendous pity, however, that in so huge a continent, so much of which is still unoccupied by any Christian body, that there should be any invasions such as this, or rivalry such as is scarcely avoidable following such an invasion.[2]

The Catholic 'invaders' opened their first station in the district at Ilondola, approximately 20 miles from Lubwa. Not long after the White Fathers had settled in and had opened their first schools they were joined by a group of White Sisters. Their order, 'Les Soeurs missionaires de Notre Dame d'Afrique', had been founded by Cardinal Lavigerie in 1869, only a year after he founded the White Fathers society. At Ilondola, the girls' school was run very efficiently by Sister Fidelia and her colleagues. Flanking one side of the school compound, the Sisters' house was always immaculately clean. In an atmosphere of polish and incense, the Sisters radiated purpose and piety as they went quietly about their duties. By contrast, the Fathers' living quarters always looked to be in need of a thorough spring-clean; the visitor was greeted by the smell of stale tobacco smoke and over-cooked cabbage. Once I asked the Father Superior what differences there were between the rules of the White Sisters and those of the White Fathers. 'None,' he replied, 'the only difference is that they keep them.'

I made a good many visits to the White Fathers' mission station at Mulanga; it made a good centre when I was inspecting schools in Chief Chibesakunda's area. The priest-in-charge was Father Kohle, a heavily built German in his 60s. He had been more than 30 years in the country. I asked him once how many converts he had made in that time. He thought long and hard. Eventually he said, 'There is only one of whom I can be really sure.' I thought that was a poor harvest from so much effort over so many years. 'But you see,' he said, 'one is enough. That one soul saved will assure me of a place in Paradise.' Father Kohle had a mischievous sense of humour. When I told him that he looked and sounded wise enough to be the Pope, he said: 'I shall write to the Vatican immediately and ask for my name to be considered at the appropriate time.' It happened that I was near Mulanga when Pope Pius XII died in October 1958. I called to express my condolences. 'We have said a mass for the Holy Father,' said the good Father. 'Now I am packing my suitcase so that I shall be ready when the call comes.' When I saw him again a few weeks later and commiserated with him that he had not been elected, he smiled ruefully: 'I forgot that those Cardinals elect only Italians, and I'm only a poor German peasant.'

99

During a visit to Mulanga, I was stung on the temple by a wasp. I thought nothing of it until 2 o'clock the next morning when I woke up in my tent to realise that I was swelling rather like a balloon. The swelling had closed both my eyes. With one hand I managed to hold an eye open while with the other I eventually succeeded in lighting a Tilley lamp. I dressed as best I could and set off to find the headmaster's house where my driver was sleeping. My bangings on the door brought a response and the startled driver then drove me to Lubwa mission hospital. We managed to rouse the doctor, David Wilson. It took some time for David to recognise me. He gave me a shot of an antihistamine drug and told me to stay in bed for two days. Within 48 hours, I was back to normal. We all suffered at some time or another from the creepy-crawlies with which Africa abounds. One bout of malaria, which I caught despite taking my paludrine very conscientiously, left me as weak as the proverbial kitten. For most of the time, however, the strenuous outdoor life kept me very healthy.

My responsibilities at Chinsali were similar to those I had had in the Eastern Province: to manage the Local Education Authority schools which previously had been run by the Church of Scotland, to inspect the schools managed by the White Fathers, to encourage the native authorities to repair and maintain the village school buildings and to chase up truants and their parents, and to represent the PEO on the district education authorities. I was fortunate to have very efficient and loyal assistant managers, Dason Mukupa and Yonam Mpuku in Chinsali District, and Jekott Bwali in Isoka District. Between them, they had more than 60 years' experience as teachers and headmasters. They could sniff out trouble in a school much better than I could. They knew when to praise and when to wield the heavy stick. They were tactful but firm in dealing with chiefs and village headmen. They were honest and trustworthy. At any one time, at least two of us were on tour, sometimes on bicycles but usually in a Landrover. This helped us keep in touch with the teachers on whom, much more than on us, the quality of the work done in the schools depended.

I was responsible for paying the teachers in the LEA schools and this provided another opportunity to meet them regularly. Each month, one teacher from each of the LEA schools in Chinsali

District cycled to the *boma* on a Saturday morning to collect the salaries for his or her school. In Isoka District, we had to organize a pay run by Landrover every other month. Our route would take us up to the border with Tanganyika and then down a road through the hills, sometimes in Nyasaland and sometimes in Northern Rhodesia, to Muyombe, more than 200 miles from Chinsali. The teachers were poorly paid. Most teachers in the primary schools were graded as T4s; they had taken a two-year training course after passing Standard 6. The average T4, depending on years of service, received £9 a month. At the top of the tree was the T2 teacher. He (and they were nearly all men at this time) had passed the Cambridge School Certificate examination at Munali and had trained for two years; his average salary was £20 a month. At the opposite end of the scale was the poor T5 who would have had only one year of teacher training after passing Standard 4. Such teachers could expect to receive £6–7 a month, a very small sum, indeed, on which to feed and clothe a family. Even the best paid teachers found it difficult to save. Custom required them to share their income with members of the extended family – uncles, aunts, cousins, nephews and nieces, as well as their immediate parents and children – who were in need. In a country where the government provided no form of social security, this practice had much to commend it; it usually ensured that no-one starved or became destitute.

As we travelled the districts, we waged a constant battle to get more girls into the schools. When children enrolled in the lowest class, sub A in the average village school, the ratio of boys to girls was usually 3:2. Three years later, in Standard 2, the ratio was unlikely to be better than 3:1 and could easily be 6 or 7:1. Parents in the rural areas were generally unconvinced of the value or relevance of education for their daughters. The girls themselves often saw little point in going to school and preferred to stay at home, helping their mothers and preparing themselves for marriage. By contrast, the mission-station boarding schools, such as the ones at Ilondola, Lubwa and Mwenzo, were well attended by girls. In such schools, well-trained staff, often expatriate, offered a range of stimulating activities which sustained the girls' interest. Parents were confident that their daughters would be safe in such establishments and that what they learned was useful and could lead to employment opportunities.

But the mission-station schools could cater for only a tiny minority of the girls. If progress was to be made on a broad front, we had to get more girls into the ordinary village schools. It was an uphill struggle. We would hold meeting after meeting with chiefs, headmen and parents. Such meetings could not be hurried. Sometimes we would sit for hours under a tree listening to what seemed to be an interminable string of objections from parents whose daughters were being kept at home. 'She is too young,' said some; 'She is too old,' said others. 'She will be spoiled for marriage. What does a girl want with reading and writing? She will write letters to boyfriends when she is married.' These were just some of the objections which were raised. We would try to answer these points. If the Chief spoke strongly in favour of girls going to school, the meeting usually ended with a general agreement that the girls would be sent to school; such promises, of course, were not always kept. For our part, we tried to ensure that each school had a woman helper, often a teacher's wife, who would assume responsibility for looking after the girls and for teaching them simple housewifery, cookery and needlework.

Northern Rhodesia was fortunate in attracting some outstandingly good women education officers to promote and supervise girls' education in the provinces. Those I knew over the years, Mair Parry, Phyllis Trowse, Jane Pine-Coffin, Barbara Moore, Paddy Harbinson and Mary Mann, were not only highly skilled but had the knack of conveying their enthusiasm to the women teachers and helpers, and the girls with whom they worked. They thought nothing of setting off into the bush with a driver and messenger for a week-long tour of schools far from the *boma*.

Sometimes, months of confidence-building were undone overnight. At one upper primary school, we mounted a year-long campaign to persuade parents to allow their daughters to stay at school until they had completed Standard 6. The headmaster, one of the few T2s in the district, was an excellent teacher. I noticed one day that he had put curtains on the windows of his office. He told me he was sure the girls would do well in the forthcoming Standard 6 examinations; he was giving them extra coaching in the evenings. I feared the worst and confided my misgivings to Dason. He was sure that I was wrong. Alas, I was right. Three weeks before the examinations, two of the girls were found to be pregnant. The headmaster was accused in the Chief's court and was found guilty of causing both pregnancies. Sadly, he had to go. Not unnaturally, the confidence of the parents was shattered and several girls were withdrawn from the school. It would be years before the incident was forgotten and numbers would build up again.

In spite of our efforts to visit schools often, teachers were left to their own devices for months at a time. Often many miles from the *boma*, and with a very irregular postal service to contend with, they were professionally isolated, with no-one to turn to except their colleagues at the same school. To provide some professional stimulus or, on occasion, to introduce a new textbook, we would hold refresher courses. One or two tutors from teacher training colleges would come to help run the course. Usually, I would ask the District Commissioner to talk to the teachers on development issues in the district or to discuss the changing political scene. This always aroused their interest. The official view, of course, was that teachers should not become involved in politics. It was becoming increasingly difficult to achieve this aim. At headquarters level, the change from complacency to concern could clearly be seen in Jock Cottrell's reports. In 1954, he wrote:

During the year, there has been a decline of interest in politics among teachers. The great majority of teachers now understand the reasons for keeping politics out of their schools. More and more are recognising that their first duty is to promote right thinking and right action in their schools and communities and in public affairs. Many of them are making a positive contribution, through cool discussion as responsible citizens, to the solution of social problems and the development of inter-racial co-operation.[3]

By 1957, however, the Director was starting to become alarmed. 'A difficulty that is likely to increase,' he reported, is that some teachers – particularly those who are younger and less mature – seem to find it difficult to remain impartial in their civics lessons. It has therefore been necessary to issue a circular recently on 'Educational efficiency in schools and the ban on politics.' It is not intended to debar teachers from political thought, provided their work is not in any way subversive. It has, however, been stressed that political considerations must not be allowed to interfere in any way with efficient education and the inculcation of right principles of thought and behaviour.[4]

Cottrell was right to be concerned. The political situation was evolving rapidly. Schools were bound to be affected by political influences. No teacher could remain impartial, least of all in Chinsali District. To understand the changing political scene, we must go back to 1953.

In July of that year, the Royal Assent was given to legislation in the British Parliament setting up the Federation of Rhodesia and Nyasaland. Constitutionally, this was the most significant development in the history of Northern Rhodesia since the territory was declared a Protectorate of Britain in 1924. It had been the consistent policy of the Colonial Office that in any conflict of interest between the indigenous population and the minority immigrant races, African interests would prevail. To many, the imposition of the Federation, against the wishes of the vast majority of the African people, was a shameful abandonment of that policy. Henceforth, instead of a policy guaranteeing the paramountcy of African interests there was to be 'partnership' between the races. This partnership, woolly and ill-defined, was conceived by many whites, including the Federal Prime Minister, Lord Malvern, as similar to the partnership which exists between a horse and its rider.

The African National Congress (ANC), led by Harry Nkumbula, based its campaign aganst federation on a fear that the Federation would be dominated, economically and politically by Southern Rhodesia, and that the paternalistic policies and practices pursued by that country would be forced on Northern Rhodesia and Nyasaland. The ANC's long-term goals of universal adult suffrage

104

and independence, it was argued, would be quite unattainable if Northern Rhodesia were to be yoked to its southern neighbour.

Even if it had been brilliantly conceived and vigorously executed, the ANC campaign would not have prevented the Federation from becoming a reality. In fact, the campaign was poor in its planning, inept and amateurish in its organization; it failed to develop any real momentum. In August 1953, when it was clear that the Federation would come into being on schedule on 23 October, 400 ANC delegates met in a Lusaka welfare hall to hold a post mortem and to plan for the future. After a great deal of bitter recrimination, Nkumbula was re-elected as President. The other office-bearers all lost their posts. To the key position of Secretary-General, the delegates enthusiastically elected a young man who, until then, had been Congress secretary for Chinsali District and then Organizing Secretary for the Northern Province, Kenneth Kaunda.

In one of his first communiqués to the press after his election, Kaunda wrote: 'Serious trouble lies ahead. The imposition of Federation has made this trouble more certain than ever.'[5] Trouble did not erupt immediately. Nkumbula and Kaunda continued to inveigh against 'this dreadful monster, Federation', but their main task was to strengthen the ANC, to recruit members, collect subscriptions, and to establish Congress's credibility as a vehicle for expressing majority African opinion. As they moved from district to district, holding public meetings where possible and instructing the local Congress leadership, they aroused public opinion on topics such as colour discrimination in public places, promotion for Africans in the territorial and federal civil services, the need for more and better education and health facilities, the extension of the franchise.

The imprisonment of Nkumbula and Kaunda for two months in 1955 for possessing prohibited literature and a campaign of boycotting selected shops, post offices and cafés, kept the ANC in the public eye in the towns. In the Northern Province, Robert Makasa, the ANC Provincial Organizer, led a successful boycott of a trader in Kasama and was gaoled for 18 months for his pains.[6] Elsewhere in the province, as in other rural areas, controversy centred on the relationships between the chiefs and the ANC.

105

Chiefs had the power to authorize or to forbid the holding of political meetings in their areas. Sir Gilbert Rennie, the Governor, warned: 'All Chiefs must realise where their true interests lie and that no good can come to them or their people by following the bad advice of misguided men.'[7] Chiefs who allowed Congress to hold meetings and to organize were officially considered to be unsound. Some were deposed and replaced by more compliant individuals. Those who took a firm line against Congress were rewarded. When Paramount Chief Chitimukulu banned the ANC from his area in 1958, the Governor gave him a chiming clock. Gradually, the cumulative effects of the ANC's programmes of meetings, boycotts, press communiqués, demonstrations and protests began to be felt. More and more people, in remote villages as well as those in the towns, became sensitized, however imperfectly, to social, economic and political issues and began to see that not only was there need for change but that there were credible and persuasive leaders determined to bring about such change.

A powerful voice was added to the Congress team when Simon Kapwepwe returned from studying in India. Son of the head messenger at Isoka *boma*, a former school friend of Kenneth Kaunda at Lubwa, he had a strong following among the Bemba people. He was elected Treasurer-General of Congress in 1956. A militant, he became increasingly critical of Nkumbula's laid-back style of leadership. During a visit to London in 1957, Kaunda himself began to doubt Nkumbula's ability to provide the firm and determined leadership which the future would undoubtedly demand. He was urged to challenge Nkumbula for the presidency but, out of loyalty to 'the old man', as Nkumbula was known, declined to do so. The break, however, could not long be delayed. In October 1958, Kaunda, Kapwepwe and other leaders left the ANC and founded the Zambia African National Congress. Kaunda was the unanimous choice as President, Kapwepwe was elected Treasurer-General and Munukayumbwa Sipalo, a Lozi, Secretary-General. Within weeks ZANC, as it was known, had won widespread support from Congress branches in the north, the Copperbelt and parts of the Eastern Province. The Provincial Commissioner, Kasama, reported: 'When the ZANC was founded, almost all the adherents of ANC turned over to ZANC. ANC virtually ceased to exist in the Province.'[8]

The constitution of the new party stated that its intentions were to 'work relentlessly by non-violence for the attainment of self-government and national independence.'[9] The need for non-violence was frequently stressed by Kaunda whose natural inclination towards peaceful methods of resolving disputes was strengthened by a visit to India in 1958. Nevertheless, by the beginning of 1959, both the Federal and Territorial Governments were increasingly worried at the prospect of widespread violence. Dr Hastings Banda, who had lived in exile in Britain for many years, had been allowed to return to his homeland, Nyasaland, in July 1958. He had been given a rapturous welcome. Although Banda himself had not advocated violence, there had been numerous violent incidents involving his followers and the police. In Southern Rhodesia, the Land Husbandry Act was leading to turmoil in the rural areas. In 1960, there was to be a conference to consider advancing the Federation to dominion status within the Commonwealth. In reaction to the announcement by the British Government, Sipalo told a ZANC rally at Chingola: 'We must have self-government and a democratic constitution now in Northern Rhodesia. We must get it before 1960 or face the prospect of dominion status.'[10]

Alarmed at what he considered to be a rapidly deteriorating security situation, Sir Roy Welensky, Federal Prime Minister, called a meeting in Salisbury in February 1959, of the Governor-General of the Federation, the Governors of Northern Rhodesia and Nyasaland, and the Prime Minister of Southern Rhodesia. Welensky argued for firm action and promised the use of Federal troops should they be needed. Thereafter, events moved quickly. States of emergency were declared in Southern Rhodesia on 26 February and in Nyasaland a few days later. In the belief that the man in the street and in the village was being led astray by a small minority of power-hungry militants, both governments arrested their Congress leaders. In Northern Rhodesia, too, the authorities refused to believe that in demanding self-government and universal suffrage Kaunda and his colleagues were speaking for the African people as a whole, not just for themselves. A general election, under a new constitution, was due on 20 March. ZANC decided to boycott the election on the grounds that it would give inadequate representation to the African people. Calling on Africans not to register as voters or to vote, Sipalo said that anyone who disobeyed this instruction would be 'punished'. Other ZANC leaders made similar inflammatory statements. Kaunda himself spoke in what were interpreted as menacing terms; 'ZANC's policy,' he said, 'is to warn the Government three times on any issue and then to take action. Whatever the consequences, we are prepared to pay the price of freedom. I shall not rest until the Union Jack is pulled down and something better is put in its place.'[11]

Against this background, the arrest and detention of Kaunda and his colleagues was widely anticipated. At Chinsali, we noted that Ted Pamphilon, an officer in the Special Branch of the police, was spending a lot of his time closeted with the DC. In the evenings, he was rarely to be seen. He was out in the district, meeting his informers – Africans who would give him information on the movement and conversations of known ZANC members in exchange for a few pounds. The expected round-up took place in the early hours of 12 March. The first I knew of it was when the DC woke me at dawn. Several ZANC officials had been apprehended in the district and, as part of a carefully worked out plan, were on their way to the other side of the country. The authorities had calculated, rightly, that tribal antipahties would ensure that no attempt would be made to release the detainees if they were sent to areas far from their own tribal bases. Kaunda, for instance, was sent to Kabompo, in the Northwestern Province where he had no following, Kapwepwe to Mongu, in Barotseland, far from his Bemba tribespeople. The DC and his staff were tired, having been up all night. He asked me to report to the Provincial Commissioner by radio at 9 o'clock that the operation in Chinsali district had been successfully carried out. As I listened to the radio reports from other *bomas*, it was clear that the round-up had been extensive and that ZANC members in the province would be leaderless.

The early morning news broadcast from Lusaka gave prominence to an announcement by the governor, Sir Arthur Benson. He had banned ZANC, he said, because its leaders had initiated a reign of terror, had practised witchcraft and had threatened to kill

108

innocent women and children. He compared ZANC with 'Murder Incorporated' in the USA; its leaders he condemned as 'gangsters' and 'racketeers'.[12] It was a strange speech, couched in intemperate language; it did nothing to defuse an explosive situation. Nevertheless, it served its immediate purpose. The general election took place as planned on 20 March without incident. The United Federal Party secured a large majority. One of its African members, Gabriel Musumbulwa, an official on the copper mines, was appointed Minister of African Education, the first person to hold this newly created position.

Deprived overnight of their leaders, the rank and file members of ZANC, now banned, took some little time to react. When they did so, the reaction was sporadic, unco-ordinated and localized. In Lusaka, some cars were stoned and shop windows were smashed. On Chilubi Island in Lake Bangweulu in Luwingu District, part of the Northern Province, the District Officer and District Assistant were wounded by spears and four Africans were shot dead. In Chinsali District, trouble was on a small scale. A dormitory was set on fire and destroyed at Kalonga primary school on the night of 29 March, and a week later the cattle *kraals* at Chinsali *boma* and Lubwa mission were burnt, resulting in the loss of several animals. Retribution was swift. Within two weeks, the arsonists had been apprehended; they were tried by the DC in his courtroom at the *boma*. Dennis Frost, the tough, no-nonsense DC, thought that stiff penalties would deter other trouble-makers. He sentenced four of the men to 10-years' imprisonment with hard labour and thirteen to seven years. 'That will keep the b . . . quiet,' he said. But within 24 hours there were further arson incidents. The court house at Chief Nkweto's *musumba* went up in flames. Chief Chibesakunda narrowly escaped death when arsonists attempted to burn down his house while he was sleeping inside.

I wrote to all headteachers urging them to arrange for parents to guard their school buildings at night. I knew, however, that this was not really feasible. Practically all the school buildings in the district had grass-thatched roofs. Water was usually not available in any quantity. Once the thatch was alight – and it ignited easily – there was little hope of dousing the flames. It was not possible for parents, even if they were willing, to watch all the buildings in the average school compound – classrooms, teachers' houses and dormitories – although they might succeeed temporarily. Three attempts, for instance, were made to burn down the classrooms at the school at Senior Chief Nkula's *musumba*. Three times the arsonists were thwarted and fled. On the fourth occasion, however, they soaked a piece of cloth in paraffin, tied it to an arrow and fired it high on to the roof of the main classroom block. Only smouldering ashes remained when I reached the scene early the next morning.

As the Chief, the headmaster and I stared gloomily at the remains of a building which had been constructed with a great deal of effort, and had been destroyed in a matter of minutes, I asked why the ZANC members or sympathizers should choose schools as the targets for their fire-raising attacks. After a little reflection, the Chief gave the answer. First, he said, the schools were easy targets. It needed neither daring nor skill to set them on fire. 'These people,' he said, 'want to rule this country. They cannot become the government until they get rid of the present Government and the chiefs. When they burn the schools, they see them as symbols of the Government in Lusaka and of the Native Authority. I think,' he concluded grimly, 'we must expect more of our schools to be spoiled by these men. After all, if you were one of them, how would you tell the Government that you are angry because your leaders have been locked up?'

The Chief's prediction that there would be further trouble was to prove correct, but not immediately. One or two more arson incidents took place in April 1959, and for a time I slept with a loaded shotgun under my bed. But the widescale disturbances which the Government expected did not materialize. The reaction to the detention of the ZANC leaders never amounted to more than an irritation. In Chinsali District, as the threat to peace for political reasons died away, a new cause for concern made itself apparent in the shape of Alice Lenshina and the Lumpa Church. For the next few years, Lenshina and her church were never out of the news for long.

In the history of the Christian Church in Africa there are numerous examples of breakaway movements where groups of black Christians have seceded from their white-dominated congregations and set up their own, distinctively 'African', churches. Some of these breakaway churches have resulted from consciously anti-European motives; others have had no political aims, at least initially, but have later become irresistibly involved in political controversy, sometimes with tragic results. The Lumpa Church in Northern Rhodesia, with its headquarters just a few miles from Chinsali, was a classic example of a seemingly harmless schismatic movement which began in spiritual fervour and ended in bloodshed and disaster. In the six years that I spent in the Northern Province, the Lenshina Movement, so called after its founder, Alice Lenshina Mulenga, grew from small beginnings into an organization of considerable significance. From being a curiosity, and a minor irritation to the establishment, it became a thorn in the flesh of the orthodox churches and presented a challenge to the forces of law and order which could not be ignored.

Little is known of Alice Lenshina's early life. She was born at Kasomo, near Chinsali *boma*, in about 1920, into a polygamous and non-Christian family. At an early age, she married Petros Mulenga and bore him five children. She was an ordinary village woman; short, stout and rather dowdy. Her interests centred on Kasomo village. Her friends included several members of the church at Lubwa mission. Lenshina herself was not a member of the church although she worshipped there on occasion and had started a course of instruction.

In September, 1953, this unremarkable village housewife had a religious experience. Her subsequent accounts of the experience varied considerably but this much seems clear. While looking for mushrooms near Kasomo, she became faint and 'died'. She went to heaven where the 'Lord' told her to put her headcloth on the ground. On the headcloth, the 'Lord' placed a 'book of life'. The 'Lord' then explained to her the teachings of the 'book of life' and taught her many hymns. He told Lenshina to return to earth, to bear witness to him and to preach against evil. She was not told to start a new church. Rather, she was to go to Lubwa mission station and report to the missionary in charge.[13]

Lenshina did as she had been told. At Lubwa, she was well received by the Reverend Fergus Macpherson who arranged for her to be given further instruction in the catechism. Soon afterwards, Alice was baptized at Lubwa church. Macpherson and the other missionaries at Lubwa were satisfied that Alice had undergone a profound religious experience. They sought to use this in the service and witness of the church. Alice was encouraged to tell others her extraordinary story and to teach them some of the many hymns which the 'Lord' had given her.

Lenshina's message was simple and direct. She told the people of her death and resurrection. She said that she had met the 'Lord' face to face. She could not describe him in detail because his face was dazzlingly bright. The 'Lord', she said, had told her that he was much stronger than the Evil One, that he could overcome all evil spirits and that the people must turn away from witchcraft and sorcery. The message was a powerful one. Mixed with lively hymns and choruses of a simple evangelical nature and sung to catchy tunes with African rhythms, the appeal was irresistible to an unsophisticated audience.

In the Northern Rhodesia of the 1950s and 1960s, belief in the power of witchcraft was widespread. (It is probably not much less widespread nowadays.) Everything that takes place in the world, it was believed, is controlled by forces emanating from the spirit world. Thus, death, disease and drought do not have natural causes; they are brought about by an intervention of the *imipashi* (disembodied souls, generally well disposed if properly propitiated),the *ifiwa* (badly disposed souls), the *ngulu* (superior spirits), the *shamfumu* (spirits of deceased chiefs) or by the representatives on earth of these spirits, the *baloshi* (sorcerers or witchdoctors). Because they are so powerful, it is important to propitiate the spirits and to show them the respect which is their due. Thus, a calabash is frequently placed in the corner of a hut and is used to receive regular offerings of meal, beer or beads. The spirits of chiefs require greater sacrifices. At the death of important chiefs such as Paramount Chief Chitimukulu, human sacrifice was necessary. Practices varied considerably between the tribes. In order to keep on the right side of the spirits which controlled the growing of crops, ritual sacrifice was regularly practised in some tribes. At Mweru wa Ntipa, it was said, a young girl was ritually killed each year in order to ensure that the salt harvest would be good. Some protection against the machinations of ill-disposed spirits was thought to be provided by the wearing of amulets and by carrying lucky charms but these would not suffice if a powerful spirit was determined to cause harm or even death.

Fear of witchcraft permeated every facet of life, from birth, through childhood, adolescence, marriage, farming, hunting and sickness until death. Europeans generally scoffed at the fear of witchcraft; to them, such thinking was irrational, if not ludicrous. For Lenshina, however, these fears were real. She wanted to use her meeting with the 'Lord' to free people from the fear of witchcraft by assuring them that the 'Lord' would overcome any evil spirit which threatened a believer. Accordingly, the people should be baptized, throw away their amulets and other charms, and put their trust in the 'Lord.'

The popular response to her message was phenomenal. People flocked to Kasomo to hear Lenshina preach. To begin with they came from nearby villages. Soon they were trekking to Kasomo from all over Chinsali District and then from other parts of the Northern Province. Her influence did not stop there. My first contact with Lenshina's movement had been in Lundazi District in the Eastern Province, in 1956. Teachers were complaining that their schools were being affected by poor attendance, caused by parents taking their children across the river Luangwa and then up the Muchinga mountains to Kasomo to see and hear Lenshina, the prophetess, a round trip of three–four weeks. In one village in the Luangwa valley, I stopped to rest in the hut provided for travellers. The headman came to greet me. As we talked, I saw in the roof of the hut a handsome fly switch made from the tail of a wildebeest. Its handle consisted of the bottom half of a bicycle pump. Noting my interest, the headman asked if I would like the fly switch. 'Whose is it?' I asked. He explained that it had been left there by a man returning to Lundazi after visiting Lenshina at Kasomo. In the handle were some small dried bones and some pieces of animal skin. These had been used by the owner in the practice of witchcraft. While at Kasomo he had been converted by Lenshina and no longer had need of these grisly items. 'Take the switch,' said the headman. 'No-one here dare touch it. But it cannot hurt you because you are a white man.' The belief that Europeans were immune from the effects of witchcraft was very common.

113

Many discarded symbols of witchcraft were left at Kasomo. The 1955 report of the Department of African Affairs stated, 'The charnel house of surrendered bones and horns and other witchcraft paraphernalia at Lenshina's village represents a far greater reality to the average African than the windy talk of politicians who seem sometimes to forget the real problems of the people.'[14]

For a time it looked as if Lenshina and her followers could be contained within the United Church of Central Africa in Rhodesia (UCCAR) (of which Lubwa mission was a member). Late in 1954, however, Fergus Macpherson went to Scotland on long leave and his departure seems to have triggered off a deterioration in relations between Lubwa and Lenshina, culminating in the schism which took place in 1955. Soon, Lenshina and her husband began to baptize those who professed a wish to join her movement. These included a number of Roman Catholics from Ilondola and a group of UCCAR members who had been suspended from Lubwa because of alleged misconduct. Members had to promise to follow the rules of the Lumpa church.[15] Rule 1 stated: 'The Lumpa Church is a church in which God and His Son, Jesus Christ, are to be praised. It is not a political organization.' Other rules laid down high standards of conduct:

> A Christian must take no part in backbiting, boasting, lying, theft or cruelty ... must be of good character whether in private or public ... must go with others for prayers from time to time and on every appointed day of worship ... must not be a polygamist ... must not come to worship if he has taken some beer (even a little) ... must not bring cigarettes, a pipe or snuff into the church.

The need to shun witchcraft was spelt out very clearly: 'A Christian must avoid witchcraft ... witch-hunting ... sorcery ... bewitching ... should not participate in any mourning festival ceremonies. There should be no invocation of the spirits.' Finally,

> Anyone who does not obey the rules is not liked by our Lord, the Almighty God, and that is why our Lord said: 'Stop practising witchcraft and live in my love.' Anyone who is

found practising witchcraft will suffer more when his time comes to an end because he or she will be heavily punished.[16]

The missionaries at Ilondola and Lubwa condemned Lenshina as a heretic but, to begin with, there seemed no reason to suppose that the setting up of a separate church would provoke trouble with the Government. As the movement grew, however, Lenshina's followers, their confidence increasing, began to resent having to accept any authority other than that of Lenshina herself. Petros, her husband, and some of her more hot-headed followers, appeared bent on defying both central government and the power of the native authorities. The first serious breach of the peace came in September 1956, when a Lumpa church member was imprisoned for calling one of the priests at Ilondola a wizard. Demonstrations followed at Chinsali *boma* and a number of arrests were made. Among those arrested was Petros. He was convicted of proposing violence to an assembly and was sentenced by Paramount Chief Chitimukulu to two years' hard labour.

Initially, relations between Lenshina and the chiefs were good. Indeed, several chiefs joined the Lumpa Church in its early stages. Gradually, however, relations began to deteriorate. It became clear that Lenshina could command more respect and support than the chiefs. Lenshina and her deacons showed increasingly less respect to the traditional authority of the chiefs. The chiefs, for their part, became worried at this challenge to their authority. In particular, they objected to the unauthorized movement of their people from one chief's area to another and the setting up of new villages without the approval of the chief.

For Senior Chief Nkula, a major cause of concern was Lenshina's home village of Kasomo, which had grown out of all recognition. There were more than 60 Lumpa Church buildings in Chinsali District by 1958. By far the largest and most magnificent was the cathedral which Lenshina had built at Kasomo. Two hundred and fifty feet long, and 45 feet wide, it was one of the largest church buildings in the country. It held several hundred worshippers; women sat on the left facing the altar, men on the right. Robert Rotberg, a student of history and politics from the USA, attended a service there in 1959. He described the interior of the cathedral in these terms:

> Behind the altar, the wall is decorated black, yellow and white around a green crescent and an eight-pointed red and blue star. The side walls are pink and green, with blue curtains over the small, high-placed windows. Pillars run the length of the large nave; above the pillars, on a sloping wall to the peaked ceiling, is a plain yellow decoration, topped by a thin blue line and white above the peak of the roof. Little windows are glazed and painted yellow. The floor is cement. It was built exclusively by African labour, and with funds collected from the faithful, in November 1958. Its size remains a symbol of Lenshina's strength.[17]

Living at Kasomo and attending the services there, were hundreds of Africans who had moved there without getting permission from their chiefs. Lenshina had persistently refused to tell her followers to obtain such permission before they left their villages, where they were registered, and moved to Kasomo. She had also ignored the Native Authority's demand to register Kasomo. Chief Nkula decided that the time had come to assert his authority. He sent some *kapasus* (messengers) to Kasomo. There they were mocked and beaten by Lenshina's followers. The District Commissioner then sent some of his *boma* messengers to warn Lenshina that the illegal settlers in her village must leave; if they did not do so, force would be used to remove them. The *boma* messengers met with a hostile reception. Dennis Frost, the DC, now had to appeal to the Provincial Commissioner for support. Before long, two platoons of the Mobile Unit of the Northern Rhodesia Police arrived at Chinsali and camped near the *boma* offices. The Mobile Unit had a reputation throughout the country for toughness and for rough-arm tactics. It was said that no-one was allowed to join the unit whose education had gone beyond Standard 2. 'The thicker, the better,' one of their officers told me. The unit went to Kasomo on 7 May and were attacked with spears and stones. It was only after the Mobile Unit had shown its strength and several of the Lenshinas had been wounded by gunfire,

116

that it was possible to arrest some of the ringleaders and bring them to Chinsali. They were tried by a resident magistrate from Kasama, convicted and sentenced to terms of imprisonment. For a time, an uneasy peace prevailed. Lenshina and her followers licked their wounds and lay low. Next time, they would be better prepared. The Mobile Unit returned to Lusaka. We wondered how long it would be before it returned.

After the school burnings of March and April and the violent clash at Kasomo in May, a period of peace and quiet was welcome. We got on with the less exciting but more profitable daily routine. My father and my stepmother, Kathleen, arrived at the end of April. It was the first time he had been abroad since being wounded at Arras in 1917, and she had never previously left Britain. Despite my misgivings, they fitted well into the Chinsali scene and made many friends. Fortunately, they adjusted rapidly to being driven around by Landrover or in a vanette piled high with sacks of meal, *nshembe* (small dried fish), exercise books and boxes of chalk, as they occasionally accompanied me on visits to schools.

As always, my work was varied and kept me on my toes. Glyn released funds for a new upper primary school at Chinsali *boma* to replace an old and unsafe collection of rather shabby buildings. The classrooms and teachers' houses were to be built in burnt brick with corrugated iron roofs. Glyn had a building foreman in Kasama who made periodic visits to Chinsali to see how things were going. He sent a very reliable young African foreman, Safeli, to be in charge of the day to day operations. My role was to supervise. But how? I knew nothing about building, had never laid a brick in my life, and hardly knew the difference between a joist and a rafter. Fortunately, help was at hand in the shape of the *Field officer's manual* which was issued to all civil servants in bush stations. This book, a veritable treasury of information, told you everything you needed to know about building, from the making of the bricks and mixing of mortar to calculating the number of six-inch nails in a pound and how to apply the final coat of paint. It was particularly useful on brick-making and firing. A gang of labourers, using moulds made locally, made some 60,000 bricks on the edge of the school site. Once these had partly dried, they were built into a kiln. Meanwhile, another gang went off in the five-ton lorry and brought

117

back branches of trees to be used as firewood. Once the kiln had been fired, sufficient wood had to be ready for feeding into the kiln, keeping it at the right temperature for several days and nights. To ensure that those responsible for firing the kiln had not fallen asleep, I would set my alarm at three-hourly intervals throughout the night and make spot checks. Happily, all went well.

Much more up my street was the professional side of the work. Because the education system was so highly competitive, great importance was attached to the Standard 4 and Standard 6 examinations. Only if they did well in the Standard 4 examination, which was set provincially and marked at district level, could a boy or girl go on to Standards 5 and 6. Similarly, children had to get very good marks in the Standard 6 examination to have any chance of being selected for a place in Form 1, the start of the secondary cycle. I conducted the oral English exam in each of the upper primary schools in the two districts. Each pupil would first read a passage to me. Then came aural comprehension; I would read to the pupil and ask questions on the passage. Finally, we would exchange a few sentences of general conversation. By the time you had dealt with a class of 30 or 35, you were pretty exhausted. I had a battery-operated tape recorder which I would sometimes switch on during these interviews. When the exam was over, the class would assemble to hear my comments on their performance. When the recording was played back, the effect was often sensational. Gasps of astonishment (for they had not previously encountered recorders) would give way to shrieks of delight as they recognized their friends' voices, followed by groans of anguish as mistakes were spotted. The errors of the children, of course, frequently mirrored those of their teachers. At one school, for instance, the expression 'hoping you' was much in evidence. The conversation would go: 'Good morning, how are you?' 'I'm all right. Hoping you.' What was meant, of course, was 'I hope you also are all right.' The person responsible for teaching the expression was the Standard 6 teacher. He could not remember where he had picked it up. At many schools, teachers did not have the opportunity of conversing at all regularly with people whose mother tongue was English. Bad habits, once learned, became ingrained. The wonder, though, is not that the standard of English was poor but rather that it was

118

so good. The English vocabulary, understanding and powers of expression, both orally and in writing, of the average Standard 6 pupil were far superior to the laboriously acquired skills in Cibemba of all but a handful of whites.

By November 1959, the political scene in the Northern Province was quiet enough for Gabriel Musumbulwa, Minister of African Education, to make a visit. Glyn said that he would bring him to Chinsali. A few days before he arrived, the classroom block at Musunsu lower primary school was burnt down, a reminder that political troubles were not far below the surface. The Minister, however, was confident that the disturbances of earlier in the year were a thing of the past. He thought it would build up the Chinsali people's confidence in the Government and in the Federation if a secondary school was built in the district. He asked Glyn to look for a suitable site for such a school. Musumbulwa's reasoning sounded naive but the news that a secondary school would be allocated to the district was very welcome. The DC and I did some spadework and lined up a list of possible sites. Early in 1960, the Provincial Commissioner, Glyn, the DC and I inspected all the sites and chose one near Chinsali *boma*. Things looked promising.

Meanwhile, on the political front, important events were taking place. It would be tedious to describe these in detail but some of the highlights must be recorded.

Within a few weeks of the banning of ZANC and the detention of its leaders, there emerged new political groupings which, by October 1959, coalesced into the United National Independence Party (UNIP). By the end of January 1960, Kaunda, Kapwepwe and Sipalo had been released from detention and had taken over the same positions of president, treasurer-general and secretary-general of the new party as they had held in ZANC. Kaunda was released in time to meet Harold Macmillan, the British Prime Minister, who visited Lusaka in February 1960. Kaunda and Nkumbula told Macmillan that they were not prepared to meet the members of the Royal Commission, headed by Lord Monckton, which Macmillan had appointed to advise on the future of the Federation. As far as they were concerned, the whole concept of federation was anathema and there was no point in considering how it might be made more acceptable. Before going to Lusaka,

119

Macmillan had spent a few days in South Africa. On 3 February, he addressed both houses of Parliament in Cape Town. He startled his audience with words which reverberated around the African continent and beyond:

> We have seen the awakening of national consciousness in peoples who for centuries lived in dependence on some other power. The most striking impression I have formed since I left London a month ago is the strength of this African national consciousness . . . In different places it takes different forms but it is happening everywhere. A wind of change is blowing through this continent, whether we like it or not . . . Our national policies must take account of it.

The wind of change, in fact, was but one of several factors which determined Britain's policy towards the colonies. Apathy and ambivalence were two other factors. The passage of time had long since eroded belief in Britain's imperial destiny, with which Rhodes and Kipling had inspired an earlier generation. Popular interest in the colonial empire was lukewarm. Gratitude for the way in which the colonial territories, as well as the dominions, had stood by Britain during the war, many suffering grievous losses of their young men, was giving way to irritation over the aggressive nature of the campaigns for self-government which were springing up in many territories. A weariness with empire and its responsibilities was resulting in a growing feeling among the British people that no useful purpose would be served by Britain attempting to retain its territories against the wishes of the indigenous peoples. 'If that [independence] is what they want,' many were prompted to say, 'let them get on with it.'

Successive British governments had projected Britain as a trustee for the indigenous peoples of her colonial territories.[18] Britain, it was claimed, ruled in Africa and elsewhere, not for its own benefit but for the good of the native peoples. Britain's guiding principle, said the Colonial Office, was the paramountcy of native interests, not of the settler communities. Because of this, Britain protected indigenous populations against colonists who wanted their land, their minerals and their labour. For the same reason, as a responsible trustee, Britain accepted its responsibility for promoting the social and economic development of its colonial possessions and for preparing them for self-government and eventual independence.

So much for the rhetoric of trusteeship; what of the practice? To claim the role of trustee was one thing; to translate the principle into practice was, of course, quite another. The progress of the colonies towards independence was not conceived in Westminster or Whitehall as a matter of urgency. Independence was regarded as a distant goal to be achieved, if at all, after decades of gradual development. The economic and social development of the Empire was seen by Britain as primarily a responsibility of the governments of the colonies; only very limited support could be provided by Britain. When a more generous spirit prevailed in London, and Colonial Development and Welfare Acts were passed, the level of assistance was raised significantly but there was never adequate funding to prime the pumps of industrial and agricultural development in all the far-flung dependencies and to provide all the roads, bridges, hospitals and university colleges which were demanded.

As for the political advancement of the indigenous populations, the Colonial Office had to contend not only with the demands of native nationalist movements but also those of the expatriate colonists. In many colonies, settlers made a vital contribution to the economic life of the country. Their rights could not be ignored. How those rights could be reconciled with the rights of the native peoples, within the framework of a policy of trusteeship, and in a manner acceptable to British and international public opinion, presented a severe test for British statesmen of the 1950s and 1960s.

Where a settler community was large and well-established, it was likely to demand the maintenance of white supremacy, at least in the short to medium term, in order, it was said, 'to maintain civilized standards'.

Most settler communities, however, did not seriously challenge the principle of trusteeship as long as it could be safely assumed that preparation for majority rule would be a lengthy process spanning many generations. The crunch came when irresistible nationalist movements demanded immediate black majority rule and independence. It was then that hard decisions had to be made;

ambivalence was no longer possible. To her credit, though not always with good grace, Britain adhered to the principle of trusteeship and the paramountcy of native interests. The position in Africa in 1960 was that British Somalia and Nigeria were about to follow in the footsteps of Ghana which had been given its independence in 1957. Tanzania already had an African majority in its legislature; independence would come there and in Cameroons and Sierra Leone in 1961. There could be little doubt that Uganda's independence would not be long delayed. Even in Kenya, where the murderous activities of the Mau Mau movement had aroused strong feelings in Britain, it could only be a matter of time before the nationalists succeeded in gaining control. In these countries there were white settlers who felt that they had been betrayed and that Britain had reneged on her promises to them. But, comparatively speaking, they were few in number and they commanded little sympathy in the international community.

In the Central African Federation, however, the way forward was unclear. There were the wishes of more than a quarter of a million well-organized and determined whites to consider. The British Government remained convinced that the Federation was a good thing which, given time, would be seen to be working to the advantage of blacks as well as whites. Iain Macleod, Macmillan's Colonial Secretary, was prepared to see Northern Rhodesia's Africans advance quite rapidly towards holding a majority of seats in the Legislative Council. At the same time, he was intent on maintaining the Federation if it was at all possible. Meanwhile, Kaunda and Nkumbula, leaders respectively of UNIP and the ANC, had set their sights firmly on achieving both black majority government and the break-up of the Federation. For his part, Sir Roy Welensky, Federal Prime Minister, began to hint that the Federation would be maintained by force, if necessary. In this situation, how would Britain discharge its responsibilities as trustee?

During the long, tense months of 1960 when the Monckton Commission went about its business, Kaunda repeatedly condemned violence and urged his followers to be calm and patient. I met him for the first time when he came to visit his mother at Lubwa and asked the DC for permission to hold a political meeting at Chinsali *boma*. On balance, the DC was in favour of allowing the meeting to take place. He believed Kaunda would order UNIP members in the district to follow a path of non-violence. 'Everybody in the district knows that Kaunda is here,' he told me. 'If I refuse to authorize the meeting, there's no telling what might happen.'

'Then why not let the meeting go ahead?' I asked.

Gloomily he told me: 'I've no choice in the matter. Orders from the PC. When Kaunda comes to see me tomorrow, I'll have to tell him the answer's "No". I'd like you to help me. Give me ten minutes alone with Kaunda and then come and interrupt us. Don't leave it any longer or I'll have run out of reasons for not letting him have his meeting.'

From my office window, I watched Kaunda approach the *boma* on the next morning. To a man, the *boma* messengers received him with great civility and respect. Ten minutes after he entered the DC's office, I went in and 'reminded' the DC that he was late for a meeting. The DC got up at once and told Kaunda that he would have to ask him to leave. 'My people will be disappointed that you will not let me speak to them,' said Kaunda. 'I shall do my best to restrain them, but you must not hold me responsible for any incidents that may follow.' Shamefacedly, the DC and I watched him leave, both of us sure that he had rumbled our little deception.

The report of the Monckton Commission, signed by all but two of its 25 members, was released in October 1960. It stated that it was desirable, on economic grounds, for the Federation to continue. It recognized that in both Northern Rhodesia and Nyasaland opposition to federation was 'widespread, sincere and of long standing. It is almost pathological.' In order to overcome African hostility, there was need for 'drastic and fundamental changes' in the Federation's structure; more power should be devolved on the territorial governments, leaving the Federal Government with responsibility only for external affairs, defence and the control of the economy. The report went on to recommend that Africans should have a higher percentage of seats in the Federal Assembly, and that 'unfairly discriminatory legislation' should be removed in all territories. Members of the Commission noted with approval that Nyasaland had already been given a new constitution under which Africans were assured of a majority of seats; they recommended that similar provision should be made for Northern Rhodesia. On the highly controversial issue of whether territories should be allowed to secede from the Federation, the commissioners used tortuous langauge: 'A declaration of the intention of Her Majesty's Government to permit secession by any of the Territories, if so requested . . . would have a very favourable effect, and might be decisive in securing a fair trial for the . . . association.'[19] This seemed to mean: The best way of maintaining the Federation is to give the territories the right to secede if they so wish.

By this time I was on home leave. I flew to London in August 1960. Ken was working in Iraq and he and Moyna invited me out to Baghdad for a holiday. An army coup had recently toppled King Faisal and his government; after a good deal of bloodshed, General Kassem had seized power. While I was there the atmosphere was tense and further bloodshed was expected. It duly came but not while I was there. Kassem was overthrown and his severed head was displayed on television as proof that he was, indeed, dead. One could be forgiven for hoping that Northern Rhodesians would choose the British, rather than the Iraqi, way of conducting their political affairs.

Leave over, I sailed to Cape Town and drove my new Triumph Herald 2,000 miles northwards, arriving back in the Northern Province in February 1961. My posting was to Kasama where I was to be second in command to Glyn, the PEO, with special responsibility for Kasama, Luwingu and Mporokoso districts. This was new ground for me and I enjoyed the touring. With my driver, Michael Mumba, who had been with me in Chinsali and who was a good friend as well as a safe and reliable driver, I covered thousands of miles while visiting and inspecting schools, delivering food and equipment, attending meetings with parents, teachers, headmen and chiefs.

My mind, however, was not entirely on my work. For some time, I had been writing to Evelyn West, a teacher employed by the Church of Scotland. We had first met at Mwenzo mission in Isoka district soon after she arrived from her home in Banffshire, Scotland. We had seen more of each other when she was transferred to the primary school at Lubwa mission. A graduate and a trained teacher from Aberdeen University, and with a very sympathetic ear, she was the ideal person to whom I could pour out my worries and exchange news. Now she was a tutor at a new teacher-training college at Serenje, 300 or so miles from Kasama. We became engaged on Easter Sunday and decided that the wedding would be in July at Lubwa mission, about 100 miles from Kasama and 200 from Serenje.

While Evelyn and I made our wedding plans, the political atmosphere steadily deteriorated. In February, Macleod had produced a White Paper proposing a new constitution for Northern Rhodesia. There was to be a legislature of 45 members. Of these, 15 would be elected by mainly white voters, 15 by Africans, and a further 15, sitting for so-called 'national' seats, would be elected by both sets of voters together. There was no question of universal suffrage. The right to vote would be restricted to about 25,000 Europeans, 3,000 Africans and 2,000 Asians who qualified for the upper electoral roll and to some 70,000 Africans who had the necessary educational and/or property qualifications for the lower roll.

Both UNIP and the ANC objected strongly to Macleod's proposals as falling far short of what they considered to be just and reasonable. They put forward demands for changes which would increase the possibility of African candidates winning the 'national' seats. They acknowledged however, that elections under the proposed constitution, defective though it was, would produce a majority opposed to the Federation. As an interim measure, therefore, it was hinted that the constitution could be accepted.

Sir Roy Welensky had also been making his calculations; he did not like what he discovered. He denounced Macleod's proposals as a betrayal of white interests (Welensky had been prepared to accept African majority rule in Nyasaland). Poor, and with a white settler population of only 8,000, Nyasaland was something of an embarrassment to the Federation; its secession would leave the Federation stronger rather than weaker. Northern Rhodesia, on the other hand, with its 70,000 settlers, and the source of enormous wealth from its copper mines, was a very different story. Northern Rhodesia must be retained in the Federation at all costs. In

125

appealing to Macleod to reconsider his proposals, Welensky could point to widespread violence and bloodshed in the Congo, now Zaire, where the Belgian colonial rulers had withdrawn and left the country in a state of virtual anarchy. It was not difficult, said Welensky, to envisage similar chaos developing in Northern Rhodesia if an African government came to power. A massive propaganda campaign in Britain, orchestrated by Welensky, had its effect. It was estimated that a third of the Conservative Members of Parliament supported Welensky's demands that Macleod's draft constitution should be amended to ensure that a European-dominated pro-federation majority would be assured.

Alarmed, Kaunda warned in language which was unusually intemperate for him, that if Britain yielded to the demands of Welensky and the Federal Government, trouble would break out which 'would make Mau Mau look like a child's picnic.'[20] As Welensky began to hint at a possible unilateral declaration of independence and called up the white territorial army batallions in both Northern and Southern Rhodesia as a means of showing his strength, Kaunda told a rally on the Copperbelt that he was ready to launch a 'master plan'[21] which would paralyse the country. It was clear that whatever Macleod did would alienate one side or the other.

In June, Macleod announced his decision. He amended his earlier proposals in such a way as to tilt the balance of power in favour of the pro-federationists. Welensky was jubilant. He described the amended constitution as a 'reasonably workable document'. If the Federal Party played its cards well, he said, 'it would emerge from any election with a substantial majority.'[22]

By contrast, UNIP and the ANC were dismayed by Macleod's amendments which they saw as a gross betrayal. On 9 July Kaunda addressed 3,000 UNIP delegates at Mulungushi. He asked them, in spite of much provocation, to remain 'patient, non-violent in thought, word and deed'. As he spoke, shouts of 'Cha-cha-cha' became insistent. This was a reference to a popular form of community dancing which was starting to acquire sinister overtones. Kaunda took up the idea. 'Cha-cha-cha means real dancing,' he said. 'Europeans will take part along with Africans. Young children and those unborn will join in the dance. Hens, dogs and all our domestic beasts will join in. Yes, even the Queen will dance Cha-cha-cha. Cha-cha-cha is for all.'[23] It may be assumed that Kaunda meant that the whole community, black and white together, would join in opposing Macleod's constitution and in working for freedom. Some of his followers, however, interpreted Cha-cha-cha as a call to violence. Within a few days of the Mulungushi meeting, trouble broke out on the Copperbelt. It could be only a matter of time before it reached the Northern Province.

Amid mounting political tension, we pressed ahead with our wedding preparations. A wedding of Europeans on a bush station was a rarity. We invited 100 or so friends, black and white. Many of them cheerfully put themselves to considerable inconvenience and travelled long distances to share in the festivities. Bill McKenzie, the minister in charge of Lubwa, agreed to marry us with the help of the Revd Paul Mushindo. Bill thought he should check to see that Lubwa was properly registered as a place where Europeans could be married. He found that it wasn't, which meant that the last Europeans to be married at Lubwa, some 30 years earlier, had not been married at all in the eyes of the law. He decided not to tell them! Margaret, Bill's wife, took the place of Evelyn's mother as hostess of the reception which followed the wedding service. Everyone on the mission station and at Chinsali *boma* rallied round and a splendid meal was laid on. My part in the proceedings was to provide 15 large chickens which were to be flown up to Kasama from Lusaka for the occasion. When the plane arrived, there was no sign of the chickens. When I reached Lubwa, empty-handed, messengers were urgently despatched to the surrounding villages and 30 of the local fowls were assembled, slain and cooked. Bev Packer, Principal of Serenje Teacher-Training College, gave Evelyn away; Claude Slater, the Agricultural Supervisor at Chinsali and a good friend, stood as my best man. Neither Evelyn's mother nor my father could make the long journey from Britain to be at the wedding, but Evelyn's sister, Rosemary, came out from Scotland to be bridesmaid.

As the guests drove home to Kasama and Serenje, several came across trees felled across the roads. Cha-cha-cha had reached Chinsali District. As luck would have it, we had chosen to go east for our honeymoon and encountered no sign of trouble either on the Nyika Plateau in Nyasaland or in the Luangwa valley, where we stayed in two game camps. Then, honeymoon over, we hurried back to Kasama.

Glyn had been transferred to Lusaka and it would be several months before he would be replaced as Provincial Education Officer. While I was acting as PEO, Evelyn and I lived in the PEO's house, a large, rather rambling establishment with a wide verandah enclosed by mosquito gauze netting. At the back of the house was a guest house and beyond that were the offices of the Ministry of African Education. The front of the house looked on to the nine-hole golf course of Kasama Club. Number 5 'green', actually made of sand, was just across the road, immediately in front of the house. The house itself had been built by a previous PEO named Miller. It was after him that we named the junior secondary school, the opening of which was made possible by Evelyn's arrival on the scene. Just before the wedding, Clifford Little, by now Secretary for African Education, sent us his personal good wishes. In the same envelope was an official minute informing me that approval had been given for me to employ Miss Evelyn West as a temporary mistress. This was a typically Clifford joke, which Evelyn did not really appreciate. It meant, however, that for the first time the Northern Province had a girls' secondary school, even though it initially consisted of only 30 girls.

While Evelyn coped with the problems of opening the new secondary school, my first few months of married life and as PEO were taken up with dealing with a serious outbreak of arson. As might be expected, Chinsali District, where John Daniell was now Education Officer, was the centre of the trouble. As in 1959, villagers wanting to show their anger at 'government' – a vague concept which might cover the Native Authority, the DC, the Governor, Legislative Council, Sir Roy Welensky or the Colonial Secretary in London – had difficulty in finding suitable targets at which to direct their protests. They possessed no guns, apart, perhaps, from a few shotguns, and they had no explosives. In any case, they were not terrorists as the term is now understood, and their aim was not to kill. While in some other countries, the struggle for independence was highlighted by murderous attacks on white farmers, traders, missionaries and civil servants, the pent-up fury and frustration of Zambia's freedom fighters was mostly directed towards inanimate targets: bridges, cattle *kraals*, dip tanks, roads and schools. Like most European civil servants in Kasama, I was sworn in as a special constable and spent some long, dreary nights patrolling the low-density area of the town on the lookout for trouble which never came.

Of 64 arson incidents at schools which took place in the country between July and October 1961, 47 occurred in the Northern Province. Of these, 24 happened in Chinsali District. The arson resulted in the destruction of 120 classrooms, 7 teachers' houses, 28 dormitories and 38 ancillary school buildings. In most of the affected schools, furniture and equipment went up in flames together with the buildings. As a result of the destruction, nearly 200 teachers became temporarily redundant and some 8,500 children were unable to attend school.[24]

While the burning of schools in 1959 had taken place by night and in secret, the arson campaign of 1961 was quite blatant. A gang of UNIP men would arrive at a school in daylight, often while lessons were in progress. The children would be ordered to leave their classrooms. Sometimes the teachers were allowed to remove books and other items from the office, sometimes not. The class-rooms were then set on fire while the children and their teachers watched.

Visiting the blackened shells of the schools was a sad and sickening experience. When the DC, Chinsali, refused to let me go to some schools unless I travelled with an escort of two lorry-loads of armed soldiers or policemen, I had to wonder whether the three years I had spent in the district, trying to build up the confidence of the teachers, the village headmen, the chiefs and the parents had not been time wasted. I found it tragic that disagreement over the small print of a constitution drafted in London should be the cause of so much senseless destruction in little village schools on the Bemba plateau where the people, as I knew from experience, were basically patient and peace-loving. Like them, I felt angry and frustrated. I expressed my anger by writing an open letter to the chiefs in Chinsali District telling them that their people seemed to have gone mad and that the secondary school which had been promised to the district would now be allocated to another district

129

where the people appreciated education and did not burn down their schools.

There is no doubt that the school arson in the Northern Province was perpetrated by followers of UNIP. Equally, I have no doubt that it was done with the approval of the mass of the village people. UNIP produced a document, 'A grim peep into the north', which attempted to show that many of the schools were burnt down by the security forces.[25] Certainly, there were large numbers of soldiers and the notorious police Mobile Unit on duty in the Northern Province at the time. Certainly, they were guilty of the wanton destruction of many village houses and grain bins, and of the theft of cattle and other livestock. Certainly, they were brutal in their handling of those whom they suspected of being 'trouble-makers'. But I know of no evidence that the security forces burned down schools. All the evidence that I knew of, gathered from teachers who were eye-witnesses, pointed unmistakably to UNIP as the arsonists. Kaunda implicitly recognized this when, writing his autobiography, '*Zambia shall be free*', a year later, he declared:

The days that followed the Mulungushi conference were anxious days. Most of the country remained peaceful but in the Northern Province the long years of frustration spilled over into violence. In went the Mobile Unit of the Northern Rhodesian Police and the white troops of the Federal Army. Schools were burnt down, whole villages were gutted by fire; about eight Africans were killed in various incidents by the security forces of Welensky's Army. No one regrets more than I the violence that took place in the Northern Province, but if you drive an animal into a corner and torment it, you may expect that in its fear and rage it will slash back at you.'[26]

In fact, much of the heat was taken out of the disturbances in September 1961 when the British Government announced its intention to reopen discussion on the Northern Rhodesian constitution. Welensky, predictably, was aghast and accused Macmillan of giving way in the face of violence, 'in the tradition of Munich',[27] he added scornfully. Reginald Maudling, who had replaced

Macleod as Colonial Secretary, visited Lusaka in November but it was not until the end of February 1962 that he announced the final form of the constitution. UNIP and the ANC had won some minor concessions. Welensky was furious but his United Federal Party in Northern Rhodesia accepted the new arrangements. After a long and bitter discussion, UNIP's leaders acepted Kaunda's advice to participate in the ensuing election rather than to agitate for further concessions. Kaunda ended his autobiography with these words:

> There are always those who say that violence pays and that it was what happened in the Northern Province that made the British government once again change its mind. It is not for me to say what goes on in Whitehall. All I know is that now in 1962 we have been given a constitution in which we have decided to work for majority rule in Northern Rhodesia. For the first time in our history we may be able to use the ballot box to break up this ugly Central African Federation. For a long time I have led my people in their shouts of KWACHA (the dawn). We have been shouting in the darkness; now there is the grey light of dawn on the horizon and I know that Zambia will be free.'[28]

The election campaign began in earnest in September 1962. There was little doubt that UNIP would win the lower roll seats in the Northern Province. To gain any of the 'national' seats, it had to secure the votes of at least 10 per cent of the upper roll, mainly white, voters. With this in view, the UNIP leadership did its best to win respectability in European eyes. When Kaunda spoke to a mainly white audience at Kasama, he was accompanied by John Mwanakatwe whom I had not seen since leaving Munali eight years earlier. Their theme was one of reconciliation and of working together for a peaceful and prosperous future. On the other side, the United Federal Party played on Europeans' fears of being swamped by black nationalists who were portrayed as vicious, violent, irresponsible and inexperienced. Europeans who intended to vote for UNIP candidates were condemned as 'traitors'.

The election took place on 30 October. I was appointed Presiding Officer at Nkolemfumu, a village some 20 miles from Kasama.

Voting was to begin at 6.30a.m. which meant making an early start from Kasama so that there was time to rig up a polling booth in a classroom of the village school and to show representatives of the candidates that the ballot box was empty. By 6.15 there was a queue of a score of villagers anxiously waiting to exercise their democratic rights for the first time. Some had difficulty in marking their ballot papers. As Presiding Officer, I had the responsibility of going with them into the polling booth, ascertaining their wishes and marking their papers for them. I was left in no doubt that UNIP commanded the loyalty of nearly every voter. By 8 o'clock, all but two of the 70 voters on the electoral roll had cast their votes. Of the two absentees, I was told that one was sick and would not be coming. The other had gone fishing; no-one was sure whether he would be back in time to vote. It made no difference to me. The poll had to remain open until 7.30 in the evening, irrespective of the number of voters who might turn up. The UNIP candidate was Simon Kapwepwe. He arrived just before dusk and spent the last two hours discussing with me the likely political development of the country. He had little doubt that Northern Rhodesia would win its independence within two years and would be known as Zambia. We were both pleased when, just before the poll closed, the missing fisherman turned up to cast his vote.

That Kapwepwe would win his seat was never seriously in doubt. He was one of 14 UNIP members returned on the lower roll. In the contest for the 'national' seats, however, UNIP suffered a humiliating reverse. The polling figures clearly showed that very few Europeans and Asians were prepared to entrust the government of the country to Kaunda and his colleagues. In the Chambeshi 'national' seat constituency, for instance, the UNIP candidate, Sir Stewart Gore-Browne (a pillar of respectability) won over 11,000 African votes but could muster only 55 from Europeans.[29] I think that fear was the main factor, at that time, in UNIP's failure to win the support of non-African voters. The events of 1961 and especially of Cha-cha-cha were still fresh in their minds. My European colleagues in the civil service certainly had no love for Sir Roy Welensky or for the Federation. Most of them considered the Federation to be a millstone around Northern Rhodesia's neck and, to change the metaphor, a drain on the country's wealth.

132

Many, I think, were quite prepared to see African majority rule, a black government, the end of all forms of discrimination based on colour and, if that was what the people wanted, independence from Britain. The parting of the ways came over the question of timing. Black nationalist opinion demanded black majority rule now, the end of the Federation now, independence now. Moderate and progressive Europeans thought that to accede to these demands immediately would lead to disaster. Time was needed – and estimates varied between five and 25 years – in which to provide significant numbers of Africans with higher education and to train them to assume increasing responsibility for running the country's economic, social and political life. There was a genuine fear that if the nationalists came to power immediately the country could easily sink into the same state of bloody chaos as appeared to be the fate of Zaire from which the Belgians had precipitately withdrawn, having failed lamentably to train people to take over the running of the country from them.

Temporarily, at least, the ANC and UNIP leaderships settled their differences and combined to form a coalition which governed the country, uneasily, throughout 1963. Kaunda was Minister of Local Government and Nkumbula held the portfolio of African education. Although they managed to give the appearance of working together, their supporters at grass roots level made no attempt to conceal their dislike for each other, a dislike based more on tribal than on ideological grounds. Clashes between rival ANC and UNIP supporters broke out on the Copperbelt and the violence resulted in some deaths. At the height of the trouble, the British Government, which had already conceded to Nyasaland the right to secede from the Federation, made the same concession to Northern Rhodesia. Facts had at last been faced: the Federation could not continue in the face of African intransigence. Macmillan and his colleagues in London and Sir Roy Welensky and his government in Salisbury had to accept defeat; the Federation was dead. It was formally dissolved at the end of 1963, just ten years after it had come into existence.

The disturbances on the Copperbelt did not spread this time to the Northern Province. In Kasama and the surrounding districts UNIP reigned supreme. Any supporters of the ANC kept their opinions to themselves. It was good to get on with the business of administering education without political distractions. Now that it was clear that the Federation was on its way out and that independence would not be long delayed, villagers set to with a will to repair or to replace the school buildings which had suffered in the earlier disturbances. As I moved around the province, breaking new ground in Abercorn and Mporokoso districts, I sensed a determination to make up for the time that had been lost during Cha-cha-cha and to prepare for independence and the challenges and opportunities that would bring.

We went on home leave in April 1963, taking with us our young son, Nicholas West, who had been born the previous August. Evelyn's mother, Barbara Ann West, at the age of 64, had gamely come out to help with the new arrival. Granny came from a community of sturdy, God-fearing fisherfolk. She had never previously been out of Britain, but quickly became a seasoned traveller. She had not only flown out to Kasama, via Ndola, but had also made trips to Kasaba Bay on Lake Tanganyika, Victoria Falls and to the eastern districts of Southern Rhodesia. Now she welcome us to her home in Gardenstown, a fascinating and picturesque fishing village on the Moray Firth. For Evelyn, it was a case of going home and being reunited with her relations and friends. For me, it was an introduction to a new way of life and to the warm hospitality of north-east Scotland. It was wonderfully relaxing. As we helped two of Evelyn's cousins to haul their lobster creels, explored Tayside and Deeside, or (on a trip to the beautiful west coast) sat quietly in the abbey on the island of Iona, the problems of Northern Rhodesia receded, rightly, into the far distance.

We returned to Northern Rhodesia in August 1963, taking with us a sturdy Peugeot 403 which we had collected in Paris, and now drove the long 2,000 miles from Cape Town to Kasama. By this time there was no doubt independence was near. In an envelope marked 'Top Secret' came instructions from Lusaka for the disposal of all incriminating papers. As PEO, I had to handle the exercise myself and not delegate it. It meant going through all the files in the registry and removing any papers which contained information detrimental to those who were, or were likely to be, our political leaders. It also involved searching for and removing all papers in which civil servants had expressed opinions derogatory to the same actual or potential political leaders. I could see the purpose of the exercise, which extended to all ministries and which was common practice in all British colonies as they approached independence. Nevertheless, as I completed weeding the files and burning the offending pages, I could not help regretting that historians were being deprived of a good deal of valuable and irreplaceable material. The file I burnt on Kenneth Kaunda, for instance, who had taught at Lubwa before going into the political world, would have been a fascinating source of material for his future biographer.

Another innovation was the system of 'shadows'. It was important to give outstanding African civil servants training in their future posts as permanent secretaries, under-secretaries, ambassadors, directors and so on. This was achieved by appointing them as 'shadows' to the substantive holders of these posts, all of whom were white. To begin with, the shadow merely observed his boss. Then, as he gained in experience and confidence he took over some of the simpler tasks then, gradually, the more difficult until it was felt he had learned enough to assume the full duties of the post. At that point, the shadow was appointed to the substantive post and the former boss was often appointed as an adviser. Our ministry had more African graduates on its strength than any other and it was natural, therefore, that we should lose many of our high fliers. Some of those selected as shadows failed to make the grade and were returned to their original posts. Others proved great successes. One of these was the District Education Officer at Abercorn, Dominic Mulaisho. Still in his 20s, very intelligent, a person of integrity and modesty, Dominic had been with us for not much more than a year when I was informed that he was to report to ministry headquarters where he was to 'shadow' the Under Secretary, the second most senior post in the ministry. As I never doubted, Dominic rose to the challenge, worked very hard and took over in due course as substantive Under-Secretary. Subsequently, he became Permanent Secretary of several ministries before being appointed Special Economic Adviser to the President.

The coalition government which the Macleod–Maudling 15:15:15 constitution had produced was an uneasy compromise which fully satisfied no-one. A new constitution, providing for

135

universal adult suffrage and a legislature of 75 seats was announced in August. More than a million Africans were enrolled on the new electoral register, compared with fewer than 100,000 under the previous constitution. For the general election which was to be held in January 1964, I was appointed Returning Officer for Luwingu constituency. My first task was to receive and check the nomination papers of the candidates. Nominations were due to close at noon on 21 December. The UNIP candidate, Unia Mwila, arrived the previous day. His papers were in meticulous order. He already carried the walking stick with a carved handle that was to become *de rigueur* for cabinet ministers. I told him that the ANC candidate had not yet been to see me. Mr Mwila did not seem surprised. Rather, he made it clear that he expected to be unopposed. Sure enough, when the time for nomination passed the next day, there had been no sign of the ANC candidate. But there had been foul play. UNIP supporters in Mpika had got wind of the fact that four ANC candidates for constituencies in the Northern Province were travelling together in one car. They ambushed the car and held the candidates prisoner until the time for the receipt of nominations had passed.

When it was known what had happened, the period for receiving nominations was extended by one week. Again, I waited in my office for the ANC candidate. He arrived, Dismas Bwalya, at five minutes to noon. When I examined his papers I found, to our mutual dismay, that they were defective. The regulations were quite clear. There was no way in which I could accept his nomination. I could not help but wonder whether, in his heart of hearts, the lugubrious Dismas was not relieved. He must have known that he could not possibly win the election and that his life might well have been in danger had he tried to hold election meetings in some parts of Luwingu District. I had to prepare a statement for the Registrar of the High Court giving my reasons for rejecting the nomination papers. It was a relief, but hardly a surprise, to know that my decision had been upheld.

In the election held in January 1964, UNIP was unopposed in 24 main roll seats and won 31 others, leaving the ANC with 10. The National Progress Party, which had replaced the United Federal Party, won all ten of the reserved, European, seats.[30] Kenneth

Kaunda was appointed Prime Minister of the country's first all-African cabinet. Kapwepwe was Minister of Home Affairs, Arthur Wina was given the Ministery of Finance, John Mwanakatwe, Education, Nalumino Mundia, Local Government.

John Mwanakatwe's appointment as Minister of Education was especially significant. While the Federation was in existence, the education of Africans was a responsibility of each of the three territories. The education of European, Asian, and coloured children, on the other hand, was a responsibility of the Federal Government. Now, with the Federation dead, Northern Rhodesia had regained control over the education of all its children. As John Mwanakatwe tried to fashion a single, integrated education system, major changes were certain. Nowhere would these changes be more difficult or more bitterly contested than on the Copperbelt.

Within ten days of Mwanakatwe taking up his appointment I learned that I was to be transferred immediately to Ndola, capital of the Copperbelt. I was sorry to leave the Northern Province where, for more than six years, I had had the opportunity to observe, often at close quarters, the country's exciting and, at times, painful evolution from being a British protectorate to becoming an independent republic. Although Zambia would not be officially born for a few more months, the main political struggle was over. A black government, for so long no more than a dream, an unattainable goal, was now a reality. Independence was just around the corner. Compared with many other countries, Zambia achieved its independence with remarkably little loss of life. The policy of non-violence consistently followed by Kaunda and his senior colleagues undoubtedly saved many lives. When disturbances did break out, such as during the Cha-cha-cha emergency of 1961, they were on a small scale compared with the bloody insurrections and civil wars which sometimes preceded independence elsewhere. During the Mau Mau crisis in Kenya, for instance, 10,000 people were killed. Southern Rhodesia was destined not to achieve its independence until 1980 by which time 40,000 of its citizens would have perished in a bitter and protracted struggle between black and white, black and black.

Politically, then, there was much to be thankful for. Personally, the years spent in Chinsali and Kasama had been no less rewarding.

Independence and Beyond

Evelyn and I were happily married; Nicholas was thriving and a second child was well on the way. Letters from the Minister and the Permanent Secretary indicated that I had won my spurs as a provincial education officer. All the same, it was a big surprise to know that we were going to Ndola. The post of PEO, Western Province, was reckoned to be the most demanding posting outside the top three posts in ministry headquarters. As the youngest of the PEOs, and having spent nearly all of the previous ten years on bush stations, I knew that Ndola and the Copperbelt were going to be very different and very challenging.

Notes

1 'Report of the Livingstonia Misssion, 1907', quoted in W. V. Stone, 'The Livingstonia Misssion and the Bemba', in *Bulletin of the Society for African Church History*, Vol. 2, No. 4, (1968).
2 R. D. McMinn, *Lubwa Misssion Report, 1934*, Church of Scotland Archives.
3 *African Education Department Annual Report* (1954).
4 *African Education Department Annual Report* (1957).
5 Quoted in K. D. Kaunda, *Zambia shall be free* (London: Heinemann, 1962), p. 57.
6 Kaunda, *Zambia*, p. 73.
7 *Hansard*, No. 78 (April 1953), quoted in Hall, *Zambia*, p. 174.
8 Quoted in Hall, *Zambia*, p. 183.
9 *Ibid.*, p. 187.
10 *Northern News* (19 February 1959), quoted in Hall, *Zambia*, p. 186.
11 *Northern News* (16–17 February 1959), quoted in Macpherson, *Kenneth Kaunda*, p. 271.
12 Hall, *Zambia*, p. 188.
13 Robert Rotberg, 'The Lenshina movement in Northern Rhodesia', in *Rhodes-Livingstone Journal*, No. 29 (Manchester: Manchester University Press, June 1961), pp. 63–78. (This article draws on unpublished reports by the Revd Fergus Macpherson and the Revd W. Vernon Stone.)
14 *Department of African Affairs Annual Report* (1955), quoted in Hall, *Zambia*, p. 177.
15 'Lumpa' derives from a Chinyanja word meaning 'supreme'. Lumpa Church, therefore, means highest or supreme church, a claim which gave great offence, of course, to the Church of Scotland, the White Fathers and to other denominations.
16 *Report of the Commission of Enquiry into the former Lumpa Church*, Appendix A (Lusaka: Government Printer, 1965)
17 Rotberg, 'The Lenshina movement', p. 75.

Education and the struggle for independence

18 The Fabian Society made valuable contributions to the understanding of trusteeship. See Rita Hinden (ed.), *Fabian colonial essays* (London: Allen & Unwin, 1945) and A. Creech Jones, *The Labour Party and colonial policy, 1949–1951* (London: New Fabian Colonial Essays, Hogarth Press, 1959). It was the concept of trusteeship which inspired the mandatory system set up by the League of Nations after the First World War. This required the countries which were mandated to govern the colonies taken from Germany and Turkey to promote the rights of native populations and to prepare them for self-government. After the Second World War, the United Nations appointed the Trusteeship Council to ensure that these responsibilities were faithfully discharged.

19 *Monckton Report*, C 1148 (London: HMSO, 1960), p. 16.
20 *Central African Mail* (14 February 1961), quoted in Hall, *Zambia*, p. 203.
21 Macpherson, *Kenneth Kaunda*, p. 330.
22 Hall, *Zambia*, p. 207.
23 Macpherson, *Kenneth Kaunda*, p. 345.
24 *Ministry of African Education Annual Survey* (1961).
25 UNIP, *A grim peep into the north* (Lusaka: UNIP, 1961).
26 Kaunda, *Zambia*, pp. 159–60.
27 Hall, *Zambia*, p. 211.
28 Kaunda, *Zambia*, p. 160.
29 Hall, *Zambia*, p. 220.
30 *Ibid.*, p. 227.

5

Independence and after

Harold Holmes and Ron Brown greeted our arrival at Ndola. Harold had been Provincial Education Officer for several years and knew the Western (now Copperbelt) Province well. Ron was the Regional Director of Education, appointed by the Federal Government and responsible for European, Asian and coloured education. Their two jobs, which had kept them both at full stretch, were being merged into one, into me.

'Roughly speaking,' said Harold, at the end of our hand-over discussions, 'the school population for which you are responsible is about 100,000 spread over nearly 200 schools.' His hand swept across a map studded with coloured pins. Now he pointed to a neat row of filing cabinets. 'You've got about 2,000 teachers to take care of. Their files are all there. You'll find they make interesting reading, if ever you get the time.' I must have looked concerned. 'Keep a close watch on your budget,' he said, 'and you'll be alright.' He got into his car for the 200-mile drive down to Lusaka where he was to take over at Ministry headquarters as Assistant Secretary in charge of personnel matters. 'And the best of British luck,' he called, giving a cheery wave.

Ron stayed just long enough to initiate me into the non-African education system which had developed on very different lines from the African system with which I was familiar. After a hesitant beginning in the days of the British South Africa Company, European education had expanded rapidly, with scant regard to cost.[1] Staffed by expatriate, mainly British, teachers, many of whom were trained graduates, inspected regularly, housed in substantial and well-equipped buildings, and provided with excellent facilities for sports and other extra-curricular activities, the schools for European children reached a very high standard which could bear comparison with similar establishments in South Africa and Britain. Ron was highly respected in these schools as a caring professional who had contributed a great deal to the first-class reputation which they enjoyed. He was clearly apprehensive. 'Standards are bound to suffer,' he said gloomily, 'when you open the floodgates.' He commended to me the small group of advisers led by Paul Bowler, who were staying on and who would help develop a curriculum and teaching/learning materials which would be suitable for use in all types of school. He suggested I might join them in their work on the English and history syllabuses. I showed him my diary for the week, a seemingly endless round of visits and meetings – with the Provincial Commissioner, representatives of the teachers, district education authorities, parent-teacher associations, building contractors and others. 'Yes, you've got your hands full alright,' he said, and departed to keep bees on Dartmoor. I felt overwhelmed.

After Kasama, Ndola itself was, indeed, overwhelming. As the administrative capital of the Western Province, including the Copperbelt, an important commercial and industrial centre with a sprawling business area, extensive railway marshalling yards and an international airport, it was a town of considerable significance. The population exceeded 100,000. By comparison, Kasama was a glorified village. Stretching northwestward from Ndola, in an area of undulating bush country roughly 90 miles long and 30 miles wide, lay Zambia's economic heartland – the mining centres of Luanshya, Kitwe, Mufulira, Chingola, Chambishi, Kalulushi and Bancroft (now Chililabombwe). It was the copper mines around which these towns had developed, owned by the Anglo-American Corporation and Roan Selection Trust, that produced the wealth on which Zambia depended. Few countries in the world have been so dependent upon a single commodity as Zambia was (and remains) upon copper. Nearly all the country's foreign exchange earnings derived from sales of copper on the London Metal Exchange. Over half the Government's revenue came from taxes paid by the mining companies.

141

In the towns of the Western Province lived some 600,000 people, representing approximately 60 per cent of the urban dwellers in Zambia. In 1964, the labour force employed in the mines amounted to about 50,000. Of this number, approximately 6,000 were expatriates; it was they who ran the mines. They occupied not only all the top managerial posts; they were the mine captains, the section heads and the shift bosses. They had a virtual monopoly of technological expertise and of the higher technical skills. Their trade union made it their business to ensure that African mineworkers, with very few exceptions, were employed as labourers; only a handful of blacks held positions of any responsiblity. With independence on the horizon, and the new government now stressing the need to Zambianise first the middle level and then some of the more senior posts, the mining companies had no choice but to accelerate and expand their efforts to train Africans for more skilled and responsible positions. But this would take time. Mining is a complicated and highly skilled operation; you cannot take short cuts or reduce safety margins. In the meantime, it was vitally necessary to retain the services of the white miners, many of them from South Africa, who regarded the incoming black government with grave suspicion if not outright hostility. In order to maintain their confidence, it was essential to ensure that high standards were kept in the schools. For the Afrikaner shift boss this meant leaving things as they had been in the federal era. But in its election manifesto, UNIP had promised to end segregation in education. The new government had wasted no time in implementing this pledge. In a schedule to an ordinance amending some earlier legislation, all the former federal schools had been listed and declared to be open to children of all races. When they realized that African children were to be admitted to the scheduled schools, as they were now called, which hitherto had been reserved exclusively for European children, many white parents became alarmed. The arguments I heard as I moved around the Copperbelt were similar to those which had been advanced in Alabama, Georgia and Louisiana. Some were blatantly racist: 'It's not right for decent white kids to be taught alongside kaffirs.' 'Blacks are slow at learning; they'll hold back our kids.' 'Sexually, Africans mature more quickly than Europeans; they'll rape our daughters.' 'Do you

142

want your kids to be taught by a coon?' Others were genuinely apprehensive about the quality of the education which would be provided in the schools once they became multiracial. Was there not a danger that European teachers would leave and would be replaced by less well-qualified black ones? How would African children cope when English was the language of instruction? Since Africans usually started school at a later age than white children, would the teachers be able to handle classes with a very wide age range?

As Minister of Education, John Mwanakatwe was well aware of the strength of white feeling. He made this clear when he visited Ndola a few days after we arrived. He also pointed out that African parents had their own reservations about sending their children to the scheduled schools. They feared that an inadequate command of English would put their children at a disadvantage, that they would be made to feel inferior, that the teachers, all white, would neglect them. 'Politically,' he said, 'it is important that we get a good number of African children into the scheduled schools. On the other hand, from the point of view of the national economy and the efficiency of the administration, we cannot afford to alienate expatriate miners and civil servants by letting in too many Africans. I'm sure you'll be able to strike a satisfactory balance between these two objectives.' I interpreted this as meaning that I should not take too seriously his public pronouncements calling on African parents to enrol their children in the desegregated schools. The national interest, for the time being at any rate, required that the number of Africans to be admitted should be kept small.

In the event, the desegregation of the schools presented few problems. The number of Africans applying for places in the scheduled schools in 1964 was quite small. In allocating places, heads were told to give preference to the children, irrespective of race, who lived nearest to the school. Since the scheduled schools were all situated in low-density, almost exclusively white, residential areas, this ruling effectively meant that black children from the high-density African townships could be excluded on the grounds that they did not live within the school's catchment area. There were financial as well as geographical constraints. Some African parents were deterred by the imposition of modest fees, £24 or 48 *kwacha* a year, which were a recognition of the fact that the cost to government of educating a child in a scheduled school was considerably higher than in an unscheduled school.[2] Where African parents were prepared to pay the fees, they sometimes found the cost of providing their children with expensive school uniforms was beyond their means.

The net result of all these constraints was that, in the country as a whole, of 11,000 children in scheduled primary schools in 1964, only 200 were African. In the secondary schools, Africans took only 140 of the 4,500 places.[3] White parents were delighted, but remained apprehensive. Government took stock and decided it must be made easier for African children to get into the scheduled schools. In 1965, John Mwanakatwe announced that tuition fees would be halved in the scheduled primary schools and that extra classes would be arranged for those children, white or black, who needed help with their English. Enrolment of African children promptly rose to more than 1,100. By 1967 it reached over 2,700, equivalent to about 20 per cent of overall enrolment. By that time, the number of European children in the scheduled primary schools had fallen from 8,500 to 6,200, a reflection of the gradual exodus of white families whose contracts expired or who decided to take advantage of the generous 'golden handshakes' which many were offered.

In the scheduled secondary schools, tuition fees for Form 1 pupils were abolished in 1965 and the maximum age for entry to secondary schools was raised to 16. The effect on enrolment was dramatic. The 140 pioneers of 1964 increased to 4,000 by 1967. In that year, Africans made up nearly 70 per cent of the total enrolment. The number of European children, by contrast, sank in the same period from 3,600 to a little over 800. There were several reasons for the rapid fall in the number of European children receiving their education in Zambia's secondary schools. A decision had been taken that entry to the University of Zambia, due to open in 1966, would be at Ordinary rather than Advanced level. As a consequence of this decision it was decided to phase out Advanced level courses, which were required for entry to universities in Europe, and M level courses which gained admission to South African universities. In addition, many firms gave their European

144

employees generous education allowances so that their children could be educated in South Africa or in Britain. Finally, it was found that once Africans made up more than a third or so of the enrolment in a school, and there were signs that the percentage would rise, many white parents accepted the inevitable and redoubled their efforts to make alternative arrangements for their children's education.

The gradual integration of the scheduled schools into the mainstream of the country's education provision was a minor success story. A good deal of my time had to be spent in building bridges between the former European and African education systems. This meant assuring white parents that they had nothing to fear and that standards were being maintained, while encouraging African parents who could afford it to take advantage of the opportunities which were now open to them. Contrary to the expectations of many, there were very few racial incidents in the integrated schools. Extremists on both sides of the colour divide kept their views to themselves. Children do not experience colour consciousness and racial antagonism to the same extent as their parents. In the scheduled schools, where children of all races sat, learned and played together, mutual respect, understanding and friendships developed across racial barriers. Youngsters who in colonial days would have never met, let alone mixed, grew up together, formed associations and developed mental attitudes which would last into adulthood. In this way, the desegregation of the schools contributed to the achievement of the Government's aim of building a non-racial society where a person's worth was measured by factors others than the colour of his or her skin.

Inevitably, there were some problems. Dr Monica Fisher, the Schools Medical Officer, whom I had first met when Chris Hoyte and I went to Luanshya in 1951, telephoned from Kitwe one afternoon to ask if she could see me urgently. 'Of course, Monica,' I said, 'But what's wrong?'

'I'd better not speak about it on the phone,' replied Monica, 'but it could be very serious.' Within the hour she was in my office. Grim-faced, she told me that four white girls at a scheduled school for infants at Kitwe had been provisionally diagnosed as suffering from a form of gonorrhea. The diagnosis was based on a micro-

145

scopic examination of organisms found in the girls' vaginal discharges. I listened dumbfounded. There was a ray of hope, Monica said. Other bugs were morphologically similar to those which caused gonorrhea. The organisms were being cultured by Dr Fine at Kitwe Central Hospital. It was possible that they would prove to be relatively harmless. She would have the results in a day or two. Monica did not know how the girls could have become infected with gonorrhea, if this was what the trouble was. In many years of examining children in the federal schools, she had never previously met such a case. What she was afraid of was that the parents of the girls would put the blame on one or more of the newly admitted African children for bringing disease into the school.

Monica had been all too right in saying that her news could be serious. It could be catastrophic. If Monica's suspicions were confirmed and news leaked out, as it was bound to, no amount of reassuring speeches would persuade European parents that their worst fears had not been justified. The opponents of the Government and particularly of multiracial education, would have a field day. Nevertheless, our responsibilities were clear. If the trouble proved to be a form of venereal disease, there would be no alternative but to close the school until all risk of further infection had been eliminated. 'Perhaps we should close the school at once, as a precaution,' she suggested. I shuddered at the thought. 'We'll give it 48 hours,' I said. 'In the meantime, mum's the word.' Two days later she rang me. 'It's alright,' she said, the relief in her voice very obvious. 'It's not gonorrhea. Dr Fine is quite sure of that. The girls will soon be well again. So there's no need to close the school.' We could breathe again.

Other incidents blew up equally unexpectedly. All schools were provided with posters showing the members of the cabinet and with photographs of President Kaunda sitting at his desk in State House. Heads usually displayed the picture of the cabinet on the school noticeboard, while in each classroom the President smiled benignly from a place of honour above the blackboard. One day the UNIP office at Mufulira telephoned me to say that the local organizer of the Party had a serious complaint to make. In one of the scheduled schools in Mufulira, the poster of the cabinet was not to be seen and the portraits of the President were not on display. UNIP was demanding the immediate suspension of the headmistress of the school. Her failure to display the photographs was clear evidence, it was said, of a lack of respect for the Government of the country and of the President. This complaint was particularly embarrassing because it came from Mufulira. The other Copperbelt towns were solid in their support of UNIP. Mufulira, however, had traditionally favoured Harry Nkumbula. Perhaps the headmistress, it was hinted, was a member of the ANC. The headmistress was completely taken aback when I told her of the accusations which had been made against her. She took no interest in politics. She had forgotten all about the photographs, she said. They must be in a drawer in the stockroom. In federal days, she had never displayed a photograph of the Queen or of the Governor-General or of the Governor in her classrooms. Why should she show photographs of the President now? It took three visits to Mufulira and protracted meetings with UNIP officials, the headmistress and her equally naive colleagues, before the issue was resolved. UNIP withdrew their accusations of lack of loyalty against the head and her staff. Photographs of the President were displayed in all classrooms. The UNIP District Secretary would come to teach the children the Zambian national anthem which was to be sung each day at the raising of the national flag and, *mirabile dictu*, was invited to present the prizes at the next school open day. We could all feel relieved as the District Secretary and the headmistress shook hands and smiled broadly at each other. The incident had been a trivial one and no lasting damage had been done. But it could easily have blown up into something serious in the highly charged and emotional atmosphere that independence engendered. As two cultures which had previously kept themselves apart met, and different political philosophies rubbed against each other, the opportunities for misunderstanding and worse, were numerous. Metaphorically, I held my breath for months on end and half-expected that each telephone call would bring news of a flare-up. In the event, however, the number of racially or politically inspired incidents in the schools was very small. Most of the teachers in the scheduled schools went out of their way to accommodate themselves to the changed circumstances, and showed extraordinarily good sense. Many found that teaching multiracial classes gave a welcome new dimension to their work and provided them with insights into the indigenous culture and way of life which they had previously lacked. In response, African parents were anxious to avoid confrontation and readily adapted to what many must have regarded as strange practices.

Keeping a close eye on the scheduled schools took up a great deal of my time. I had to keep reminding myself that the children in these schools made up less than 10 per cent of the total school population in the province and that my main responsibility was towards the 90,000 or so African children in the unscheduled or non-feepaying schools. In this sector, expansion was the order of the day. For years, African political leaders had clamoured for increased educational opportunities for African children. UNIP had come to power on a wave of promises – better housing., more jobs, higher wages, more hospitals, cheaper food, more and better schools. Now the time for delivery had arrived. Until a full-scale national development plan could be framed, short-term programmes known as the Emergency Development Plan and the Transitional Development Plan were launched. Through the implementation of these plans, government aimed to provide many thousands of extra primary school places in all provinces so that, by 1970, there would be a place in Grade 1 for all of the 160,000 children who it was estimated would reach the age of seven in that year. Provision was to be made for three-quarters of those who enrolled in Grade 1 to remain at school until they had completed Grade 7. Some idea of the magnitude of the task to be tackled can be gained from this statistic: in 1964, fewer than 11,000 pupils completed the top primary class. In 1976, if all went well, the number would be 120,000. If these ambitious targets were met, Zambia would be well on the way towards achieving the targets set for the year 2,000 by a Unesco conference of African states, held at Addis Ababa in 1961.

To meet the targets, a massive building programme was necessary and the training of thousands of new teachers had to be provided for. On the Copperbelt, we were very fortunate in that the mining companies came forward with offers of assistance in building many of the new classrooms which were needed and in allocating more houses in the mine townships for the additional teachers. Elsewhere, self-help was the order of the day. In the rural areas, the party machinery, the chiefs, headmen, businessmen, farmers and ordinary villagers were asked to clear sites for new classrooms, to make bricks and to infill the steel frames which government provided for classrooms. To begin with, the response was excellent and rivalled the achievements of the astonishing *harambee* movement in Kenya. The initial enthusiasm, however, did not last. In Kenya, civil servants and business and professional people living and working in Nairobi and other towns maintain close links with their home villages and visit them regularly at weekends. They are the main contributors to self-help or *harambee* appeals. There is no such tradition in Zambia. Many villages are almost denuded of the men who could contribute either cash or labour to self-help programmes.

In the urban areas such as the Copperbelt, building regulations were such that the use of voluntary labour in constructing new school buildings was not feasible. Instead, parents were asked to meet the cost of the furniture required for new schools. In 1964, we asked 70,000 children each to bring four shillings for the provincial furniture fund. We pulled out all the stops in publicizing what was known as *Ubushiku bwa Kwafwana* – the day of helping each other – and were delighted when over £14,500 was raised.

The teachers co-operated splendidly over this exercise but difficulties arose over other issues, particularly salaries and housing. The political campaign leading to independence had aroused many hopes. African teachers compared their salaries and their living conditions with those of expatriate teachers in the scheduled schools. Not unnaturally, they looked forward to big salary increases when the education systems were integrated and to the building of better teachers' houses. Alas, the new salary scales, when they were announced, were a bitter disappointment to the average African teacher. They were based, as was right and proper, on educational qualifications, teacher training and years of experience. The salary differential between a trained graduate teacher, which many of the Europeans were, and a T4 teacher (who had passed only Standard 6 before doing teacher training) was very considerable. An African teacher of a Grade 4 class in an unsched-

149

uled school would earn less than a quarter of the salary paid to a European teaching the same grade in a scheduled school. The difference was not due to colour discrimination but to qualifications; but it was difficult to explain this to a meeting of disgruntled African teachers.

Another source of friction was that the building programme placed more emphasis on constructing new classrooms than on replacing antiquated staff housing. The National Union of Teachers began to talk of a strike. When I met their provincial committee they made it clear that they had no quarrel with me. They accepted that it was government which had determined the new salary scales and that it was the Minister who had decided to allot comparatively small sums of money for better teachers' housing. At my request, John Mwanakatwe came to Ndola to meet the teachers' representatives. He could speak to them in a way which I would not have dared. Always polite and moderate in tone, he nevertheless left no-one in any doubt that Kenneth Kaunda's Government would not put up with any nonsense. All sections of the community were required to make sacrifices, he said. Teachers were fortunate to be employed and to be so well paid. When resources permitted, teachers' housing would be improved. In the meantime, other requirements merited higher priority. He wished to hear no more talk of possible strike action which he would regard as sabotage and which would result in serious consequences.

For the time being, at least, the teachers accepted defeat. I encouraged the Provincial Inspectorate under Paul Bowler to try to wean the Teachers' Union away from its preoccupation with salaries, allowances and housing and to invite them to become more involved in professional matters. Many African teachers had a good deal to contribute, for instance, to the work of the subject committees which were revising and remodelling syllabi which had been left undisturbed for years. Others were willing to participate in literacy classes and to teach adult education classes. The increasing involvement of teachers in professional issues and the forging of closer links between teachers and inspectors were signs of a willingness on the teachers' part to play a responsible part in the education revolution which was going on around them. It had to be recognized, however, that they had genuine grievances and that occasional disruptive action was inevitable. Their willingness to put up with low pay and difficult conditions could not be taken for granted. When they protested, they should not be branded as trouble-makers. A little more carrot and a little less stick was the best way of securing their co-operation.

There were teacher-training colleges at Kitwe and Mufulira which provided two-year training courses for lower and upper primary teachers. In order to speed up the output of new teachers required to staff the new classes, it was decided that students starting their training in 1965 would be given a one-year residential course followed by one year in school as student teachers. During this year of on-the-job training a comprehensive follow-up programme was arranged which included holiday courses, professional guidance under the supervision of the Provincial Inspectorate and training college lecturers, Saturday morning seminars and lessons by radio and television. In the Western Province, where the inspectorate was strong and where communications were comparatively easy and distances short, the scheme worked well. In the rural provinces, however, it was rarely possible to provide the student teachers with adequate guidance on a regular basis and they were left to their own devices for far too long. The rapid expansion of education facilities was a feature of all newly independent countries. More schools usually meant a fall in teaching standards because of the employment of untrained or semi-trained teachers. Zambia was more fortunate than most African countries in that, at independence, some 95 per cent of the teachers were trained. With this solid base on which to build, the Minister could, for a few years, justifiably reduce the training period for new teachers without producing disastrous consequences.

The date for independence was 24 October 1964. Celebrations were planned not only in Lusaka where the Princess Royal, on behalf of the Queen, would hand over the instruments of state to President Kaunda, but throughout the land. Children were to play a big part in the festivities. Rehearsals for callisthenics displays, exhibitions of dancing, pageants of history, sports, choral concerts and so on began in the schools months before the big day. Sadly, they were overshadowed by growing tension between UNIP and the Lumpa Church. On the Copperbelt, there was little direct involvement other than the burning down of some Lumpa churches by UNIP supporters. In the Northern and Eastern Provinces, however, in areas which I knew well, a grim and tragic story unfolded in the months preceding independence.

After the Mobile Unit's intervention at Kasomo in May 1959, Lenshina and her followers lay low for a while. Relations with government and with the native authorities remained strained but not seriously so. Relations with political parties, first the African National Congress, then ZANC and finally with UNIP were good. Many UNIP followers were also supporters of Lenshina. Robert Kaunda, for instance, Kenneth's brother, was one of Lenshina's deacons as well as being active within the Party. There seemed to be no reason for a clash between the politicians and the Lumpa Church leaders. Gradually, however, as Lenshina and her deacons regained their confidence after the events of 1959, a certain arrogance and intolerance grew up within the Church. Claims were made that only members of the Lumpa Church were true Christians; those outside it were condemned as heretics or worse. For their part, UNIP leaders in the Northern Province were emboldened by the success, as they saw it, which the Cha-cha-cha disturbances of 1961 achieved. They became more assertive, more aggressive and demanded the total loyalty of their members. Those who were not with them must be against them. Anyone, therefore, who would not become a member of UNIP and carry a Party card must be regarded as an enemy. Gradually, tension and mistrust grew to the point where membership of the Lumpa Church was no longer compatible with membership of UNIP, and vice versa. By early 1963, minor clashes between Lumpa followers and UNIP members were becoming commonplace in Chinsali District. The burning of a Lumpa church in one village would be followed within days by an arson attack on houses in a strongly pro-UNIP village. In attempts to resolve the differences between the two sides both Simon Kapwepwe and Kenneth Kaunda made a series of visits to Chinsali District during 1963. They listened to the complaints from both sides. Lenshina's followers alleged that members of the UNIP Youth Brigade burned their churches, that UNIP officials prevented Lumpa Church members from attending Sunday worship and insisted that they attend political meetings instead; Lumpa members, they said, were harassed by UNIP officials demanding to see their Party membership cards; the UNIP leadership, it was alleged, had threatened to proscribe the Lumpa Church after independence. On their side, UNIP complained that Lumpa leaders had organized the burning of Party membership cards, that UNIP members of the Lumpa Church had been expelled from the Church, that Lenshina had said that no-one could be a Christian and belong to UNIP. Worse, Lenshina had allegedly said that no UNIP member who had died in the 1961 troubles would go to heaven.

'There was,' adjudged the Commission of Enquiry which investigated the causes of the tragedy which was to follow, 'a certain element of truth in all these allegations.'[4]

The intervention of Kapwepwe and Kaunda, both of whom, of course, knew Chinsali District well, produced a temporary reconciliation between the two sides, but it could not last. To escape from the harassment and intimidation to which they said their followers were subjected, Lumpa leaders decided to set up their own villages. Some of these they surrounded by stockades made of bush poles; none was authorized by the native authorities. Local UNIP leaders took a serious view of this development; it was said that Lenshina was trying to set up a state within a state and that various anti-UNIP elements, such as Welensky and Nkumbula, were encouraging her to do so. The Lumpa Church leaders were becoming more firmly convinced that UNIP was determined to wipe out the church. Encouraged by the more fanatical and irresponsible of her deacons, Lenshina told her followers to prepare for a violent struggle. At the same time, as the Commission of Enquiry subsequently declared, 'there can be little doubt that, despite the efforts and pleas of their political leaders, a large section of the non-Lumpa community (effectively, UNIP), particularly the youths, was not prepared to make the effort to reach reconciliation.'[5]

The stage was set for violence and tragedy. On 13 July 1964, Kaunda flew to Chinsali and held meetings with both Lenshina and local UNIP officials. He instructed both sides to resume friendly relations. Lenshina's attitude was hostile; she put the entire blame for the unsatisfactory situation on to UNIP. She ignored Kaunda's explicit instructions that Lumpa Church followers living in unauthorized settlements must return to their original villages. On 24 July came the spark which precipitated the explosion we were fearing. The diary of events prepared by the Commission of Enquiry gave a graphic and sickening account of the unfolding of the tragedy.

24 July 1964

A platoon of the Mobile Unit left Chinsali at 0820 hours to carry out a normal patrol to Mpundu (Lenshina) village, which was 65 miles south of Chinsali *boma*. The patrol was motorised and consisted of Assistant Inspector Smith and twenty men. En route, they encountered two district messengers and a *kapasu* who reported that they had been chased away from Chapaula (Lenshina) settlement which was situated about 23 miles north of Chinsali on the Great North Road and about four miles off the road to the east. It was inaccessible to motor vehicles. Asst Inspector Smith's patrol was diverted to investigate the Chapaula report.

The patrol parked its vehicles four miles from Chapaula and advanced on foot. They met one African carrying a stick to which was attached a bicycle chain. He fled on seeing the patrol. On approaching Chapaula, it was found to be surrounded by a stockade. One woman was seen running away. Mr Smith appeared to have gained the impression that the village was empty and entered it with a constable, Mpapa, leaving the remainder of the platoon twenty yards behind. As they passed through the gate, Smith received a wound in the back from a spear which had been thrown by a man hidden outside the gate. The spear remained in Smith's back but he caught his assailant. A shout of "Jericho" went up in the village and large numbers of people, armed with spears, sticks and *pangas*, attacked Smith. A woman also attacked constable Mpapa who struck her down with his rifle butt. Smith called to Mpapa for help. They were about four yards apart. Mpapa fired at Smith's attackers who had taken his rifle. Firing his revolver, Smith reeled back through the gate but fell down after he had gone about ten yards. His attackers followed him shouting 'Hallelujah" and speared him repeatedly. Mpapa was forced to retreat, firing at the attackers, and he finally rejoined the platoon which was forced to withdraw to its vehicles. In this action, in addition to Inspector Smith, an African constable, Chansa, was killed and his body was mutilated, and driver Sergeant Kabiba was seriously injured.

Trouble now became widespread and Lumpa followers attacked other villagers. Three UNIP villages in the Siachepa area were attacked; four people were killed and two wounded.

An operation was mounted to recover Smith's and Chansa's bodies but the two platoons of Mobile Police sent were not sufficient to deal with the strong opposition again encountered at Chapaula. Owing to recent events, the morale of the African Police had reached a low ebb, and no action took place. Chansa's body was found but villagers would not give up Smith's body.[6]

The poor showing on this occasion by the Mobile Unit was a source of great encouragement to Lenshina's followers and stiffened their resolve to defy those who attacked them. The police authorities, on the other hand, knew that they must regain the ascendancy over untrained villagers armed with nothing more modern than muzzle loaders and spears. Retribution followed swiftly, as the Commission of Enquiry later recorded.

25 July 1964

Further Police reinforcements were despatched and the operation was placed under the command of Assistant Commissioner of Police, J. D. O. Bird. Strong opposition was again met at Chapaula by the three platoons of the Mobile Unit which engaged them. The villagers opened fire on the Police who were forced to retaliate. Twenty nine Lenshina supporters were killed or seriously wounded and two Police other ranks suffered flesh wounds. Smith's body was found near a river, some 150 yards from the village.

The action was a difficult one as African Police morale was still low and the Lenshinas were extremely ferocious in their attack. Asst Insp. Standaloft was speared in the back during the action. Some of the firearms lost by the Police in the previous action at Chapaula were recovered. A number of muzzle loaders and other weapons were also seized. The casualties among Lenshina supporters, 14 dead and 15 wounded, included women and a child. This was unavoidable as the women seemed to have a complete disregard to the effectiveness of bullets and were exhorting the men to resist throughout the action which took about 1½ hours. The wounded were dealt with as expeditiously as circumstances permitted.

The Lumpa followers were armed with muzzle loaders, bows and arrows, spears, axes and machetes. Prior to and during the action at Chapaula, the District Commissioner, Chinsali, Mr Hannah, had talked without success to the villagers through a loud-hailer, requesting them to lay down their arms and give themselves up.[7]

The events of 24 and 25 July were but a foretaste of what was to come. Each day, the radio and newspapers brought news of further bloodshed. Since the police could not cope with the situation, the Governor, Sir Evelyn Hone, and the Prime Minister decided to send two battalions of the Northern Rhodesia Regiment to Chinsali District. On 30 July, the 1st battalion attacked Kasomo, now known as Sione (Zion) village, the headquarters of the Lumpa Church. The village had been heavily stockaded. The Lenshinas ignored the DC's call to surrender. As the troops slowly advanced into the village, making for the church building at its centre, they were attacked with what the Commission of Enquiry later described as 'frenzied fanaticism.'[8] Their account continued:

They were armed with bows, arrows, spears and an assortment of firearms. The troops were obliged to use automatic weapons as the Lenshina forces showed the utmost determi-

156

nation and a complete disregard for their own lives. The opposition gradually weakened and the troops burst into the village meeting fierce resistance by males, and women and children who had concentrated in the area of the church. The Police were called upon to use tear smoke. A last-ditch attempt at resistance by women and children who had occupied the church was finally overcome by the use of tear smoke. A European Police Office was injured in the action, as were five soldiers, two seriously. One of the soldiers subsequently died in hospital.

The security forces then cleared the area. A five-ton truck load of weapons, including firearms, was accumulated as a result of this action. Alice Lenshina, the leader of the sect, was found not to be in the settlement. Fifty-nine male and seven female Lenshinas were killed in the action and there were 110 wounded.

The size of the death toll was appalling. It was difficult to avoid the conclusion that the Government, yielding to Party pressure, had overreacted and was using a sledgehammer to crack a nut. *The Daily Telegraph* in London voiced the misgivings of many in an editorial on 4 August: 'It is unfortunate that the Government of Northern Rhodesia should have entangled itself so deeply in the disgraceful suppression of the Lumpa sect.' The sect's adherents, said the *Telegraph*, had been officially represented as 'bloodthirsty fanatics whose strange creed had impelled them to rebellion and murder. Yet the only crime of the Lumpas, apart from what they have been driven in desperation to do, was and is, that their creed strictly forbids them to engage in politics in any form.' It was for this reason, the *Telegraph* went on, 'that they had refused to join the United National Independence Party. This soon made them targets for political intimidation. Their huts and crops were burned, they were attacked and some were killed. They built isolated stockaded villages where they defended themselves against all comers.'[9]

But sympathy for the Lumpa cause evaporated quickly when, on the same day as the *Telegraph* editorial appeared, news came of a massacre at Lundazi. It was, perhaps, in retaliation for the capture

157

of Sione that on 3 August a gang of some 200 Lenshina followers from Chipoma village attacked Lundazi township by night, capturing the police station and killing 150 people before fleeing at dawn. A wave of horror swept through the country. The *Northern News* expressed a popular viewpoint in its editorial.

> Any remnants of sympathy that may have been felt for the Lumpa church followers after the Chinsali fighting, on the grounds that they were ignorant men tragically misled, disappeared with the crazy, bloodthirsty attacks on Lundazi and its neighbourhood. It was a mass slaughter of innocent people, for which there is no possible excuse. Freedom of worship is an admirable thing, but always provided churches preach good and condemn evil. But, as Dr Kaunda emphasised yesterday, Lenshina has been teaching her followers not only to prepare themselves to die, but to kill other people. She has taught hatred. And in filthy rites, her followers have smeared themselves in the belief that they were making themselves immune to bullets. Such practices and such beliefs cannot be dignified by the word religion. There is no reasoning with fanatics. In the north, this is no less than a 'holy' war against law and order, and the only way to save more innocent lives is by ruthless suppression.[10]

Retaliation for the attack on Lundazi was swift in coming. On the very next day, two companies of the 1st Battalion of the Northern Rhodesia Regiment, who had been hastily transferred from Chinsali to the Eastern Province, moved on Chipoma village. Eighty-one Lenshinas were killed and 43 wounded.

For many weeks, the carnage continued, mostly confined to Chinsali and Lundazi Districts, both of which I knew well. From the safety and comfort of Ndola, I found it terribly sad to read in the *Northern News* of the bloodshed that was taking place in the peaceful villages I had known. From Lundazi District, for instance, came news of the murder by Lumpa members of Chief Chikwa and ten other people. I remembered the Chief being very concerned when I camped near his village and the pug marks of a leopard were found next morning at the entrance to my tent. On another occasion, he had sent a big basket of mealie meal to my camp when I shot an impala and presented him with the two hind legs. At Pikamalaza, also in Lundazi District it was reported that 17 people had been killed by marauding Lenshinas. Had the head-master of the school survived, I wondered? What a waste it would be if such a bright and determined young man fell victim to a spear thrust before he had the chance to develop his undoubted potential. A group of 500 Lumpa followers were said to be operating in Chief Lundu's area. They must include, I realized, some of the cheerful and hard-working women who had greeted me so warmly when I went there with carriers in 1955.

Alice Lenshina surrendered to government forces in Kasama District on 11 August and was detained in Mumbwa prison.[11] Hostilities, however, continued until the end of 1964. By that time the official death toll was 700. Unofficially the figure was con-siderably higher. Within a few months, religious fanaticism in conflict with political intolerance had killed ten times as many people as had died in all the years of the political struggle for independence.

Alice Lenshina's vision of September 1953, had started a move-ment which, at one time, had seemed to be a force for good. This simple village woman, however, had proved incapable of control-ling the forces she had unleashed or of preventing her deacons from challenging black nationalism in the form of UNIP. But if Lenshina had much to answer for, the local leaders of UNIP were by no means blameless. In their zeal to win more members for the Party, they turned a blind eye to the bully-boy tactics employed by some of the young thugs who, perhaps more than anyone else, precipitated the outbreak of violence. All political leaders are apt to be embarrassed and dismayed by the behaviour of some of their followers. As he prepared to assume the office of President, Kenneth Kaunda, a sensitive and humane man, must have had bitter regrets that his home district should have been the setting for carnage on a scale which had not been equalled at any time during the colonial era. Perhaps, like me, he could not help but feel that wiser and firmer leadership, exercised earlier, might have averted the tragedy.

There had been serious faults on all sides. Lenshina had been wrong to defy the Native Authority and to ignore the warnings given her by the Governor, Kaunda, Kapwepwe, Senior Chief Nkula and the DC. By her actions as well as her rhetoric she had fanned the flames of fanaticism which gripped her followers. For their part, government and the Native Authority had waited too long before trying to clamp down on the illegal movement of Lenshinaites to unregistered villages. UNIP leaders, from Kaunda downwards, had not made serious efforts, at a time when violence was only just beginning, to stamp on the undisciplined louts of the UNIP Youth Brigade and others who terrorized Lenhsina's followers and provoked retaliation. Too little leadership, and too late, had caused the dispute to escalate to a point where a bloody showdown was inevitable.

It had been the security forces which had defeated Lenshina and the Lumpa Church. But there were many in UNIP who saw the outcome as a victory for the Party whose authority Lenshina had dared to challenge. It would take years to heal the deep wounds which the Northern and Eastern Provinces had suffered and to reintegrate the former Lenshina followers into the community. The Commission of Enquiry, reporting nearly a year after the end of the disturbances, stressed the need for tolerance, patience and understanding. Unusually, it severely criticized the Resident Minister of the Northern Province for his intolerant attitude towards the former Lumpa followers. The Resident Minister was not only the senior government representative in the province, he was also the provincial head of the Party: he was a key man whose attitude was critical. 'Your Commissioners consider it necessary,' wrote the Commissioners, 'to recommend that the Resident Minister, Northern Province, be made aware of the need to adopt a genuinely tolerant attitude and to ensure that the regional Party officials in his Province follow suit.'[12] Brave words. Unfortunately they did little to curb the arrogance, brutality and petty-minded stupidity of some of UNIP's more militant members.

Independence Day, 24 October 1964, was sunny, hot and joyful. The main events, of course, took place in Lusaka where the Princess Royal represented the Queen at the official ceremonies. Sir Evelyn Hone, the highly respected Governor, stood side-by-side with Kenneth Kaunda, the Prime Minister, while the Union flag was lowered during the playing of 'God save the Queen'. Then, on the stroke of midnight, the new national Zambian flag was hoisted for the first time and fluttered proudly in the glare of the searchlights while the huge crowd sang 'Stand and sing of Zambia, proud and free,' then roared its approval and beamed with delight. For those watching on television, or listening to their radios in distant villages throughout the land, as well as for those seeing and hearing it at first hand in the stadium, it was a heart-stirring moment. After so many years of hoping and praying, struggling and enduring, after so much frustration, disappointment and anticipation, it was hard to grasp that independence had actually come.

The new flag had been designed to symbolize patriotism and the nation's wealth. Against a green background, representing the country's natural resources, an orange coloured fish eagle was depicted in flight over a rectangular block of three vertical stripes in red, black and orange. The red stood for the struggle for freedom, black for the people of Zambia, and orange for its mineral wealth. The fish eagle in flight symbolized freedom and the ability to rise above the country's problems. Enough paper flags had been produced to ensure that all schoolchildren had one to wave at the celebrations which took place in the football stadium in Ndola. Displays, games and sports by the children, football matches and dancing for the adults, the unveiling of a monument, a civic reception and a grand fireworks display combined to produce a day which was memorable as well as enjoyable. To round it off there was a speech on radio and television by Dr Kaunda, now His Excellency the President of the Republic of Zambia. He called on everyone to forget their differences of race, tribe, religion and colour and to work together to develop the new country. 'We must become,' he said, 'one Zambia, one nation.'

Listening to the President's words, Evelyn and I were conscious for the first time that we were now living in a foreign country. The British Protectorate of Northern Rhodesia, governed by a small white minority of which we were part, no longer existed. The Union flag, that reassuring symbol of British power, had been lowered for the last time. The British national anthem would not be heard again. Now, there was not only an African government (to which we were becoming accustomed) but an African head of state. The President was about to move into Government House, now to be known as State House. Like Sir Evelyn Hone, some of our friends were leaving. An era had ended; they did not want to be part of the new dispensation. For our part, however, we could see no reason why we should leave. We had each come to help serve the people of Northern Rhodesia. The fact that they were now Zambians did not mean that we no longer had a role. Rather, with increased resources for education now becoming available, expansion of facilities was proceeding rapidly. To help direct that expansion and to suggest how the new-found enthusiasm might be usefully channelled seemed to us to be a worthwhile challenge. We decided to stay for as long as we felt we could be useful and while domestic circumstances permitted.

One of the fruits of independence was that government acquired the remaining assets of the British South Africa Company. In Ndola, these included two handsome double-storey houses, a rarity in Zambia where the normal 'house' was, in fact, a single-storey bungalow. To our surprise, the Provincial Commissioner allocated to us one of the big houses which stood on an acre plot surrounded by a high brick wall, in a quiet residential area. It was an ideal place in which to bring up a young family. Andrew Michael had arrived on the scene in April 1964. We hoped to complete our family with a little girl and were delighted, therefore, when Rosemary Ann was born in November 1965. Granny came out again from Scotland to help Evelyn when Ann was due. As before, she settled in marvellously well and loved to accompany me on day visits to schools. Sometimes she would babysit while Evelyn took some English classes at the Ndola Adult Education Centre which we opened to provide a second chance for those whose earlier education had been curtailed, usually for financial or domestic reasons. Granny got on particularly well with Brush, our loyal and resourceful cook. Brush, a Chewa from near Msoro in the Eastern Province, had joined me in 1956. Usually, when bachelors married, their cooks had to go because their wives resented their presence in the kitchen. Brush, however, survived my change of status; he and his family were to remain with us until we finally left the country.

Brush's standing, like ours, improved with our move to the prestigious double-storey house. It was no longer enough for us to employ James as a houseboy. We had to take on Peter, too, as a gardener. In the school holidays, Chisanga, whose education we were supporting, came to us by bus from Kasama and helped out with the domestic and gardening chores. We had no wish to employ so many servants but the size of the house and garden was such that we had no choice. Having servants conferred responsibilities as well as privileges. As employer, you were expected to look after not only the servant himself and his wife and children (all of whom lived on the premises), but also distant relatives who periodically appeared and assumed that they would be maintained. To them, we must have seemed to have so much, while they had so little. Evelyn made sure that the children were properly fed and decently clothed, and were taken to hospital when they were sick. We sorted out disputes. When relatives died in distant places – and the casualty rate in Brush's family seemed suspiciously high – we gave leave and, as likely as not, paid the bus fares so that the mourning rituals could be observed. Perhaps we were too soft. All the same, it was generally a happy relationship from which we all benefited.

Chisanga was especially useful in keeping down the weeds in the vegetable beds. These lay to the side of the house between two avocado pear trees and a small clump of mango trees. Without the benefit of any attention, these yielded prolifically. As I note the absurdly high prices charged for avocado pears and mangoes in modern supermarkets, I often think of the large numbers of succulent fruit which, in season, rotted in our garden because we could not catch up with them.

Having a large house was certainly a bonus from the entertainment point of view. Friends from the Northern Province going on or returning from leave found Ndola a very convenient place in which to spend a night or two. There were frequent 'official' visitors from Lusaka who required meals and sometimes accommodation. On the local scene, we avoided the cocktail or sundowner circuit as much as possible but entertained and were, in turn, entertained by, the provincial heads of other ministries, and, of course, colleagues in education. Fortunately we had a friendly relationship with the Resident Minister, a political appointee who represented the President in the province. Andrew Mutemba was always thoughtful and considerate in his official dealings with me. When I needed his help, he was always ready to bring his political 'clout' to bear. When I wanted him to stand off, he was happy to let me get on with things myself.

Most of our friends, in contrast to our official colleagues, came from the church. In Kasama, there had been a small inter-denominational church where visiting clergy would sometimes conduct services. Most Sundays, however, a group of us arranged the services ourselves, taking it in turns to lead the worship. In Ndola, it was a joy to find St Andrew's church with a full-time minister and a lively congregation. Evelyn was soon roped in as relief organist and I became a member of the board of stewards. It was a warm, outward-looking fellowship. In January 1965, an important event occurred when the Methodist Church in Zambia, the Church of Scotland, the United Church of Canada and the London Missionary Society sank their differences and joined forces to form the United Church of Zambia. The first public service of the new church took the form of a big rally at Kitwe where the sermon was preached by Dr Donald (later Lord) Soper. It was a joyful occasion. By taking this major step towards unity in the church, Zambia gave a lead to the ecumenical movement which, unhappily, few other counties, Britain included, have succeeded in following.

John Mwanakatwe as Minister, and Henry Thornicoroft, his Parliamentary Secretary, were frequent visitors to the province. With his polished and urbane manner, and calm delivery, the Minister was especially good at addressing speech-day gatherings, and meetings of chambers of commerce and rotary clubs. On 11 November 1965, we were together at a luncheon meeting of Mufulira Rotary Club when news came through that, after months of dithering, Ian Smith, Prime Minister of Southern Rhodesia, had unilaterally declared his country to be independent of Britain. John returned to Lusaka immediately to attend an emergency meeting of the cabinet, leaving me to stand in for him at a meeting of Ndola Rotary Club the next day. Smith's UDI, as it was called, dealt a

164

devastating blow to the Zambian economy, although none of us appreciated it at the time.

Harold Wilson, the British Prime Minister, told Commonwealth heads of government that UDI would be brought to an end 'in a matter of weeks rather than months' through the imposition of economic sanctions against the Smith regime.[13] Others wanted sterner measures to be taken to end the rebellion. Boumedienne in Algeria, Nasser in Egypt and Nkrumah in Ghana demanded that the Organization of African Unity should send troops to oust Smith and bring about majority rule in Rhodesia. Kaunda and his colleagues were fearful that any military intervention by the OAU, in the unlikely event that it could be organized, would bring severe retaliation on Zambia by Smith's air force and army, and the cutting off of electricity supplies from the Kariba power station. They were also aware that white miners on the Copperbelt had held celebration parties on the evening of 11 November and had toasted 'good old Smithy'.[14] Inter-racial tension was suddenly acute. If racial conflict broke out on the Copperbelt, it was by no means certain that the Zambia police, where the majority of commissioned officers were still white, would contain it. The Government was in a dilemma on the action it should take. Fortunately, the bellicose proposal to invade Rhodesia with troops from north and west Africa came to nought. Not for the first time, nor the last, the OAU failed to reach any agreement. There were coups in Nigeria and Ghana. Tanzania made the gesture of breaking off diplomatic relations with Britain but Nyerere's lead was not followed. Britain sent a dozen Javelin fighters to defend Zambia against possible air attack from Rhodesia; no such attack was launched. Gradually, the heat went out of the situation and we all breathed that much more easily.

Nevertheless, UDI was to have a profound effect on Zambia for many years. Most of the country's oil supplies were imported from Beira, on the Mozambique coast, through Rhodesia. Many other imports and the vitally important copper exports also used the southern route. Economically, Zambia could not live without the co-operation of Rhodesia. This stark truth was underlined when Britain imposed oil sanctions against Rhodesia and blockaded Beira. Since neither Portugal, which administered Mozambique, nor South Africa had the slightest intention of refusing to supply Ian Smith with all the petrol he wanted, the only victim of the oil sanctions was Zambia. Cut off from its traditional sources, Zambia had to be rescued from the crippling effects of the oil shortage, at first by an airlift of petrol and oil organized by Britain, Canada and the United States. But the cost of the airlift was prohibitive, and the planes were soon replaced by a large fleet of lorries which took copper to Dar-es-Salaam and brought back supplies of petrol, a round trip of some 2,000 miles. Ironically many of the lorries on the so-called 'Hell-run' were driven by Afrikaners and the exercise was made possible by the purchase of 40,000 petrol drums from South Africa. Later, petrol supplies were improved by the completion of an oil pipeline from Dar-es-Salaam which was laid by an Italian firm. The amount of petrol allowed to private motorists under the rationing scheme, which had sometimes been as low as two gallons a week, was then increased.

UDI brought home to the Government and the people Zambia's extreme vulnerability. Land-locked, it had to rely on the co-operation of friendly neighbours for its imports and exports. It must seek to replace its traditional trade routes through Rhodesia and South Africa by increasing the flow of traffic through Dar-es-Salaam and Mombasa in the east, and Benguela in Angola. But Zambia's vulnerability was not confined to its trade routes. The crisis which UDI had precipitated pointed sharply to the need to accelerate the pace of Zambianization, to replace as quickly as possible expatriates whose loyalty was in question, whether they were in the army, the police, the mines or the civil service. 'There are enemies within as well as without,' said the President, and gave instructions that new targets should be set for the advancement of Zambians to positions of responsibility. The need to expand the stock of educated manpower was never clearer. In recognition of this truth, John Mwanakatwe was able to secure the allocation of generous resources for education in the new national development plan which was launched in July 1966.

Amid the excitement and anxiety created by UDI, life went on much as before. I was fortunate in having a strong team of colleagues. In the provincial office, David Semple, deputy PEO, knew the province very well and was a first class administrator. He

166

Chris Hoyte, Chepasani and the elephant, Luangwa Valley, 1952.

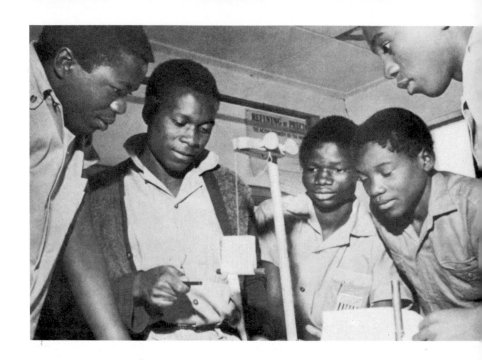

Above. Form 1 boys in the physics lab., Munali Secondary School (Photo: R. Krag-Olsen). *Below.* Nkula school, 1959. *R to L:* Senior Chief Nkula, Glyn Goddard, Gabriel Musumbulwa, Philemon Mwambazi.

Above. A lower primary class in the Northern Province, *c*. 1960. *Below*. Wedding day at Lubwa, 1961. The Reverends Bill McKenzie and Paul Mushindo with Rosemary West and Claude Slater.

Above left. Jekott Bwali, manager of schools, delivering equipment and paying teachers, Isoka District, 1959. *Above right*. Michael Mumba, driver and family friend. *Below*. Lenshina's Lumpa church at Kasomo, Chinsali District (Photo: Claude Slater).

Above. Father Kohle and John Daniell survey the remains of classrooms at Mulanga destroyed by arson, 1961. *Below*. Sir Evelyn Hone (Governor), at Timba school with Sir Stewart Gore-Browne, Robin Foster and Mr Kasote, 1960.

Above. Upper primary schoolboys building dormitories at a community service camp, Chinsali District, 1960. *Below*. Andrew Mutemba (Resident Minister), Reuben Kamanga (Vice-President), and John Mwanakatwe at Ndola Adult Education Centre, 1965 (Photo: Zambia Information Services).

Above. Kansenji Secondary School, Ndola, becomes multi-racial, 1964 (Photo: *Zambia News*). *Below L to R:* Bob Walsh, Basil Kabwe, the author, R. Messiter-Tooze, Martyn Sibson and Ping Lee (World Bank), Mufulira Mine, 1966.

Above. Marlborough House, home of the Commonwealth Secretariat.
Below. President Kenneth Kaunda, Wesley Nyirenda and Arnold Smith at
a conference of Commonwealth Youth Ministers, Lusaka, 1973 (Photo:
Zambia Information Services).

One of the thousands of students supported by the Commonwealth Fund for Technical Co-operation (Photo: University of the South Pacific Media Centre).

Above left. Namibian refugees en route from Zambia to Jamaica for education and training programmes (Photo: Jim Houston). *Above right.* Sonny Ramphal greets Rajiv Gandhi at Marlborough House, 1986 (Photo: Commonwealth Secretariat). *Below.* Caribbean regional seminar, Barbados, 1981. *L to R:* Gareth Aicken, Henry Forde (Minister of External Affairs), Doris Shepherd (Photo: Barbados Government Information Office).

Above. African regional seminar, Nairobi, 1985, opened by Dr Robert Ouko, subsequently murdered when he began to expose corruption in the Kenya Government. *Below*. Lord Soames (Governor of Rhodesia), with members of the Commonwealth Observer Group and Commonwealth Secretariat staff. Government House, Salisbury (Harare), February 1980.

Above. Congratulating Prime Minister Lauti on Tuvalu's Independence. Funafuti, October, 1978. *Below*. Chief Emeka Anyaoku with Sam Nujoma (President of SWAPO and subsequently of Namibia) (Photo: Commonwealth Secretariat).

took a particular interest in the Education Television Service which we ran from the Kitwe studio of Zambia Television. We put Wilfred Chilangwa in charge and encouraged him to develop programmes in subjects where there were shortages of specialist teachers in the secondary schools. Not many schools in the country could receive television but it was worthwhile to provide the service for schools on the line of rail where transmissions could be picked up.

Yonam Mpuku, whom I had first met when he was headmaster of Lubwa and then as a manager of schools in Chinsali, was outstanding as one of a small group of Zambians appointed to be education officers. He rapidly made the transition from a rural province to the hurly burly of the Copperbelt and was soon as much at home in primary schools of a thousand and more pupils as he had been in the village schools of the Northern Province. In each town we had at least one Zambian manager of schools. Messrs Chikolokoso, Chipowe, Kanyense, Lombe, Mwondela, Nyirenda and Samusungwa were a good group who bore the heat and burden of the day in the African townships. It was they who posted and paid the teachers, equipped the schools and were the front men in handling disputes. It was more difficult to get Zambians into the Provincial Inspectorate; good and experienced teachers were needed as head teachers and could not, at that time, be spared for inspection duties. The Inspectorate, therefore, was made up of expatriates: Paul Bowler, Tom Potter, Jim Hardman, Muriel Miles and Barbara Moore from Britain; Heather Howie from Australia and Robert Walsh from New Zealand. These all spent a good deal of their time visiting schools, advising teachers, running refresher courses and endeavouring to help teachers raise their professional standards. In mid-1965, the Government decided that English, rather than a vernacular language, would be the medium of instruction in all Zambian schools, starting with the reception class, Grade 1, in 1966. The main task of the Provincial Inspectorate was to prepare materials and to train teachers for the implementation of this bold initiative, as well as to impart to Zambian teachers some of the modern sophisticated methods which had been successfully used elsewhere. While these colleagues helped the heads and teachers to keep the

167

schools running, I was free to give time to policy issues such as the planning of new schools, to controlling the budget and to public relations.

Life was busy, sometimes hectic, never dull. It was also exhausting. I was more than glad when in May 1966, we went on home leave. Four months later, a good leave under our belts, I was equally glad when we flew back to Ndola feeling that this, perhaps, would be our last tour of duty. We had assumed that we would spend the tour, whether or not our last, on the Copperbelt. but two weeks after we returned, and had just completed our unpacking, the new Permanent Secretary of the Ministry, Fwanyanga Mulikita, telephoned. The Minister and he had decided that I should be transferred to headquarters as an assistant secretary. When I asked why I could not remain in Ndola, the answer was vague. I was required for 'special duties'. Hurriedly, and not in the best of humours, we packed and made our reluctant way to Lusaka, a city I had never liked.

Inevitably, there was a period of adjustment. In Ndola, we had been quite big fish in a moderate sized pond. In Lusaka, we were small fish in a big pond. This was reflected in our housing allocation. Gone was the two-storey house set in its own extensive grounds. In its place we had a very modest bungalow in a cul-de-sac off the Great East Road. There were advantages, of course. We could now make do with only two servants since the house and garden were very much smaller and we were no longer required to do anything like as much entertaining as was necessary in Ndola. Another plus was that we were warmly received into the United Church of Zambia congregation where Hugh Fielder was the minister; soon, both of us were elected to the eldership.

Very noticeably, my workload was considerably less heavy than it had been and the buck no longer stopped with me. On the Copperbelt, I had been on duty virtually 24 hours a day and was liable to be disturbed at any hour of the day or night. In Lusaka, when I left the office, I could 'switch off' almost completely, confident that neither teachers, parents nor the press would try to contact me.

The 'special duties' to which the Permanent Secretary had referred turned out to be a mixed bag. My first task was to write the ministry's annual report for 1965. Like its predecessors, this 60-page document recorded the main events of the year, summarized policy changes and gave a wealth of statistical details which were a convenient source of reference at the time and would provide invaluable material for the historian of the future. Compiling the report was a wearisome chore but at least it gave me the opportunity to become better informed on the work of sections of the ministry which, while I was in the provinces, had not really concerned me. Now that I was at headquarters, I had to try to think in terms of the country as a whole, rather than in the context of a single province. It took time to learn to draft a circular which, when read, would make as much sense to, say, the Education Secretary of the Capuchin Fathers in Mongu as it would to the District Education Officer in Mbala, at the other end of the country.

Joe Mwemba had been Permanent Secretary of the ministry in 1965, and it was he who signed the report for that year. My draft suffered few amendments at his hands and he let pass the rather purplish prose in which I gave my assessment of the year:

The year 1965 was the most exciting, most challenging and most dramatic in the history of education in Zambia. It was a year of consolidation in the sense that the integration of the old Federal and African education systems was carried forward without mishap; a year of development and achievement in that an enormous education building programme was successfully carried out; a year of preparation as policies and priorities were re-appraised and plans were scrutinised for inclusion in the First National Development Plan.

The Ministry of Education is in the forefront, indeed, is the spearhead of the Government's attack on the national enemies of ignorance, poverty and disease. In these pages, an attempt has been made to give an account of the Ministry's stewardship and to show how we have endeavoured to carry out our responsibility of providing the nation with the education it needs and must have if Zambia and her people are to develop to their full potential.

The formal language of an official report cannot tell the

full story of educational development. Education concerns people: infants, teenagers and adults; children, parents and grandparents. Nearly everyone in the country is affected by the success or failure of the Ministry of Education to provide educational facilities at the various levels throughout the length and breadth of this large country. The real story of the Ministry's work in 1965 cannot be told here. It can only be told by the villager who made bricks in the hot October sun; by the little girl who was able to find a place in grade one in the new primary school on the hill; by the carpenter in the building co-operative who made roofs for the new teachers' houses; by the father who left sub B many years ago and enrolled in 1965 in an adult education class; by the mother who bought the uniform for her son and proudly watched him catch the bus which would take him to the new secondary school at the *boma*; by the form 5 leaver who learned that he had been accepted for the new University; by the teacher who switched on his radio and heard his former training college tutor talking to him. These, and tens of thousands like them, are the people who know – because they were part of it – what the Ministry attempted to do in 1965. They are the ones who will keep alive the events of the year when the official reports are gathering dust on the shelf. It is good to know that for thousands of people, in hundreds of villages throughout Zambia, 1965 will always be 'the year the school was built'.

The period 1964–70 may be likened, in athletic terms, to a 'hop, step and jump'. We made the 'hop' in 1964 when the Emergency Development plan was successfully implemented: we have covered further ground in 1965 with the 'step' of the Transitional Development Plan; we look forward with confidence to the 'jump', nay, the major leap forward in the First National Development Plan for which we are now poised.[15]

The FNDP was, indeed, intended as a major leap forward. It provided the framework for all aspects of the country's development in the period 1966–70. If implemented, it would transform and strengthen the national infrastructure and produce an unprecedented expansion in the country's resource base and in the services, including education, provided by Government. The planners estimated that expenditure during the plan period would total £434 million, a colossal sum for a country such as Zambia. The plan had its critics. 'Grotesquely over-optimistic and over-ambitious', was the verdict of Dr Charles Elliot, reader in economics at the University of Zambia (and a future director of Christian Aid).[16] 'By the end of 1968,' subsequently wrote Richard Hall, former editor of the *Northern News*, 'the Plan was in ruins; it had almost ceased to exist.'[17] But if the plan as a whole was poorly conceived, led to serious inflation and should have been modified in the light of Rhodesia's UDI, it nevertheless provided the impetus and resources for very significant education expansion, especially in secondary education.

The need to provide increased opportunities at the secondary level had been well-documented in a survey of the economic development of Zambia, conducted in 1963 under the sponsorship of the United Nations Economic Commission for Africa and the Food and Agriculture Organization. According to the survey, the distorted shape of Zambia's education pyramid

implied that of every 100 Africans who start primary school, 82 would reach the fourth year, 42 the sixth, and 21 would complete their full primary course. Of these 21, only 6 would find a place in secondary school; of these, only 3 would enter a senior secondary form and only 2 would end up with a school certificate.[18]

For years the colonial government had severely restricted education opportunities for Africans beyond Standard 2. As we saw in Chapter 1, the Department of African Education had given priority to providing four years of elementary education to as many children as possible. It had made inadequate provision for upper primary education. It had delayed first in starting and then in expanding secondary education. The cumulative effects of the department's policies were spelt out in the survey: only 32,000 Africans had completed the full primary school course by 1963; only 4,420 had passed the two-year junior secondary course, and a

171

mere 961 were known to have passed the Cambridge School Certificate examination.[19] There was some improvement in these figures in 1964 but the fact remains that Zambia embarked on her independence with crippling shortages of educated people capable of moving into positions of responsibility. The full extent of these shortages was not statistically known until the end of 1965 when the government's Manpower Report, the first in the country's history, was published. The report, covering the full scope of the activities of government, industry and commerce, provided valuable guidance on the numbers of people who were, or would be, required up to 1980 in a comprehensive range of occupations in both the public and private sectors, the levels at which they would be required to operate, and the education and training they would require. Manpower planning and analysis is an inexact science. The planners are forced to make a number of assumptions, some of which may be seriously wrong. The margin of error in their projections inevitably increases the further ahead they attempt to forecast. For all its imperfections, however, the 1965 Manpower Report made it clear beyond doubt that the output from the country's secondary schools had to be significantly and quickly increased.

In fact, the Manpower Report provided the statistical justification for the action which the Government had already taken. At the start of the year, 31 new Form 1 classes and 18 new Form 3 classes, either as extensions to existing schools or as the first phase of completely new schools, had opened. A year later, the intake of Form 1 pupils at Local Education Authority and mission schools was doubled with the opening of no less than 120 new classes. As the *Times Education Supplement* commented: 'In 1966, Zambia doubled its secondary school intake, thereby creating in one year more new secondary opportunities for Africans than had been supplied in the whole seventy years of Company, Colonial and Federal rule.'[20] Total enrolment in the non-scheduled secondary schools rose from just over 8,000 in 1964 to almost 17,000 in 1966, an increase of more than 100 per cent, a veritable explosion in the country's secondary school population. Out of the 47 administrative districts into which the country was divided, only

172

two of the most inaccessible, Kabompo and Feira, were without at least one secondary school.

Providing the necessary buildings, facilities and equipment for the new classes and recruiting sufficient qualified staff placed a tremendous burden on the ministry. Building contractors, many of whom had their head offices in Europe, enjoyed a bonanza. The amount of new construction work waiting to be carried out, not just in education but in almost every sector, was so great that the builders could pick and choose among the many attractive projects and could virtually name their own prices for the contracts for which they tendered. UDI in Rhodesia, and the resulting problems of obtaining supplies, gave the building firms the opportunity to demand that their contracts be renegotiated, and provided them with ready-made excuses for the slow pace at which work some-times proceeded. Several of the new schools opened long before the building work was completed or the electricity supply had been installed. Many suffered from inadequate water supplies. In schools where the total population exceeded a thousand, empty water tanks and dry wells created severe health problems as well as much inconvenience.

It would be many years before Zambia could produce enough of its own secondary school teachers to staff all the schools. It was, therefore, necessary to recruit suitably qualified and experienced teachers from overseas. In 1966 alone, some 300 secondary school teachers were recruited from outside Zambia. Before independence, Britain had provided virtually all Zambia's expatriate teachers. Now, the recruiting net was cast widely. Teachers came from east and west Africa, Europe, India, Sri Lanka, Australasia, the USA, the Caribbean, Scandinavia and even Iran. Negotiations were completed for the appointment of teachers of science and mathematics from Moscow and Leningrad. Zambia's secondary schools thus acquired a strong international flavour. This had its advantages in broadening the experience of the pupils and in bringing in new ideas. It also meant that teachers did not always use the same methods or share the same goals. A further, serious drawback was that the spoken English of some of the teachers was appallingly bad. There were disturbing reports of teachers who could not make themselves understood in the classroom. The recruitment section in the ministry learned the hard way that possession of even a first class degree of certain universities was no guarantee of competence in a subject, let alone of teaching ability or of command of the English language. Far fewer bad appointments were made after it was decided that applicants from certain countries would not be offered employment unless they had been interviewed and assessed by a small team sent from Lusaka for the purpose.

By any standards, the rate at which Zambia's secondary education system expanded in the years immediately following independence was very impressive. Much of the credit for this must go to John Mwanakatwe whose determination and enthusiasm overcame all opposition. It was he who persuaded cabinet to agree that the secondary school population should increase from nearly 17,000 in 1966 to more than 54,000 in 1970. He achieved this in face of strong arguments from the Office of National Development Planning. The ONDP, as it was called, was staffed by economists, mainly expatriates; they were responsible for manpower planning and development, among other things. It was clear to ONDP that Zambia was seriously short of educated people at independence. It was equally clear to them that the shortfall could be made up within a few years after which the employment market would soon reach saturation point. Thus the ONDP challenged both the scale and the pace at which John Mwanakatwe proposed to expand the education system. 'By building all these schools, by employing all these teachers,' they argued, 'you are swallowing up resources which are needed elsewhere. Moreover, you are educating people for unemployment.'

There were those in the ministry who sympathized with the ONDP case. They included the Minister's Adviser on development, Alan Chorlton, Director of Education for Oxfordshire, whose services were made available by Unesco. Alan's main task was to advise on the setting up of a planning unit within the ministry. It was to be the responsibility of the unit to collect and analyse statistical data, to determine the costs of the various inputs into the education system, to quantify, where possible, the benefits derived from the inputs, to keep in close touch with the ONDP, to provide the Minister with a range of policy options from which he would plot the path ahead, to monitor the implementation of the current development plan and to look ahead to the next. It was a formidable remit, made no easier for Alan by the Minister's reluctance to consult him regularly. After the tremendous expansion of facilities which had taken place at independence, Chorlton urged that there should be a breathing space, a period of consolidation, before the programme of rapid growth was resumed. John Mwanakatwe would have none of this. Politically and on grounds of social justice, he had a strong case. For his cabinet colleagues, education, like motherhood and apple pie, was a good thing. They readily accepted his policy formulation which would ensure that one-third of primary school-leavers would proceed to Form 1; that two-thirds of the output from Form 2 would go on to senior secondary: and that boarding fees in the non-scheduled secondary schools should be abolished.

The Government's policy of expanding education opportunities in all sectors – primary, secondary, technical and vocational, teacher-training, adult and higher – as rapidly as possible, was shared by most countries as they achieved independence. Independence, whether in Africa, Asia, the Caribbean or the Pacific, unleashed a surge of expectations. Governments responded with a strategy of linear expansion which aimed to enlarge their existing education system in its old image, in order to increase the numbers and proportions of each age group enrolled at each level of the system. Unesco arranged regional conferences, such as the one for Africa, held in Addis Ababa in 1961, which set quantitative targets against which countries could measure their progress. Judged against these statistical criteria, Zambia's progress towards reaching the Addis Ababa targets was brilliantly successful. But there were worries. The capital costs of the school building programme were high; the recurrent costs of the expanded education system were huge; and unit costs were rising. Education already accounted for 20 per cent of government expenditure; it could not expect to receive a more generous allocation.

There was also increasing uneasiness about the curriculum and the relevance of what was being taught to the real needs of pupils, particularly secondary school students, and their life prospects. These doubts, however, did not unduly disturb the head of the inspectorate. Martyn Sibson, Chief Inspector of Schools, was a traditionalist rather than an innovator. He had been a highly regarded headmaster of a grammar school in Manchester. Now, towards the end of his professional career, he had been appointed not only to head the inspectorate but also to guide the development of the curriculum so that it would be responsive to the changed needs of the new nation. He was content to leave responsibility for the primary school curriculum in the hands of others, but he kept a tight rein on the secondary school curriculum and strongly resisted change. Having spent all his working life in grammar schools, he could think of no better model for Zambia's secondary schools to follow than the English grammar school. The English grammar school has many virtues. Clifford Little had modelled Munali on such an establishment. That was appropriate when Munali was the only school in the country taking students up to School Certificate level. It was definitely not appropriate when Zambia had more than 50 secondary schools. Not all their graduates, by any means, would go into traditional white-collar kinds of employment. The curriculum needed to be broadened to include pre-vocational types of education which would provide a jumping-off point for those whose future lay in agriculture, industry, commerce and the service industries. Sibson was not the man to provide the lead for this kind of change. The lead, in fact, came from a World Bank/Unesco team who made it a condition of Zambia receiving financial assistance for its secondary school development programme that the traditional curriculum should be diversified to include rural science, commercial subjects, agriculture and home economics.[21]

The debate within the ministry on changing the school system to fit new circumstances, rather than simply to expand the system as it had been for many years, went on for several months. I did not fully come into it until the middle of 1967. By then, Alan Chorlton had returned, rather disgruntled, to Oxford. The young Planning Unit he had set up was in difficulties and I was given the job of putting it on its feet. I soon found that there was little time to think about where we were heading. The demands of the job were such that it was all one could do to cope with the latest crisis: a complete breakdown of the water supply at a school in Choma; an accident to a lorry taking food supplies to Sesheke; a paper to be prepared for cabinet on savings which could be effected in the secondary school building programme; a parliamentary question on unemployed school leavers from the Member for Petauke. There was little opportunity to consider what was being taught in the classrooms. Getting the school buildings completed on time and within the budget, and ensuring that the staff were in place, had to be the top priorities. Unbeknown to us at the time, we were typical of those who contributed to the so-called 'world education crisis'. This was the title of an international conference, held at Williamsburg, USA, in 1967. As Dr Philip Coombs subsequently recalled, great concern was expressed at the conference at the 'growing imbalance between the rapidly expanding output of educational systems and the capacity of employment markets to provide appropriate jobs for the newcomers. The politically lethal problem of the "educated unemployed" was just around the corner in many countries'[22] Time would show that this was certainly true of Zambia. Coombs went on to describe the most fundamental cause of the world educational crisis as 'the inflexibility and inertia of educational systems themselves and their over-powering tendency to cling to the familiar, and to perpetuate the inherited curriculum, teaching methods and all the other paraphernalia of the traditional system in the face of great changes in the composition, needs and life prospects of their expanding clientele'. The crisis, in a nutshell, was a crisis of growing maladjustment between tradition-based educational systems and the rapidly changing world which those systems served.

There was a good deal in Coombs' judgement which applied to Zambia. It was not good enough simply to open scores of new schools and to set them traditional grammar school objectives. With the benefit of hindsight, one can see that we paid too much attention to quantitative expansion and not enough to the quality of what was taught or its relevance. We should have been thinking more about the content of education and should have advised the Minister, as Alan Chorlton urged, to proceed more cautiously and to give higher priority to curriculum reform and development. Of course, the political pressures on the Minister were very strong; almost every day, a delegation of Party officials, headmen and parents could be seen waiting in the corridor outside his office.

177

Whether he would have been able to slow down the rate of expansion, had he wanted to, is doubtful.

As Minister, John Mwanakatwe was in great demand to perform opening ceremonies at new or expanded schools and to be guest of honour at speech days. I soon became his chief speech writer. Through the Permanent Secretary, the Minister would send me a note saying that he was going to school X or Y and that he intended to speak on such and such a topic. Sometimes he would give me an outline of the points he wished to make, but usually not; he relied on me to guess the line he wanted to follow. Sometimes, he would speak on the university. One of the first decisions taken by the new government in February 1964, was to accept the main recommendations of a commission, headed by Sir John Lockwood, a former vice-chancellor of London University, that a university should be established, of full degree-awarding status, as soon as possible. The entrance qualification for the four-year first degree courses would be O level passes. Government undertook to provide half the capital costs. Britain gave a million pounds and smaller amounts were given by other countries. Clifford Little, a staunch supporter of the university, agreed to head a local fund-raising campaign which touched the hearts, as well as the pockets of the nation. The appeal, which raised half a million pounds, reached the smallest village in the most remote part of the country. Thousands of schoolchildren played their parts by holding concerts, organizing flag days and selling badges. The Minister used his speeches to thank the children and their parents for the contribution they were making to the appeal and to give progress reports on the setting up of the university: the selection of the site on the Great East Road outside Lusaka, the erection of the first buildings, the installation of President Kaunda as Chancellor, the appointment of the vice-Chancellor and other staff, the arrival of the first students and the formal inauguration of the university in August 1966. Historically, the establishment of the university was an event of great significance to the nation, for it was the university which would ultimately make Zambia self-sufficient in high-level manpower. Zambia would soon no longer have to look to universities such as Fort Hare, Makerere and Roma for the training of its professional men and women. When fully fledged, the University of Zambia would provide the doctors, the engineers, the geologists, the agriculturalists, the graduate teachers, the scientists, the journalists, the economists and so on, whom the nation required.

Another favourite speech-day theme was that of national unity. Many Africans had little sense of belonging to a country. Their first loyalty was to their family, their clan, their chief and to their tribe. The idea that they were also fellow citizens of a country, Zambia, was one which had to be nurtured. To encourage children to think in national, rather than provincial or tribal terms, a number of primary school leavers from each province were sent to other provinces for their secondary education. But this would benefit only a tiny proportion of the total school population. For the vast majority, national unity and citizenship had to be fostered by exhortation and by the raising each day of the national flag while the national anthem was sung. The legal power to require children to sing the national anthem and to salute the national flag was conferred on the Minister by the regulations made under the Education Act of 1966. The same regulations made it clear that no pupil would 'be required to sing the national anthem or to salute the national flag as part of any religious ceremony or observance.'[24] We included this proviso in the regulations in the hope that it might satisfy the members of the Jehovah's Witness sect who were strongly opposed to both the singing of the anthem and the saluting of the national flag. Such practices, they contended, were against God's will as revealed in the Ten Commandments. I had first encountered the Jehovah's Witnesses, or Watchtower, sect in the Eastern Province. At one school in Lundazi District, parents would not allow their children to play football or rounders because there was no record in the Bible that the children of Israel played these games. I had long since learned that no useful purpose is served by swapping Biblical texts with Jehovah's Witnesses. In my experience members of the sect have a very limited understanding of the Scriptures and are seriously in error. They hold tenaciously to their beliefs and will not be shaken from them. So it was with the national anthem and national flag. No amount of argument would persuade the Jehovah's Witnesses that to salute the flag and to sing the anthem were exercises in the promotion of national consciousness and had no religious significance. John Mwanakatwe took the view that since education was not compulsory, parents were free to withdraw their children from school if they did not like any feature of the life of the school. Similarly, government had the right to prescribe what was taught in the schools, and to insist that all children, on pain of exclusion, took part in all school activities. Take it or leave it, was the message. When scores of Watchtower children obeyed their parents, rather than their teachers, and refused to comply with the regulations on the flag and the anthem, they were first suspended from school and then expelled. When the sect brought a test case to the High Court, protesting against one of the expulsions, the Chief Justice dismissed the appeal and ruled that the regulations were reasonable.[25]

It was not difficult to write speeches for John Mwanakatwe. He had no pretensions to oratory and delivered his speeches much in the same way as he would read an essay. The President, however, had a distinctive speech-making style. He built up his argument slowly and carefully; he frequently repeated his points; he expressed himself on difficult issues in language which an unsophisticated audience would understand. He liked to keep them alert with a little humour, or a song; he was not afraid of tugging at the heartstrings and of displaying emotion, whether of anger, joy or sadness. Writing the education section of a speech for him, as I was sometimes required to do, was a demanding and time-consuming assignment. Only by reading each sentence out loud as I went along could I hope to find the words and rhythm that would suit his style of delivery. The reward sometimes came in hearing on the radio some of the phrases which had taken so long to produce.

One of the spin-offs from speech-writing for the Minister was unexpected. When he visited a mission station, he liked to make reference to some of the pioneer missionaries who had laboured there in the past. Searching in the National Archives for information on the early mission educationists, I realized that there were enormous gaps in the recorded history of the country's educational development. The first schools and the gradual spread of facilities until well after the end of company rule, were largely the result of the work of dedicated missionaries from more than 20 churches and societies. The story of their achievements and disappointments, successes and failures, was scattered in mission archives, in books long out of print and in the memories of ageing mission workers who were unlikely to commit their thoughts to paper. Here, I thought, was a gap which should be filled. Unless the material on the country's early educational development was brought together quickly, it was likely to be lost. The Minister encouraged me to work along the lines which I outlined to him. Clifford Little was enthusiastic and gave me the use of his very extensive library. Evelyn agreed that this was a worthwhile task and undertook to help with the collection of material and the typing. Before I really realized quite what was happening, I had committed myself to writing a book. Two or three afternoons a week, on leaving the office, I would cycle to the National Archives and search the files of 50 or 60 years earlier. Then, when supper was over and the children were in bed, I would try to make some sense of the notes I had taken and would write a few hundred, or on a good night, a thousand words for Evelyn to type. It was hard work for us both, but as the chapters were finished and the final shape of the book became clear, we were very glad that we had made the effort.

In African political life, the disruptive influence of tribalism is rarely far below the surface. It erupted in August 1967 when elections took place for the key posts in UNIP. Kaunda said later that the power struggle within the Party had been waged 'viciously along tribal, racial and provincial lines.'[26] He had been astonished, he said, to observe the 'spate of hate' among his colleagues. An alliance between Bemba and Tonga groups within the Party led to Reuben Kamanga of the Eastern Province, Vice-President of UNIP and of Zambia, losing his position to Simon Kapwepwe. Arthur Wina, a Lozi, the Party treasurer and Minister of Finance, was beaten in the election by Elijah Mudenda. A cabinet reshuffle followed. Kamanga accepted the Ministry of Foreign Affairs. Wina was more difficult and needed time to consider his position. Kaunda appointed him Minister of Education, moving Mwanakatwe to the rather less prestigious Ministry of Lands and Mines. There was intense speculation in the press, not to mention the ministry, as to whether Wina would accept the post. Rumours flew thick and fast while the minister's office remained empty. Wina

181

was deeply hurt, it was said; he could no longer trust his Bemba and Tonga colleagues and was going to resign; he was leaving politics and going into business. After an interregnum of ten days, Arthur Wina reported for duty, a comfortable, relaxed figure, keenly intelligent and with a rich sense of humour.

Like the Minister, Fwanyanga Mulikita, permanent secretary of the ministry, was a Lozi. In the Zambian context, it was not acceptable to have people from the same tribe occupying the top political and top civil service posts in the ministry. Mulikita would certainly have to go in the next reshuffle of permanent secretaries. The President moved his top people around frequently. His critics thought that he did so too often. Ministers and permanent secretaries hardly had time to settle into their posts before they were on the move. The lack of continuity in key positions and the uncertainty generated by the reshuffles led inexorably to indecision in government. Mulikita was a prime example of the paralysis which the system produced. Never a very decisive person, he was in a state of perpetual dither after Arthur Wina arrived. Papers requiring his decision lay untouched on his desk. Files piled up until he almost disappeared from view. When asked to make a decision on a matter of real urgency, he would say: 'How can I say yes or no when I do not know whether I shall be here to implement it?' He was very unhappy and it was a great relief to all of us when the next reshuffle of permanent secretaries took place. As frequently happened, the first news came on the radio: Mulikita was to go to Foreign Affairs. He came round the offices to say goodbye. He apologized for having failed to give his ruling on several matters. 'You must be very pleased to be leaving,' I said. 'In Foreign Affairs, you will be able to make decisions and keep on top of the files.'

'But how can I,' he asked plaintively, 'when I don't know how long I shall be there?'

Arthur Wina was not troubled by the same indecisiveness. He kept the files moving briskly across his desk. He enjoyed getting out of Lusaka and meeting teachers. I found him a pleasant and easy-going companion. I flew with him to the opening of the Kenneth Kaunda Secondary School near Lubwa mission, a few miles from Chinsali. He was intrigued to learn of my interest in the work of the early mission educationists but was dismayed to know that I had never been to his home province of Barotseland. On his next visit he insisted that I accompanied him. We flew to Mongu, the provincial capital, in a small plane of the government flight. It was a thrill for me to go with him to the Barotse National School and to Sefula mission, both of which I had written about at some length when researching for John Mwanakatwe. We spent a whole day travelling down the Zambesi from Mongu to Senanga. It was October, and the water level, even in the mighty Zambesi, was quite low. Wina had a shotgun. As we rounded each bend of the river, a gaggle of spur-winged geese, resting on a sandbank, would raise their heads and peer at us curiously as we approached. The Minister would then fire into their midst. At that range he could hardly miss. Soon the cockpit of the launch was full of geese, each weighing upwards of ten pounds. I protested at the slaughter and suggested it would be more sporting to fire at the birds in the air instead of on the ground. He thought it would be a waste of ammunition but lent me his gun and a couple of cartridges. Round the next bend, sure enough, yet another group of geese were sunning themselves on a sandbank. Arthur and the driver shouted and waved their arms until the birds took fright and lumbered into the air. I fired twice, but a solitary feather, spiralling into the Zambesi, was all there was to show for my efforts. Arthur laughed uproariously. 'So much for British sportsmanship,' he shouted above the roar of the engine, as he clapped me on the back.

Relationships in the office, then, were good and I still felt that I had a worthwhile contribution to make to the ministry's work. On the domestic front, Evelyn was frustrated at not being able to teach, the three children taking up all her time, but we were comfortably situated and had much to be thankful for. Nevertheless, as 1967 wore on, our thoughts turned increasingly towards Britain. Obviously, there was not a full career for me in Zambia. Sooner or later we would have to make a fresh start. I was 40; the longer we delayed, the more difficult it would be to start another career. Evelyn's mother was nearly 70; my father was in his late 70s; they would both be glad if we returned home. There were, then, strong factors drawing us towards Britain. At the same time, there were others which were edging us away from Zambia. The euphoria which had accompanied independence had not lasted long. The politicians had united, with some difficulty, to bring the colonial era to an end. But they could not sink their differences for long. As disenchantment set in, politically motivated thuggery and violence appeared on the streets. 'It pays to belong to UNIP' was the unfortunate campaign slogan adopted by the Government to encourage its opponents to join their ranks. This message was interpreted by some Party youths as a mandate to roam the streets demanding to be shown Party membership cards and to prevent those without cards from boarding buses or entering beerhalls. Government seemed to be powerless to stop these bully-boy tactics. Indeed, some of the speeches made by senior members of the Party, who should have known better, actually encouraged lawlessness and incited victimization of non-UNIP members. We were in no danger ourselves, but we found it increasingly uncomfortable to live in a country where law and order, as we had known it, seemed to be breaking down and where the media uttered not a word of criticism of the Government which controlled it.

It was the bizarre incident of Mrs Kamanga's turkey which triggered off our decision to leave Zambia. Mrs Kamanga, the wife of Reuben Kamanga, was a customer of a Greek butcher at Longacres in Lusaka. After Christmas, the butcher had some turkeys unsold. He decided to give them to his favoured customers, among whom was Mrs Kamanga. When Mrs Kamanga went to cook the turkey, she found that it was 'off'. Feeling insulted, she complained to the butcher; angry words were exchanged. The Lusaka branch of the UNIP Youth Brigade was informed of the incident. Their secretary led a gang of his members to Longacres for a noisy demonstration in the course of which the butchery was wrecked and the butcher had to flee for his life. The Youth Secretary was duly charged, convicted and sentenced to a term of imprisonment. Further demonstrations followed. The President, exercising his powers of clemency, ordered that the Youth Secretary should be freed. White opinion was shocked. If those who encouraged political intimidation and violence could get away with it unpunished, the outlook seemed bleak.

On its own, the turkey incident would not have led us to quit, but coming, as it did, after a number of disturbing incidents, it tipped the balance in favour of our going. Arthur Wina was sorry to know that I had sent in my letter of resignation. Word came from State House that it would be appreciated if I would stay on for at least another year.[27] But, having decided to go, we would not change our minds. Far better to go, we reasoned, while we were still wanted than to hang on and then be told, as had happened to some of our friends, to leave as soon as possible.

Evelyn had been ten years in the country, I had been 14. We had met in Zambia, and married there; the three children had been born there. As a family, we felt in many ways that we belonged as much to Zambia as we did to Britain. Pulling up our roots, disposing of many of our belongings, arranging for our cook, Brush's, future, saying goodbye to many friends, black and white, and handing over my duties to my successor, was difficult and sad. Had we known how quickly and comprehensively Zambia's economy would deteriorate, and the disastrous effects this would have on the nation's schools and, indeed, on all aspects of national life, we would have found it easier to leave. But in 1968 Zambia's slide into economic ruin, galloping inflation, widespread corruption, urban unrest and a vicious one-party state lay in the future. It was as well we did not know then of the decline which would soon begin. Had we known, we might have thought that our time in Zambia had been largely wasted.

We decided that we would not fly direct to London but would break our journey somewhere in order to get over the shock of leaving. Thus it was that when we left Lusaka in early March 1968, we headed not for London but for Dar-es-Salaam and Arusha. Our last nights in Africa were spent in tents on the rim of the magnificent Ngorogoro crater, listening to the roar of the lions and the whooping of the hyenas coming up from the darkness below. Via Nairobi, we flew to Israel and spent a memorable three weeks in Jersualem and Tiberias visiting the Biblical sites and holy places and marvelling at the way the Israelis were developing their country.

We landed at Heathrow on 1 April. It was snowing. Nicholas, Andrew and Ann, now 5 and a half, nearly 4 and 2 and a half, were delighted; this was the first snow they had seen. For Evelyn and me the snow seemed symbolic. We had left behind the warmth of Africa and many friends. Now we had to make a new start in an environment which was likely, in every sense, to prove much colder.

Notes

1 See Snelson, *Educational development*, chapter 10.
2 Unscheduled schools were so called because they were not on the schedule of fee-paying ex-federal schools referred to above. They had previously been under the control of the Ministry of African Education. Virtually all the pupils were Africans.
3 *Ministry of Education Annual Report*, (1964).
4 *Report of the Commission of Enquiry, op.cit.*, p. 11.
5 *Ibid.*, p. 13.
6 *Ibid.*, p. 22.
7 *Ibid.*, p. 23.
8 *Ibid.*, p. 24.
9 *Daily Telegraph* (4 August 1964).
10 *Northern News* (4 August 1964).
11 *Report of the Commission of Enquiry, op.cit.*, p. 28.
12 *Ibid.*, p. 16.
13 Quoted in Richard Hall, *The high price of principles* (London: Hodder and Stoughton, 1969), p. 124.
14 *Ibid.*
15 *Ministry of Education Annual Report* (1965).
16 Quoted in Hall, *The high price.* p. 175.
17 *Ibid.*
18 Quoted in J. M. Mwanakatwe, *The growth of education in Zambia since independence* (Lusaka: Oxford University Press, 1968), p. 24.
19 *Ibid.*, p. 37.
20 Quoted in *Ministry of Education Annual Report* (1966).
21 Ping-Lee, *Educational priority projects for development*, identification mission report (Paris: UNESCO, 1966).
22 Keynote address by Philip Coombs in, *Report of the seventh Commonwealth Education Conference*, Ghana, 1977 (London: Commonwealth Secretariat, 1977), p. 59.
23 *Ibid.*, p. 60.
24 *Education (Primary and Secondary Schools) Regulations of 1966*, Section 25 (4).
25 Mwanakatwe, *The growth of education*, pp. 252–5.
26 Quoted in Hall, *The high price*, p. 194.
27 The President had a very good memory. On a visit to Lusaka several years later, I was very gratified to receive a copy of the President's book, 'A humanist in Africa' which he had inscribed:
Peter,
Zambians remember only too well your contribution to their country's development in the field of education . . . For all this we shall always

be grateful. Please keep it up, and remember to keep smiling all the way.
God's blessings.
KK
13/8/79   State House, Lusaka.

6

Into the Commonwealth

'What I want,' said the Secretary-General, 'is a really good paper on Southern Rhodesia's education set up. We've got to show next month's heads of government meeting that the system is heavily loaded in favour of the whites and that blacks get a bad deal.' The pale December sunshine streamed through the windows which overlooked The Mall. Beyond the Secretary-General's shoulder, I could see Big Ben and the towers of Westminster Abbey on the other side of St. James's Park. 'Unless we can give them chapter and verse showing how Ian Smith discriminates against Africans – not enough schools, poor teachers, that kind of thing – we'll never get them to agree to expand the programme for the refugees.'

Arnold Smith had been a senior member of Canada's diplomatic service when, in 1965, he was elected the first Commonwealth Secretary-General and thus executive head of the Commonwealth Secretariat. Before the Secretariat came into being, intra-Commonwealth affairs had been the responsibility of the British Government. That it was no longer appropriate for Britain to exercise this role was a feeling expressed by several heads of government when they met in London in July 1964. It was Kwame Nkrumah of Ghana who first suggested that the Commonwealth should have its own secretariat.[1] He was supported by Abubakar Tafawa Balewa of Nigeria, Milton Obote of Uganda, Eric Williams of Trinidad and Tobago and Ayub Khan of Pakistan. The proposal found favour with the other presidents and prime ministers. In the communiqué issued at the end of their meeting, they included a paragraph supporting the concept of a secretariat which would be 'a visible symbol of the spirit of co-operation which animates the Commonwealth'. The Secretariat they considered,

> would be available, *inter alia*, to disseminate factual information to all member countries on matters of common concern; to assist existing agencies, both official and unofficial, in the promotion of Commonwealth links in all fields; and to help co-ordinate, in co-operation with the host country, the preparations for future meetings of Commonwealth Heads of Government and, where appropriate, for meetings of other Commonwealth Ministers.[2]

Now in December 1968, nearly three and a half years into his term of office, Arnold Smith was entitled to a feeling of satisfaction that the Secretariat had overcome several of its teething problems, that it was achieving credibility in the international arena and that it was winning for itself a reputation for excellence in the quality of its work and the calibre of its staff. 'I don't think you need have any worries, SG,' said Hugh Springer, Assistant Secretary-General, and my boss. 'Peter has a lot of experience of that part of Africa and I'm sure he'll produce the paper quickly.'

'I'd like to read it over the weekend,' said Smith. I blanched. It was Monday, my first day in the Secretariat. The thought of producing within a few days a detailed exposition of Rhodesia's education system, about which I knew little, which would be read critically by the prime ministers, and presidents of the Commonwealth, or at least, by some of their senior advisers, filled me with apprehension. Springer's confidence was reassuring, 'I'll see you get it on Friday,' he said. As we left the office, which had been Queen Mary's bedroom until her death in 1953, the Secretary-General turned to watch a detachment of Life Guards pass Marlborough House on its way to the changing of the guard ceremony at Horse Guards Parade. Like most Canadians, he was fascinated by the pageantry and strong sense of tradition that London provides. As Hugh and I walked down the stairs, past the murals by Louis Laguerre showing bloodthirsty scenes from Marlborough's victories at Blenheim, Malplaquet and elsewhere, Hugh smiled: 'You're going in at the deep end.'

A job in the Commonwealth Secretariat was but one of several posts for which I had applied in the summer of 1968. When we left Zambia, I assumed that I would probably join a local education authority in Britain. Conscious of the fact that I was out of touch with the British educational scene, I arranged with the County Education Officer for Cambridgeshire to spend some weeks in his office bringing myself up to date. But although I did not have any serious doubts about my ability to cope successfully with a middle level position in a borough or county education office, this was clearly not the view of the interviewing boards before whom I appeared. I grew to recognize the way in which the eyes of the chairman of the board (whose experience of 'overseas' probably went no farther than Majorca or Dubrovnik) would become glazed as I endeavoured to explain the extent and the relevance of my experience in Zambia. Subsequently, I was to be profoundly grateful that I had not been appointed to any of the positions for which I had applied with local education authorities. At the time, however, it was depressing to find myself an 'also ran'. Ironically, while I was trying in vain to find a local education authority in Britain which would employ me, I received an offer from the Ministry of Overseas Development to become Director of Education in the Bahamas. Initially, I was tempted by the invitation but, as Evelyn pointed out, we had not left Zambia because we did not like Zambia but because the time had come to make a new career in Britain. Going to Nassau, or anywhere else overseas, would simply delay the settling-down process.

I was excited, therefore, to read in *The Times* an advertisement for two senior education officers who were required by the Commonwealth Secretariat.' Applicants,' said the advertisement,

should have a good university degree and should have wide practical experience in education, preferably in more than one Commonwealth country. A knowledge of educational planning and educational administration is also desirable. Duties will include the collection of information about planning and development in all fields of education in Commonwealth countries and assisting their programmes.

I felt at once that the advertisement had been aimed especially at me and was encouraged in this view by the Overseas Services Resettlement Bureau, which helped people like me to find suitable jobs when they were made redundant by the Colonial Service or resigned. By the time I was called for interview, I had read all I could find on the Commonwealth Secretariat and the reports on Commonwealth education conferences. The advertisement had attracted more than a hundred applications. The interview went quite well, I thought, but there followed some anxious weeks of waiting. Then, at 8 o'clock one Friday morning, the Director of the Education Division at the Secretariat telephoned to say that I was being offered one of the posts. Could I start on Monday morning? Evelyn and I had a hurried consultation across the breakfast table. 'I'll start a week on Monday,' I told the Director. That gave us just a week in which to find a house. At the time were were living in a small maisonette in Cambridge. We would need to move closer to London but also keep within easy reach of Cambridge where my father was still living. We swung an arc on a map. It cut through Bishop's Stortford, Epping, Welwyn Garden City and Hatfield. We visited all of them, found a house we liked in Welwyn Garden City and made an offer for it which was accepted. It was four months before we could get occupation. I spent the winter of 1968–9, therefore, commuting to London each day from Cambridge; the discomfort and expense were a small price to pay for getting started on a new career.

The contrast between the living and working environment could hardly have been greater. Our maisionette in Cambridge was tiny. Marlborough House was spacious, elegant and full of history. One of the royal palaces, Marlborough House had been offered by the Queen as a home for the Secretariat while the proposal to establish it was still under discussion. The history of the house goes back to the beginning of the eighteenth century when John Churchill, Captain-General of the British Army, led a highly successful campaign against the French. He was rewarded by Queen Anne with a dukedom and a large sum of money. For his country seat, he built Blenheim Palace, near Oxford. His wife, the former Sarah Jennings, was a friend and confidante of the Queen, holding the positions of Mistress of the Robes and Keeper of the Privy Purse.

191

Sarah prevailed upon the Queen to lease to the Marlboroughs part of the garden of St James' Palace, then the official residence of the royal family. Sir Christopher Wren was commissioned to design the house; Sarah laid the foundation stone on 24 May 1709. By the time the house was finished, Sarah had quarrelled with the Queen and had lost her position at Court. The Duke died in 1722 but Sarah continued living in Marlborough House until her own death in 1744. She must have been an extraordinary woman, tempestuous in temperament and a striking beauty. As a girl, she lived for some years at Waterend, just a few miles from the present-day Welwyn Garden City, and had associations with St Albans. She quarrelled with everyone. At one stage she wanted to build a more imposing entrance to Marlborough House. This would have involved buying and then demolishing some houses in Pall Mall. To thwart her, Sir Robert Walpole, the Prime Minister, whom she had crossed, promptly bought the houses. The entrance archway, which Sarah had already built, had to be bricked up, as can still be seen. Despite her sharp temper, Sarah had many friends and entertained lavishly. She lived in such style that Marlborough House quite outshone the Court of St James's opposite.[3]

The Marlborough family continued to live in the house until 1817 when it passed to the royal family. The most glittering period in its history began in 1863 when it became the residence of the newly-married Prince and Princess of Wales. For nearly 40 years, London's upper crust social life revolved around the couple at Marlborough House rather than Queen Victoria who, following the death of the Prince Consort in 1861, was a virtual recluse at Buckingham Palace. When Victoria died, the Prince and Princess, now King and Queen, moved up The Mall to Buckingham Palace. When King Edward died in 1910, Queen Alexandra returned to her old home and remained there for the rest of her life. Some of her pets, six dogs and a rabbit, are buried in a tiny cemetery in the shrubbery at the back of the house. Each has its own headstone. A later occupant of Marlborough House was Queen Mary who moved there after the death of King George V in 1936. She died, in what is now the Secretary-General's office, in 1953.

Marlborough House, then, is full of history. No-one can fail to be impressed by what is now the conference room, a room of perfect proportions, dominated by glittering chandeliers hanging from a heavily decorated gilt ceiling, the scene of many important meetings; or the reading room on the first floor where, it it said, the flirtatious Prince of Wales used to seduce his lady friends while his loving Alexandra embroidered in the drawing room. I must have walked down St James's Street, across Pall Mall and into Marlborough House, a few thousand times. I never did so without experiencing a feeling of privilege and excitement that I was entering a house which had known great pageantry and had been the scene of many important moments in history. This feeling was particularly strong when, for some months, my office was Queen Mary's private sitting room. It was here that King Edward VIII came one evening in December 1936 to tell his mother that he was going to abdicate in order to marry Wallis Simpson.

When I joined the Secretariat at the end of 1968, I knew less about the Commonwealth than I did about the United Nations Organization. The United Nations came into being in 1945 after a great deal of detailed planning. UNO had a clearly defined purpose, a variety of carefully designed instruments for achieving its aims, a constitution, an enormous budget and a very large staff. By contrast, the Commonwealth was planned by no-one. It simply grew or, more accurately, it evolved from a series of historical events. In 1968 its aims had not been defined with any exactitude; it had no constitution; it had only a tiny Secretariat, with a very limited mandate and a shoestring budget, to help it reach whatever goals it might set itself.

The Commonwealth of 1968 was significantly different from the Commonwealth of today. It was even more different from the Commonwealth I had known as a boy. Then, we spoke not of the Commonwealth but of the Empire. Large areas of the world map were coloured satisfyingly red to mark the boundaries of an empire on which, literally, the sun never set. We sang 'Rule Britannia' and accepted, as if it were part of the divine dispensation, the concept of 'the white man's burden'. We celebrated our imperial heritage each year on 24 May, Empire Day. The term 'Commonwealth' was confined to the handful of former colonies – Australia, Canada, Newfoundland, New Zealand and South Africa, together with Eire – which had achieved dominion status. They were described in the

Statute of Westminster in 1931 as 'autonomous communities within the British Empire, equal in status, in no way subordinate one to another in respect of their domestic or external affairs, though united by a common allegiance to the Crown and freely associated as members of the British Commonwealth of Nations'.

Despite the fact that full members of the Commonwealth were legally equal in status, Britain was still very much the senior partner. The pre-war image of the Commonwealth was one of a wheel, with Britain at the hub and the dominions at the end of the spokes. The rim of the wheel was very thin and there was little contact between the dominions except through Britain. Ties with 'the mother country' were very close. Britain was 'home' to many second and third generation New Zealanders and Canadians. They liked to feel that they shared a common way of life with their kith and kin in 'the old country'. Coming mostly from the same British stock, they were united by bonds of colour, language, religion and culture. They owed allegiance to the same king. One of the highlights of Christmas was the wireless programme when the whole Commonwealth family at home and overseas was united by radio and, as a climax to the programme, the King, as head of the family, sent his royal greetings to all the members. In some families, it was the custom to stand to attention in front of the wireless set while the national anthem was played before and after the King spoke. But the links were stronger than those of blood and sentiment. The Commonwealth was underpinned by important agreements on trade and defence. A series of measures negotiated at Ottawa had refined a system of imperial preferences in trade aimed at insulating Commonwealth countries from the worst effects of the world depression of the 1930s. Intra-Commonwealth trade was of the greatest importance both to Britain and the dominions. Britain, before the 1939–45 war, was a major military and naval force, willing and able, it was claimed, to go to the assistance of any dominion or colony which might be attacked. The concept of the Royal Navy, ready and able to defend the sea routes of intra-Commonwealth trade, generated confidence and inspired a feeling of unity.

By 1968, the picture was very different. The Anglocentric, homogeneous, white, wealthy Commonwealth had evolved into a multinational, multicultural, predominantly black Commonwealth, embracing some of the poorest and least-developed nations of the world. Of the old dominions Newfoundland had become a province of Canada in 1947, the same year as Eire had decided to leave the Commonwealth. South Africa had withdrawn in 1961 when its policy of apartheid became abhorrent to other members. This left only four of the old, white countries – Australia, Britain, Canada and New Zealand. To their number, beginning with India and Pakistan in 1947, had been added 24 other countries which, by 1968, had made the transition from colonial status to independence and had chosen to become members of the Commonwealth. Only Aden, Burma and Somaliland had become independent and opted to sever their links with the association.

Little remained of the traditional links which had bound the Commonwealth together. Shared blood and a common way of life were no longer the unifying force since, by 1968, seven out of every ten Commonwealth citizens were Asian, one was African, one was white and one was a member of another ethnic group. Intra-Commonwealth trade, though still important, had declined appreciably as a proportion of the total trade of Commonwealth countries. Imperial preferences had been steadily eroded and would virtually disappear when Britain entered the European Economic Community. In the military arena, Britain was no longer a major world power and the Commonwealth was in no sense a military alliance; its two largest countries, India and Pakistan, were soon to be locked in war. Some Commonwealth countries were non-aligned between East and West. Others were members of regional defence organizations which relied to a greater or lesser extent on the United States of America, rather than on Britain, for their 'muscle'. The Queen reigned in only seven Commonwealth countries. The other 21 countries which made up the membership at that time were either republics or, in the case of Lesotho, Malaysia, Swaziland and Tonga, had their own monarchies. They also recognized the Queen as 'the symbol of their free association and, as such, Head of the Commonwealth'.[4]

Most of what gave the old Commonwealth its reality, its unity and its sense of purpose had gone. It was probably for that reason that the Commonwealth was receiving more than its fair share of abuse. 'Commonwealth countries have little in common and no wealth,' sneered one commentator. An imperial fossil, a tool of neo-colonialism, a ghost of empire, an irrelevance, were some of the uncomplimentary epithets that were directed at the Commonwealth. Twenty years later when I left the Secretariat, the Commonwealth, like the UN and all other international bodies, still had its critics. But by that time, the Commonwealth had won, from most fair-minded observers, recognition as a force for good in a troubled world. No fewer than 21 countries were welcomed into the Commonwealth between 1968 and 1987, bringing the total number of countries to 49. There are now more than a billion Commonwealth citizens, that is, nearly a quarter of the world's population. They live in six continents, are of every major race, culture, colour and creed. Between member countries, there are great differences in political systems and in levels of economic development. Put another way, the Commonwealth is a cross-section of the world community, straddling the main divisions of mankind between regions, between races, between the rich and the poor, the north and the south, the first world and the third. Over the years, Commonwealth leaders have progressively come to use the association to help bridge these divisions, to increase understanding and mutual respect, and to foster co-operation. In this process, the Secretary-General has played a key role. At the same time, the Secretariat has been given increasingly important functions, to the extent that it is critical to the Commonwealth's effectiveness.

Working within a framework of great diversity, the role of the Secretary-General is a difficult one. Some governments encourage him to give a lead, to take the initiative; others, particularly the larger ones, watch him closely to see that he does not exceed his authority or stray outside his mandate. He needs the wisdom of Solomon, the patience of Job, and the saintliness of the Archangel Gabriel to keep most member governments happy for most of the time. Arnold Smith was certainly wise for much of the time and was very patient. He made up for any lack of saintliness by his skills in diplomacy, his combativeness on behalf of the Secretariat, his refusal to be brushed aside, particularly by Britain, and by his tremendous enthusiasm. He gave his staff a lead in working hard and playing hard. An outburst of strong words would be followed by a laugh and a slap on the back. He had little sense of self-importance and made you feel that you were working with him and not for him. He wanted his staff to share his vision of what the Commonwealth could become and to work together to make it a reality. Of course, he had his faults. He was not always a good judge of people and some of the appointments he made turned out to be unfortunate. Nevertheless, it was Arnold Smith who laid the foundations of a strong secretariat on which Sonny Ramphal was subsequently able to build.

With few tangible resources at his disposal, Arnold Smith's strategy for promoting Commonwealth co-operation was to build on existing strengths and shared similarities. The Commonwealth has an enormous advantage over other international groupings and associations because of the many things which member countries have in common. Many of these derive from the former association with Britain. First is the English language which is common to nearly all Commonwealth countries and which helps bridge the gulf which so often separates politicans and professional people of different countries. Although there are clear differences in English usage and pronunciation between, say, Africa and the Carribean, between Asian countries and those in the Pacific, all speak the same language and understand each other. Thus Commonwealth meetings can take place without the need for interpreters or simultaneous translations, which characterizes the work of the United Nations. Then there is the heritage of ideas and institutions, such as parliamentary government, judicial systems, educational systems, the organization and techniques of public administration, the ethics and practices of many of the professions, the traditions and working methods which are shared in many fields. It is these similarities which facilitate collaboration between countries which, in all other respects, are at very different stages of development. Nowhere is this more true than in the field of education as I soon discovered when I joined the Secretariat's Education Division.

Bilateral co-operation between Commonwealth countries in education has a long history. For decades, Britain sent lecturers, tutors, teachers, administrators and advisers to the colonies, and provided

197

places in her universities and colleges for thousands of students from these territories. At the request of the countries concerned, the British continued to offer this service after they had gained their independence. Similar assistance was given by Australia, Canada and New Zealand to the countries with which they had special relationships. In 1968, the concept of multilateral, rather than bilateral, co-operation was still compartively new. The first Commonwealth conference on education was held at Oxford in 1959. From this conference came two important decisions. The first set up the Commonwealth Scholarship and Fellowship Plan under which graduates were enabled to take higher degrees in Commonwealth countries other than their own. The awards – 1,000 in the first instance – were to be made to people 'of high intellectual promise who may be expected to make a significant contribution to life in their own countries on their return from study overseas.'[5] The second decision was to set up in London a committee composed of representatives of each member country of the Commonwealth. The main task of the committee was to follow up progress on the schemes of assistance, agreed to by the conference, in teacher training, technical education and industrial training. The committee, recommended the conference, would be serviced by a small administrative unit. In this way, there came into being the Commonwealth Education Liaison Committee and the Commonwealth Education Liaison Unit. In 1965 the Liaison Unit was absorbed into the Commonwealth Secretariat and became its Education Division.

The main task of the Education Division was to encourage and facilitate Commonwealth co-operation in education. We did this by collecting, analysing and disseminating information on matters of interest to member countries. We held seminars, workshops and conferences. We arranged a limited number of exchange visits which enabled key people from developing countries to study at first hand innovations in other such countries. We tried to make ourselves familiar with the educational problems of the developing countries through visits as well as through reading and correspondence. We made ourselves available as consultants, but a chronic shortage of funds severely restricted the amount of time we could spend overseas.

Into the Commonwealth

There is little doubt that the work of the Education Division, and the Education Programme as it is now called, has proved valuable, particularly for the smaller countries. It is extremely difficult for a minister of education and the senior officials in a ministry of education in many Commonwealth countries to keep abreast of international developments in, say, curriculum reform, science education, youth employment programmes, the use of new technologies, distance education, and the economic use of resources. The Secretariat's publications, seminars and advisory visits facilitate the sharing of information and experience between governments, institutions, professional associations and individuals. They also help combat the feeling of professional isolation which often afflicts those who are not in the mainstream of development and do not have regular access to books and journals. Similar work in other fields, such as health, the law, agriculture and youth affairs, is carried out by other divisions of the Secretariat.

Following the success of their 1959 meeting in Oxford, Commonwealth education ministers met at three-yearly intervals. In 1971, the fifth Commonwealth Education Conference was held at Canberra, Australia. This was the first of many major Commonwealth meetings in which I was involved. Later, I was to attend meetings of heads of government, senior officials, ministers of health, ministers of labour and employment, ministers responsible for youth affairs and a host of seminars and workshops. The theme of the Canberra meeting was 'Matching needs to resources'. The tremendous expansion in education which had taken place in all the developing countries in the years following their independence had stretched their resources to the limit. Some countries were spending as much as 20 per cent of their recurrent budget on education. Some were beginning to ask if they were getting value for their money. In any case the emphasis was shifting from quantitative expansion to qualitative improvement. It was not enough to build more schools and train, or half-train, more teachers. The curriculum, inherited from the colonial era, needed reform; new teaching and learning materials had to be written and produced; new technologies had to be acquired. As teachers were asked to accept new responsibilities, they were demanding higher salaries. Priorities had to be established among the many competing claims for limited resources.

Ministers and their officials from 28 countries – nearly 200 all told – met at the Australian National University in Canberra for two weeks to discuss these issues. The Australian Prime Minister, John Gorton, opened the conference; messages were exchanged with the Queen; it was a big occasion. For months beforehand our lives in the Education Division were dominated by the conference: invitations had to be drafted and issued; the agenda had to be composed and the timetable agreed; arrangements had to be made for flights and hotels; lead speakers had to be identified who could be guaranteed to be gently provocative; security and protocol arrangements had to be taken care of, and documentation had to be provided. This last was my responsibility. There were agenda items on the training, supply and status of teachers, further and higher education, technical and vocational education, education media, the school curriculum, out-of-school education and training, and educational planning and administration. Countries were invited to submit papers on any or all of these subjects. My task was to mastermind the writing of 'umbrella' papers on all the agenda topics, to edit all the papers received from countries and write a summary of each. In all we had 93 papers, totalling over 500 pages. Clearly, this was absurd. No delegate, however serious and conscientious, could possibly cope with such a mountain of paper. At subsequent conferences we drastically reduced the volume of documentation. No-one complained. No-one, I think, even missed the familiar heaps of paper because no-one had read them.

It had been the practice at previous conferences for the printed and bound report of the conference, running to a hundred or more pages, to be distributed to delegates on the last day. We determined to keep up the practice at Canberra and, with the help of the Government Printer, managed to do so.[6] For Secretariat staff, I soon discovered, conferences were hard work. Each evening, the minutes of the day's proceedings in five working groups had to be written, edited, typed, cyclostyled and delivered to delegates' hotels so that they could be read over breakfast the next morning. Briefing notes had to be written for the chairman of the conference and the

200

Secretary-General. Return flights for the delegates had to be confirmed with the airlines, or sometimes cancelled and replaced by new arrangements. Disgruntled delegates – and each conference produced a few – had to be cossetted. Interesting items had to be fed to the press. There was always something to be done. It was rare for Secretariat staff to get to bed before midnight and it was by no means unusual to work until two in the morning, or later. For most delegates, of course, the pace was much more leisurely. Countries with small delegations were hard pressed since much of the work of the conference was conducted in five committees. Countries with only 2 or 3 delegates had to decide which committees they would attend or rush madly from one committee to another. Members of larger delegations could concentrate on the work of whichever committee was most relevant to their interests and expertise.

It never ceased to amaze me that some delegates would sit through a whole conference without opening their mouths either in committee or in the plenary sessions. By contrast, others wearied us with the frequency of their interventions and the length at which they spoke. Those who made the biggest impression were the ones who could think internationally (rather than constantly referring to their own countries), and could express themselves succinctly and with occasional flashes of humour. Some delegates were serious and would spend their evenings catching up with the documentation or preparing a speech for the next day. At the other end of the scale were those who were much less assiduous. It did not take many conferences to make me realise that a small minority of those attending conferences, usually at very considerable cost to their countries, have little interest in the proceedings and scant understanding of what is happening. They include those whose main aims are to have a good time and, if possible, acquire some hard currency.

The success of any conference, whether of education ministers, health ministers, finance ministers or heads of government, depends on the work of a few who have the intellectual capacity and the will to think in Commonwealth terms, and to consider how decisions will affect the association as a whole. Important decisions and ringing declarations of principle do not emerge spontaneously from conferences. They have to be planted carefully and nurtured assiduously, often for many months. Arnold Smith took great pains to see that conferences, other than heads of government meetings, were cut and dried in advance, with little left to chance. He involved himself very actively in the preparations for a conference, identified the 'desirable outcomes', as he termed them, at an early stage, and then spent a good deal of effort ensuring that these would be achieved. In 1974, when education ministers met in Kingston, Jamaica, he arrived only a day before the conference opened. On the drive from the airport, he wanted to see the draft of the communiqué which would be issued to the press at the end of the conference. He was furious to find that there was no such draft. 'I haven't come here to listen to a debate on education,' he snapped. 'The purpose of the meeting is to get approval for new Secretariat initiatives. I'm off to see Michael Manley. By the time I come back, I want to know what this conference is all about and what the Secretariat will get out of it.' We hastily drafted a communiqué and gave it to him when he returned from seeing the Prime Minister. Two weeks later, when the conference ended, only minor amendments were necessary before it could be given to the press.

Conferences cost a lot of money. The cost to the host country, which is expected to provide a social programme as well as the normal conference, protocol and security facilities, can be a real burden. Is it worth it? Often I have doubted it. Many Commonwealth conferences I have attended have done little to advance the frontiers of knowledge. Many of their recommendations have been platitudinous or of the 'praising motherhood' variety. And yet heads of government, ministers and their officials go on attending them. The heads of government meetings in particular are extraordinarily popular. Most presidents and prime ministers attend in person. No other organization, including the United Nations, succeeds in bringing together so many heads of government for a week's concentrated debate on some of the major issues of the day. They would not go unless they got something out of it. The friendly club-like atmosphere in the conference room has something to do with it. The absence of resolutions, votes and lobbying helps to keep the temperature down. Of course, there are no walk-outs.

Indeed, to walk out of a meeting as a mark of protest would be a most unCommonwealth thing to do. Other factors contributing to the success of Commonwealth meetings are the excellent hospitality normally provided by the host country and the unobtrusive efficiency of the Secretariat which helps to keep everything running smoothly and copes with any difficulties which arise. But perhaps the single most important reason why conferences continue to attract so many participants, irrespective of the cost, is the opportunities they provide to make really useful contacts with people, ministers, officials and professionals from other countries. These contacts and the conversations which take place over coffee and in the corridors and hotels are far more important in the long run than the discussions, often dreary and predictable, in the conference chamber. For this reason, it is very unlikely that the teleconference, now technically feasible, which enables people to discuss matters and to reach conclusions without leaving their office, let alone their country, will replace the traditional face-to-face conference, for all its imperfections.

When heads of government decided to establish the Secretariat in 1965, they envisaged that the Secretary-General and his staff would have a very limited role. As they saw it, the Secretariat's main responsibility would be to facilitate consultation, which was 'the life blood of the Commonwealth associaton.'[7] Circulating information, preparing for and servicing meetings were seen as the main work of the Secretariat. To ensure that the Secretary-General stuck to his limited mandate and did not attempt to acquire an executive role, the Agreed Memorandum setting up the Secretariat required that 'the Secretariat should not arrogate to itself executive functions'.[8]

But there are ways other than by arrogation of acquiring executive functions. Arnold Smith explored and exploited them all. He made it his business to see that the Secretariat was given executive responsibilities by direction of heads of government and other ministerial meetings, and by the Secretariat absorbing bodies such as the Commonwealth Economic Committee and the Commonwealth Education Liaison Unit which already had executive roles. Smith strove to give the Secretariat some teeth. In particular, he set his heart on persuading government that the Secretariat should be given the funds and the responsibility to run a technical assistance programme. Most of the developing countries needed no persuasion; they were prepared to welcome any proposal which would help them to meet some of their developmental needs. The scheme would never get off the ground, however, without the backing of the rich, white nations. Of these, Australia and Britain were initially opposed to the idea. New Zealand was cautiously in favour, but could not provide the resources which would get the programme on the road. Pierre Trudeau of Canada supported Smith, his fellow-countryman, but could not give more resources to the Commonwealth than he gave to the Francophone quasi-equivalent, L'Agence de co-opération culturelle et technique. Patiently and skilfully Smith went to work. Sometimes cajoling, sometimes hectoring, he made his case. Success was finally achieved at the heads of government meeting in Singapore in 1971. This meeting was dominated and embittered by discussion on Britain's proposal to sell arms to South Africa. 'Break-up of Commonwealth imminent,' screamed the tabloid press, as a number of countries, including India, Nigeria, Tanzania and Zambia, threatened to leave the Commonwealth if Britain went ahead with its plans. Happily, Edward Heath, Britain's Prime Minister, backed down and a major setback for the Commonwealth was averted. On the last day of the conference, in the mood of euphoria generated by the resolution of the arms issue, the heads gave their approval to the establishment of a multilateral technical assistance programme to be known as the Commonwealth Fund for Technical Co-operation.

The setting up of the CFTC, as it was known, was perhaps the most significant decision taken by heads of government while I was at the Secretariat. It was a decision which revolutionized the work of the Secretariat. Until the CFTC came into being, the Secretary-General was largely concerned with facilitating, informing and encouraging consultations, in preparing for and servicing meetings. He had virtually no capacity to offer technical assistance to member countries, however desperate their needs might be. Now, with the inauguration of the CFTC, he was in a position to provide a range of assistance in response to their requests. With this new dimension added to its role, the Secretariat was going to become an increasingly satisfying organization in which to work.

The setting up of the CFTC had important personal implications for me. The Memorandum of Understanding which established the CFTC provided that the fund, in addition to making available the services of experts and advisers, 'may also finance education and training of personnel from one developing country in another developing Commonwealth country in such fields and under such terms and conditions as may be agreed by the Board of Representatives'. It was not until mid-1972 that Arnold Smith decided to activate this clause. He sent for me one morning and said he wanted me to draw up a blueprint for a third country education and training programme. 'If you make a good job of it,' he said, 'and the Board buys it, I'll give you a chance to run the programme.' Did he have any specific instructions or guidelines, I asked. 'Keep it flexible,' he said. 'The needs of countries vary enormously. You might find it useful to imagine yourself back in Zambia and to think of the sort of things that Kaunda wants for his people and how other countries could help provide them.' It was good advice.

In all developing countries, as in Zambia, independence had generated a tremendous expansion of education facilities not only in primary and secondary schools but also at the tertiary level. New universities had been opened, new technical institutions had been established, and training opportunities for entry to the professions had multiplied. These new facilities had a critical role to play in producing the human resources required for both the public and private sectors. The shortages of skilled manpower and womanpower, particularly at the middle and senior levels, were a major constraint on national development, as I knew all too well from my Zambian experience. Despite the rapid expansion of facilities, none of the developing countries had all the institutional and financial resources it required to train all the skilled people it needed. The smaller countries could never hope to sustain a full range of institutions and were obliged to look to other countries for many basic and intermediate training courses as well as those at a more advanced level. Even the largest and most richly endowed countries, such as India, needed to send their people abroad for sophisticated training in some of the more specialized skills. Against this background certain things were clear. The principal aim of the CFTC's Education and Training Programme must be to assist countries to meet their manpower development and training needs and to increase the numbers of trained personnel with the skills and expertise necessary to run the machinery of government and to implement national development plans.

The strategy for achieving this aim must be to encourage and facilitate the sharing of education and training resources. Countries with spare capacity would be willing, I felt sure, to accept students from other countries into their universities and colleges provided they were not a financial burden. To overcome this constraint, the programme would need to provide scholarships. The value of these would have to be carefully calculated to cover the costs of tuition and other fees, board and lodging, books, stationery, medical expenses, pocket money and, of course, travel. Since all students would be trained in countries other than their own, heavy expenditure on travelling was inevitable. CFTC, then, would provide scholarships to enable people from one developing country to go and study or train in another developing country. But in what subjects, and at what levels? How would the people be selected, and how would they be placed in appropriate institutions? The answers to these questions, I soon realized, could be given only by the governments we were trying to assist. We must avoid a heavily centralized or directive system. It would be folly, if not impertinent, to sit in London and tell governments what their priority manpower requirements were. Some donor governments did exactly that in their bilateral aid programmes. We should avoid making similarly arrogant mistakes. It must be left to each government to decide whether it wished to apply CFTC scholarships to the training of agriculturalists or electrical technicians, or auditors, or business managers, or town planners or meteorologists. The only criterion we should apply would be the very general one that any education or training that the CFTC was asked to support would contribute to economic and social development. This meant that we would draw the line at providing scholarships for the study of purely cultural subjects and that we would not support training for

206

the armed services. Otherwise, virtually everything could be considered for assistance.

We must also respect the wishes of governments regarding the level of education and training for which we would give support, provided it was at the post-secondary level. Governments knew far better than we did whether their priority need was for graduates, diplomates, technicians or craftsmen. As things turned out, the majority of awards were requested for middle-level training, this being the category for which most developing countries had the most pressing need.

In order to avoid duplicating the work of the Commonwealth Scholarship and Fellowship Plan, it was decided that CFTC awards would not normally be made for higher degree and research studies. Exceptions could be made, however, for those who were nominated to take such degrees as part of the staff development programme of a university or other institution of higher learning. This provision was to prove particularly helpful to universities wanting to enhance the academic standing and international experience of their staff. Makerere University in Uganda, which lost many members of staff during the vicious and obscene regime of Idi Amin, was one of the universities which were to benefit from being helped by CFTC: some of its promising young lecturers went to well-established universities in Ghana and Nigeria to gain higher degrees.

If flexibility was to be one of our watchwords, we had to be ready to support not only formal courses of education and training but also informal kinds of learning such as training attachments and study visits. Experience had taught me that a good deal of time and effort in the developing world is spent in reinventing the wheel, at least in a metaphorical sense. Many of the problems and difficulties faced by one country have been already experienced by other countries. Solutions which have been successfully devised in one country can rarely be transplanted without modification to others; there are always important differences of detail. But to see at first hand how their opposite numbers in other countries have tackled problems, and dealt with difficulties, can often provide useful pointers to civil servants, business men, agriculturalists and those working in industry. While study visits and training attachments can be a waste of time if they are not carefully planned, they can be very valuable if time and trouble are spent in designing programmes which will familiarize trainees with relevant innovations, research and practice in countries at a comparable stage of development, and are tailored to meet specific needs in the trainees' home countries.

The Memorandum of Understanding on the CFTC, already mentioned, deliberately confined the operations of the Education and Training Programme to the developing countries. It was not to be used, in other words, to provide scholarships tenable in Australia, Britain, Canada or New Zealand, these being the so-called industrialized or developed countries of the Commonwealth. It meant, for instance, that a Zambian could be given an award tenable in Kenya and Nigeria or, further afield, in India or Trinidad. A Zambian could not, however, be given an award for study in London or Sydney. There were very good reasons for this decision. First, the more developed countries were already providing, under bilateral arrangements, scholarships for the developing countries so that they could send their people for training in Europe, North America and Australasia. It would be pointless for the CFTC to duplicate these arrangements. Secondly, training in another developing country, or third country training as it was called, offered positive advantages: the syllabus of an institution in a developing country was likely to be more relevant than that of, say, an institution in Britain to the needs of a Third World student. The student would live in conditions similar to those from which he came and in which he would be working on his return home; hence, the culture shock would be less. Students would be trained on the same kind of equipment they would be likely to find in their home countries, rather than on high-tech machines and apparatus which would not be available. A further consideration was that the cost of training in Third World institutions would be considerably less than in, say, London or Montreal. By encouraging students to study at institutions in their own regions, we could help the development of these institutions. Some, as time went on, would emerge as centres of excellence. A final point was that third country training would reduce the incidence of 'brain drain', the phenomenon whereby students from developing countries go to, say,

Europe for their education, are seduced by the style of living they find there and fail to return home.

Several drafts of a paper embodying thoughts along these lines circulated in the Secretariat before we were ready to put firm proposals to the Fund's Board of Representatives. This was composed of all high commissioners and a senior official from the British Foreign and Commonwealth Office. I was apprehensive before the meeting, but the paper was approved with little discussion. George Kidd, Managing Director of the CFTC, scribbled me a note as the Board moved on to the next item. 'Congratulations,' it read. 'You're in business.' I did not know it at the time, but the next 15 years of my working life were to be spent in inaugurating, running and developing the programme which the Board had approved.

Notes

1 Arnold Smith with Clyde Sanger, *Stitches in time: the Commonwealth in world politics* (London: André Deutsch, 1981), pp. 4–5. This book gives a blow-by-blow account of Arnold Smith's tenure of office as Commonwealth Secretary-General.
2 Quoted in *ibid.*, p. 10.
3 John Glasheen, *St James's, London* (Chichester: Phillimore & Co., 1987), pp. 75–7.
4 For the origins of this expression, see Smith with Sanger, *Stitches*, p. 267.
5 HMSO, *Report of the Commonwealth Education Conference*, Cmnd. 841 (London: HMSO, 1959).
6 *Report of the fifth Commonwealth Education Conference* (Canberra: Government Printer, 1971).
7 Smith with Sanger, *Stitches*, p. 13.
8 *Ibid.*, p. 14.

7

Human resource development and special assignments

In the period 1972–87, the Education and Training Programme I had helped to devise, and which the Board had blessed, took me to nearly every country in the Commonwealth, to scores of universities, to hundreds of technical institutions, to thousands of meetings. It gave me the opportunity to meet heads of government, ministers, vice-chancellors, principals, directors, bursars, civil servants of every grade, officers of non-governmental organizations, refugees, the high and the low, the good and the bad. Perhaps those whom I most enjoyed meeting were some of the 25,000 or so students who received CFTC scholarships in that time. From small beginnings there grew something in which we could all take pride.

My first task in 1972 was to inform governments of the programme and get their nominations for the award of the first scholarships. I also needed to gather information on as many as possible of the large numbers of post-secondary education and training institutions in the developing countries of the Commonwealth. All the universities were meticulously recorded in the Yearbook of the Association of Commonwealth Universities (of which my former boss, Hugh Springer, was now Secretary-General),[1] but nowhere was there a comprehensive listing of non-university tertiary institutions. The task before me was a daunting one. I had a secretary, but no other staff. Until such time as its operations expanded, the programme would be virtually a one-man band.

Each government had already been asked to appoint a ministry or department to liaise with the CFTC on education and training matters. These agencies, or points of contact as we called them, had a key role to play in the programme's operations. In many countries our point of contact was a ministry of economic development or ministry of manpower development. Some countries nominated their Ministry of Education for the task. Others chose the Ministry of Foreign Affairs or their Establishment Division. The programme was to depend heavily on the points of contact for a variety of services. As sending countries, the points of contact were to be responsible for providing information on priority training requirements, for defining the kinds of training required, for selecting students and trainees and helping them to obtain passports, tickets, visas, etc. As receiving countries, the points of contact would be responsible for giving information on their training institutions, for placing students and trainees from other countries in appropriate institutions, recommending suitable rates of allowances to be paid to foreign students, sometimes paying those allowances on our behalf, and generally safeguarding their welfare. Since the successful operation of the programme would depend so heavily on the efficiency and co-operative attitude of the points of contact, it was important that I should get to know them. They needed to be able to put a face to the signature at the bottom of the numerous circulars and letters which, in the first few weeks, I despatched to Commonwealth capitals.

I thus embarked on a series of 'sell the programme' peregrinations around the Commonwealth. I had been invited to take part in a seminar on education planning in New Zealand. I could justify my attendance only if my going could be combined with other work. En route to Wellington, therefore, I visited our points of contact in Delhi, Colombo and Singapore. On my way back, I stopped in Suva to visit the university and other institutions and to talk to the Ministry of Foreign Affairs, our point of contact. Next came West Africa. In two busy weeks, I 'did' the Gambia, Ghana, Nigeria and Sierra Leone. Southern Africa – Botswana, Lesotho and Swaziland – came next. After that I went to the Caribbean, concentrating on the 'big five', Guyana, Trinidad and Tobago, Barbados, Jamaica and Bahamas. Then it was time for East Africa and Mauritius, followed by a sweep through the Pacific. 'How exciting,' said friends and neighbours when they saw me between trips. 'You're really one of the jet set now,' said others (a particularly stupid and meaningless expression I have always thought). In fact, if the truth were known, so much travel was very hard work, very exhausting and very tedious. The more trips I made, the more wearisome it became. There are those who are excited by airports, who thrill as their 747 gathers speed down the runway and rises into the air, who really enjoy their flight, and who marvel at the new sights, sounds and smells which greet them at their destination. Good luck to such people; they should count themselves fortunate. I suspect they do not travel often, at least, not on business. For many of us, air travel means hanging around airports because of delayed or cancelled flights, being treated like a sheep, having insufficient legroom during long flights, eating indifferent food, coping with unwelcoming and inefficient customs and immigration officials, staying in over-priced hotels. I exaggerate, of course, but only a little. The first time my travels took me round the world, I was quite excited. The tenth time, I found it distinctly tiresome, particularly when sitting in a cramped position for several hours precipitated a deep vein thrombosis in my leg.

It was not long before the barrage of letters and circulars and my frenetic travel programme began to bear fruit. Information poured in on polytechnics, technical colleges and a wide variety of other training institutions in the developing countries. It became clear that just about every training need imaginable could be met, from accountancy, advertising, air traffic control, animal husbandry and apiculture to water engineering, weights and measures, welding, wood technology and wool production. All the data was systematized, edited and put together in a directory which was sent to our points of contact for wide distribution. This ensured that they had at their fingertips details of over 400 institutions of good quality which were able and willing to accept students from other developing countries of the Commonwealth. The first students to be put forward for awards were nominated by the Establishments Secretary of the Gambia. Next came a batch from St Lucia in the Caribbean, closely followed by a dozen or more forms from Swaziland. Soon the trickle became a steady flow. It looked as if the programme was taking off.

George Kidd agreed that I needed an assistant. We advertised and received large numbers of applications. I sent a copy of the advertisement to a young man, James Allie, who had been very helpful when I visited Sierra Leone where he was a senior assistant secretary in the Ministry of Development. James applied for the post and was short-listed. He interviewed well and was offered the job. His proved to be an excellent appointment. He was good at appraising requests for assistance, quick at dealing with large amounts of paper, and highly successful at getting on with people. He was a bundle of energy and good humour, who brought high spirits and laughter into the sometimes stuffy corridors of Marlborough House. I gave James responsibility for developing the programme in Africa. As the work expanded Sabanayagam Mahendra, a very experienced Sri Lankan working with the Colombo Plan Bureau, joined us to look after Asia, and Paul Sotutu from Fiji, with a good record both in teaching and in development administration, came on secondment from his government to handle the Pacific region. A highly conscientious and hard-working New Zealander, Garry Milne, was Project Officer for the Caribbean. It was a small team. It lacked a woman, but was otherwise well-balanced. Without letting go of the reins, I encouraged each of them to be bold and innovative in developing the programme in his region. When requests arrived from a point of contact, the appropriate regional officer would appraise them. He would consult where necessary colleagues in the specialized divisions of the Secretariat, or outside the Secretariat, and would then bring his recommendations, with preliminary cost estimates to me for discussion. Initially, I sought the endorsement of the Managing Director for my view on an application. As time went on, however, he came to trust my judgement and was content to leave decisions to me. It was always understood that where points of principle were involved, or where the proposed expenditure on a project was above a certain figure, the Managing Director's approval would be obtained before the project went ahead. By keeping the appraisal procedure simple, although rigorous, we avoided long delays in processing applications for assistance. Delays, we knew, would frustrate and irritate governments, students and institutions. It was a pleasant surprise to find that we had built up a reputation for flexibility and speed of response.

Before long, we reached a point where the main constraint on the programme's activities was not a shortage of applications or a shortage of staff but a shortage of financial resources. The CFTC received its funds from voluntary contributions made each year by member governments. Canada and Britain (in that order) were the main contributors, followed by Australia, New Zealand, Nigeria and India. All governments gave something, although in the case of some of the smaller and poorer countries, their contributions were only a few thousand pounds. Since all countries contributed, the usual distinction made by aid programmes between givers and receivers was, if not removed completely, considerably blurred. After a slow start, contributions to the fund reached £4 million in 1975. This was divided between the three programmes through which CFTC initially operated. Half the resources were allocated to the General Technical Assistant Programme. GTA, as it was known, made available to governments the services of 'experts'in a wide range of economic and social development fields. The other 50 per cent was shared between the Export Market Development Programme, which provided technical assistance geared to the expansion of a country's exports, and the Education and Training Programme. In 1975, we could report that Education and Training had used its share, amounting to a little over a million pounds, to provide scholarships for more than 1,100 students and trainees, drawn from 35 countries.[2]

We could point to some interesting examples of the kinds of projects which the Education and Training Programme was supporting. The largest single project had been the training in India of 25 technicians from Tanzania who, on their return home, would be responsible for promoting small-scale industries in rural areas. Most awards had been made for single trainees or for small groups. Malawi, for instance, had been helped to send three telecommunications technicians for training in Malaysia. Three St Lucians had begun diploma courses at the East Caribbean Institute of Agriculture and Forestry in Trinidad and Tobago. Students from Zambia had attended a forecaster's course in meteorology in Nairobi. A group of young men from Papua New Guinea were taking nautical courses at the Honiara Technical Institute in the Solomon Islands, and in Swaziland, 43 trainees from 13 countries had successfully completed courses in farm management. Bachelor degree students from several countries were being supported in practical subjects such as agriculture, electrical engineering, forestry, geology, meteorology, mining and veterinary science.

We could give several examples of the support provided for non-formal types of training. A mining engineer from Lesotho, for instance, had received practical training in mine safety and explosives in Zambia's copper mines. A young accountant from Western Samoa had spent three months in the office of the Auditor-General, Malaysia. A produce inspector from Malawi had gained experience in food storage methods in Kenya. An estate manager from Dominica had studied the processing of citrus fruits in Cyprus. A scheme supported by the programme in the Caribbean, with the object of improving teaching standards in that region, had enabled 24 teacher training college tutors to spend three months on attachments to the University of the West Indies.

It was a good start and provided a pattern for the future development of the programme. It showed that technical co-operation between developing countries, or TCDC, about which the United Nations were starting to get excited, could work very successfully. In his last report to heads of government before retiring, Arnold Smith pointed with justifiable pride to the success achieved by the CFTC in its short existence. Already, he claimed, it had proved itself 'by a long way the most cost-effective channel for multilateral economic assistance'.[3] He pointed to the indisputable fact that, as a percentage of overall expenditure, CFTC's administration costs were much lower than those of United Nations agencies. Smith urged the major donors to the fund to increase their contributions. This plea was taken up eloquently by Sonny Ramphal when he took over as Secretary-General in July 1975.

Ramphal came to Marlborough House with a glowing reputation. Whereas Arnold Smith, with a civil service and diplomatic service background, was a cautious, sometimes diffident, man and kept a fairly low profile, Ramphal was ebullient, ambitious and charismatic. He rapidly established himself as 'Mr Commonwealth', a role to which Arnold Smith never aspired. He exuded confidence, even when troubled by doubts. It was Arnold Smith's misfortune that while he was Secretary-General, the Commonwealth suffered one crisis after another. When not simply ignoring the Commonwealth, the press speculated on its imminent dissolution. Ramphal soon changed that. 'It is no longer relevant to discuss whether the Commonwealth has a future,' he said magisterially. 'The urgent need is for a debate on where the Commonwealth can lead the rest of the world.'[4] Good, stirring stuff. We all held our heads a little higher.

Ramphal had a good background for a secretary-general.[5] His great-grandmother was transported from India to British Guiana in the 1860s to work as an indentured labourer. Shridath Surendraneth Ramphal was born in Georgetown in 1928, the son of a teacher. After doing his secondary education in British Guiana, he read law and qualified as a barrister in London. He first worked as a civil servant in the Legal Department in British Guiana and then with the Federal Government of the West Indies. When the federation broke up, he practised as a barrister in Jamaica. As Guyana approached independence, he accepted the invitation of Prime Minister Forbes Burnham to return home to become Attorney-General and to draft Guyana's independence constitution of 1966. In 1972, he became Foreign Minister and in the following year was made Minister of Justice as well. In the meantime, he was establishing a reputation for himself as an advocate of Caribbean regional integration and of Caribbean solidarity with the rest of the Third World through the Non-aligned Movement and the Group of 77. His very considerable negotiating skills were mobilized when the developing countries of Africa, the Caribbean and the Pacific entered into protracted and complex negotiations with the European Economic Community. These led to the first Lomé Convention. Ramphal's sharp mind and silver tongue enabled him to play a central role in welding the ACP countries, as they were called, into a unified negotiating group. He was spokesman and negotiator for all the ACP countries on the trade regime which formed the centrepiece of the Lomé Convention. He was made a Knight Bachelor in 1969 but made it clear that he still wished to be known as Mr Ramphal. The outside world referred to him as Sonny. In the Secretariat, we addressed him as 'SG'.

We had held Arnold Smith in high regard. Now we had to get to know the new man. Ramphal impressed us all as a leader of quality. You did not need to spend long in his presence to realize that here was a man of great ability, formidably intelligent and highly articulate, who would drive himself to the limit for a cause in which he believed, and who would expect high standards of efficiency and loyalty from his staff. He was concerned for the welfare of Secretariat staff and was mostly jovial and caring in his relationships with us. At the same time, he could be tough and ruthless when necessary. His interests, we soon discovered, lay in weighty issues on the international stage rather than in the day-to-day administration of the Secretariat. This would not have mattered had he been prepared to delegate. He preferred, however, to keep many matters in his own hands rather than to entrust them to his two deputies. Since he was frequently out of the country for considerable periods, this meant that decisions on comparatively minor matters could be delayed for unreasonable periods. In spite of this, he was an outstanding Secretary-General. When Kurt Waldheim finally and reluctantly came to the end of his term of office as Secretary-General of the United Nations, Ramphal would have made an excellent successor. By then, however, he had expressed contentious views which had won him enemies as well as friends and his candidature never seriously got off the ground.

The Secretariat gave Ramphal a platform from which to involve himself in issues of global concern. He played a leading part, for instance, in the work of the Brandt Independent Commission on International Development Issues. He was also a member of Olaf Palme's Commission on Disarmament and Security, the Independent Commission on International Humanitarian Issues and of the World Commission on the Environment and Development. This helped place the Commonwealth in the vanguard of international efforts to make the global society safer and more equitable. The fact that the Secretary-General was recognized as a person of international stature enhanced the reputation of the Secretariat and gave us all a good feeling.

I first got to know something about Ramphal as a man when I went with him to two meetings in Canada. He had agreed to open

217

a seminar at Regina University in Saskatchewan on links between universities and industry. It was not a subject in which he had much interest. He accepted the invitation only because he was going to be in Canada at the time on other business. I had drafted a speech for him but he was unhappy with parts of it. He called me to his hotel bedroom at 8 o'clock in the morning. Still in his pyjamas, he was sitting at the portable typewriter he always took with him when he travelled. 'I'm stuck,' he told me. 'I don't know how well what you have given me will go down, and I can't think of anything better to say.'

I tried to reassure him. 'The speech I've written is professionally sound. It may be a bit lacking in humour, but it will be appreciated by the people here.' He looked a bit dubious but eventually agreed to leave the speech as it was. That evening he delivered the speech with his usual panache. At the end, the audience applauded enthusiastically. Clearly, he had made a hit. He gave me a great wink and a broad smile. Thereafter, we got on well. He was content to leave the running of the Education and Training Programme in my hands. For this I was very grateful. As Secretary-General he received numerous letters from eminent people in governments overseas, high commissions in London and elsewhere, seeking scholarships for their children, nephews, nieces and cousins. There were times when Ramphal must have been sorely tempted to instruct me to award scholarships to those who sought his favour. Not once, however, did he attempt to bring any pressure to bear on me. His secretary would pass the soliciting letters to me. I would reply direct or would draft an answer for Ramphal's consideration. At no time did he query my decisions which, in nearly every instance, were negative.

Ramphal's arrival meant that two of the five top posts in the Secretariat were held by people from the Caribbean. James Maraj, Assistant Secretary-General, removed any embarrassment this might have caused by accepting an invitation to be Vice-Chancellor of the University of the South Pacific. His going was a real loss to the Secretariat. He was imaginative and innovative and I had been glad to seek his advice when I ran into difficulties. He had defined a clear role for the post of Assistant Secretary-General and had

218

brought a sense of purpose to the post which his immediate predecessors had lacked.[6]

Among these was Yusuf Lule, a former principal of Makerere University and Minister of Education in Uganda. Lule never fitted into the Secretariat's modus operandi. One reason was that he made frequent visits to Dar-es-Salaam where he met other Ugandans in exile and helped plan how best to end the bloody regime of Idi Amin. The latter had led a military coup d'état which had overthrown President Milton Obote while he was attending the Singapore heads of government meeting in 1971. Lule left the Secretariat to take up the post of Secretary-General of the Association of African Universities. I met him a few times in Accra. He telephoned me in London one day in 1978 and asked if we could meet. We had lunch together and I asked him when he thought that Milton Obote might be restored to power. 'Why do you keep talking about Obote?' he asked. 'There are several of us who could be President.' I was taken aback to realize that he had political ambitions for himself. He had made no mark in the Secretariat; he was nearer 70 than 60. I found it hard to believe that he was strong enough to make a success of being President of Uganda. In due course, Tanzanian troops invaded Uganda and Amin was overthrown. Yusuf Lule was installed as President in April 1979. In the Secretariat, we wondered how we could have under-estimated his ability. But it was not to last. The Uganda National Liberation Front which Lule headed was a coalition of disparate groups who soon fell out. In the turbulent situation that followed Amin's hasty departure, Lule's attempts to provide strong leadership and to prepare for Uganda's rehabilitation aroused such animosities that he was replaced within two months by Godfrey Binaisa. He, in turn, was overthrown within less than a year and the way was clear for the return of Milton Obote. Uganda then embarked on yet another chapter of bloody and corrupt tribalism and civil war. Yusuf Lule died a sad and disappointed man. It was not until I attended a memorial service for him in London in 1985 that I fully realized how highly regarded he was by many Ugandans, especially those from Buganda, and in what affection he was held. It was clear that we in the Secretariat, where he had seemed so ill at ease, had seriously misjudged him.

The expansion of the CFTC, and with it the growth of the Education and Training Programme, was seriously checked in 1979 and 1980. In these years, the fund's income fell sharply. Reduced resources coupled with increased training costs and higher air fares meant that the number of scholarships we could give dropped significantly. Knowing the needs of governments for trained personnel in key sectors of their economies, I found it acutely depressing to have to turn down requests for the training of agricultural assistants, health workers, technicians and managers who were required in order to increase productivity, raise living standards or improve administrative efficiency. It was equally galling to have to reduce support for the training activities of regional bodies and non-governmental organizations.

By 1983, happily, we had recovered quite a lot of the lost ground and were able to give scholarships to over 1,500 students, a figure which increased steadily. By this time we had made arrangements with a number of regional institutions to support their students on a block grant basis. These institutions provided training in sectors which were important to all or many of the countries in a region. The Mananga Agricultural Management Centre in Swaziland was one such institution; it provided courses in agricultural management to which all Commonwealth countries in Africa (and elsewhere) wished to send their farm managers and agricultural supervisors. The Caribbean Meteorological Institute in Barbados, the Asian-Pacific Institute for Broadcasting Development in Malaysia, the Telecommunications Training Centre in Fiji and the Cyprus Forestry College were others among a group of 15 institutions which participated in the scheme. We gave scholarship funds to the institutions and left it to them to award the scholarships in accordance with guidelines I had previously agreed with them. This arrangement speeded up the consideration of applications and the award of scholarships. Both the institutions themselves and the nominating governments benefited. The advantage to us was that our administrative workload was lightened and we could keep our overheads down.

One of the many controversial actions of Mrs Thatcher's Government in the early 1980s was to make British universities increase very substantially the fees which they charged students from overseas. Students from oil-rich countries in the Middle East had little difficulty in paying the new fees but many Commonwealth developing countries could no longer afford to send their students to Britain. Several British institutions approached us for scholarships in order that they could continue to accept students from their traditional partners in the Commonwealth. We could not provide the scholarships, tenable in Britain, which they wanted. Instead, we encouraged them, where it was feasible to do so, to take their courses to the developing countries. Liverpool School of Tropical Medicine, for instance, ran courses in tropical community medicine and health for non-physician health staff. Most of their students – nurses, rural health officials, public health inspectors and nutritionists – came from West Africa. When staff from Liverpool asked us to give scholarships so that they could continue to run the course in Liverpool, Kihumbu Thairu, our medical adviser, suggested that the course should be transferred to the medical faculty of the University of Sierra Leone. To begin with, the Liverpool people were very sceptical but were willing to give the proposal a trial. A package of support was put together: the British Council met the expenses of the Liverpool team of lecturers and paid for equipment and text-books; the CFTC, through the Education and Training Programme, gave scholarships to the students (from the Gambia, Ghana, Nigeria and Sierra Leone) who attended, and, through the General Technical Assistance Programme, covered the expenses of tutors from West African institutions. The first course was a great success; the cost was considerably less than if the students had gone to Liverpool; the contribution made by the indigenous staff and the use made of local materials, clinical cases and epidemiological situations made the course more relevant to West African needs. The Liverpool School had no hesitation about running subsequent courses in Sierra Leone. The success of this experiment helped us to persuade other British institutions to 'export' their specialist courses.

In addition to responding to requests from governments to send students on existing courses, colleagues and I endeavoured to identify training needs which were common to several countries but were not being adequately met. In these circumstances, CFTC

221

would assist an institution, by providing expertise and scholarships, to plan and mount a suitable training programme. The Institute of Financial Management in Madras, India, for example, was helped to run a series of courses in aspects of financial management for people from several countries in Africa. This was but one of numerous institutions in India which participated in the programme's activities. Among the Commonwealth's developing countries, India has an unparalleled range of educational institutions and training facilities. Among its 100 and more universities, there are those which can match in academic excellence and up-to-date facilities the best universities in the world. We made full use of the education and training opportunities offered by India right across the development spectrum. At one time, for instance, we had students in Indian institutions studying forestry, sugar-cane technology, poultry husbandry, rice research, inland fisheries, education planning, manpower planning, industrial management and the design of air-conditioning plants. The fact that we were able to place so many students in Indian universities and colleges was due to the Indian Government's willingness to share its facilities and also to the work of Jim Houston, one of our chief project officers. Jim was untiring in his efforts to foster good relations with Indian institutions, in coping with New Delhi's bureaucracy, and in helping to devise tailor-made programmes to meet specific training needs.

The Commonwealth Secretariat has no offices overseas. All its staff are based in London. It was, therefore, very difficult for us to keep in touch with, and to counsel, the students whom we were supporting. Monitoring the progress of students was, of course, an essential part of our work. Programme staff maintained an extensive correspondence wth students. We accumulated a lot of experience in anticipating difficulties, in resolving problems before they reached crisis point, and in providing long-distance counselling. We received reports regularly from both students and their institutions and this information was supplemented by face-to-face meetings with staff during overseas visits.

In my office, a map of the Commonwealth dominated one wall. Coloured pins indicated the locations of the students whom we were supporting. Sometimes I sat and looked at the map and thought: 'Those pins represent more than 2,000 students. Someone, somewhere, is in trouble.' In fact, the vast majority of the students completed their study programmes without running into difficulties and returned home without causing us any anxiety. But inevitably there were some who had problems, whether academic, financial or personal. Their files grew thick as the months went by.

There was the enigma of Emmanuel, a student from West Africa, who was quite incapable of using a computer.[7] In virtually every branch of scientific research nowadays, familiarity with computer language and ability to work with a range of software is essential. Emmanuel, otherwise a very intelligent young agricultural officer, had a mental blockage every time he sat down at a keyboard. He touched the keys as if the computer was unclean or contained an evil spirit. The university where he was studying gave him every help and encouragement but eventually Emmanuel had to be transferred to a course of study which did not have a statistical component.

Jeremiah's problem was different. He came from a small Caribbean island and was sent to Jamaica to train as an electrical technician. There seemed nothing very special about either his appearance or his personality. In course of time, however, it became clear that there was something irresistibly special about young Jeremiah. 'Everything here is fine,' he assured us. 'I just love Jamaicans.' Indeed, he did. First one and then another of his fellow students succumbed to his charms and became pregnant. At the request of the principal, we had to repatriate Jeremiah hastily.

While we had no sympathy for the amorous and irresponsible Jeremiah, we had a lot for Fatma, a vivacious but naive young lady from a country in Asia. She came from a poor family and had rarely strayed far from her village. She was nominated by her government to study in Singapore. The contrast between the poverty of her home and the affluence of Singapore must have been startling. She had six months' living allowance in her handbag. In one glorious shopping spree, she spent it all, buying gifts, not for herself, but for her family back home. She had nothing left to live on. In shame and despair, she wrote to admit her foolishness. Rather than see what seemed to be a promising career ruined, we

223

had no alternative but to make a telegraphic transfer of money to her and to follow it up with a stern letter of admonition. It was a very pleasant surprise when, a year or so later, she repaid the money.

And then there was Abraham. Poor, dear Abraham. Abraham was a Namibian refugee and his story perhaps belongs more to the next chapter than to this. He was one of a group of Namibians whom we were helping to train as car mechanics in Malta. He first came to my notice when, one Good Friday, Malta's High Commissioner in London telephoned me at home to say that Abraham was suffering from acute kidney failure. He needed dialysis. Unfortunately, there were very few dialysis machines in Malta. Patients were dialysed only to keep them alive for a transplant operation. Could I guarantee that Abraham would be given a transplant? If so, he could be dialysed. Without such a guarantee, there was nothing the hospital could do to help. 'I'll have to consult my colleagues,' I told the High Commissioner. 'I'll let you know the answer after the holiday weekend.'

'But, Peter,' said the High Commissioner, 'my people tell me that he won't live more than 24 hours unless he's given dialysis.'

I had no alternative. 'Go ahead, then. Put him on the machine. We'll arrange a kidney transplant as soon as we can.'

It was some weeks before Abraham was well enough to be flown to London. He was not eligible, of course, to be treated under the National Health Service. We arranged for him to go to a private hospital for dialysis three times a week while the hospital looked for a replacement kidney. We discovered, to our dismay, that the only way in which we could obtain a kidney was by buying one from a privately-run organ bank in Houston, Texas. A kidney would cost US$10,000. We had by now passed the point of no return. So much money had been spent already that there could be no question of denying Abraham the opportunity of having an operation which would enable him to live a comparatively normal life. We swallowed our reservations about the organ bank and placed an order for a kidney. Twice kidneys were flown across the Atlantic for Abraham. Twice they turned out to be unsuitable. The third time, the match was perfect. Abraham had his operation and made a good recovery. The Christian Fellowship at the Secretariat,

224

which met every week for Bible study and prayer, prayed regularly for Abraham. They were delighted when I brought him along to one of the meetings. Their pleasure was shared by the Swedish International Development Authority which was making a major contribution to the costs of our scholarship programme for Namibians and generously offered to share the costs of Abraham's treatment.

Armed with a supply of tablets which would help ensure that the transplanted kidney was not rejected, Abraham returned to Malta. He completed his course successfully and was posted to Lusaka where he helped maintain SWAPO's fleet of vehicles. He married the charming young lady who had stood by him throughout his long illness and convalescence. It seemed like a fairy-tale ending to a tense and traumatic story. But one of the conditions that Abraham had to observe was that he must keep clear of alcohol. He began to drink, first a little and then rather more. The kidney could not stand it. We learned that he was in Lusaka hospital, then that he had been transferred to Zimbabwe. Terry Dormer went to see him in Harare hospital. The damage was irreversible; there was nothing more the doctors could do. Abraham died, leaving us all with a feeling of great sadness.

But life, of course, went on. We devised a range of questionnaires to determine as systematically and objectively as possible the relevance, effectiveness and impact of each training project in the light of its objectives. All projects of more than three months' duration were evaluated by the students themselves and their employers six months after completion. A representative sample was re-evaluated two years later. It was encouraging to find that, in nearly every case, the training objectives had been achieved, the main needs of the trainees had been met, and that they were employed in posts in which the knowledge and experience they had gained was being put to good use. It was also good to find that the pass rate in examinations usually averaged 95 per cent. Perhaps most important of all, we confirmed that all the students – apart from the unfortunate few who died while overseas – returned to their home countries when they had completed their study programmes. In 15 years only one student refused to go home and was thus 'lost'.

Occasionally we attempted to make an evaluation of the Education and Training Programme as a whole, as distinct from assessing individual projects. We brought together representatives of governments, education and training institutions, and regional organizations at meetings in Nairobi (twice), Bridgetown (Barbados) and Apia (Western Samoa). These meetings took a critical look at the operations of the programme and recommended ways in which it could be made more responsive to countries' needs. They were useful in suggesting how we could streamline the administration of the programme. They also pinpointed areas in which the training facilities of the region were inadequate, and made proposals for filling the gaps, either by the Secretariat or by the multilateral and bilateral technical assistance agencies which were represented at the meetings.

One gap which was crying out to be filled was in industrial training. In many countries, people were graduating as civil engineers, for instance, or electrical technicians. They had extensive textbook knowledge but little or no practical experience. The lack of such experience was a handicap to the industrial development of their countries. As a contribution to meeting this need, we drafted a programme which aimed at providing practical training and experience in industry for people from the public, parastatal and private sectors. The main beneficiaries would be technologists and technicians but training officers, craftsmen, supervisors, managers and trade union officials would also be eligible for assistance. I wanted the new programme to offer opportunities for skills development and for familiarization with advanced technologies which were not available in the trainees' home countries. The programme had to be planned in such a way that we would be able to make use of the facilities of the more industrially advanced among the developing countries, especially India, and also of those in the more developed countries, Australia, Britain, Canada and New Zealand.

Obtaining approval for the programme took longer than expected and involved my attending three meetings of Commonwealth ministers of labour and employment at the International Labour Organization (ILO) headquarters in Geneva. By the end of 1985, however, we had the approval of heads of government for the establishment of what was to be known as the Commonwealth Industrial Training and Experience Programme, CITEP for short, as a means of helping countries to improve their industrial performance. It was appropriate that India should provide the Chief Project Officer, Raj Nagarajan. He had extensive experience in industry, management and training and was the right man to get CITEP off the ground. His discussions with ministries of industry and labour, parastatal organizations, small industries development organizations, chambers of industry and commerce, confederations of employers, trade unions and others made it clear that there was widespread and enthusiastic support for the new programme. I was confident that CITEP would soon develop as an important component in the service which the Secretariat provides to governments.

Colleagues in the Economic Affairs Division and the Industrial Development Unit were very helpful in getting CITEP approved and launched. I could find little support for another ambition I had – to get approval for a Commonwealth volunteer service. Several countries, including Australia, Britain, Canada and New Zealand, run volunteer programmes. There is also a United Nations Volunteer Programme and International Voluntary Service. Although there are differences between them the programmes have a common aim: they each provide an avenue whereby people can volunteer to share their skills and experience with people from other countries. At the same time, the programmes help the countries who receive the volunteers to implement development projects.

While working in Zambia I had met some British volunteers, young men and women who wanted to spend a year or two in Africa before going to university. The need for this kind of volunteer disappeared as the developing countries began to produce their own 'A' level students. Volunteer programmes adjusted to the changing needs and began to recruit volunteers who had already obtained their professional and technical qualifications and had some work experience.

The idea of a Commonwealth volunteer service came to me in October 1980 when I accompanied Sonny Ramphal to a Commonwealth Parliamentary Association conference in Lusaka. Before the conference, delegates had been given the chance of travelling in

227

some of Zambia's rural areas. One of the delegates from Malta, Dr Micallef, had made a point of visiting a number of rural clinics. He had been distressed, he told me, to find that they were not only short of medicines but they were also seriously understaffed. It was not uncommon for a poorly-qualified medical assistant to have to treat serious illnesses and injuries which required the attention of a medical practitioner. People were suffering unnecessarily, he said, because there were not enough doctors who were willing to work in the rural areas. He told me that he would be willing to return to Zambia on a voluntary basis and to work for some months in rural clinics. He would not require a salary, provided his expenses could be covered. Did the Commonwealth, asked Dr Micallef, have a scheme which would help him to work in Zambia as a volunteer? The answer was 'No'. We could employ him as a CFTC expert and pay him quite a generous salary. There was no way, however, that we could utilize him as a volunteer who did not require a salary. Here, clearly, was a ridiculous anomaly. I could imagine Alec Dickson, founder of Britain's Voluntary Service Overseas and Community Service Volunteers programmes, snorting with indignation and teasing me about it. I had been fortunate to get to know Alec during seminars in which we had both participated in Nairobi and Regina, Saskatchewan. He bubbled over with ideas and had enormous enthusiasm. He would certainly not let pass an opportunity like this.

Over a cup of tea I helped Dr Micallef work out a little speech. The next day he delivered it to the conference. 'Developing countries,' he said,

are short of skills and expertise in many areas of development. Governments find that the cost of employing expatriate experts is often prohibitive. Sources of technical assistance cannot meet all the needs. We know that there is a vast reservoir of professional expertise in the Commonwealth but, for financial reasons, developing countries cannot make use of it. Some of that expertise, I believe, is ready to make itself available on a voluntary basis. I, for instance, would be willing to come back to Zambia as a volunteer, to work with my Zambian colleagues, and to put my medical training at the disposal of the Zambian people. I believe there are many professional people, like myself, who would be glad of the opportunity to serve as volunteers in Zambia and other developing countries. Can we begin to think in terms of a Commonwealth volunteer service? Such a service might include doctors, dentists, teachers, agriculturalists, economists, architects, engineers, lawyers, journalists, accountants. The list of skills that could be utilized is almost endless. On investigation, the idea may prove to be unworkable or too costly. But it is my belief that the suggestion is worth exploring. I am convinced that the fund of goodwill towards the developing countries has not yet been fully tapped.

Dr Micallef went on to suggest that the Commonwealth Secretary-General should be asked to look into the feasibility of setting up a Commonwealth volunteer service under the auspices of the Secretariat. The conference agreed.

Back at Marlborough House, the idea found few friends at a senior level. The Secretariat, it was felt, could not propose such a major initiative; the proposal should come from a member government. As far as I am aware, no government has so far put forward such a proposal. But if the Commonwealth Volunteer Service is destined to remain only a pipedream, I still believe it is an idea which has many merits. I am confident that a service could be devised which would not simply replicate other volunteer programmes but would have a distinctive Commonwealth flavour and orientation. Of course, there would be problems over the recruitment of the volunteers, the matching of the volunteers with requests received from governments, the briefing of the volunteers, the provision of support services in the field, and, of major importance, the funding of the service. But it would not be beyond the wit of the Secretariat to resolve these problems if the will was there.

After I left the Secretariat, Evelyn and I spent two years as mature VSO volunteers in a developing country. This experience convinced me of the value of volunteering both for the volunteers and for the receiving country. By failing to provide a practical channel through which men and women who are committed to the ideals of co-operation and interdependence can involve themselves

229

in Commonwealth affairs and share their skills and experience with people in other countries, the Commonwealth is missing a big opportunity. And development projects in many countries, especially the small countries which constitute much of the Commonwealth's membership, are languishing for lack of the very assistance which volunteers are willing to offer.

A two-tier system of remuneration operates within the Secretariat. Most members of the staff are employed on local conditions of service; their salaries are based on those of officers of a similar grade in the British Civil Service. The top 10 per cent or so of Secretariat staff, from Assistant Director up to Secretary-General, are known as 'diplomatic' officers. As a director I was technically a diplomatic officer and my name duly appeared in the Diplomatic List. Being British, I could not enjoy, of course, the privileges and immunities of a foreign diplomat and I was not entitled to the same allowances as colleagues from overseas. In fact it cost the Secretariat two and a half times as much to employ a director from, say, Australia or Zambia as it did to employ me. Not that I had any reason to complain. My salary was enough to ensure that we could live reasonably comfortably. One of the few perks that my job conferred was being able to go to garden parties at Buckingham Palace. Each year the Queen gives four or five of these parties. Some 8,000 people are invited to each, so there is nothing very exclusive about going. Nevertheless, most people regard it as a signal honour to be invited. Ladies go to a great deal of expense in buying new outfits to wear; men hire morning suits. Evelyn and I were able to go a dozen or more times. Ann, our daughter, became eligible at the age of 18 (to the astonishment of her friends and the irritation of her brothers) and she came with us on three or four occasions. However often we went, it was still a thrill to receive the beautifully printed card: 'The Lord Chamberlain is commanded by Her Majesty to invite . . .' When we first went, the children assumed that the Queen and the Duke of Edinburgh had sat down together and made a list of those who were to be invited to have tea with them. 'Let's ask the Snelsons,' said the Queen. 'Good idea,' said the Duke and wrote down our names. They also assumed that the Queen stayed up late the night before the party and made all the sandwiches and cakes. When we slipped one or two goodies into Evelyn's handbag and took them home, they were regarded with considerable awe: here was a sandwich which the Queen herself had made!

If it was a thrill to receive the invitation, it was an even greater thrill to be driven down The Mall in one of the Secretariat's Daimlers and then to sweep past the curious spectators at the gates of Buckingham Palace and into the courtyard. Each year the routine was the same. From the terrace at the back of the palace, you have a splendid view of the gardens. In the centre is the main lawn where the Queen, the Duke, Prince Charles and, sometimes, the Queen Mother slowly make their way from one selected couple to another, chatting with each for a few minutes while hundreds form an avenue and watch from a discreet distance. On either side of the lawn are long open-sided marquees where tea, iced coffee, orange juice, tiny sandwiches and cakes are served by waitresses. To the right along the wall separating the palace grounds from Constitution Hill are magnificent herbaceous borders, beautifully maintained and ablaze with colour. It was our practice to walk along the borders, through the rose garden and to a leafier part of the garden where, in a clearing, lie two tennis courts and a large pool which is home to groups of colourful flamingoes. Away from the stiff formality of the lawn, some guests are smoking, some loosen their collars while many of the ladies are clearly wishing they had worn less stylish and more 'sensible' shoes. We come back to the lawn and reach the marquee reserved for members of the Diplomatic Corps. At the same time, the royal family arrive at the tent which they share with the heads of Diplomatic Missions. At 6 o'clock, it is all over; the Queen, the Duke and the other members of the royal party walk across the lawn to the palace, preceded by the Lord Chamberlain, while their guests politely applaud. Then it is time to join the departing throng, passing through the palace and the courtyard and returning to Marlborough House.

More exciting than the garden parties were the diplomatic receptions which the Queen gives each November. These are truly splendid occasions. Each embassy, high commission and international organization is entitled to nominate a specified number of members of staff to receive invitations. Ladies adorn themselves in long dresses; tails and white tie are *de rigueur* for the men. You are asked to arrive between 9.30 and 10 o'clock in the evening. A liveried footman opens your car door at the Grand Entrance and you are ushered up a richly carpeted staircase to the first floor. Champagne is served while you wait in the area assigned to your delegation. At a signal from one of the Gentlemen of the Household who are on duty, each delegation lines up as the Queen approaches. The Lord Chamberlain presents the leader of the delegation, in our case the Secretary-General, to the Queen. Her Majesty, wearing the royal blue sash of the Order of the Garter and with several miniature portraits of members of the royal family pinned to her ball gown, exchanges a few words with the Secretary-General and his wife, and with two other couples who are presented to her. She then moves on to the next delegation. The Duke of Edinburgh, looking faintly absurd in the breeches of the Order of the Garter, now approaches and the same procedure is followed. Other members of the royal family follow. The presentations over, you are free to go to the state dining room where a buffet supper is available. You can dance in the state ballroom where the band of one of the Guards regiments is playing, or simply wander around, bumping into cabinet ministers, church dignitaries and other notables. At midnight, you ask for your car to be called. A Secretariat Daimler soon appears at the Grand Entrance. A footman opens the door for you, salutes, and you slip quickly and easily from the fairy-tale world of Buckingham Palace to the reality of everyday life.

One year, the Secretary-General, the two Deputies and the two Assistant Secretaries-General were all away at a conference. As the senior Secretariat officer in London I had to lead the Secretariat group to the palace. Evelyn practised her curtsey and I rehearsed what I would have to say. I had a terrible fear that in presenting my colleagues to the Queen I would tread on her foot. Perhaps she would scream, the Lord Chamberlain would fling me to the floor, and I would be taken to the Tower of London! In the event, of course, it all went without a hitch. The Queen has enormous experience of meeting people and putting them at their ease, and there was never the slightest danger that I would tread on her toes. After the Queen came the Duke of Edinburgh, the Prince of Wales,

Princess Diana, Princess Alexandra and the Hon. Angus Ogilvy. It was a magical and memorable evening.

Deputising for the Secretary-General sometimes brought surprises. His private office asked me once to stand in for him at a ceremony at County Hall, Westminster, where a petition for the release from detention of Mrs Winnie Mandela was to be launched. 'Do I have to make a speech?' I asked.

'No, nothing like that,' his PA assured me. 'Just turn up and smile.'

Arriving at County Hall, I found the occasion was a press conference. I sat down among the newsgatherers. On the platform sat Illtyd Harrington, chairman of the Greater London Council, and Ken Livingstone, leader of the GLC. There was an empty chair beside them. I wondered idly who was to join them. I was suddenly conscious of Ken Livingstone waving at me and calling me to the platform. Aghast, I took my seat. My embarrassment deepened as I heard Livingstone say: 'The Commonwealth Secretary-General was to have addressed us this morning. He's been called away but has sent Peter Snelson in his place.' If ever there was a moment when I wished the floor would open and swallow me up, this was it. Fortunately, by a stroke of great good fortune, I had with me a copy of the communiqué which had been issued at the end of the last heads of government meeting. It contained several paragraphs on South Africa and the evils of apartheid. Around these I hastily concocted a short speech.

It was a relief when we moved on to the signing of the petition. 'I sign this on behalf of the six million people of London,' said Illtyd Harrington, and wrote his name. For one intoxicating moment I was tempted to upstage everyone and say: 'I sign on behalf of the billion people of the Commonwealth.' But my nerve failed and I simply signed on behalf of the Secretary-General. Ken Livingstone is a good publicist and had invited a fair number of people from the world of television and theatre. Over coffee, I enjoyed a conversation with Paul Eddington, alias the Right Honourable Jim Hacker of *Yes, Prime Minister*. Photographs were taken. When I took them home, the children said: 'Look, there's A, and there's B, and you never said that C was there.' Alas, A, B and C were not known to me, even though the family assured me that they were household names.

One of the particular pleasures of my work was that it brought me into regular contact with sections of what is known as the 'unofficial Commonwealth'. Some definitions must be attempted. The official Commonwealth may be said to comprise member governments, the Commonwealth Secretariat, the Commonwealth Foundation, and certain regional inter-governmental organizations such as the Caribbean Community Secretariat and the South Pacific Bureau for Economic Co-operation. The unofficial Commonwealth is not so easily defined. It is concerned with people rather than with governments. A conference held at Dalhousie University, Canada, in 1976, concluded that it consisted of 'the totality of non-governmental relations among the peoples of the Commonwealth'. That definition, though vague and question-begging, is probably as good as any. The fact is that the unofficial Commonwealth defies precise definition. It manifests itself in a multiplicity of personal and non-governmental links which crisscross the Commonwealth in almost every field of human endeavour. These links, particularly those which have come together, however loosely, in non-governmental organizations, constitute some of the strongest and most enduring strands in the Commonwealth fabric and make a powerful contribution to the vitality and cohesion of the association.

Perhaps the best organized of the non-governmental organizations, or NGOs as they are called, are the Commonwealth professional associations which operate on a pan-Commonwealth basis. For several years, I represented the Secretary-General on the Board of Trustees, subsequently Board of Governors, of the Commonwealth Foundation. John Chadwick, director of the Foundation for the first 14 years of its existence, had the foresight to persuade the board to assist more than 20 pan-Commonwealth professional bodies – comprising lawyers, medical doctors, veterinarians, journalists, librarians, human ecologists and so on – to get themselves properly organized.[8] Once that had been achieved, the professional associations were given assistance with their developmental activities. These included the holding of seminars and conferences, the publishing of learned journals and newsletters, and the delivery of educational and technical programmes. Most of the professional associations, such as the Commonwealth Association of Surveying and Land Economy, the Commonwealth Association of Architects and the Commonwealth Nurses Federation, are run very efficiently. They keep their members throughout the Commonwealth in touch with new trends in their fields; they contribute to the professional development of their members; and they put their expertise at the disposal of the official Commonwealth. The same is true, to a lesser extent, of the smaller NGOs which usually operate in their own countries and do not cover the whole Commonwealth.

NGOs are usually led, for no financial reward, by people with a lifetime of experience and who are totally dedicated to their profession. They are not hidebound by red tape; the best of them are flexible, pragmatic, imaginative, sometimes adventurous in their approach to problems. From a deep fund of enthusiasm, expertise and goodwill, they have much to offer the Commonwealth.

Most divisions in the Secretariat established and fostered informal relations with the NGOs operating in their fields of interest. In the Education and Training Programme, for instance, we found it valuable sometimes to seek the advice of NGOs in identifying suitable training places for students, in assessing the strengths and weaknesses of training institutions, and in utilizing their expertise in running short training courses. In return, we provided financial assistance for their training activities when the opportunity arose. The Forum of African Science Educators, based in Lagos, the Commonwealth Association of Polytechnics in Africa, working from Nairobi, the Commonwealth Association for the Education of Adults, with headquarters in Britain, and the Standing Conference of Supervisors of Schools in Southeast Asia and the Pacific, operating from Darwin, Australia, were samples of the NGOs we were able to assist.

The feasibility of making fuller use of the expertise and potential strength of the NGOs in development programmes and in increasing public understanding of the Commonwealth was explored at a conference held at Dalhousie University, Canada, in 1976. Subsequently, Sonny Ramphal appointed an Advisory Committee to propose 'concrete steps to promote mutually beneficial ties between the official and unofficial Commonwealth.'[9] Chief Emeka Anyaoku, Deputy Secretary-General at that time, and I represented the Secretariat. In its report, *From Governments to Grassroots*, the Committee addressed a series of recommendations to governments. They included one which caused hackles to rise in some capitals: 'Governments should recognise that the maintenance of the integrity and personality of NGOs is essential to a healthy society. They should consider ways of assisting them without infringing their independence, and convince them that such assistance is possible.' The Committee further recommended that a 'NGO desk' should be set up in the Secretariat for a trial period of three years, 'to serve as a central point of contact with Commonwealth NGO's and with NGO liaison units which might be set up by member governments.'[10]

Ten years later, when I left the Secretariat, the NGO desk had still not materialized. The fact is that there are stark differences among governments in their attitudes towards NGOs. In some countries, especially the older, more developed countries, NGOs often play a significant part in public life. They lobby ministers and members of parliament; they campaign through public meetings and the media; they criticize their governments for following what they perceive to be wrong policies or for being dilatory, parsimonious or corrupt. In these countries, NGOs are generally tolerated and even encouraged, provided they stay within the limits of the law. They are thought to provide healthy and constructive criticism which keeps the authorities on their toes. By contrast, other governments, with different traditions, and faced with different political and social circumstances, tend to regard NGOs with suspicion and even hostility. 'Not everyone,' as Sonny Ramphal diplomatically observed, 'accepts the legitimacy of the NGO as a pressure group on Government. An adversary relationship between governments and NGOs that in some countries is regarded as healthy and productive will in others be regarded as inimical to good government.'[11] Put another way, in some countries, governments are not prepared to tolerate criticism and therefore want NGOs kept firmly under control.

Since there was not a consensus to set up a NGO desk in the

Secretariat, the proposal was dropped. Successive heads of government meetings contented themselves with declaring that NGOs were an underutilized resource and that means should be found of promoting further collaboration between the official and unofficial Commonwealth. There were plenty of fine words but we seemed to be getting nowhere.

It was the Royal Commonwealth Society in London which kept the pot boiling. Periodically the society convened meetings of NGOs based in Britain and pressed for the greater involvement of NGOs in official Commonwealth programmes, including the Commonwealth Fund for Technical Co-operation. Two practical measures were proposed. The first was for the setting up in each country of NGO liaison units, linked internationally, to assist development programmes. The second proposal was for the allocation of additional resources to the Commonwealth Foundation, specifically to support the developmental work of NGOs.

In'oke Faletau of Tonga, who became Director of the Commonwealth Foundation in 1985, enthusiastically supported these proposals. He persuaded his board of governors to agree to support a series of regional meetings to arrange for the setting up of NGO liaison units at national and regional levels. The creation of these liaison units means that the unofficial Commonwealth is less amorphous and better organized than it was before. It has facilitated the forging of closer links between the official and unofficial Commonwealth. Much remains to be done but it is a mark of the progress that has been made that a Commonwealth NGO Forum, the first of its kind, was held in Harare, Zimbabwe, in 1991, just three months before Commonwealth heads of government met in the same city. Both Robert Mugabe, President of Zimbabwe, and Chief Emeka Anyaoku, Commonwealth Secretary-General, publicly stressed the need to strengthen the role of NGOs at the grassroots level in the social and economic development of Commonwealth countries. Gradually, I am sure, their words will be translated into action. Such action, which uses the vigour and skills of the NGOs in the interest of development, can only be beneficial.

Every so often, I was asked to undertake special assignments. In October 1978, Tuvalu was to celebrate its independence. The Government had applied to join the Commonwealth as a special member. This meant that it would have all the benefits of Commonwealth membership but its prime minister would not be able to attend meetings of heads of government. As Secretary-General, Sonny Ramphal was invited to attend the independence celebrations. He was unable to go and asked me to represent him. I had already been to the South Pacific half a dozen times and had visited Fiji, the New Hebrides (now Vanuatu), Nauru, the Solomon Islands, Tonga and Western Samoa. I was due to attend a meeting of the Development Board of the University of the South Pacific in September and could easily adjust my programme to take in Tuvalu – once I could find it on the map!

Tuvalu was the Ellice Islands part of the Gilbert and Ellice Islands. These two groups of atolls were ruled by Britain as a single colony. As independence approached, the Polynesian Ellice Islanders made it clear that they no longer wished to be associated with their Micronesian neighbours in the Gilberts. In 1979, the Gilbertese would achieve their independence as citizens of Kiribati. First, the Ellice Islanders would celebrate the winning of their own nationhood. By any standards, Tuvalu is a microstate. It consists of nine coral atolls scattered over hundreds of thousands of square miles of the Pacific Ocean. The most northerly atoll is 600 miles north of Fiji. The total land area is 15 square miles, give or take one or two, depending on the state of the tide. The highest point above sea level is six feet. If the so-called 'greenhouse effect' causes the polar icecap to begin to melt, Tuvalu will simply disappear beneath the waves. On these tiny atolls live some 8,000 souls. A further 1,500 work abroad and it is their remittances home, together with modest exports of copra, and revenue from the sale of postage stamps, which keep the economy going.

The main celebrations were to take place in Funafuti, the capital, by far the largest settlement, with a population of not much less than 3,000. Funafuti boasted only one hotel and its five bedrooms were already booked for the independence period. Where, then, would the guests stay? Ships, I was informed, would be anchored offshore and a berth would be found for me. How to get to Funafuti? A charter flight, it was thought, would convey guests from Fiji to Tuvalu. I should enquire in Suva when I got there.

If I was to be a guest of the Prime Minister, it seemed right to take a gift to him. Not at all, said the Secretary-General's private office. This was not the custom. 'Tell the Prime Minister that we are sending copies of all the Secretariat's publications for the last five years. Tell him about CFTC and the kinds of assistance we can provide.' All the same, I decided to take a small personal gift. At the bottom of my suitcase I carefully packed two bottles of Chivas Regal and, as an afterthought, put in a Commonwealth Secretariat tie, which displays the Commonwealth logo.

In the arrivals hall at Nadi airport, I found that Air New Zealand had omitted to unload my suitcase, and that its precious contents of whisky and tie were on their way to Auckland. Worse, I had nothing to wear except the clothes I was standing in. Happily, the suitcase was rapidly identified in Auckland and quickly returned to me. The whisky was intact. In Suva, I found that Tuvalu main-tained an office in one of the backstreets. A charming young lady answered my questions. Yes, Air Pacific was running a special flight to Funafuti on Friday. Yes, I could stay on the *Cenpac Rounder* which was anchored in the lagoon off Funafuti.

Dawn broke as the taxi took me from the Grand Pacific hotel in Suva to Nausori airport to join the others who were going to Funafuti. There were cabinet ministers from several countries, as well as staff from high commissions and embassies in Suva. Thirty or so of us climbed aboard the HS748 which rose into the sun and then headed northwards across the vast, empty Pacific. It was three hours later that the pilot banked the plane to give us a first glimpse of Tuvalu. The main island lay below us, some three miles long, shaped like a boomerang. The arms of the boomerang were barely 100 yards wide but, where they met, the centre of the atoll widened to perhaps as much as 400 yards. Here, clearly, was the heart of Funafuti. We could see a cluster of buildings and, as we circled lower before landing, we realized there was a crowd waiting for us. The plane came to a halt, the rear door was opened and the steps were put into position. As we left the plane, a great waft of heat engulfed us. At the bottom of the steps, a well-built figure clad in a palm skirt, with strips of bright red pandanus leaves about his chest, warmly greeted us. This was Chief Minister Lauti who had overcome the doubts of his compatriots and had led Tuvalu to its imminent independence. Garlands of frangipani were placed around our necks; our heads were also bedecked with flowers. Members of the cabinet, each as gaily dressed as the Chief Minister, shook our hands. Champagne, doubtless ice-cold when it was poured, but now lukewarm, was served in the palm-leaf shelter by the side of the airfield. Nearby, lay a set of goal posts. The airfield doubled as the island's football ground and sports field. The goal posts were removed two or three times each week when planes were expected.

The whole island was *en fête*. All the adults and the very young were wearing traditional costumes of skirts and coloured tops. Only the schoolchildren wore Western style dress; they were in newly-washed and pressed school uniforms. Preceded by dancers, we walked slowly down the main street of the town, under a triumphal floral arch where *Tulofa* – welcome – had been picked out in hibiscus blooms, to the little hotel. Here, in the bar-cum-dining room we drank coffee while the band of the Fiji police played outside. We were asked to clear one table. No sooner had we done so than Princess Margaret arrived. Despite the heat and the blazing sun she looked cool in a simple summer dress and wide-brimmed hat. With her little entourage, she sat down at the table we had just vacated, asked for a gin and tonic, and lit a cigarette which she smoked in a long holder. It was not the place for formality and soon the Princess was chatting happily with the other guests.

Now we made our way to the *maneapa* or meeting place, an open-sided meeting hall, about 60 feet long by 30 feet wide, beautifully decorated for the occasion with palm fronds and flowers. Finely woven mats covered the floor on which we were invited to sit. At one end on a low wooden stool, sat Princess Margaret; at the other, the Chief Minister. The rest of us were placed according to rank around the edge of the *maneapa*. We sat cross-legged; to sit with your legs stretched out before you is a terrible insult to the person opposite you. Teenage girls wearing palm-leaf skirts and short blouses, came to kneel before each guest; they proffered bowls of water, soap and towels so that we could wash our hands. Now young men, wearing only skirts, brought a tray of food for each guest. Neatly set out on a banana leaf was a whole chicken, a whole fish some 18 inches long, pieces of taro (a

240

kind of yam), various fruits, including a large bunch of bananas. I ate what I could of this feast while the young lady who had washed my hands gently fanned me. When I indicated that I could eat no more, my tray was taken away and the food was distributed among the villagers who sat outside the *maneapa* watching every movement of the guests.

From where I sat I could see Princess Margaret very clearly and was curious to see how she would cope with the tray of food, which had been served without the benefit of knife or fork. Life in the royal palaces did not seem to have prepared her at all adequately for a Tuvaluan feast. Delicately, she broke off a banana, peeled it and ate it elegantly. This, however, was the extent of her meal. The royal fingers, it seemed, were not trained for handling the other items on the tray. Now the Princess shocked everyone by taking out her case and holder and lighting a cigarette. The idea of a woman smoking in public, in the *maneapa*, and while the men were still eating, was something new to the Tuvaluans. That it should be the sister of the Queen who committed such an outrage was a sensation. A buzz of excitement went round the *maneapa* as the smoke drifted up to the roof for all to see. Chief Minister Lauti started. Clearly, it had not crossed his mind that the guest of honour would desecrate the *maneapa* by smoking. He recovered quickly and summoned an aide. A shell was rapidly produced and was placed at the Princess's side to be used as an ashtray.

The feast over, we repaired to the government offices to see an exhibition of handicrafts. Then it was time to find our accommodation. Anchored offshore were frigates from the Australian and New Zealand navies, together with smaller ships from the United States and Fijian navies. It was these ships which were providing the hardware – crockery, cutlery, chairs and so on – for the celebrations. Beyond the naval ships lay the *Cenpac Rounder*, a vessel of 5,000 or more tons which, as the name indicated, travelled round the central Pacific carrying goods and passengers. A small boat took us to the ship where our suitcases were already waiting. By this time I had discovered that Chief Minister Lauti was a teetotaller. The captain of the *Cenpac Rounder* was not, and he gratefully accepted the Chivas Regal I had brought from London. In the evening, we all returned to the island for a reception at

Government House, another feast in the *maneapa* and a display of traditional dancing. Prayers brought the day's proceedings to a close.

Overnight, the heavens opened and the sports meeting which had been planned was cancelled. There was other bad news. From the New Zealand frigate, *Otago*, came word that Princess Margaret was indisposed with chest pains and a temperature of 103°. Let my diary take up the story:

Saturday, 30 September, 1978

We were guests of the Philatelic Bureau for pre-lunch drinks. Tuvalu derives considerable revenue from the sale of stamps. The drawing up of the designs and the printing of the stamps is handled by a firm in Bristol. The Bureau in Funafuti employs 60 people making up and despatching orders received from overseas. Some of the guests, myself included, were presented with a very handsome album of Tuvalu stamps. I am tempted to hold on to it rather than to hand it over when I return to Marlborough House. Another feast in the *maneapa* was followed by the presentation of gifts to the heads of delegations. We each received a finely woven mat, a basket, a model canoe, a necklace and two fans. The amount of work that has gone into the making of these items is phenomenal. How I shall get them back to London is another matter. Feagai, my schoolboy ADC, carried them to the jetty for me when we returned to the ship. Rested a bit before showering and changing for an excellent buffet dinner at the home of Chief Minister Lauti. The Fiji police band and a local choir entertained us while we ate and there was dancing in the *maneapa*. At 11.30, we assembled in the grandstand. A short religious service was followed by the lowering of the Union Jack, which has flown here for the last 80 years, and the raising of the new Tuvalu flag. As the flag was broken on the stroke of midnight, the people gave a great shout, but otherwise remained quite quiet throughout the ceremony. The American ship in the lagoon sent up some rockets and we watched these while sipping champagne. I got back to the *Cenpac* at 1.00a.m. after a long, memorable day.

Sunday, 1 October

The alarm woke me at 6.00a.m. We assembled again in the grandstand. On parade were detachments from the four navies, the Fiji police, scouts, guides, etc. The sun beat down; there was no wind; it was swelteringly hot. Within ten minutes, I was soaked with perspiration and spent most of the day mopping my streaming brow. We began with prayers; surely this tiny country needs the protection and blessing of the Lord if it is to survive, let alone to prosper, in this world. Next came the swearing in of the new Governor-General, resplendent in white ducks and a pith helmet. Princess Margaret is still sick but her aide, Lord Napier, deputized very ably. He read a good speech and handed over the instruments of independence to Lauti, who is now Prime Minister. He made a very sensible speech, acknowledging Tuvalu's continuing dependence on other countries and international agencies for its survival. Proceedings ended with a stirring march-past, and a cup of coffee. After this interlude we returned to the grandstand for a service of thanksgiving and exhortation on the theme 'The Lord built Jerusalem'.

While Feagai went to the *Cenpac Rounder* to collect my suitcase, the mat and other gifts, I called formally on Prime Minister Lauti. He is a good, humble man. On behalf of the Secretary-General, I congratulated him on leading Tuvalu into the Commonwealth as its 38th member. As a symbol of Tuvalu's membership, I presented him with the Commonwealth tie. He was wearing a *sulu*, or skirt, with pieces of matting around his chest and waist. Numerous strips of dyed pandanus leaf hung around his waist and shoulders. It crossed my mind that it would have been difficult for me to have chosen a less appropriate present than a tie. In the three days that I have been in his company, Mr Lauti has not even worn a shirt, let alone a tie. Nevertheless, he graciously thanked me for the gift and asked me to tell SG that he will be a very welcome visitor to Tuvalu as soon as he can find the time.

There were tearful scenes at the airstrip as we thanked our hosts for the wonderful hospitality they had given us. That everything has gone so smoothly is a tribute to their planning ability and their generosity of spirit. As we took off and turned towards Fiji, I offered up a prayer for Tuvalu. Small is beautiful, according to Kurt Schumacher. It is also very vulnerable.

There was a sequel; there usually is. In July 1981, when numerous Commonwealth presidents and prime ministers gathered in London for the wedding of Prince Charles and Princess Diana, Sonny Ramphal held a reception on the lawns of Marlborough House. There, looking rather lost among so many guests, were Mr and Mrs Lauti. To my great joy, he was wearing 'my' tie. 'What else could I wear on an occasion like this?' he laughed. Evelyn asked Mrs Lauti how she was enjoying London. 'There is so much traffic here,' she said, 'not like Tuvalu.' I remembered the main street of Funafuti and could easily understand the difficulty the Lautis were having in coming to terms with Hyde Park Corner and Trafalgar Square. 'In Funafuti,' said the Prime Minister nostalgically, 'only the Governor-General and the Prime Minister have cars. There's only room for one of us to be on the road at a time. Before I go out, I always check to see if the Governor-General is using his car. If he is, I go by bike.'

In 1983, the Education and Training Programme changed its name and we became part of a new grouping. These changes resulted from one of the reviews which were periodically made of the Secretariat's management structure. A review in 1982 recommended that those divisions in the Secretariat which had the primary task of assisting the development of human resources in Commonwealth countries should collaborate more closely under the umbrella of what was to be the Human Resource Development Group. Senior Officials, meeting in Tanzania in December 1982, confirmed this recommendation. Thus it was that early in 1983 we were metamorphized into the Fellowships and Training Programme and became the nucleus of the new group, known as HRDG.

We had always co-operated pretty well with other Secretariat divisions. We utilized their experience when we needed it and, in return, helped to fund seminars and other training activities which they arranged. Now we were formally linked to five of these divisions, henceforth to be known as programmes. Biggest of these was the Education Programme, headed by Professor Peter Williams who came to the Secretariat from London University's Institute of

Education. Two other former professors, Sir Ken Stuart of Barbados and Kihumbu Thairu of Kenya, successively directed the Medical Programme. Dorienne Wilson-Smillie, a charming human dynamo from Jamaica, as Director of the Women and Development Programme, had a catalytic role to play in bringing women into the mainstream of development. Another programme which operated across the development spectrum was the Commonwealth Youth Programme. Raja Gomez, a highly intelligent and imaginative Sri Lankan, was its director. A former director of the Indian Institute of Management, Ahmedabad, Mohan Kaul, was head of the Management Development Programme. It was a strong, highly articulate team. Our monthly meetings, which I chaired for the first two years, were lively affairs. Co-operation and consultation between the programmes, which had previously been spasmodic, now became a habit. A realization steadily grew that each programme could enrich the activities of the others. We also found that a more collegiate style and a multi-disciplinary approach enabled us to respond more positively and comprehensively to the needs of governments. There were structural advantages, too, in that we could share common services through, for instance, the pooling of secretarial services, photocopying, and by setting up a resources centre to serve the whole group. Although we all complained at the amount of time that was taken up in meetings and reading each other's papers, we acknowledged that the creation of HRDG, a brainchild of Sonny Ramphal, increased our effectiveness and enhanced our ability to contribute to development in the developing countries.

I now had two bosses. The Fellowships and Training Programme was part both of the CFTC and of HRDG. As Managing Director of CFTC, George Kidd had been replaced first by Tony Tasker, then by David Anderson and, when he retired, by Bob McLaren. Bob came to us on secondment from the Canadian International Development Agency. He combined a lot of experience in development with a deceptively laid-back management style which concealed an ability to make tough decisions and to stick to them. My other boss was an assistant secretary-general, Moni Malhoutra from India. Politically very sharp, he had a diplomatic rather than development background. In theory, I was responsible to Malhoutra for projects and to McLaren for expenditure. In practice, the distinction could not be maintained. Fortunately, McLaren was happy to leave the running of the programme in my hands and Malhoutra was too busy supervising the other programmes and with other duties to have much time for Fellowships and Training.

It was very gratifying to be able to expand the Fellowships and Training Programme's activities during the last three years of my time in the Secretariat. Governments' confidence in the way the CFTC operated was reflected in bigger contributions to the fund. Increased resources meant that we were able to provide more scholarships. We made nearly 1,800 awards in 1984–5 and this grew to 2,750 in 1986–7. In the same year, we enabled more than 350 people to take part in training seminars and workshops. This brought the total number of people who received assistance up to 3,100. The students and trainees were placed in some 170 institutions in more than 40 countries. This was a measure of the varied use that governments made of the programme. A few examples, taken from the Caribbean, Africa and Asia, will show the range of training we supported.[12]

As a small island country in the Caribbean, with few post-secondary training institutions of its own, St Vincent and the Grenadines is heavily dependent on other countries for the training of its people. The awards we provided in a typical year were in several sectors. In health, assistance was given for courses in Jamaica in advanced nursing education, public health, radiography, dental nursing, and operating theatre techniques. Teachers were supported on courses in education and in physics and geography at the University of the West Indies, and in electrical engineering, home economics and industrial arts at institutions in Jamaica. Customs and excise and tax officers took short courses in Trinidad and Tobago. Other awards were made for studies leading to a law degree, a diploma in public administration and a certificate in social work as well as a short course in broadcast journalism and an attachment in industrial relations.

By contrast, Ghana has extensive education and training facilities and looks overseas only for advanced and specialized training. We gave awards for postgraduate courses in seed technology at the University of the West Indies and for a degree course in petroleum engineering at the University of Ibadan in Nigeria. Several awards were given to Ghanaians for training in the promotion and financing of small industries at India's Small Industry Extension Training Institute, Hyderabad. Ghana also received help towards strengthening its administration and management base through awards in statistical training at Makerere University, Uganda, a postgraduate management course in Cyprus and a study visit to Kenya and Zimbabwe by Public Service Commissioners. Other specialized training for Ghanaians included a course in agricultural credit control in Swaziland, training in hotel management in Bahamas, courses in museum techniques at Jos, Nigeria, in meteorology and diplomacy at the University of Nairobi, in education of handicapped children at the University of Ibadan and in electrical engineering and computer technology at the University of Ilorin, Nigeria.

Bangladesh received significant training support across a broad range of sectors, reflecting the Government's major developmental objectives. Consultations with manpower planners in Dhaka indicated that short-term training programmes would be particularly useful. Arrangements were then made for training in project management in Malaysia, fish-hatchery management in India, financial management in Sri Lanka, among a varied tailor-made programme. Thirty Bangladesh officers were given training in small industries promotion in India. Facilities at the port of Singapore were used for the training of ports and inland waterways personnel.

It would be tedious to give more examples. Catalogues of past training projects make dull reading. But at least they give an indication of the variety of training with which we were concerned, much of it at a middle level and designed to update and to improve the efficiency of people in mid career.

Arranging these projects was our bread and butter. It took time, a lot of local knowledge and some experience to draw up a programme of assistance with each government, to identify appropriate training placements, to make travel arrangements for the selected students, to ensure that they received their correct allowances, on time, to monitor their progress and to counsel them. This was the work of the chief project officers and project officers. As the programme grew we gradually added to the staff. Christine

Oduro from Ghana helped James Allie with the programme's activities in Africa. She fussed over her students like a mother hen. They loved it and called her Mama Christine. We were sad when she rejoined her government's service but shared her pleasure when she was appointed Ghana's Ambassador to Yugoslavia. For several years, Gareth Aicken was primarily responsible for our work in the Caribbean but we also used his professionalism in other regions. Another very professional colleague was Doris Shepherd who joined us on secondment from her post as Principal Training Officer for the Government of Barbados. As a team, we had good and loyal backup from our executive officers, Bhanu Vyas of India, Jasim Jasimuddin of Bangladesh and Basheer Ali. The composition of the secretarial team varied but I was very fortunate in having Praxede Weerasinghe from Sri Lanka as my personal secretary for many years. A quick, accurate and efficient secretary, as Praxede was, can make all the difference to one's ability to keep abreast of the flow of paperwork. We were also well served in this respect by Ida Chau from Hong Kong, Lily Semwogerere of Uganda, Siew-Kee Lim (Singapore) and Shirin Khan (Bangladesh) among others. The multinational character of the team reflected the composition of the Secretariat as a whole, making it a particularly interesting place in which to work.

Broadly speaking, the project officers handled the country programmes, each being responsible for one or more regions, while I dealt with the international and regional bodies whose training activities we supported. These included the South Pacific Commission, the South Pacific Bureau for Economic Co-operation, the Caribbean Community Secretariat and the Southern African Development Co-ordinating Conference. We also collaborated with a wide range of organizations which included the Commonwealth Telecommunications Bureau, the International Ocean Institute, based in Malta, the World Maritime University (in Sweden), and the Commonwealth Agricultural Bureaux. These last included the Commonwealth Institute of Entomology, the Commonwealth Institute of Parasitology and the Commonwealth Mycological Institute. Each ran highly specialized courses which were of great value to agriculturalists in Commonwealth developing countries. The courses could only be held in Britain where all the specimens of insects, mites, helminths, fungi and bacteria had been assembled over many decades. Support for these courses was one of the rare exceptions we made to the general rule that we would assist only training which took place in developing countries.

By 1987, when the time came for me to retire, it was clear that we had come a long way since 1972 when the programme began. From very modest beginnings and a tiny staff, a tentative pioneer of third country training, the programme had developed to a point where it was making a real contribution to meeting the education and training needs of Commonwealth developing countries, particularly the smaller ones. Our administrative procedures worked well. We had a reputation for cost-effectiveness. No less important, the programme had a human face. Without being complacent, I felt that I was handing over an enterprise which was in good shape and good heart.

Sonny Ramphal was more than generous in bidding me farewell. 'You leave,' he wrote, 'after a career of dedicated service to the Commonwealth. We will miss you greatly but your contributions are imperishable particularly through the lives of the young people you have helped.' I was grateful for the reference to young people. For 33 years I had been concerned with the education and training of young people, first in Northern Rhodesia/Zambia and then in the broader Commonwealth context. As I cleared my desk, I had a deep sense of gratitude that, among the many blessings the Lord had bestowed upon me, He had given me these opportunities.

Notes

1 Subsequently Sir Hugh Springer, Governor-General of Barbados.
2 Commonwealth Secretariat, *Report of the Commonwealth Secretary-General* (1975), (London: Commonwealth Secretariat, 1975), pp. 47–8.
3 *Ibid.*, p. 15.
4 Quoted in an article by Celia Curtis in *The Times* (17 November 1983).
5 London: Information Division, Commonwealth Secretariat.
6 Dr Maraj was subsequently appointed the first President of the Commonwealth of Learning, a pioneering distance education institution set up in Vancouver, Canada, in 1988.
7 The names of the students have been changed.
8 For an account of the work of the Commonwealth Foundation, and

the contribution to development made by NGOs, see John Chadwick, *The unofficial Commonwealth* (London: George Allen & Unwin, 1982).

9 *Commonwealth Heads of Government Communiqué* (1977).

10 Commonwealth Secretariat, *From governments to grassroots, report of the advisory committee on the relationships between the official and unofficial Commonwealth* (London: Commonwealth Secretariat, 1978).

11 *Ibid.*, p. 29.

12 Commonwealth Secretariat, *Report of the Commonwealth Secretary-General* (1987), (London: Commonwealth Secretariat, 1987), pp. 76–8.

8

Southern Africa – education, training and liberation

In the Commonwealth, which links 50 white and non-white countries across the world on a basis of equality, non-racism is a basic principle. This is true not just in a negative sense but in the form of a positive partnership of peoples of many different races. Active opposition to racial prejudice, therefore, is not only a necessary consequence of the Commonwealth's membership; it is an expression of its deepest beliefs.

Following the victory of the National Party in the election of 1948, South Africa embarked on a sustained policy of apartheid, or the separate development of the different peoples who make up the South African community. Important human rights were denied to the black and coloured races as racism was enshrined in law and political philosophy. Over the years, South Africa developed a way of life based on racial inequality which held in virtual bondage the black majority in the country. The ideology and practices of apartheid, exercised through a battery of laws and regulations, systematically excluded non-whites from any meaningful share in the running and rewards of their society, and threw a tightly woven mesh of oppression over 80 per cent of the population, denying them citizenship, political rights and civil liberties. South Africa came to represent the very antithesis of the Commonwealth's most fundamental aims. Appalled by the evidence of brutal oppression and legalized injustice to the black community, Commonwealth leaders committed themselves deeply and irrevocably to the total and speedy abolition of apartheid. In 1961, a year after the infamous Sharpeville massacre, South Africa was forced to leave the Commonwealth. This marked merely a milestone in a long and unrelenting campaign, the pursuit of which, perhaps more than anything else, gave the Commonwealth an important role and a distinctive voice in international affairs down the years.

In its opposition to racism in South Africa, and its support for the struggle for majority rule, not just in South Africa but also Zimbabwe, Namibia, Angola and Mozambique, the Commonwealth found a cause, a *raison d'être*. Here was an issue on which Commonwealth leaders could work together and be almost unanimous. Here was a cause – for some, almost a crusade – into which the Commonwealth could sink its teeth and not let go. While other countries might weary of the seemingly hopeless task of removing racism and bringing democracy to Southern Africa, the Commonwealth acted as the world's conscience. It would not let the international community forget the injustice and oppression which the black majorities in Southern Africa were enduring. It kept alive the dream of creating just and non-racial societies once apartheid had been abolished.[1]

It was less than three months after Arnold Smith took up office as Commonwealth Secretary-General that Ian Smith, Prime Minister of Southern Rhodesia, made his Unilateral Declaration of Independence (UDI). When the break-up of the Central African Federation became a possibility in 1961, the British government made it clear that independence could be granted to the member countries only if constitutional provision was made for 'unimpeded progress towards majority rule'. Nyasaland and Northern Rhodesia, with black governments elected by universal adult suffrage, became independent in 1964. Southern Rhodesia, by far the most economically developed of the three countries, but ruled by a white minority which would not share political rights with the black majority, remained a colony, albeit self-governing, of Britain. On 11 November 1965, Smith's Government defied Britain and the international community and declared Rhodesia's independence. Smith vowed that majority rule would not come to Rhodesia 'for a thousand years'.

There were many who felt that in the events preceding UDI, as it was called, Britain should have taken a firmer line. Because he ruled out in advance the use of force to keep Rhodesia a colony, the Prime Minister, Harold Wilson, was accused of virtually encouraging Smith to seize independence illegally. Wilson retorted that with a majority of only three in the House of Commons, and with a considerable body of opinion in Britain in favour of Ian Smith, he was in no position to take a tough line.

Contrasting Wilson's stance over Rhodesia with the obduracy shown by Britain in handling independence movements in countries which did not have as large a white population as Rhodesia, some African leaders spoke of leaving the Commonwealth in order to show the depth of their disgust at the British Government's attitude. Alarmed, Arnold Smith pointed out that the Commonwealth did not belong to Britain but to its members. Withdrawal from the Commonwealth would not hurt Britain but would seriously damage the association; it would also diminish the influence which a country could bring to bear on Britain. It was better to stay in the Commonwealth, Smith urged, and to work with the other members to bring collective pressure on Britain to end the Rhodesian rebellion. It was the kind of argument that he had to use many times before some heads of government came to understand the changed nature of the Commonwealth.[2]

The Secretary-General warmly welcomed a proposal by Sir Abubakar Tafawa Balewa, Prime Minister of Nigeria, that Commonwealth heads of government should meet in Lagos in January 1966 to discuss the Rhodesia crisis.[3] It was to be the first of many meetings, always anxious and frequently acrimonious, which dominated Commonwealth relations for the next 14 years. At heads of government meetings in London, later in 1966 and in 1969, in Singapore in 1971, Ottawa in 1973, Kingston, Jamaica, in 1975, London again in 1977 and Lusaka in 1979, Rhodesia was a major item on the agenda. This is not the place to attempt to record the extraordinary twists and turns in the story of the Rhodesian rebellion, the attempts by Britain to reach an acceptable agreement with the Smith regime, the lies and deceptions, the scandalous breaches of the sanctions imposed upon Rhodesia by the United Nations, the work of the Pearce Commission, the growth of guerrilla armies, the horrors of the civil war. The story has already been ably told, not least by Arnold Smith in his book describing

253

his period as Secretary-General.[4] My concern is much more narrowly focused. The Lagos meeting of January 1966 set up two committees. One was the Commonwealth Sanctions Committee which was to monitor the effectiveness of the economic and financial sanctions against Rhodesia. Subsequently, the Sanctions Committee developed into the Commonwealth Committee on Southern Africa. It was the pressure exerted by this committee, meeting frequently in London, together with the influence of the periodic heads of government meetings which, more than anything else, made it impossible for Britain to conclude a settlement with the Smith régime on terms which would have been unacceptable to most Commonwealth members. It was the same committee which kept up the pressure for the maintenance of sanctions against Rhodesia and extracted from Britain a grudging consent to NIBMAR – no independence before majority African rule. Among senior officials in the Foreign and Commonwealth Office, one of the least popular assignments was to speak for Britain at the Commonwealth Committee on Southern Africa. Many a time in the conference room of Marlborough House, I watched an unfortunate under-secretary from across St James's Park attempt to convince a well-informed and highly sceptical audience of high commissioners from Africa, Asia, the Caribbean and the Pacific that 'sanctions were beginning to bite' and that the Smith régime would soon collapse.

The other committee set up by the Lagos meeting was given responsibility for coordinating a Special Commonwealth Programme of assistance in educating and training Rhodesian Africans. When Rhodesia eventually achieved independence under a democratic constitution, Africans would have to assume positions of responsibility for which completion of higher education and professional training would be necessary. A Commonwealth Programme designed to provide advanced education and training opportunities for Africans would help to produce the high-level manpower which would be required.

When heads of government decided to set up this new programme, I was Provincial Education Officer in Ndola. It was not until I joined the Secretariat at the end of 1968 that I became aware of the committee's existence. By that time, the committee had achieved only limited success. With no funds to disburse, the committee could not award any scholarships. All it could do was to exhort governments to make available to Africans from Rhodesia places in their universities, colleges and other training institutions, and to cover the costs of their courses of study or training. Few countries, other than the four rich, white ones, Australia, Britain, Canada and New Zealand, could afford to provide this kind of assistance. The role of the Secretariat's Education Division was to examine the scholarship applications which were received from Rhodesian Africans, select the most promising, obtain references, and then send all the documentation to whichever government was most likely to be able to assist. It was not a very demanding or constructive role; nor was it very successful. It became part of my responsibilities when I joined the division. It did not require much imagination to see that the Secretariat could play a more active part in the so-called Special Commonwealth Programme only if it had funds to use for awarding scholarships.

A conversation with a friend in the Canadian High Commission may have helped us to secure the important breakthrough. His government, he said, were becoming increasingly concerned that black Rhodesian students were remaining in Canada when they had completed their studies. The Government understood why the students did not wish to return to Rhodesia while the Smith régime was in power. They did not understand why the students were reluctant to go to other countries in Africa. The problem would not have arisen, I suggested, if the students had been trained in Africa or in a developing country elsewhere. Would the Canadian Government not consider giving the Secretariat money to run a scholarship programme for Rhodesian Africans? I was pretty sure that we could obtain study and training places in developing countries around the Commonwealth if we had the funds to meet the costs of tuition, boarding, and so on. 'Give us the money,' I said, 'and we'll take the Rhodesian Africans off your hands.'

It was some time later, in 1972, that the Canadian High Commissioner informed Arnold Smith that his government wanted to enter into an agreement with the Secretariat on the training of Rhodesian Africans. Canada would provide the Secretariat with funds; the Secretariat would use the funds to run a scholarship programme for educating and training the students in developing countries of the Commonwealth. Ten per cent of the funds could be used to meet the Secretariat's administrative expenses. Arnold Smith needed no urging from me to accept the Canadian offer. He could see that it provided a lever with which to attract contributions from other countries to what would soon become a significant scholarship fund. Sure enough, Britain soon followed Canada's example. Australia and New Zealand were not far behind.

We appealed for contributions not only to the rich countries but also to the poor ones. The response, in terms of offers of study and training places, was overwhelming. Twenty-five countries, often at considerable sacrifice, offered places in their universities, technical colleges and other training institutions. Among the most generous contributors were India, Malta and Sierra Leone, but we were also able to place students in Caribbean countries and as far afield as Fiji. Zimbabweans became the wandering scholars of the 1970s. As news spread that the Secretariat was giving scholarships for post-secondary studies, applications poured in from Zimbabweans in many parts of the world. I could not possibly handle the volume of work and we recruited Terry Dormer to help out. He had previously worked as a teacher in Uganda and Nigeria. He was totally committed to non-racialism and the struggle for political justice in Southern Africa, and was prepared to work long hours to get the programme going and to make it a success. No-one could have had a more dedicated colleague than Terry in helping to initiate and subsequently to develop the Secretariat's programmes of humanitarian assistance.

Terry soon took over the day-to-day running of the Commonwealth Zimbabwe Scholarship Programme, as we now called it. The declared purpose of the programme was to provide assistance for Zimbabweans who had 'O' level qualifications, or above, who had left Rhodesia for political reasons or in order to obtain education, training or employment which was not available to them in Rhodesia because of the discriminatory policies and practices of the illegal régime. To begin with, we referred all applications to a subcommittee of the Sanctions Committee. As we expected, the members soon became disenchanted with the laborious business of sifting through scores of forms, letters of commendation and so on, and were content to leave things in our hands on the understanding that we would refer to the committee for decision any important points of principle. This we scrupulously did.

The school system for Africans in Rhodesia was highly competitive. The numbers who could take 'O' and 'A' level courses was small. They were usually very bright. As a result, we had little difficulty in placing them on degree, diploma and certificate courses in subject areas such as accountancy, agriculture, education, medicine, forestry and technical subjects where trained Africans would be required when independence eventually came. Frequently, Zimbabwean students did extremely well in their studies and successfully adjusted to living in what to them were strange countries. Some, of course, had chips on their shoulders and behaved as though the world owed them something. Occasionally, there was trouble between students who supported rival political parties. On more than one occasion, Terry or I had to drop everything and rush to some distant campus to help the local authorities sort out difficulties, sometimes violent, which had erupted between those who supported the Zimbabwe Africa National Union (ZANU) and the Zimbabwe African Peoples' Union (ZAPU). On the whole, however, the programme ran very smoothly and the students, even though separated from their families and homeland for many years, were excellent ambassadors of the future Zimbabwe.

We endeavoured to obtain an assessment of each scholarship applicant from his or her former school. These were usually commendatory, of course, but none more enthusiastically so than a recommendation for the delightfully named Moreblessing Mutambara. Her deputy headmaster wrote in glowing terms:

For the four years I have known her, Miss Moreblessing has demonstrated great potential. Her Cambridge results do not truly reflect her ability. She carries a graceful body, full of attraction and dignity. She wears a cheerful face almost without exception, and strikes to me personable as well as influential to her peers. Before she ever sat in my class, I had known her already for her athletic standing in the school. She sprints as well as performs in long and high jump events and wins with apparent felicity. Otherwise, she is seen in the church choir group and in the United Methodist Fellowship activities. So athletic as she is, she has managed to keep an even 'shapelier' frame. She looks energetic and absolutely healthy. I am positively confident that she will go through her course, endowed as she is with nimble fingers, good posture, keen observance, eloquence and superb comprehension.

Despite this boost, we were unable to place Moreblessing.

Students living within Rhodesia were not eligible for assistance and we did not wish to encourage them to leave their homeland in the hope, which might not be fulfilled, of obtaining a scholarship. Rather than offering them nothing, it was decided to extend the scope of the Special Commonwealth Programme to include correspondence education within the country. Australia and New Zealand, which had long traditions of education by correspondence, provided funds for this new initiative. We launched the scheme in 1975 by arranging with a correspondence college in Britain to provide 'A' level and first degree courses for 100 black students in Rhodesia on a trial basis. Unfortunately, we were not able to implement plans to give the students tutorial support on the ground. The absence of face-to-face assistance undoubtedly contributed to the high rate of drop-out among the students. But the percentage who persevered with their studies and achieved success in their examinations, was sufficiently high to encourage us to expand the scheme to 300 students.

By the time Zimbabwe achieved its independence in 1980, we were able to report, with no little satisfaction, that the Special Commonwealth Programme had assisted more than 4,500 students. The scholarship fund which we administered was an important part of the programme. We used it to provide awards to more than 1,000 students at 153 institutions in 25 developing countries of the Commonwealth.[5] As Robert Mugabe, the incoming Prime Minister of Zimbabwe generously recognized, the Commonwealth made a vital contribution to the creation of the new country's impressive stock of high- and middle-level manpower. I could not help but reflect that, in this regard at least, Zimbabwe was much better prepared for independence than Zambia had been. Shortly before independence, we provided the new administration with data on more than 900 trained Zimbabweans living outside Zimbabwe who had told us that they wanted to return home and work for the development of the country. We subsequently contacted – a mammoth task for our small staff – a further 5,000 Zimbabweans living in many different countries, and sent them employment application forms which they could complete and return to the Zimbabwe Government.

But this is to anticipate a little. We need to look at developments which took place in 1979 and 1980. These were developments from which the Commonwealth derived great satisfaction. They culminated in the ending of the Rhodesian rebellion and the birth of a free and independent Zimbabwe.

As the 1970s wore on, bloodshed and destruction in Rhodesia mounted steadily. From its bases in Mozambique, ZANLA, the military wing of Robert Mugabe's ZANU, first launched raids into the eastern half of Rhodesia and then virtually took control over whole districts. The army of ZAPU, known as ZIPRA, was based in Zambia. ZAPU's leader, Joshua Nkomo, was cautious about sending his guerrillas across the Zambesi, but gradually large areas of Matabeleland, his home province, came under ZIPRA control. Both armies followed classical guerrilla warfare tactics which had been learned in the USSR and China. They avoided major confrontations with the Government's security forces, concentrating on raiding European farms, ambushing convoys, blowing up bridges and power lines, generally harassing the enemy and controlling the Tribal Trust Lands. Ian Smith's army, better armed than the guerrillas, was consistently frustrated by its inability to come to grips with a fast-moving and elusive enemy. In the battle for the hearts and minds of the people, both sides were guilty of ruthless and abominable practices which appear to be the hallmark of civil wars throughout the world. In general terms, Smith's Government easily retained control of the towns; increasingly, ZANLA and ZIPRA dominated much of the Tribal Trust Lands. Neither side, it seemed, could win the war; the stalemate could last indefinitely. The possibility of armed intervention from outside, and of the conflict escalating into one of international dimensions, was always present.

259

Periodically, attempts were made to end hostilities and to bring about a negotiated settlement. What were known as the Anglo-American proposals were announced in September 1977, by Britain's Foreign Secretary, David Owen, and President Carter's roving Ambassador, Andrew Young. They aimed at ending the war and bringing about the transition to majority rule by means of a negotiated ceasefire, which would be monitored by a United Nations force, and the holding of internationally supervised elections which would be organized by a resident commissioner from Britain. Sonny Ramphal immediately commended the proposals to heads of government as providing a new and constructive framework for a negotiated settlement.[6] Here, surely, was a chance for peace. Throughout the ensuing months, Ramphal remained in close touch with the British and American Governments, the presidents of Angola, Botswana, Mozambique, Tanzania and Zambia, the so-called Front Line States, and the nationalist leaders of Zimbabwe. He also had discussions with Kurt Waldheim, UN Secretary-General, who was using his own best endeavours on behalf of the Anglo-American proposals.

It was to no avail. Ian Smith, who made a number of secret visits to Lusaka at this time for discussions with Presidents Kaunda and Nyerere and the nationalist leaders, succeeded in sowing discord among them. Negotiations dragged on and eventually ran out of steam. Meanwhile, in Salisbury, Ian Smith was having meetings with black leaders inside Rhodesia and, in February 1978, was able to announce that he had reached agreement on an internal settlement with Bishop Muzorewa, the Rev Ndabaningi Sithole and Chief Chirau. This agreement provided, *inter alia*, for the creation of an executive council composed of Smith and the three black leaders, a ministerial council with equal numbers of black and white ministers, and for the holding of elections on the basis of a so-called 'majority rule' constitution. The internal settlement was immediately rejected by Robert Mugabe and Joshua Nkomo and by the Front Line States. Both the OAU and the UN Security Council called on the international community not to recognize the internal settlement. Behind a facade of legitimacy, the new constitution preserved white domination of Rhodesia in all important respects. Ramphal described it as 'a tactic for buying time and preserving the reality of minority rule behind a new facade. It promises neither majority rule in the real meaning of the term, nor any diminution of the armed struggle.'[7]

Elections, in which the Patriotic Front of ZANU and ZAPU took no part, were held in April 1979. Bishop Abel Muzorewa, leader of the United African National Council, became Prime Minister and head of what was termed a government of national unity.

In Britain, there were many on the right of the political spectrum who were prepared to recognize Muzorewa's Government. The Rhodesian problem had gone on since UDI in 1965. Surely it was time to end it. That the problem must be resolved was certainly the view of Lord Carrington who became Britain's Foreign and Commonwealth Secretary in May 1979 when the Conservatives, under the leadership of Margaret Thatcher, swept into power. Economically and strategically, Carrington argued, Rhodesia was of little significance to Britain. Its importance was largely negative in that the Rhodesian issue soured Britain's relations with other countries and took up a great deal of Foreign Office time which would be better devoted to major issues such as Europe and the Middle East.[8] It was plain to Carrington that opposition to recognition of Muzorewa's Government was very strong in the European Community, the Organization of African Unity and the United Nations. Any lasting settlement must involve Mugabe and Nkomo as well as the internal leaders. It would be necessary, therefore, to work for a conference at which all the contending parties would be present.

Lord Carrington's first task was to convince Mrs Thatcher that it would be dangerous for Britain to go it alone in recognizing the Muzorewa Government. It seemed, however, that the Prime Minister, elated by her crushing electoral victory, was seriously considering recognizing Muzorewa and giving Rhodesia its independence. Rhodesia, she maintained, was a British colony and was therefore Britain's responsibility. It was for Britain, not for the Commonwealth or any other body, to decide the time and circumstances of Rhodesia's transition to independence. The right-wing press in Britain gave her its full support. The response from Commonwealth countries was swift. Nigeria, in particular, reacted angrily. If Britain recognized Bishop Muzorewa, Nigeria, with a population of 80 millions and one of Britain's major trading partners, would impose a boycott on British imports. To drive home the point, Nigeria nationalized British Petroleum installations in the country. Other countries went so far as to threaten to expel Britain from the Commonwealth if it gave independence to Rhodesia's unrepresentative government. Nothing daunted, Mrs Thatcher, on a visit to Australia in June 1979, suggested to a startled news conference that she would lift economic sanctions against Rhodesia when the parliamentary order expired in November. Extending recognition to the Muzorewa régime, she said, 'would take a little longer'.[9] Other voices were now added to Lord Carrington's in urging caution. Powerful among these was that of Malcolm Fraser, Prime Minister of Australia, who had won credibility among African heads of government and could present their strongly held points of view in moderate but unmistakable terms. Commonwealth heads of government were to meet in Lusaka in the first week of August. For Margaret Thatcher, this would be her first major international conference. Would she be ready to listen and learn, or would she live up, or down, to her reputation as the Iron Lady? Friends in the Foreign Office were uncertain and worried.

Clearly, the Lusaka summit was going to be an important occasion, not just for Zimbabwe but for the Commonwealth. 'Few Commonwealth meetings,' Ramphal subsequently wrote, 'have convened with a greater sense of potential disaster.'[10] About the one positive factor was that Joshua Nkomo agreed to a cessation of operations, a virtual ceasefire, on the Zambian–Zimbabwean border during the period of the conference.

I was glad to be included in the Secretariat team which serviced the conference. My role was that of an adviser but I also offered to help with the editing of the record of the proceedings. This meant that I sat in each day on one or more sessions and made notes of the speeches. Meanwhile, highly competent stenographers took down in shorthand everything that was said and rapidly transcribed it on their typewriters. The editor was then responsible for turning the spoken words into reported speech, eliminating the irrelevancies, and presenting a coherent account of what had been said. The draft of each day's proceedings was distributed to delegations overnight. Where necessary, which was rare, corrections could be made before the final conference report was prepared.

The conference was held in Mulungushi Hall on the outskirts of Lusaka. I shared an office with five other Secretariat directors, Mike Faber, Roland Brown, John Syson, Peter Brooks and Selva Selvanathan. Mulungushi and the National Assembly motel where we slept, were 'home' for the next ten days. The first two days of the conference were taken up, as was customary, with a wide-ranging debate on world economic and political issues. The discussion on Rhodesia took place on the Friday morning. I noted in my diary:

> At Kaunda's invitation, Julius Nyerere opened with a very lucid and reasonable statement. He concentrated on the common ground between the various parties involved and put forward a three-point plan for a solution. He was followed by arap Moi of Kenya, but he added little. Margaret Thatcher spoke next. She was very moderate and, a vital admission, acknowledged that Rhodesia's present constitution had important defects. A new constitution was necessary, she said, before genuine, black majority rule would be achieved. A good speech which was well received. It was clear that the warning voices which have bombarded Mrs T. for the past several weeks have had their effect.[11] She has made a U-turn which will put an end to the stresses and strains within the Commonwealth and will lead to credible independence for Zimbabwe. For this reason, it was a speech of critical importance. You could almost hear a collective sigh of relief as it became clear that Britain was not going to recognize Muzorewa's Government.

There was still a lot of work to be done, of course. There were those who were reluctant to believe that Mrs Thatcher's conversion was complete. My diary entry continued:

> After coffee, Godfrey Binaisa of Uganda soured the atmosphere by an unhelpful speech accusing Britain of failing to arrest Smith, who was guilty of treason, etc., etc., and

Muzorewa of being a woman because he was not taking part in the war. Adefope, Foreign Minister of Nigeria, was low-key but serious. He said that unless Mrs Thatcher gave more details of her proposals, and inspired confidence that she would implement them, Nigeria would have to reconsider her membership of the Commonwealth.

It is the practice at Commonwealth heads of government meetings that, after the first two or three days, the presidents and prime ministers with the Secretary-General and one or two of their most senior advisers go into 'retreat', and relax in an informal atmosphere. The value of these retreats in bringing about agreements on issues where there had previously been deadlock, and in providing opportunity for quiet reflection, away from the pressures of the media and officials, has been proved on several occasions. So it was in Lusaka in 1979. The retreat took place in the grounds of State House, President Kaunda's home. A group of eight – Manley of Jamaica, Fraser, Kaunda, Nyerere, Thatcher, Carrington, Adefope and Ramphal – put their heads together and produced what was to be known as the Lusaka Accord. Final agreement on the wording was reached by the eight on the Sunday afternoon and was informally welcomed by the other heads of government when they met at a barbecue hosted that evening by Malcolm Fraser at the Australian High Commissioner's residence. Formal agreement was reached when the conference reconvened the next day. It was a triumph for the Commonwealth and a triumph for common sense. It was also a personal triumph for Sonny Ramphal.

But if anyone imagined that the Rhodesian issue had been resolved, they were badly mistaken. The Lusaka Accord required that Britain, as the responsible power, would call 'a constitutional conference to which all the parties would be invited'. Early in September, only five weeks after the heads of government meeting in Lusaka, the conference opened in Lancaster House, London. There they all were – Muzorewa, Nkomo, Mugabe, Sithole, Chirau, Ian Smith, each accompanied, of course, by his advisers. Lord Carrington was chairman. Before the Conference began, he had sent to all the parties an outline of his proposals for an

Southern Africa – education, training and liberation

independence constitution, a cease-fire and election. It was around these proposals that discussion raged for the next 14 weeks.

It was never expected that the going would be easy. Mugabe, Nkomo and Smith were commanders of armies which had been fighting each other for years. It was unlikely that they would find it easy to agree. It was not simply a case of black against white. There were deep divisions between the blacks and also between the whites. It might have been helpful if Sonny Ramphal had been given observer status at the conference. Carrington firmly ruled this out in an assessment of the Secretary-General which was less than generous. 'I remember having to keep Sonny Ramphal from interfering,' he subsequently wrote. 'Totally committed to the Patriotic Front, he had no credibility as an impartial observer.'[12] In fact, although not present at the Lancaster House meetings, Ramphal worked tirelessly to promote a successful outcome. During the long weeks of the conference, he was in close touch with the delegation leaders. Moreover, he arranged 30 meetings of Commonwealth representatives at Marlborough House, including a number of occasions when they met formally as the Commonwealth Committee on Southern Africa. These meetings monitored the progress of the conference, point by point, and emphasized the importance which Commonwealth governments attached to continued adherence to the principles of the Lusaka Accord.[13]

Other forces were also urging the conference delegates towards reaching a settlement. All sides were conscious of a general war-weariness and had to recognize that, despite all the blood which had been shed, no side could realistically expect to win an outright military victory. South Africa, which had supported Smith since before UDI, now found him an embarrassment. South Africa had enough problems to contend with in its relations with the international community without incurring further opprobrium by continuing to send men and materials across the Limpopo to bolster the faltering Muzorewa/Smith régime. Mugabe, in turn, was under pressure to end the war. Mozambique had many difficulties and Samora Machel's Government was weary of playing host to Mugabe's ZANLA, members of which were often pursued back into Mozambique by Smith's forces. Nkomo's men, too, had outstayed their welcome in Zambia. They were accused of robbing

265

villagers of their food and of raping their women. When Smith sent soldiers by helicopter to raid Nkomo's house in Lusaka, it was said that Zambians waved and cheered as the helicopter flew low over Lusaka's Cairo Road.

As Chairman, Lord Carrington drove the delegates hard. He stood firm when they threatened to walk out. 'Nkomo and Mugabe knew,' he later wrote, 'that if they went home we should recognise the "internal settlement", come what may.'[14] (This was an extraordinary statement, given that the internal settlement had been rejected by Britain and the rest of the world.)

On 21 December, Lord Carrington's style of diplomacy succeeded and the Lancaster House Agreement was signed. This provided, *inter alia*, for a ceasefire and for the guerrilla forces of ZANLA and ZIPRA to move to assembly points where they would remain until after elections had been held. Rhodesia would revert to the constitutional situation which had existed before UDI: it would be ruled by a governor appointed by Britain. Elections would be held based on universal adult suffrage. Independence would come after elections which were deemed to be free and fair.

With the departure of the Lancaster House delegations, interest now turned to the elections. The Lusaka Accord had stated that there should be 'free and fair elections properly supervised under British Government authority and with Commonwealth observers.' What did the last phrase mean? Certainly it was ambiguous. Britain envisaged that some Commonwealth countries which could afford to do so would send small teams to observe the elections. Sonny Ramphal saw it very differently. He wanted a group of observers to be drawn from several countries, including small ones which would not be able to send their own teams, and for this integrated group to be organized through the Secretariat. He maintained that heads of government at Lusaka had foreseen a role for Commonwealth observers that was both special and distinct from that of any other group which might observe the elections. They believed that the presence of a Commonwealth team in Rhodesia at the time of the elections would be an important element in creating the necessary climate of confidence and in helping the elected government, in due course, to secure Commonwealth and wider international recognition. Only a collective group of observers, drawn from countries across the Commonwealth, could perform the role which heads of government had intended. [15]

Ramphal's view, strongly supported by the Commonwealth Committee on Southern Africa, prevailed. With some reluctance, Lord Carrington in London and Lord Soames, who had been sent to Salisbury to be Governor of Rhodesia, agreed that a Commonwealth observer group, consisting of 11 observers and 22 assistants, should observe the elections. With even greater reluctance, Carrington and Soames conceded that the group, now known as the COG, should be present in the country not just for the poll but for the entire course of the election campaign.

In Marlborough House things moved swiftly. The members of COG, it was planned, would arrive in Salisbury on 24 January 1980. The Secretariat would have a major task in preparing for their arrival, arranging their programme and drafting their report. I had not visited Rhodesia since before UDI, 15 years earlier, but I was the only Secretariat officer who had any personal knowledge of the country. It was no great surprise, therefore, when the Secretary-General asked me to be co-director of the Secretariat team which would service the COG. I was to go out to Salisbury with a small advance party a week before the main group. Ramphal's briefing was quite short. 'I don't know Rhodesia and I've never observed an election,' he said, 'so there's not much practical advice I can give you. You'll have a week to draft a plan of action which you can put to the observers when they arrive. Keep a low profile. It's the observers who will observe the election, not the Secretariat. Don't take any unreasonable risks but try to be as self-contained as possible. Try not to let Lord Soames push you around. And remember, we're totally neutral in all this. If the people want Mugabe, so be it. But if they prefer Muzorewa or anyone else, that's their decision. We shall work with whatever government may be elected.'

We left for Salisbury on 16 January. There were seven of us. Tony Hayday had the advantage of having already made a short reconnaissance visit and had booked hotel rooms and an office. Mark Robinson was one of the Secretary-General's special assistants and would be particularly helpful in handling our relations with Government House. Stephen Chan was a very bright young

New Zealander from the Commonwealth Youth Programme; this was his first visit to Africa.[16] Peter Dunne, an old Secretariat hand, and Fred Grante from the Gambia would look after our administration and finance. Anne Mittelholzer from Sri Lanka was our secretary.

The beginning was not auspicious. When we reached Salisbury, we found that some of our luggage had gone on to Johannesburg. It would have been a friendly gesture if someone from Government House had met us at the airport but no-one appeared. Courtesy, however, demanded that we should pay our respects to the Governor so Tony, Mark and I hired a taxi and drove to Government House. It was a pleasant surprise to find that I knew Lord Soames's Private Secretary, Jim Buckley, as well as some of the other members of his staff. Sir Antony Duff, deputy to Lord Soames, was genuinely welcoming. It was clear, however, that Government House envisaged that the COG operation would be Salisbury-based. Assistance would be provided, we were assured, in arranging day trips for the observers to different parts of the country. Government House, in other words, would keep a close eye on the observers and would decide where they would and where they would not go.

This, I was sure, was not the kind of operation the Secretary-General wanted. He was anxious that the COG should be as independent of Government House as was consistent with their safety. I had already concluded that if they were to do their job properly, the observers would have to disperse, not remain in Salisbury. Whether they would agree to do so was another matter. But contingency plans had to be made for stationing groups of observers in centres away from the capital.

First, however, we had to establish a firm base in Salisbury. We needed offices which would provide a headquarters for COG. Peter and Fred tracked down an ideal set of offices above a second-hand car dealer's showroom conveniently near the Jamieson Hotel where most of the Secretariat staff would be staying. We succeeded in jumping a long queue to have telephone lines installed. We opened a bank account of £200,000. Stephen assembled information on hire rates for cars and aeroplanes. Then we hired a number of cars and secured an option on the use of a couple of light aircraft which would enable us to move around the country quickly when the need arose. I wrote to the leaders of all the political parties and informed them that the COG would be arriving shortly. We paid a courtesy call on Sir John Boynton, the Election Commissioner, appointed by Britain, and met his deputies, John Cumber (who had been released from his duties as Director of the Save the Children Fund), Martin Carruthers and Don Hodge. They were to be valuable allies in the weeks ahead.

If the observers were going to disperse, Bulawayo in the south and Gwelo in the middle of the country would be suitable centres. I asked Stephen to go to Bulawayo and Gwanda and to make provisional arrangements for setting up COG centres. I went to Gwelo. In the departure lounge of Salisbury airport, Joshua Nkomo, whom I had met on a number of occasions, was waiting for a plane which would take him down to an election rally in Bulawayo. I tried to hide behind a newspaper but soon the burly figure bore down upon me and seized me in a bear-like hug. 'Where are your observers?' he asked. 'Terrible things are happening in this country. They must come quickly.' It would not say much for the impartiality of the Secretariat or of COG for me to be seen in the arms of Joshua Nkomo or any of the other political leaders. I hurriedly assured him that the observers would be arriving shortly, and was very relieved when his flight was called and he had to leave.

Gwelo's airport is at one end of the Rhodesian Air Force headquarters at Thornhill. It was strange to land there again 23 years after leaving what was then a Royal Air Force base and had been my home for three years. Gwelo was the capital of the Midlands Province. I called on the Provincial Commissioner, Mr Ferguson. The interview was illuminating if depressing. Yes, he had heard that a group from the Commonwealth would be observing the elections. He thought the exercise would be a colossal waste of time and money. I noted in my diary

> Ferguson said it was naive in the extreme to imagine that the
> election could be free or fair; conditions in the country made
> that impossible. The guerrillas (he called them "terrs" or
> terrorists) were supposed to have gone into the assembly

points. There were still several hundred at large in his province. In the Tribal Trust Lands (TTLs), intimidation was rife. He quoted at length from a batch of situation reports he had received from his officers in the last 24 hours. Most concerned armed gangs threatening to kill villagers and to destroy their homes unless they voted for Mugabe. He hoped the observers would realize that the average villager was very unsophisticated and was easily persuaded that the vote was not secret. Many believed that Mugabe would know how they voted because he had put a black box on a Russian satellite which would record where people put their crosses. Ferguson stressed that his resources were extremely limited. At present, he had no transport with which he could move around observers. If and when the observers came (and clearly he hoped they woudn't) they should not expect five-star treatment. If they wanted to go to the TTLs, they must be prepared to sit on the back of a mine-protected vehicle; this could be very uncomfortable. If the observers succeeded in reaching the TTLs, he doubted if they would learn much. After several years of war, threats and intimidation, villagers trusted no-one. They would not risk their lives by telling their stories to a group of strangers, however distinguished they might be.

It was very sobering. I found it hard to imagine high-powered judges and diplomats being willing to sit in the back of a mine-protected vehicle, surrounded by armed troops, in order to visit a few villagers in distant *kraals* and assure them that their vote would be secret. But unless the observers went into the heart of the country and saw the situation for themselves, they would not be in a position to say whether the election had been free and fair.

I exchanged notes with the two British election supervisors who were staying at the same hotel. The Lancaster House Agreement required Rhodesia to organize the elections and Britain to supervise them. To discharge this responsibility, Britain selected some men with African experience and others with expertise in running elections. It was a simple but brilliantly successful approach. Charles Wilks and Robin Mitchison were typical of the two-man teams which covered the country. Charles had been a district commissioner in Kenya and Rhodesia and was now retired. Robin was a former town clerk of Kitwe and was now Chief Executive at Basildon. Over dinner, they underlined the Provincial Commissioner's warning about the difficulties of moving around the Province, other than in a protected vehicle. They promised their assistance. Before flying back to Salisbury, I felt sufficiently encouraged to book rooms in the hotel for a month, to hire some cars, and to put two unemployed African teachers, who had a good knowledge of English, on standby for employment as interpreters.

Stephen returned from the south. Gwanda would not make a suitable base, he reported, but he had made provisional arrangements for setting up a sub-centre in Bulawayo. From there, the observers would be able to cover the elections in the two Matabeleland provinces. Like me, he had been warned that it would be dangerous to travel far from the city unless in convoy and that it was essential to use mine-protected vehicles on roads through the bush.

Before the observers arrived I was anxious to see for myself something of the countryside away from the urban centres. With Don Hodge of the Election Commission, Mark, Fred and I flew in a little Piper Cherokee to a district headquarters at Mtoko, some 50 miles north-east of Salisbury. Here the District Commissioner and a local chief briefed us. Normal administration, they said, had ceased to exist in the district. The schools and clinics were closed, agricultural extension work had stopped, the cattle dips were unused, many of the people had fled to the towns. From my diary:

The area is dominated by ZANU (PF). We heard dramatic stories of intimidation. Perhaps they were exaggerated but we were left in little doubt that intimidation is widespread. We piled on to two Pumas and a Leopard. A Puma is about the same size as a five-ton lorry and has specially strengthened sides. We sat on raised platforms, flanked by soldiers with their G3 rifles aimed into the bush on either side in case of ambush. A 20-minute drive along a bush road brought us to a large school. The roofs and windows of all the buildings were missing and the place was deserted. The buildings, of

course, can be repaired. Much more serious is the return to
the district of anthrax, sleeping sickness and rabies, diseases
that had not been seen for many years before the present
troubles.

We arranged for the media to be at Salisbury airport when the
observers arrived. Sir John Boynton, John Willson (from Government House) and I welcomed them on the tarmac. There was some
surprise when Colin Cowdrey, the distinguished English cricketer,
came down the steps with the observers. We shook his hand along
with the others.

The observers had been selected and appointed in their personal
capacities. They functioned on behalf of all Commonwealth
governments but did not represent any of them. They came from
eleven countries in four continents and from diverse backgrounds
– diplomatic, political, legal, electoral and the public service. Nurul
Islam of Bangladesh, for instance, was a judge of the Dacca High
Court and Chief Electoral Commissioner. Sir Carlisle Burton was
head of the Barbados civil service. Gordon Fairweather was Chief
Commissioner of the Canadian Human Rights Commission. Judge
Crabbe was a justice of Ghana's Supreme Court. Oscar Tammur
was a minister in the Papua New Guinea Government. The
chairman of the group, Rajeshwar Dayal, was a former foreign
secretary to the Government of India and had held many senior
international diplomatic appointments. He was going to need all
his diplomatic skills in handling his colleagues and in his relations
with Government House.[17]

With the observers came reinforcements from Marlborough
House – Moni Malhoutra, Director of the International Affairs
Division who would now direct the Secretariat team, Jeremy Pope,
Director of the Legal Division and his secretary, Carole Costa.
Another, very welcome, arrival was Derek Ingram, head of Gemini
News, a very good friend of the Secretariat and staunch supporter
of the Commonwealth. Derek was styled a 'media adviser'. Salis-
bury was beginning to fill with media people from the press, radio
and television and we needed someone with Derek's wide experience to handle the COG's relations with them.

While the observers and their assistants settled in and began a

272

round of briefing sessions in Salisbury arranged by the Election Commission, Moni agreed that Stephen and I should make two more reconnaissance missions. Stephen went to Umtali, capital of Manicaland. I went to Fort Victoria, capital of Victoria Province. I travelled with Philip Bowcock whom I had last seen nearly 20 years before. He was one of several ex-Northern Rhodesian civil servants who were working as election supervisors. Others I bumped into were Philip Farwell, ex-Lundazi, Steve Morgan and Ian Macdonald, ex-Isoka, Mike North, former election commissioner, Reg Thompson, and Lawrence Taylor, formerly of the National Institute of Public Administration. Sometimes I felt the elections were the backdrop for an old boys' reunion. The fact that so many of us knew each other and had worked together before, even though many years previously, made for understanding and co-operation.

Philip and I travelled to Fort Victoria in a convoy. At the front and rear of the convoy of 20 or so cars was an armoured vehicle. On the back was a soldier with a machine gun mounted on a turret which swivelled. We bowled along at 60mph. Travelling in fast-moving convoys minimized the risk of ambush. We stayed at the Flamboyant Hotel in the hills overlooking Fort Victoria. Over dinner, we talked with Lt-Col Stuart Green, head of the Commonwealth Monitoring Force in the province, and General Agnew Cambua, commander of the ZANLA forces. The cease-fire arrangements which formed part of the Lancaster House Agreement required the Rhodesian Security Forces to remain in their bases and for the guerilla armies of the Patriotic Front, ZANLA and ZIPRA, to go to 16 assembly places (APs). These requirements were to be supervised by a Commonwealth Monitoring Force of approximately 1,500 members. Any alleged breaches of the cease-fire were to be investigated by a commission consisting of the Governor's military adviser, two representatives of the Rhodesian Security Forces and one from each of ZIPRA and ZANLA.

As we chatted, some of the difficulties inherent in the situation became very clear. Green was responsible for monitoring two of the APs, one with 1,800 ZANLA guerrillas, the other with 1,000. Within the APs, he said, the guerrillas retained their arms. They were jittery. Used to operating in small groups, and never staying

273

long in one place, they did not like being together in large numbers in a confined space. They were afraid that the cease-fire would not hold and that the security forces might attack them. 'Our relations with them are pretty good,' said Green, 'but it's a bit like sitting on a powder keg. If they decide that they've had enough, and break out, there's nothing we can do about it.'

General Cambua confirmed that his men were nervous. They were not convinced that the Rhodesian Army were confined to their bases. Some were genuinely afraid of going to an AP for fear of being massacred. Some had not received news of the cease-fire until late and were having difficulty in reaching an AP. Others, he had to confess, had become bandits and were living off the land. The young general – he was only 28 – was worried about the auxiliaries of the security forces who had moved into the Tribal Trust Lands as the guerrillas moved out. The auxiliaries were a kind of armed homeguard who were supposed to assist the police in maintaining law and order and in helping with reconstruction work in areas where schools and cattle dips had been destroyed. In some parts of the country, they did commendable work. In others, including Victoria Province, they were said to be agents of Bishop Muzorewa whose role was to terrorize the villagers and ensure that they voted for the UANC. General Cambua said that his mend were bitter that they were confined to the APs while the auxiliaries were free to roam the country, intimidating the villagers, beating and raping those who opposed them.

At a meeting next day of the Joint Operational Command, attended by representatives of the security forces, the police and the Provincial Commissioner, I was confused by frequent references to contacts with CTTs. These turned out to be 'Communist-trained terrorists', in other words, guerrillas. Bob Menzies, the Provincial Commissioner, and David Smith, his Security Officer, promised co-operation when the observers arrived. I said the observers would be grateful for assistance but would want to be as independent as possible. 'I can't accept any responsibility for their safety if they travel around on their own,' said Menzies. 'There's a danger of ambush almost anywhere and once you get on to the bush roads you may run over a mine.'

Before flying back to Salisbury, I called at the publicity bureau to get a map of the province. The middle-aged European lady who served me made no secret of her views. 'We can't have our lovely country taken over by a bunch of reds,' she said. 'Look how much damage they've done already. Most of the farmers around here are Afrikaners from South Africa. If it looks as if Mugabe or Nkomo will win the election, they expect Peter Walls [the general in charge of the Rhodesian Army] to take over.'

At the first formal meeting of the observers, Ambassador Dayal asked Stephen and me to report on our reconnaissance missions. We gave our reports as honestly as we could, pointing out the difficulties and possible dangers of operating in the provinces as well as the opportunities which a policy of dispersal would provide for full coverage of the elections. The observers were divided. Some were clearly shaken by the picture we painted. Many of them had never been to Africa before. They were finding life in Salisbury unexpectedly agreeable and had no wish to venture into unknown and potentially dangerous territory. They could see the necessity of ascertaining what was happening across the country; could not Secretariat officers be sent out into the provinces and then come back periodically to Salisbury to report? Other observers, equally clearly, welcomed the challenge which dispersal would present. Seeing that there was no consensus, Dayal adjourned the meeting but not before he had reminded the observers that it was they, not the Secretariat, who were responsible for observing the elections. When they met again, two days later, we expected a further difficult debate. Dayal, however, had taken the measure of his colleagues. He blandly announced that he had spoken privately to each of the observers and that a clear majority were in favour of dispersal. No-one protested; it was the end of the debate.

We needed reinforcements. Moni telephoned the Secretary-General. Three days later, Hugh Craft, Raja Gomez, Emmanuel Apea, Ned Amerasinghe, Dominic Sankey, Prakash Ramgulam and John Macpherson arrived. It was good to see them. Thirty-six hours later, we wished them God speed as they set off to set up the sub-centres; Hugh and Ned in Fort Victoria, John and Prakash in Umtali, Stephen Chan and Emmanuel in Bulawayo, Raja and Dominic in Gwelo.

Before the observers dispersed, we were invited to lunch at

275

Government House. Lord Soames and his very charming wife, Mary, could not have been more hospitable. Rather larger than life, with a booming voice and a bone-crushing handshake, Lord Soames gave the impression of being in total command of the situation. Eton, Sandhurst and the Coldstream Guards had given him an impeccable background for a career in the Conservative Party. He had added immeasurably to his credentials by marrying Mary, a daughter of Sir Winston Churchill. Later he had held office in several Tory administrations, had been an outstanding ambassador to France and had served as a European commissioner. He had been Lord President of the Council and Leader of the House of Lords when Lord Carrington had asked him to be Governor of Rhodesia. He had agreed immediately and had flown to Salisbury to take up the appointment before the Lancaster House Agreement had been formally signed. As Governor, he exercised great power and ruled virtually by decree. He was very conscious, however, that the country could easily explode into renewed violence and bloodshed. There was incipient danger everywhere. Fear might lead the guerrillas to leave the assembly places and to renew the armed conflict. The leaders of the Rhodesian Army might stage a coup. Hotheads, white or black, might kill one or more of the party leaders. Things could easily go wrong with the programme to repatriate more than 200,000 refugees, principally from Botswana, Mozambique and Zambia. There was the possibility of personal attacks on his wife and himself. As he talked with the observers, however, and posed with them for a photograph on the steps of Government House, Lord Soames gave no indication of the anxiety and apprehension he must have been feeling. Rather, he exuded confidence, told the observers how important their role was, promised them every assistance and wished them well.

The first phase of the exercise had now been successfully completed. The observers had settled in, and familiarized themselves with the main issues and had made their plans. A team spirit was starting to make itself felt. Phase two would be the hard grind of observing the election campaign across the length and breadth of the country. The third and last phase would be the scrutinizing of the polling, the counting of the votes, the declaration of the results.

As we went into phase two, a pattern quickly emerged. Each

week, small groups of observers and assistants were based on the sub-centres at Bulawayo, Fort Victoria, Gwelo and Umtali. Another group remained in Salisbury. Each group travelled as widely as possible within their provinces. The Secretariat staff in each sub-centre were responsible for arranging the week's pro-gramme. As far as possible, the groups travelled in vehicles hired by the Secretariat. Where it was sensible to do so, they used mine-protected vehicles and armed escorts provided by the Rhodesian authorities. Between them, the groups visited each of the country's 55 administrative districts. The underlying aims of the observers were to find out whether all the parties were able to campaign without hindrance and to assess whether the people believed that their votes would be secret. If the man in the street and in the beer hall, and the woman in the village or the welfare centre were satisfied that no-one would know how they voted, then the danger of intimidation became much less formidable. Week after week, the observers, the assistants and Secretariat staff spoke to thou-sands of people as they visited Tribal Trust Lands, protected villages, African townships, assembly places, army and auxiliary force bases, police camps, refugee camps, schools, hospitals, mission stations, factories, mines and farms. There were other groups, national and international, which were observing the elections. None could match, by a long chalk, the coverage of the country which was achieved by the COG. At weekends, the observers returned to Salisbury, exchanged notes, met in com-mittees, rested and then dispersed again, usually to a different province. It was gruelling work.

Moni, as Director of the Secretariat team, worked closely with Ambassador Dayal and kept in close touch with the Secretary-General in London. Jeremy Pope meticulously analysed each stage of the election process to identify possible weaknesses and then alerted the Rhodesian and British authorities as well as the observers. Derek Ingram fed stories to the media as they became available and ensured that the COG had a high profile. I had two main responsibilities. One was to arrange, with Mark Robinson, visits to the three Mashonaland electoral districts for the observers who were based in Salisbury. The second was to maintain contact with the sub-centres. Each evening, between 8 and 10 o'clock the

277

Secretariat staff in Bulawayo, Fort Victoria, Gwelo and Umtali would phone through their reports on the day's activities and alert us to any difficulties.

Charles Gunawardena, Director of the Secretariat's Information Division, came out to help draft the COG's report. The report, extending to 350 pages, is very detailed and is a model of its kind. It gives, of course, the official account.[18] My diary entries, usually scribbled the wrong side of midnight, recorded some personal impressions. These are some extracts.

Wednesday, 6 February 1980

Visited Wedza TTL with some of the observers. Chatted to a good lot of people about the secrecy of the ballot, intimidation and the activities of the auxiliaries. On our way back, we called at Waddilove mission station, founded by the Methodists in 1915. The principal recalled that twice recently the whole school, staff and pupils – all 900 of them – were herded into the church and given a political harangue by ZANU (PF) men from 9.00p.m. to 4.00a.m.!

Thursday, 7 February

Went to a meeting at the headquarters of the Rhodesian Front where we met six senior members of the party, but not Ian Smith. They expressed very moderate views, including a willingness to work with whatever government might be elected, provided it did not adopt totalitarian measures. If they had held these views ten years ago, and had acted on them, the history of Rhodesia in the last decade would have been very different and thousands of lives would have been saved.

Friday, 8 February

Visited some of the African townships around Salisbury. In Mabvuka, we went to a shopping centre, a beer hall and a market on a 'meet-the-people' tour. Crowds soon gathered and people spoke freely. Intimidation is not really a problem in the townships and people appear to believe that their vote is secret – a welcome change from the attitude in the TTLs.

Sunday, 10 February

I booked a phone call home for 11.00p.m. but the lines were busy, presumably with reporters sending back their stories of the attempted assassination of Robert Mugabe this afternoon at Fort Victoria, the second attempt on his life in a week. It is a mercy that it failed. If he should be killed, that would be the end of the cease-fire. All hell would break loose. It is ominous that the mine was detonated by remote control, which points the finger at European involvement.

Tuesday, 12 February

Today's visit was to Shamva district. We were briefed by John Burgess, yet another ex-NR man now working as an election supervisor. Most of the people have had to leave their *kraals* and are living in protected villages. We went to PV number five. Some 1,500 people live there; the whole place is surrounded by high barbed wire. In the centre of the village is a 'keep', manned by district assistants, which is a strong point to which the villagers retreat in case of attack. We met a number of *kraal* heads and talked about the election. The people welcome the protection which the PV provides but find it irksome to have to walk several miles to their fields each day. Until recently, they were not allowed to take any food with them in case it fell into the hands of the guerrillas. Most of their kraals are now in ruins and they will have a big job to rehabilitate themselves when peace eventually comes. According to this evening's radio news, Soames has given himself power to ban the election in districts where intimidation has reached uncontainable levels.

Wednesday, 13 February

Another glorious, sunny day. Drove out to the Mazoe Citrus Estate which covers no less than 53,000 acres. There was little evidence of intimidation among the workforce. At the police camp in Mazoe, we inspected the remains of a bus which was ambushed on the Bindura–Salisbury road yesterday an hour or so after we had passed. Two passengers were killed and several were wounded. It's difficult to know who could do such a stupid thing at this stage unless they want to sabotage the whole election process.

Thursday, 14 February

We visited a European-run farm near Bindura. It is clearly very efficiently managed. The farmer was a kindly, decent man, full of benevolent paternalism. He spoke of 'my Africans' in the same way as he spoke of 'my cattle' and 'my dogs'. He did not seem to appreciate that his labour force were human. We drank tea on the lawn by the house; the labourers were brought to meet us. One said he had been employed at the farm for the last 40 years; he earns $19 a month! The extraordinary thing was that there was no evidence of intimidation or unreasonable pressure from the farmer. He obviously expected they would vote UANC. 'They know when they're well off,' he assured us.

Friday, 15 February

Three bomb explosions shattered last night's peace. Two of the bombs damaged churches and part of the Monomatapa Hotel where Ambassador Dayal and some of the other observers are staying. The third exploded in a car in which were found the remains of two members of the Selous Scouts (a section of the Rhodesian army). It is assumed that they had planted the other bombs and were on their way to deliver the one which blew them up.

The BBC this evening carried a so-called interim report by COG on the auxiliaries. This was based on a confidential *aide-memoire* we prepared for the observers a few days ago. One of them must have leaked it. Dayal will give the probable culprit a piece of his mind.

280

Sunday, 17 February

For the last few days, we have had a running battle with Government House concerning the number of additional staff we can bring in to observe the poll. Tonight I was informed that Soames has agreed to 30 – a far cry from the original figure of 96 and then 55, but more than we thought likely a few days ago. Broke the good news to Moni and then to John Cumber and Mike North over supper. They professed themselves delighted. 'A triumph for the old-boy network,' John called it. John Lewis, who supervised my M. Phil. at London, is now Vice-Chancellor of the university here. He has already agreed that the support staff can stay at hostels on the university campus. This is an enormous help as all the hotels are bulging at the seams with the international press corps, observers, and the like. Dayal has written to Soames again about the distribution of anti-socialist leaflets by the security forces. On Thursday, some of the observers saw some of the leaflets being dropped from a Dakota, probably belonging to the Rhodesian Air Force. Today, in Shabani, some of Raja's observers found more. We are told that the noble lord is furious, first that the leaflets are being distributed and secondly because the observers keep on finding them.

Tuesday, 19 February

A few days ago, Government House produced a map showing the areas of the country in which intimidation, allegedly, is particularly worrying. Soames sent Dayal a copy with a request that the observers should visit the areas and advise to what extent it is possible for the parties to campaign freely. One of the areas marked red on the map and said to be 'severely affected' by intimidation is Mount Darwin District. I joined a group going there this morning. A lot of media people were on the plane. As usual, the DC and the Election Supervisor (John Mousley, ex-Luwingu), briefed us. John gave details of the many meetings which had been held in the district in the previous fortnight – 17 by UANC, 11 by ZANU (Sithole), eight by ZANU (PF) and one by ZDP. I suspected that John was unaware of the Government House map. I asked how serious was the problem of intimidation. 'It's really no problem at all,' said John. When it was pointed out to him that Mount Darwin was alleged, by Government House, to be severely affected by intimidation and that the Governor might ban the election in the district, he said that there were no grounds for banning the election. Well done, John! The pressmen were writing furiously during this exchange which must undermine the credibility of the Government House map. I was sitting next to Sir Glyn Jones, former Chief Secretary in Northern Rhodesia and then Governor of Nyasaland/ Malawi. 'That'll shake Christopher,' he said. Sir Glyn is out here as a member of a very distinguished group of 'golden oldies', chiefly former colonial governors, who are observing the election for the Foreign Office.

Saturday, 23 February

Went to the university to help brief the 30 support staff who arrived on Thursday. Many are scared but the spirit is excellent. This evening we had a get-together of the whole group at the Jamieson. Then Mark, Jeremy and Derek and I went on to a party given by the foreign press. There must have been 500 there. Chatted, among others, with Joan Lestor, Labour left-winger. She left me to talk to Gen. Walls, one of the bizarre meetings that are commonplace in Salisbury nowadays.

Sunday, 24 February

Polling starts on Wednesday. There were prayers for a peaceful election at the Anglican cathedral this morning. The cathedral was packed with people of all races. The yearning for peace is over-whelming. Phoned home again this evening. E. and the children are all well. It's 5 and a half weeks since I came here. It seems like an age.

Monday, 25 February

Spent most of the day seeing off the support staff who are going to observe the poll in various parts of Mashonaland East and

Mashonaland Central. They included a Sri Lankan going to Mtoko. We gave him a camp bed, sleeping bag, mosquito net and some vegetables; he's a vegetarian.

'Our sources,' as they say, tell us that Government House expects no party to get an overall majority. They think a Muzorewa/Nkomo coalition is the most likely outcome. We find this incredible and just wonder where Lord Soames is getting his information. All our information points to Mugabe being streets ahead. Nkomo will take all or most of Matabeleland but is unlikely to get seats anywhere else. Mugabe is firmly on top in Mashonaland and Manicaland. That doesn't leave much for the Bishop. He'll be lucky to get as many as five seats.

Today the observers met General Peter Walls. He impressed them deeply. He said that he prays every day for peace and assured them that he has no intention of staging a coup. Of course, if he is planning an army takeover, it's unlikely that he would say so![10] This evening, Dayal saw Mugabe. By all accounts, he assumes that he will be Prime Minister within the week and has already asked Lord Soames to stay on for at least a month after the election.

Wednesday, 27 February

First day of the poll. I joined Nurul Islam in visiting some of the polling stations in the northern Salisbury suburbs. Everything was very quiet and decorous, which is what you would expect in these well-heeled areas where most of the common roll voters are domestic servants. To allow time for the sub-centres to get info. from their districts, I didn't start the evening round-up until late. It was 11 o'clock before it was finished. Voting seems to have been very heavy everywhere, with few incidents.

Thursday, 28 February

Joined Gordon Fairweather and two other Canadians in visiting polling stations in Mashonaland Central. Flew by Beechcraft, first to Sipolilo and then Mushimbi Pools. Everything was very quiet and orderly. It was good to see English bobbies on duty at each station. The idea of bringing out 500 constables for this exercise was a nice touch. On to an airstrip at Angwa, where we walked a mile or so to the school where the election was being held. It reminded me very much of Nkolemfumu 18 years ago.

Back at the office, Jeremy was in his element. There is no electoral register and voters may cast their votes where they wish. It is therefore necessary to have a system which makes multiple voting impossible. Entering the polling station, the voter puts his hands into an ultra violet light box. If he has voted before, his finger tips glow white and he is disqualified. If all is well, he then places his tips of the fingers of both hands into a basin containing a pad moistened with a dye. This is invisible to the naked eye but will show up under the ultra violet light box test if he tries to vote again. Jeremy had previously carried out tests with several solvents and cleaners to see if the dye could be removed. He was satisfied that it could not. Today, however, a local journalist claimed that he had voted, scrubbed his finger tips with Coca Cola and had then voted again at a different polling station. If true, this could lead to enormous problems. Jeremy at once organized a series of tests and eventually satisfied all and sundry that the dye cannot be removed by Coke. He and Derek prepared a press statement to reassure the public.[20]

Friday, 29 February

The third and last day of the poll. According to tonight's radio news, the turnout for the election has been more than 90 per cent of the estimated electorate of 2.9 million. All the sub-centres reported a quiet day.

Saturday, 1 March

The obervers now all back in Salisbury, met to consider their interim report. This has to be issued before the results of the election are known. The final, detailed report, which will be a substantial document, will be finished in London. They had no real difficulty in concluding that the election can be considered to have been free and fair. True, there has been intimidation and coercion but this has not been a monopoly of any single party. By and large, all parties have had the opportunity to campaign freely. Most people believed that their vote would be secret, notwithstanding any attempts that might be made to intimidate them.

Monday, 3 March

Today the votes were counted, starting at 8.00a.m. We had observers at the count throughout the day. From their reports, it soon became obvious that the Bishop is 'out' and that a great and famous victory for Mugabe is on the way.

Tuesday, 4 March

An historic day. The results of the election were announced on radio and TV at 9.00 a.m. These showed:

ZANU (PF) Mugabe	57 seats
PF Nkomo	20
UANC Muzorewa	3
Others	0
	80

There was jubilation in the streets as news of the results spread. There is also some relief among the COG members. The margin of victory is so huge that it cannot be due to intimidation but must express the genuine will of the people.

Mugabe broadcast this evening. It was a statesmanlike speech: let bygones by bygones; let us beat our swords into ploughshares, etc. The Bishop, happily, has pledged his support for the new government. At long last there seems to be hope for Zimbabwe.

It was another few days before we could leave. We made farewell calls, of course, on Lord Soames and Prime Minister Mugabe. Both were very complimentary to the observers. At his home in Mount Pleasant, Robert Mugabe was full of praise. The observers, he said, had played 'a magnificent role' in the election. Their very presence had given confidence to the electorate and had also ensured that the worst excesses had been avoided. He shuddered to think what the Governor and the security forces would have done had the

COG not been there. Those of us who wondered what his own men would have done if the election had not been so closely observed kept our thoughts to ourselves.

Ambassador Dayal had been something of a thorn in the Governor's side but now Lord Soames was generous in his congratulations. He was clearly relieved that the election had passed off smoothly and that the danger of a right-wing coup, led by the army, seemed to have passed. We knew that he had not expected a ZANU (PF) victory, and had no reason to suppose that he welcomed it. Nevertheless, he accepted that the people had spoken with a very clear voice. He said that he felt he could trust Mugabe and was willing to stay on for a while to help him get his administration organized. Some of my colleagues were very critical of Lord Soames. I felt he did a first-class job in very trying and dangerous circumstances.

The farewell meeting with Joshua Nkomo was a sad one. For years, Nkomo had been the father figure of the nationalist movement. I think he had genuinely believed that he enjoyed support across the country, not just among his own Matabele people. He was bitterly disappointed by the result of the election. He maintained that his election agents in Mashonaland and Manicaland had been kidnapped by ZANU (PF), had been beaten and held prisoner for the period of the election. 'How can I work with that man [Mugabe]?' he asked. In fact, he soon agreed to serve in Mugabe's Government, although the going was rough.

And so, nearly 15 long years after Ian Smith's ill-conceived Unilateral Declaration of Independence, Robert Mugabe led Zimbabwe to its real independence. The transition from colony to independent republic within the Commonwealth had been turbulent and bloody. Tens of thousands, black and white, had died fighting for what they believed to be right, or simply as innocent victims of a savage conflict. The Commonwealth and its Secretariat, could take some pride in having helped to end the bloodshed and to give the people of Zimbabwe the chance to choose their own Government. I was glad that Arnold Smith, as well as Sonny Ramphal, was invited to the independence celebrations in April 1980.[21] Between them, they had ensured that Rhodesia/Zimbabwe was kept high on the Commonwealth's agenda. For 15 years they had provided the quiet but dogged leadership which the situation demanded and which now reaped its reward. As the Union Jack was lowered for the last time, and the new flag of Zimbabwe was raised to the roar of the crowd in the Independence Stadium, Smith and Ramphal, no less than Lord Carrington and Lord Soames, had every reason to feel both pride and pleasure. Collectively, the Commonwealth had done a good job. The Secretariat's image stood high.[22]

Now that the country was independent, we could begin to help the new government by arranging training placements in other countries, providing scholarships and generally contributing to Zimbabwe's human resource development. In addition, we were still responsible for 300 or so Zimbabwean students who had been refugees. They were free now, of course, to return home but it made sense for them to complete their courses in the countries where they were studying. We made no new awards to refugees after the Lancaster House Agreement had been signed. We could therefore anticipate a gradual running down of the programme as the students we were supporting finished their courses of training and went back to Zimbabwe. Suddenly, however, our responsibilities for Zimbabwean students virtually doubled. The circumstances were bizarre. We maintained contact with a number of organizations which worked with refugees. This helped to ensure that no student received scholarships from more than one agency (although there were several who tried) and that the value of our awards was broadly similar to that of other scholarship-giving agencies. One of the largest of these collaborators was the International Universities Exchange Fund. Based in Geneva, and run by a likeable and dynamic Swede, the IUEF administered funds provided by a dozen or more governments. The largest contributor was Sweden which, together with Denmark, Norway and Finland, has an excellent record in providing assistance to developing countries and humanitarian aid to refugees. The deputy director of the IUEF was a South African named Craig Williamson. He claimed to be an opponent of apartheid who had fled from South Africa in order to escape arrest. In fact, he was in the employ of BOSS, the South African state security organization which was remarkably successful in infiltrating its agents into politically sensitive organizations.

287

Once inside, an agent would systemically extract valuable information from files and other records and would then proceed to destabilize the organization. In the case of the IUEF, Williamson compiled a highly damaging report on the fund's financial affairs and the activities of its director. He then disappeared, but not before he had made known the contents of his report. The director had not benefited personally from the unorthodox financial administration of the fund, but there was no doubt that irregularities had occurred for which he was responsible; he had no option but to resign. Confidence in the IUEF among donor governments sank to rock bottom.

Because the director had been Swedish and because Sweden was the largest contributor to the Fund, the Swedish International Development Authority (SIDA) felt obliged to lead the rescue operation. Their director wrote to ask whether the Commonwealth Secretariat would take over responsibility for the 500 or so students, from several countries, whom the IUEF was supporting. Terry and I flew to Stockholm in July 1980 to meet the SIDA officials. It was encouraging to find that the Secretariat's stock was high with the Swedes and that our scholarship programmes were admired as efficient, developmentally oriented and cost-effective. Would we take on all the IUEF students? we were asked. I had to reply that the Secretariat had a mandate from heads of government to assist Zimbabwean students. We would be willing, therefore, to administer the scholarships of the 300 or so Zimbabweans, but we could not help with the other 200. SIDA accepted our offer and we made arrangements for colleagues to go immediately to Geneva to collect the files of our new students.

This was our first serious contact with SIDA. We soon established a good rapport with their officials. We enjoyed working with them. They seemed to find our methods of work agreeable and to like our no-frills approach. Before long, they were asking us to administer other funds for them, particularly to provide scholarships for refugees from Namibia. The Secretariat's assistance to Namibia dated back to 1975. In that year, at their meeting in Jamaica, heads of government affirmed their willingness to accept Namibia into the Commonwealth when it became independent.

They also agreed that CFTC funds could be used to provide humanitarian assistance to Namibians.[23]

Namibia, then known as South West Africa, had been colonized by Germany in 1884–5. With the defeat of Germany in the Great War of 1914–18, the colony was made a trust territory of the League of Nations. South Africa was mandated by the League to administer the territory on its behalf. Over the next three decades, this mineral-rich country became a virtual colony of South Africa. When the United Nations succeeded the League in 1945, South Africa was asked to return Namibia to international trusteeship. It refused to do so and governed the country as if it were part of the republic. The United Nations formally terminated South Africa's mandate in 1966. Pretoria retorted by imposing a full-scale policy of apartheid on the country. It ignored a ruling by the International Court of Justice in 1971 that its occupation of Namibia was illegal. By then, some members of the South West Africa People's Organization (SWAPO), led by its president, Sam Nujoma, had resorted to an armed struggle as the only means of gaining independence for their country. Several thousand of them were to die at the hands of the much better equipped South African Defence Force before independence was eventually achieved in March 1990. Namibia then took its place as the 50th member of the Commonwealth.

When, soon after the Jamaica summit of 1975, we began to plan an education and training programme for Namibian refugees, we rapidly realized that it could not be a carbon copy of the programme for Zimbabweans. There were important differences between the needs and the abilities of Zimbabwean and Namibian students. The Zimbabweans who sought the Secretariat's assistance already had at least 'O' level qualifications; they were fluent in English; many had already secured places in recognized institutions in Africa, Asia and elsewhere; they could hold their own in the training programmes of their choice. What they required from us were scholarships to cover their travel, tuition, books and living expenses. In sharp contrast, very few of the Namibian refugees had finished more than two years of secondary education; having been taught in Afrikaans, their knowledge of English, or any other international language, was very sketchy; they could not possibly cope with the level of training for which we normally gave awards.

289

These were some of the results of the discriminatory education policies pursued by the South Africans. If we were going to help Namibians to prepare for independence, we needed a new approach.

We ran the Zimbabwe Programme in as non-political a way as we could. We never asked applicants any questions about their political affiliations and did not consult ZAPU or ZANU before making awards. With the Namibian refugees, it was different. Most were living in health and education centres in Zambia and Angola which were run by SWAPO. SWAPO had been recognized by the United Nations as the sole, authentic voice of the people of Namibia. It made sense, therefore, for us to work closely with SWAPO, but without excluding approaches from students who were members of other parties, or who had no political affiliation. Our main contact was the Secretary for Education and Culture, first Linekela Kilenge then, when he was tragically killed in a car accident (like so many other very capable Africans I have known), his successor, Nahas Angula. Between us, we devised a three-pronged strategy. First, we must try to increase the numbers of refugees with 'O' levels, this being the standard required for entry into many education and training institutions in Commonwealth countries. Happily, the Gambia, Ghana and Sierra Leone were prepared to offer places in their secondary schools. James Allie and Christine Oduro, both from West Africa, arranged for the first group of 55 students to assemble in Lusaka, met them there and checked their certificates and travel documents. Christine had the good sense to insist that the girls were medically examined. Those found to be pregnant were replaced by others. The party then flew to Accra, Banjul and Freetown. James and Christine made sure that they were all properly clothed, equipped and settled into their schools before returning to London. Thereafter, they made regular visits to monitor their progress and to read the riot act occasionally when the exuberance of the Namibian youngsters, rejoicing in their new-found freedom, proved too much for their hosts.

Skills training was the second objective. Those refugees who had finished two or three years of secondary education and had a smattering of English were given the chance to follow technical courses in areas where there was likely to be a skills shortage after

290

independence. Jim Houston was particularly good at this side of the work. He established good relations with a wide range of government officials and institution heads in India. He would fly off to India, send me lengthy telexes from far-off places which I had to search for on the map, and would return triumphantly two weeks later having worked out a complete skills development programme, starting with a crash course in English, for groups of Namibians in a variety of different subjects. We guessed that many whites, occupying key positions in the Namibian economy, would leave when a black government took office at independence. It was prudent, therefore, to train black Namibians to take over some of their jobs in vital sectors such as railways, the mines and telecommunications, as well as to prepare them for work in areas such as education where independence would bring a big expansion of activity.

Jim monitored all his projects very carefully. On one visit each year, we would arrange for him to be accompanied by Nahas Angula, representing SWAPO, and someone from SIDA, which was providing some of the training funds. Nahas would bring the students up to date with the progress in 'the struggle' and would exercise 'revolutionary discipline', as he termed it, on any who were found to be lukewarm or unco-operative in their attitude. We did not consider it appropriate to ask what 'revolutionary discipline' involved, but it was doubtless very unpleasant.

The number of students we were able to support grew steadily. In 1987, when I left the Secretariat, we had 250 Namibian refugee students currently on the books. In small groups of 3 or 4, or in larger groups of 20 or more, they were following a wide range of training programmes: as secretarial instructors, literacy organizers and agriculturalists in Kenya; as automobile mechanics and teachers of English in Sri Lanka; in the maintenance and operation of railways and mines in India; in nursing in Barbados, Cyprus, Guyana and Malta; in teacher-training in Singapore and Sierra Leone; in building in Nigeria and Seychelles; as hotel and catering operators in Fiji, to mention only some.[24] SWAPO and the United Nations Commissioner for Namibia were generous in expressing their appreciation of the Secretariat's efforts. The Secretariat, of course, could only make use of the resources – money and training places – which governments provided. It was the generosity of many countries, often with very limited resources of their own, which made possible the significant Commonwealth programme which we co-ordinated.

The third element in our package of assistance broke new ground. We were concerned that there were many refugees in SWAPO's health and education centres in Angola and Zambia who had very little to look forward to and had difficulty in keeping themselves usefully occupied. SWAPO did their best to provide classroom teaching for some of the refugees, but there were many thousands of adult men and women in the centres who had very little education and had time on their hands. We could not provide traditional teaching for them but perhaps something could be done by using distance education methods. We asked the International Extension College (IEC), in the persons of Tony Dodds and Janet Jenkins, to investigate. Their report identified very clear learning needs in the centres and was cautiously optimistic that a distance education programme could be designed to meet those needs. This was a new departure and there were those within the SWAPO leadership who doubted the value of the kind of programme we were proposing. Fortunately, Sam Nujoma, SWAPO's President, came to Marlborough House at the time of indecision and I had the opportunity of explaining our proposals to him. He urged us to go ahead. With this encouragement, we arranged three meetings in close succession in Lusaka during 1980. Apart from SWAPO and ourselves, the Government of Zambia, the United Nations Institute for Namibia and the IEC were represented. At the first meeting, it was agreed to set up a Namibian Extension Unit in Lusaka which would have administrative, training and production functions. November Mthoko, a Namibian teacher, was appointed by Sam Nujoma as co-ordinator of the unit. We arranged for him to go to London University for a course in distance education. The CFTC funded two experts to help get the unit off the ground. One was Gordon Leech, who had had a lot of good experience in distance education in Africa. The other was Aldridge Adamson, a deputy secretary to the Zambian Cabinet, a very capable and experienced Zambian civil servant who was to prove invaluable in overcoming the administrative difficulties which the new unit inevitably faced. At the other meetings, run as workshops, a year's learning material was prepared in basic English and primary mathematics and the first group of SWAPO tutors were trained in the techniques of distance education and in the use of the project's learning materials. These consisted of 10 workbooks in English and 15 in mathematics, supplemented by audio cassettes. To our surprise, we found it was considerably cheaper to have the books, 50,000 in the first instance, printed in England and flown out to Lusaka than to have them produced in Zambia or any of its neighbours.

We launched the programme early in 1981 in one SWAPO camp in Zambia and in four in Angola. Before long, 2,000 students had enrolled. They would meet in small groups, often under the trees, studying under the supervision of group leaders who had received a rudimentary training from course tutors. Some groups made very slow progress; there were many dropouts; some of the leaders failed to provide adequate stimulation; others were transferred before the group members were capable of working on their own. Nevertheless, despite many difficulties, the scheme was a success. Terry and I took it in turns to represent the Secretary-General at the meetings of the project's management board in Lusaka. It was good to see and hear at first hand how the project was developing on the ground. To the courses in basic English and mathematics were added junior secondary maths, mother and child care, nutrition, environmental health and agriculture. When I retired in 1987, over 6,000 students had been helped through the project which was, perhaps, the first in the world to assist refugees in settlements using distance education techniques. One of the measures of its success was the international financial support it attracted. When we started, the CFTC met virtually all the costs. By 1987, over 90 per cent of the costs were being covered by the governments of Austria, Denmark, Finland, Norway, Sweden and Holland, the British Council, the Commission of the European Communities and several non-governmental organizations including the Africa Educational Trust, the Ford Foundation, Oxfam, the United Nations Association of China and World University Service.[25]

The chairman of the Namibian Extension Unit's board of management was Hage Geingob, Director of the United Nations

Institute for Namibia, based in Lusaka. He was one of several SWAPO leaders with whom we worked. Initially, we found collaboration difficult. Like all newcomers, we were viewed with suspicion. We had to become used to being regarded as actual or potential agents of South Africa. SWAPO leaders, we soon learned, lived and worked in an atmosphere of intrigue, plots and treachery. They found it very difficult to believe that our interest in the project was partly professional and partly humanitarian. They seemed to assume that we had some ulterior motives, that we must be plotting something. And since they could not discover what it was that we were plotting, it must be something very devious indeed. They had good reason to be constantly on their guard. South Africa recruited many informers from among Namibians. They included soldiers in PLAN, SWAPO's army, and refugees in the health and education centres. Through these agents, the South African intelligence obtained detailed information about future PLAN operations and SWAPO activities. Many Namibians died through being betrayed by their countrymen. It must have been very difficult to know which comrade was loyal and which had been seduced by Pretoria. We knew nothing of it at the time but the world later learned that SWAPO resorted to brutal methods in dealing with suspected informers. Shortly before Namibia's independence, gruesome and horrific details came to light on how suspected agents were handled by SWAPO security guards. Beatings, torture and killings were commonplace. Those who were allowed to live were liable to be kept for many years in harsh, degrading conditions, even though they might be completely innocent of the charges against them.

Gradually the barriers of suspicion were broken down and good working relationships were established. As confidence grew, SWAPO turned increasingly to the Secretariat for assistance. Thus when SWAPO decided that the main medium of communication after independence would be English, Nahas Angula sought our advice on how to implement the decision. The English language was understood by only a tiny percentage of the population since, under South African rule, Afrikaans was the official language. To change from Afrikaans to English would require a massive and deep-reaching piece of social engineering. In the schools, textbooks would have to be rewritten and teachers would have to be retrained. In the public service, civil servants would have to be taught to conduct the country's business in English rather than in Afrikaans. The media and the information services would have to be re-vamped. In the mines, factories and shops, Afrikaans would give way to English. And so on. The scale of the task facing an in-coming government would be enormous. In consultation with Nahas, we brought together a group of English-language experts from Namibia, other countries in Africa, and Britain, to analyse the problems, challenges and opportunities which the Government would face and to draw up an action plan for tackling them. SWAPO endorsed the meeting's recommendations, and we com-missioned the British Council to design some 300 discrete projects for making the plan a reality. It was then left to SWAPO to select the projects to which they attached the highest priority and to seek funding for them from the international community. For our part, we doubled the support we were giving for English-language teacher training.

Collaboration brought mutual respect and understanding. Fol-lowing SWAPO's victory in the 1990 election, President Sam Nujoma appointed Hage Geingob as Prime Minister. Nahas Angula, Minister of Education, Sport and Culture, was just one of several cabinet members who were well-known to the Secretariat. The good relations which had been established during the long and difficult years leading to independence made for easy co-operation between President Nujoma's Government and the Secretariat. This helped ensure the success of an enhanced Commonwealth pro-gramme of assistance, administered by the Secretariat, to help build the new Namibia. I was glad to learn that the Namibian Extension Unit was transferred to Windhoek and became part of the national education system.

The success of the distance education programme for Namibians prompted us to wonder whether something on similar lines could be provided for the considerable numbers of refugees from the Republic of South Africa who were living in the Front-Line-States. At their Melbourne meeting in 1981, heads of government asked the Secretariat to draw up proposals for a Commonwealth edu-cation and training programme for them.[26] But where were the refugees, and in what numbers? What were their education needs?

How could the Secretariat help meet those needs? Finding the answers to these questions took up quite a lot of time for Terry and myself and for Tony Dodds of the IEC whom we roped in to help. While Terry and Tony concentrated on locating the refugees in Tanzania, I visited Botswana, Zambia and Zimbabwe. At first, no-one was ready to talk freely to us for fear that, by accident or design, we might pass on sensitive information to those who could use it to the disadvantage of the refugees. Gradually, however, and with the help of the country representatives of the United Nations High Commission for Refugees, we succeeded in establishing our credibility with the leaders of the refugees, particularly the African National Congress and the rival Pan-Africanist Congress of Azania. Over several months, we built up a picture of where the refugees were, their education background, and their current needs. Our enquiries showed that the refugees had widely differing abilities. A few were barely literate; the majority had studied for a few years in a secondary school; a small number were qualified to pursue first degree studies. We concluded that a distance education programme in English, mathematics and agriculture would be relevant to the needs of more than half the refugees, and this should be our starting point.

Selling the idea to the ANC and the PAC, and amending it where necessary, proved a wearisome business. The leaders of the two groups in Dar-es-Salaam refused to sit down together. I would have a meeting with the ANC in the morning and would take their views to the PAC in the afternoon. They, in turn, would want changes which I had to convey to the ANC the next morning. This could have gone on indefinitely. The heat and humidity of Dar-es-Salaam, the obduracy of some of the refugees, even the sleaziness of the offices in which we met, made for slow progress. At last, however, we had a scheme which was acceptable to both groups, to the Tanzanian Ministries of Home and Foreign Affairs, to the ANC headquarters in Lusaka, and to the United Nations High Commission for Refugees.

We asked the Tanzanians to run what was to be known as the South African Extension Unit. They were delighted to do so, on the understanding that the Secretariat would provide the funds. They appointed a senior tutor from their National Correspondence

College, Egino Chale, as the unit's director. Egino had just completed a doctorate in distance learning at London University. He soon got down to finding offices, appointing a small staff, and arranging workshops, with Tony Dodds' help, to prepare course materials. He had a good manner and succeeded in getting people from the ANC and the PAC to work together in writing, editing and trialling materials, and in training the first tutors and group leaders in their use. This was a major achievement. Instead of reviling each other and plotting violence against each other as they had done for several years, the ANC and PAC, in Dar-es-Salaam at least, were co-operating.

The first beneficiaries of the scheme, enrolled in 1986, were some 250 students in four settlements in Tanzania. Once it was going well in Tanzania, we planned to extend it to another thousand or more refugees in Angola, Botswana, Zambia and Zimbabwe. In 1987, we enlarged the scope of the programme by buying 'O' and 'A' level courses from a British correspondence college and making these available to students who had requested them and whom we were satisfied could study on their own with occasional help from tutors.

We could see very clearly that, in addition to the distance education programme, there was need for a scholarship programme to help refugees who had successfully completed their secondary education, to take full-time degree and other higher education courses. If blacks were to play a major part in running a future South Africa, the need for well-qualified people would be tremendous. Unfortunately, we had neither a mandate to start such a scholarship programme nor the funds with which to run one. Through the Commonwealth Committee on Southern Africa, we succeeded in feeding a suggestion into the heads of government meeting in Nassau, Bahamas, in 1985. The meeting duly called on the Secretary-General to prepare plans for a programme of full-time scholarships for South African victims of apartheid.[27] Unexpectedly, the British Government gave an enthusiastic lead. Margaret Thatcher informed the Secretary-General that Britain proposed to increase significantly the number of South Africans studying in Britain. She was also ready to contribute handsomely to a Commonwealth scholarship fund, to be administered by the

Secretariat, provided other governments would also do so. I was to discuss the details with the Overseas Development Administration. 'No terrorists, Sonny, of course,' said Sir Crispin Tickell, Permanent Secretary of the ODA, as he explained the proposal to the Secretary-General and me. 'The PM wouldn't want terrorists to be given fellowships.'

'Better get over to ODA as soon as you can,' Ramphal told me. 'See what she means by terrorists.'

In Mrs Thatcher's book at that time, all members of the ANC and PAC were terrorists since both parties were committed to the armed struggle. Terry and I were able to point out to the officials in ODA that the programme we had in mind would be non-political, in a party sense. It would be modelled on the successful Zimbabwe programme where we had not been concerned with helping members of ZANU or ZAPU but in building up stocks of educated and trained manpower for the country. Similarly, with South Africa, we did not intend to ask applicants if they were members of ANC, PAC or any other party. Applications would be judged purely on educational grounds. Mrs Thatcher could be assured, therefore, that fellowships would be given to genuine students who would be prepared for positions of responsibility under whatever government might rule South Africa, and not to terrorists. And to make the point absolutely clear, we would be happy to give ODA advance information on all those to whom we intended to give fellowships. ODA could tell us if they had any objections. They could see that the Secretariat had nothing to hide. We heard no more about terrorists and ODA was happy to leave the selection of fellows to us.

The scheme which Terry and I devised, and which the Committee on Southern Africa endorsed, provided for two kinds of scholarships. There were to be Nassau Fellowships awarded by individual Commonwealth governments, using their own selection criteria and their own funds. There were also to be Commonwealth Nassau Fellowships, funded multilaterally and administered by the Secretariat through the Fellowships and Training Programme. When the Secretary-General appealed for funds and places, the response by governments was good. As news of the new scholarship programme spread, applications poured in from South Africans living in exile in many different countries. Selecting those who were to receive fellowships proved difficult. Colleagues in the Secretariat's Education Programme helped us make the final choice of the 100 fellows for the first year.

Attracted by the low costs of the programme, the UN Education and Training Programme for Southern Africa, based in New York, and a number of voluntary organizations offered to augment the funds we received from Commonwealth governments. I was glad that the programme had been successfully launched while I was still at the Secretariat and that its expansion seemed assured. Nothing succeeds like success; the rate of expansion exceeded all our expectations. In 1991, the Secretary-General could report to heads of government that over 250 fellowships had been awarded under the multilateral element of the scheme and that 600 more awards had been made under bilateral programmes. At the same time, he reported that some 3,000 refugees at settlements in six southern African countries were studying under the auspices of the South African Extension Unit.[28] About half were studying basic maths, English and agriculture to help them cope with the demands of life in exile and to prepare them for training in technical and vocational fields. The others were taking 'O' and 'A' level courses by correspondence in order to qualify for admission to polytechnics and universities. It was heartening to know that the Secretariat's efforts to provide practical help for some of the victims of apartheid were producing such good results.

Equally heartening was the endorsement by the 1991 heads of government meeting in Harare of a proposed programme of human resource development for a post-apartheid South Africa. This programme aims to prepare black South Africans to take senior posts in both central and local government and provides for training and work placements in top- and middle-level public administration, the professions, non-governmental organizations, trade unions and other key areas. The Commonwealth, through multilateral and bilateral arrangements, has a significant role in implementing this programme in partnership with the wider international community.[29]

The education programmes we devised were just a small part of the Commonwealth's involvement with South Africa. Politically, the Commonwealth led the international community in bringing

299

pressure to bear on Pretoria to abolish apartheid, to release Nelson Mandela and other political prisoners, to lift the ban on the African National Congress and other parties, and to start discussions on radical constitutional changes. These demands were at the centre of the Commonwealth Accord on Southern Africa, as it was called, which heads of government issued at their Nassau meeting in 1985. The process of political dialogue in South Africa was bound to be difficult. In order to help it forward, heads of goverment decided to ask a small group of eminent Commonwealth persons to visit South Africa and to do all they could to remove the obstacles to getting a dialogue going between the different parties. At the same time, the group would endeavour 'by all practicable means, to advance the fulfilment of the objectives of the Accord'.[30]

Thus was established what was known as the Eminent Persons Group, or EPG. Sonny Ramphal took immense pains over the composition of the EPG. For its views to command respect its members had to be truly eminent, had to come from different regions of the Commonwealth, had to represent a wide cross-section of opinion, and had to be willing to work as members of a team. As eventually constituted, the EPG was outstandingly successful. General Olusegun Obasanjo, who was a former head of the Federal Military Government of Nigeria, and Malcolm Fraser, a former Prime Minister of Australia, were co-chairmen. The other members were Lord Barber from Britain, Dame Nita Barrow of Barbados (subsequently Governor-General), John Macela of Tanzania, Swaran Singh of India and Archbishop Edward Scott of Canada. It was a formidable team, by any standards.

With the help of a small Secretariat team, led by Emeka Anyaoku, the EPG travelled extensively in South Africa and the neighbouring states, and consulted widely over a period of six months. They presented their report in June 1986.[31] They painted an informed and balanced picture of South Africa which commanded world wide attention. They began their report in arresting fashion: 'None of us was prepared for the full reality of apartheid. As a contrivance of social engineering, it is awesome in its cruelty. It is achieved and sustained only through force, creating human misery and deprivation and blighting the lives of millions.'

The EPG was satisfied that the black and other non-white groups were ready to negotiate with the Government without preconditions. They were very favourably impressed by the calibre of the black leaders, including Oliver Tambo and Nelson Mandela, whom they met. 'Their idealism, their genuine sense of non-racialism, and their readiness not only to forget but to forgive, compel admiration.' By contrast, Pretoria was intransigent. 'We have examined the Government's "programme of reform" and have been forced to conclude that at present there is no genuine intention on the part of the South African Government to dismantle apartheid.'[32] And again: 'The Government is in truth not yet prepared to negotiate fundamental change, nor to countenance the creation of genuinely democratic structures, nor to face the prospect of the end of white domination and white power in the foreseeable future.'[33]

Here was the stark truth for all the world to see. Because of the status of the EPG, and the moderate language it employed in assessing the situation, the group's report achieved high international credibility. Because it showed that no real change would take place in South Africa without an intensification of international pressure, the EPG report acted as a catalyst for global action and led to the imposition of further sanctions against the republic. In the Secretariat, we all took pleasure in the tributes that were paid to the members of the EPG who had approached their difficult task in a very fair-minded and professional way.

Since 1986, there have been a great many changes in South Africa. Pressures from within the country as well as international action, have broken the intransigence of the South African Goverment. The decision of the Government of State President de Klerk to abolish apartheid, to release Nelson Mandela and other detainees, and to embark on a programme of far-reaching reform was, of course, a policy revolution of tremendous significance. Commonwealth leaders believe that the long-overdue but nevertheless radical and irreversible changes made by the South African Goverment have fully vindicated the Commonwealth's role, sustained for more than 40 years, in leading international action and opinion in support of the struggle to end apartheid. 'Recent developments,' stated heads of government at Harare, 'brought into sight the goal of the eradication of apartheid and the establishment of a non-racial democracy in a united and non-fragmented South Africa.'[34]

But the final achievement of that goal is still a long way off and many obstacles have yet to be overcome before it is reached. Many white South Africans have genuine fears that they would lose everything if universal suffrage brought a black government to power. These fears are played upon by the right-wing parties, such as the Afrikaner Weerstandsbewegining, which include extremists who hold neo-Nazi views, and who have publicly announced their intention to defend white supremacy, by force if necessary. There are also deep divisions, often based on tribalism, among the blacks. The mutual suspicion and hatred is dramatically and sickeningly typified in the bloody rivalry between Nelson Mandela's African National Congress and Chief Mangosuthu Buthelezi's Inkatha Freedom Movement. In 1960 the world was shocked, and rightly so, when 69 PAC supporters were shot down by the police during a peaceful demonstration at Sharpeville against the pass laws. Thirty years later, when similar numbers are mindlessly slaughtered in yet another weekend of violent clashes between Inkatha and ANC supporters, the world shrugs off the news with weary indifference.

Against this background, it is hard to believe that the enormous problem of determining how political and economic power is to be shared between the different races can be resolved peacefully. Many observers doubt whether the whites will be willing, when the crunch comes, to surrender, or to share in any meaningful way, the power which they have enjoyed for so long, and whether the blacks will be ready to settle for anything less than a democratically elected government in a unitary, unpartitioned, South Africa.

For the pessimists, the stage seems to be set for a dramatic and bloody showdown which only a miracle can avert. It is precisely for that miracle that the Commonwealth must continue to work. South Africa's problems are going to be solved by the South African people themselves. No-one else can do it for them. But they can be helped along the road to agreement by the pressure of Commonwealth governments, sometimes encouraging, sometimes warning, always urging those principles of equal political rights, civil liberties, justice under the rule of law and non-racism which the Commonwealth endeavours consistently to uphold.

That the Commonwealth will continue to fight racism and strive to bring about a non-racial democracy in South Africa is not in doubt. Emeka Anyaoku, in his first report to heads of government as Secretary-General, made this very clear. 'Apartheid will not be truly dead and buried,' he wrote

> until a new political dispensation gives the majority popula-tion of South Africa full voting and constitutional rights. Everything must be done by all concerned . . . to ensure that progress to full negotiations of the future constitution of a democratic South Africa is not in any way imperilled. The Commonwealth remains unswerving in its support for early negotiations to end apartheid and install that new political order. It remains equally ready to render such appropriate assistance to facilitate negotiations as the parties may deem helpful.[35]

Politically, nothing is impossible. Friends of South Africa pray that the political power structure will be transformed peacefully, that patience, wisdom and determination may yet avert a catas-trophe, and that a free and united South Africa, in the not too distant future, will be welcomed back into the Commonwealth. Until that day, South Africa is 'unfinished business' for the Commonwealth.

Notes
1 For an account of the Commonwealth's role in promoting freedom and justice in Southern Africa, see Commonwealth Secretariat, *Racism in Southern Africa, the Commonwealth stand* (London: Common-wealth Secretariat, 1987).
2 Smith with Sanger, *Stitches*, p. 28.
3 *Ibid.*, p. 54
4 Smith with Sanger, *Stitches*, especially chapters 4 and 10.
5 Commonwealth Secretariat, *Report of the Commonwealth Secretary-General* (1981), (London: Commonwealth Secretariat, 1981), p. 33.
6 Commonwealth Secretariat, *Report of the Commonwealth Secretary-General* (1979), (London: Commonwealth Secretariat, 1979), p. 24.
7 *Ibid.*, p. 4.
8 Lord Carrington, *Reflect on things past* (London: Collins, 1988), p. 287.
9 Quoted in Smith with Sanger, *Stitches*, p. 236

10 *Report of the Commonwealth Secretary-General* (1981), p. 28.
11 In his autobiography, *Reflect on things past*, Lord Carrington refutes the charge that Lusaka marked a change in British policy.
12 Carrington, *Reflect*, p. 300.
13 *Report of the Commonwealth Secretary-General* (1981), p. 29.
14 Carrington, *Reflect*, p. 300.
15 *Report of the Commonwealth Secretary-General*, (1981), p. 29.
16 Stephen Chan wrote an entertaining and iconoclastic account of the election. See Stephen Chan, *The Commonwealth Observer Group in Zimbabwe* (Gweru, Zimbabwe: Mambo Press, 1985).
17 The other observers were: Keith Shann (Australia), former chairman of the Public Service Board, and Ambassador; Ivo de Souza (Jamaica), Ambassador and former permanent secretary of the Ministry of Foreign Affairs; Samuel Goomsu Ikoku (Nigeria), National Secretary of the People's Redemption Party, and university lecturer; Justice Sheku Kutubu (Sierra Leone), judge of the Court of Appeal; J. W. Subasinghe (Sri Lanka), attorney-at-law, chairman of presidential committees on the police and the armed services.
18 Commonwealth Secretariat, *Southern Rhodesia Elections, February 1980, Report of the Commonwealth Observer Group on elections leading to independent Zimbabwe* (London, Commonwealth Secretariat, 1980).
19 There is no doubt that General Walls was under great pressure from his fellow officers and disgruntled whites to seize power when the outcome of the elections became known. In a tense meeting with Sir Antony Duff and Robin Renwick at Combined Operations Headquarters on 2 March, Walls demanded that the election be declared null and void on the grounds that Mugabe had won only by intimidation. He was persuaded to back off and eventually agreed to collaborate with Mugabe in creating a single army out of the former Rhodesia Security Force and the guerrillas of ZANLA and ZIPRA. See Martin Meredith, *How Rhodesia almost stayed white* (London; *The Times*, 1 July 1985).
20 *Southern Rhodesia Elections*, COG Report, p. 65.
21 The Zimbabwe Government subsequently stated that there was a South African plot to destabilize the country just as it came into existence. On the day before independence, Claymore mines were found buried at the four corners of the VIP stand in the independence stadium. The mines, it was stated, were set to explode at the moment when the Prince of Wales was handing the instruments of state to President Canaan Banana in the presence of 50 visiting heads of state and of government, other VIPs, Prime Minister Mugabe and all his cabinet.
22 At the opening ceremony of the Commonwealth heads of government meeting in Melbourne, 1981, Robert Mugabe said: 'At Lusaka in 1979

you all resolutely put your heads together, initiating a decisive prelude which culminated in the Communiqué that led to the Lancaster House Conference, and there we produced an agreement. This led to the cease-fire, its monitoring and eventually the elections which brought us independence. This seeming miracle would not have been possible without the concerted support and sacrifices that Commonwealth Governments were willing to make.'

Quoted in Commonwealth Secretariat *Racism in Southern Africa*, p. 15

23 *Commonwealth Heads of Government Communiqué* (1975).
24 Commonwealth Secretariat, *Report of the Commonwealth Secretary-General* (1987), (London; Commonwealth Secretariat 1987) p. 15.
25 *Ibid.*, p. 16
26 *Commonwealth Heads of Government Communiqué* (1981).
27 *Commonwealth Heads of Government Communiqué* (1985).
28 Commonwealth Secretariat, *Report of the Commonwealth Secretary-General* (1991), (London: Commonwealth Secretariat, 1991), p. 28.
29 *Commonwealth Heads of Government Communiqué* (1991).
30 *Commonwealth Heads of Government Communiqué* (1985).
31 Commonwealth Secretariat, *Mission to South Africa, the Commonwealth Report* (London: a Penguin Special for the Commonwealth Secretariat, 1986).
32 *Ibid.*, p. 137.
33 *Ibid.*, pp. 132–3.
34 *Commonwealth Heads of Government Communiqué* (1991).
35 *Report of the Commonwealth Secretary-General* (1991), p. 8.

9

Postscript

The Commonwealth may be said to rest on six pillars. Remove any of them and the whole structure is seriously weakened.

The first pillar is a commitment by Commonwealth members to a number of fundamental principles. These were first set out formally in the Declaration of Commonwealth Principles agreed by heads of government at their meeting in Singapore in 1971.[1] They remain, in Emeka Anyaoku's words 'the heart of the Commonwealth's creed'.[2] Twenty years later, in Harare, a new generation of heads of government reaffirmed their continuing commitment to them:

- — we believe that international peace and order, global economic development and the rule of international law are essential to the security and prosperity of mankind;
- — we believe in the liberty of the individual under the law, in equal rights for all citizens regardless of gender, race, colour, creed or political belief, and in the individual's inalienable right to participate by means of free and democratic political processes in framing the society in which he or she lives;
- — we recognise racial prejudice and intolerance as a dangerous sickness and a threat to healthy development, and racial discrimination as an unmitigated evil;
- — we oppose all forms of racial oppression, and we are committed to the principles of human dignity and equality;
- — we recognise the importance and urgency of economic and

social development to satisfy the basic needs and aspirations of the vast majority of the peoples of the world, and seek the progressive removal of the wide disparities in living standards amongst our members.[3]

Other Declarations, for example at Lusaka (1979) on racial justice, at Melbourne (1981) on economic justice, Goa (1983) on international security, Nassau (1985) on world order, Vancouver (1987) on world trade, expanded certain aspects of these principles or sought to base practical action on them. The application of Commonwealth principles during the last two decades has resulted in a collective attitude towards political and economic issues which could be loosely described as liberal-progressive and slightly left of centre. There have developed recognizably Commonwealth positions on a growing number of issues – vehement opposition to apartheid and other manifestations of racism, advocacy of a more equitable international economic order, support for multilateralism, the United Nations and its organs, the enforcement of human rights, the observance of democratic processes.

Cynics may say, with some justification, that the practice of Commonwealth governments is often at variance with the principles they purport to uphold. In the same way, mankind has persistently fallen short of the requirements of the Ten Commandments. Like the tablets which Moses brought down from Mount Sinai, the Declaration of Commonwealth Principles, reaffirmed in the Harare Commonwealth Declaration, provides an ideal towards which all should strive and a yardstick against which all may be judged.

The Commonwealth stands or falls on the willingness of its member governments to support and to make use of it. If governments lost their confidence in the association, failed to pay their annual subventions, stayed away from heads of government and other meetings, the Commonwealth would simply wither and die. The association draws strength from the periodic renewals of commitment to the Commonwealth by member governments. This commitment constitutes the second pillar of the Commonwealth; it must never be taken for granted. Sentiment and habit undoubtedly play their part in sustaining Commonwealth loyalty, but these would not suffice to keep the association together if member countries did not perceive a practical value in supporting the Commonwealth, or found it had become irrelevant to their interests. At their meeting in Kuala Lumpur in 1989, heads of government set in train a 'high-level appraisal', as they termed it, of the Commonwealth's role in the 1990s. Ten presidents and prime ministers met to consider how best the Commonwealth should respond to the profound changes taking place on the international scene, to new needs and to emerging priorities. Their recommendations were endorsed by the full heads of government meeting in Harare in 1991. Areas of priority importance for co-operative action were identified in four major areas of political dialogue: sustainable development, environmental conservation, the promotion of good governance and of human resource development. In pursuit of the new goals they had set themselves, heads of government expressed their resolve to draw upon 'the unique strength and character of the Commonwealth which is rooted in its shared ideals, common traditions and language, in its membership which spans nearly one third of humanity and every corner of the globe, and in its ability to fashion a sense of common purpose out of diversity.'[4]

The continuing commitment of heads of government to the association was expressed in ringing terms in their Harare Commonwealth Declaration:

> In reaffirming the principles of the Commonwealth and in committing ourselves to pursue them in policy and in action in response to the challenges of the 1990s, in areas where we believe that the Commonwealth has a distinctive contribution to offer we, the Heads of Government, express our determination to renew and enhance the value and importance of the Commonwealth as an institution which can and should strengthen and enrich the lives not only of its own members and their peoples but also of the wider community of peoples of which they are part.[5]

The Queen is a pillar of great strength. She reigns in only a third of the countries which make up the Commonwealth but she is recognized by all as Head of the Commonwealth. She takes this role, which no-one has attempted to define at all closely, extremely seriously. The Commonwealth could not have a more conscientious and enthusiastic champion. She symbolizes the unity of the Commonwealth in a very personal and remarkable way. More than anyone else, she makes credible the notion that the Commonwealth is a family, its hands linked across the oceans and continents. To watch her resolutely performing her duties on yet another overseas visit, broadcasting to the Commonwealth on Christmas Day, attending the great Commonwealth Day Observance in Westminster Abbey, mingling with the guests at a reception at Marlborough House, or sitting serenely, surrounded by 40 and more presidents and prime ministers, when she entertains them on board HMS *Britannia*, is to catch something of the charm and charisma of this gracious lady.

The popular press would have one believe that it is the Queen who opens the two-yearly meetings of heads of government. This is quite wrong. It is the president or prime minister of the host country who opens the meeting. Her Majesty does not even enter the conference hall. She does, however, arrange to be present in the city where the meeting is taking place, and uses *Britannia* as her base if at all possible. In the first few days of the meeting, she receives the presidents and prime ministers one by one. Some she has known for more than a quarter of a century. None can match her in experience and length of service; she succeeded her father as long ago as 1952. She is extremely well-informed. From even the most hard-bitten president, she receives great respect and affection.[6]

The Commonwealth family is an association not only of governments but also of peoples. The multiplicity and strength of the links between the peoples of the Commonwealth constitute a fourth and often underrated pillar of the Commonwealth.

Some of the links are commercial. Some are academic, involving exchanges of staff and students between universities and other institutions of higher education and training. Links between the professions – fostered particularly by the Commonwealth Foundation – are strong in many fields. Sporting contacts are extensive and reach a high point every four years in the Commonwealth

Games. Cultural links are expanding; arts festivals are a regular feature of the Commonwealth scene; a distinctive Commonwealth literature has emerged.

Links between Commonwealth countries in the many fields of human endeavour in which they co-operate or compete are sometimes arranged at governmental level but, more usually, by non-governmental organizations and societies. These vary enormously in the type of activity in which they are involved, their geographical scope and their organizational structure. Most NGOs have a specialized focus – on education, health, the disabled, industry, international understanding, science, human rights, sport, youth and so on. Some have social functions; others provide information and act as pressure groups. Some are very actively involved in development and make available the expertise and experience of their members in assisting with the planning and implementation of projects in Commonwealth developing countries.

Together, the non-governmental organizations and societies make up an important part of the human face of the Commonwealth. Their value, as we saw in chapter 7, has been increasingly recognized, at least on paper, by the official Commonwealth. It was reaffirmed by Emeka Anyaoku in his 1991 report to heads of government:

> The activities of the NGOs strengthen and raise general awareness of the Commonwealth, both within and outside the association. It is also being widely recognised that NGOs can be effective in national socio-economic development efforts, particularly at the grassroots level. They can often achieve, even at minimal costs, what governments cannot, through their enlistment of popular participation in efforts to achieve sustainable economic development.[7]

The fifth pillar of the Commonwealth is its Secretary-General. He is elected to the post by heads of government for a period of five years. This may be renewed; Arnold Smith served two terms, Sonny Ramphal three. The Secretary-General has the right of access to the Queen, a right which Arnold Smith won, with the Queen's support, in the face of opposition from those in the British

Government who tried to insist that relations between the Head of the Commonwealth and its Secretary-General should be conducted through the Foreign and Commonwealth Office. The right of access is one which the Secretary-General uses sparingly. He also has the right of access to all Commonwealth heads of government. Whatever his personal opinion may be of their political philosophies, their policies, their methods of government, their record on human rights, or their personal lifestyle, he treats them all with great respect. Like St Paul, he must be all things to all men. Without their understanding and support, he can do little. Provided, however, he can win and retain their respect and confidence, they will allow him to set the pace on some issues. They will not allow him to take for granted their approval of any new course of action, especially if it involves expenditure. They, or their officials, will scrutinize with great care any proposal the Secretary-General may make which involves any increase in the Secretariat's budget.

The Secretary-General's job is not one for the faint-hearted. It is for one who thinks clearly and quickly, has a thorough grasp of international affairs, understands complex economic issues, has great personal charm, can write well and can speak with authority and conviction. A dynamic, innovative and persuasive Secretary-General is a *sine qua non* of the Commonwealth. Arnold Smith and Sonny Ramphal, each in his own way, met the requirements of the post with considerable distinction. For Chief Emeka Anyaoku of Nigeria, who succeeded as Secretary-General in mid-1990, theirs were hard acts to follow. Cautious, pragmatic and determined by nature, he is setting his own course. He has pledged himself to work towards a Commonwealth whose actions will foster its values. He was the driving force behind the high-level appraisal of the future of the Commonwealth. To achieve the new goals which have been set, he will build on the successful track record of Smith and Ramphal, changing tactics and adopting different strategies where necessary.[8]

Chief Anyaoku, I am sure, has the full support of his colleagues in the Commonwealth Secretariat. This is vitally important, for a strong and efficient Secretariat is essential to the Commonwealth's well-being. It is its sixth pillar. The Commonwealth has very few official institutions. Unlike the United Nations Organization, it has no General Assembly, no Security Council, no Economic and Social Council, no Trusteeship Council, no International Court of Justice and no Charter. Unlike the European Community, it has no equivalent to the European Parliament, the Council of Ministers, the European Commission and the European Court. By contrast, the Commonwealth is low-key, low-cost and loosely structured.

Because the Commonwealth has no legislature and no judiciary, it passes no laws, votes on no resolutions, issues no directives and makes no judicial rulings. Nevertheless, member governments of the Commonwealth find it useful to come together periodically at a variety of levels, to discuss matters of common concern, and to co-operate, on a purely voluntary basis, in certain subject areas. It was to facilitate such discussion and co-operation that the Commonwealth Secretariat was established and the Secretary-General was appointed. Over the years since 1965, the number of meetings, at both ministerial and official levels, has multiplied many times and the areas of co-operation have become more extensive, more specialized and more technical. Commonwealth leaders of the 1990s expect more of the Commonwealth than they did in the 1960s. They have not, however, established new bodies to handle the increased volume and variety of work; neither have they created elaborate and expensive bureaucracies to match those of New York or Brussels. Rather, in pragmatic manner, the Commonwealth Secretariat has progressively been given additional responsibilities. Each heads of government meeting has resulted in new mandates for the Secretary-General and the Secretariat. It is the Secretariat which gives the Commonwealth much of its momentum.

Thus it was that when I left the Secretariat in September 1987, soon after reaching my 60th birthday, the Secretariat, in terms of size, responsibilities and international status, was very different from the small organization I had joined in 1968. Then, the staff had numbered a bare hundred, and Arnold Smith was struggling, not always certainly, to carve out a credible role both for himself and for the infant Secretariat. By 1987 there were 400 members of staff, many of them very able and experienced, and the Secretariat could offer a high quality of service to member governments. It was acknowledged as an essential part of the Commonwealth fabric. Indeed, it was difficult to imagine the Commonwealth functioning coherently without its Secretariat. Through the machinery it provided for consultation and co-operation at numerous levels, the information and co-ordinating roles it performed in many sectors, and the work – usually unpublicized but nonetheless very valuable – of the Commonwealth Fund for Technical Co-operation, the Secretariat had reached the point of being indispensable to the Commonwealth.

Of course, the Secretariat had its tensions and animosities. Morale was sometimes low. A few appointments at diplomatic level, made in order to maintain a geographical balance or to repay a kindness, sometimes left us with colleagues who were not equal to the requirements of their posts. I believe, however, the Secretariat had a far lower percentage of misfits and time-servers than other international organizations. For efficiency, cost-effectiveness and the originality of much of its work, the Secretariat scored well.

There were, perhaps, three areas in which the Secretariat excelled (and doubtless still does). One was in bringing together experts from across the Commonwealth, getting them to discuss an issue and share their experiences for a few days, and then analysing and distilling their views and findings into a report and a series of recommendations. These were then distributed, as a service, to governments and to other relevant bodies. In this way, valuable work was done on important topics such as the problems of small states, industrial development, the rescheduling of foreign debts, food security, human rights and a number of environmental issues.

A second activity in which the Secretariat shone was the organization and servicing of conferences, seminars and workshops. Secretariat staff were good at providing the inputs necessary to ensure the successful outcome of meetings, whether a prestigious gathering of heads of government or a low-key workshop for ministry officials. These covered everything from the drawing up of the agenda, the writing of background papers, the briefing of the chairman, the feeding in of proposals for action, to the drafting of the final report, as well as all the logistical arrangements for the meeting. A conference skill which is particularly highly valued is the ability to find a form of words which will accommodate conflicting points of view. A meeting sometimes reached deadlock as advocates of differing opinions made known their seemingly irreconcilable positions. Ramphal, blessed with an extraordinarily rich command of English, was frequently able to produce a sentence acceptable to everyone. There were others who were nearly as adept at breaking through impasses of this kind. Their talents were particularly appreciated at heads of government meetings when a 20-page conference communiqué, covering many different and often controversial topics, had to be agreed by more than 40 presidents and prime ministers. When a roomful of heads of government and their most senior advisers are anxious to finalise a communiqué, but are divided over a critical paragraph, it takes a sharp mind and a cool head to find the verbal formulation which will resolve the crisis.

A third Secretariat strength was the Commonwealth Fund for Technical Co-operation. Although quite small by the standards of several other international programmes, it was tailored to the needs of the developing countries, it operated smoothly and efficiently and gave good value for money. It was a matter of pride that we responded positively and rapidly to requests from governments, that we kept formality to the minimum and that we produced results. Of those who were acquainted with its work, few would deny that the CFTC deserved its excellent reputation in international aid circles or that it was one of the Secretariat's biggest success stories.

I felt glad to have been part of a genuinely international team, multicultural and multidisciplinary, always competent, frequently imaginative, sometimes brilliant. After 19 years, it was hard to leave. Colleagues were kind and presented me with an electronic typewriter and a crystal decanter. Sonny Ramphal gave us a hand-coloured print showing a detachment of Life Guards passing down The Mall below his window in Marlborough House. Like Arnold Smith before him, he loved the view from his office windows and had a deep regard for London's pageantry.

On leaving the Secretariat, it was natural to reflect a little on the period covered by my working life, a period characterized by, among other things, the transition from empire to Commonwealth. In the 33 years which had elapsed since I first went to Northern Rhodesia as a young education officer, the Commonwealth had changed almost beyond recognition. From a nucleus of seven fully fledged members in 1954, (Australia, Britain, Canada, New Zea-

314

land, India, Pakistan and Sri Lanka), the Commonwealth now comprised 49 independent countries.[9] Seen from its headquarters in Marlborough House, the machinery of the Commonwealth and its major organs were in good shape. But what of the member states which had joined the association in that period, the countries which had taken the decisive step from dependency to independence? After two, three or even four decades of independence, how were the former colonies and protectorates faring? Had independence and self-determination brought the benefits that had been so confidently forecast by those who had worked to hasten the end of the colonial period?

The picture, of course, was very mixed, a confused jumble of pluses and minuses. India, for instance, the oldest and largest of the 'new' Commonwealth countries, had developed as a major industrial power. It had also succeeded in implementing a green revolution which meant that, except when the monsoon failed, India could virtually feed itself, a tremendous achievement considering that the population had almost trebled to 800 million since independence in 1947. But there were signs that national cohesion was breaking down: the underlying antagonism between the dominant Hindus and the large Moslem minority was periodically leading to bloody clashes; unrest was flaring up between the castes; the problem of Kashmir remained unresolved; Rajiv Gandhi had failed to find a solution to the rebellion in the Punjab which had led to his mother's assassination in 1984. No-one could foretell, of course, that Rajiv would suffer an equally horrific fate in 1991. But there were those who questioned whether India's democratic institutions and the rule of law could withstand the increasing level of violence.

As India endeavoured to maintain its cohesion, Sri Lanka was tearing itself apart in a bloody civil war. Sri Lankans had the reputation of being a gentle, peace-loving people. It was tragic to see both government troops and their Tamil separatist opponents descending to acts of unbelievable savagery and bestial atrocities as war destroyed many of the gains which had been painfully achieved since independence. Bangladesh, overcrowded, riddled by corruption, and regularly ravaged by cyclones and floods, remained one of the poorest nations in the world. Independence had brought wealth and privilege to a small élite but had done little to improve the lot of the teeming millions of urban slum-dwellers or of the rural masses. Two-thirds of the people were living below the WHO poverty line and a majority were not getting enough to eat.

In southeast Asia, there were at least two success stories. Singapore had established itself as a prosperous city-state and was riding high on the waves of advanced technology. Opponents of Lee Kwan Yew's Government received short shrift but perhaps that was a small price to pay for economic prosperity and political stability. Thanks largely to the entrepreneurial enterprise and technological skills of its Chinese and Indian peoples, Malaysia's GNP was rising steadily. Its Malay-dominated government had been successful in preventing overt clashes between the races.

Farther east, Papua New Guinea, which had been inadequately prepared for independence by Australia, was endeavouring to cope with the political problems of separatism, (particularly in Bougain-ville), the social problems associated with unemployed youth and excessive drinking, as well as the severe difficulties imposed by its geography. The mini-states of the Pacific had very few natural resources to develop but were making a living from tourism and from the sale of licences to Japan, the USA and USSR to fish and prospect in the exclusive economic zones which extended 200 miles from their shores. The largest, Fiji, had suffered a major setback in May 1987 when a military coup took place, aimed at ensuring that the reins of government would always be in the hands of the native Fijian population, even though the majority of the population were now of Indian origin. The coup and its aftermath shocked many of Fiji's friends and laid bare the racial animosity that existed just below the surface. We were reminded, if any reminder was necessary, that democracy and the parliamentary system of government are tender plants that have no depth of soil in many countries and can all too easily be uprooted. Because of Fiji's failure to adhere to accepted principles, her membership of the Commonwealth was sadly, but rightly, deemed to have lapsed.[10]

No less shocking had been events in 1983 in Grenada where Prime Minister Maurice Bishop had been overthrown and murdered by a left-wing group, allegedly supported by Cuba. I knew St George's, Grenada's beautiful capital, and was a friend of Sir Paul Scoon, the Governor-General. Grenada had seemed to be an idyllic, peaceful spot. It had been horrifying to read the graphic accounts in the media of the way in which a small group had brought bloodshed and terror to the island. Rightly or wrongly, the United States had taken it upon itself to mount a military operation which quickly toppled the rebels and restored order. Elsewhere in the Caribbean, inter-island rivalry remained strong among the peoples and governments. Events in Grenada had reminded them of their vulnerability; there was no way in which their security against aggression could be guaranteed. Their economies remained fragile; only tourism flourished, and that spasmodically. Without some form of economic integration, independence was scarcely a reality.

If the economic outlook in 1987 for Commonwealth countries in the Pacific and the Caribbean was unpromising, the future for Africa looked extremely bleak. A quarter of a century of independence had done little or nothing to raise the living standards of most citizens of that continent. Many, indeed, were worse off than they had been before independence. A few examples suffice to make the point. Colonial regimes had succeeded in putting a stop to inter-tribal fighting and had kept the peace with small numbers of lightly armed troops and police. Within a few years of their departure, bloody civil wars had broken out in several countries and were each year claiming the lives of tens of thousands of African people. Huge amounts of scarce hard currencies were being spent on the purchase of sophisticated and expensive weaponry. Before independence, there were virtually no refugees in Africa; in 1987 there were 5 million. In 1987 one could be thankful that there had been a great expansion of education facilities since independence; but the melancholy fact had to be faced that there were more illiterates in Africa in that year than there had been 20 years before and that 45 per cent of African children never gained access to formal education. In health, too, the position had worsened. Despite all the efforts which had been made to build more hospitals and clinics and to train more doctors, infant mortality in Africa, averaging 150 for every 1,000 live births, was the highest in the world; and many hospital drug stores were virtually empty.

It was sad to see the spread of corruption to countries which had previously been free from this menace. In Northern Rhodesia, whatever the faults of the colonial civil servants may have been, corruption was not among them. When President Kaunda opened Zambia's first Parliament in 1964, he spoke of three enemies which had to be combatted. These were poverty, ignorance and disease. Twenty years later, when I happened to attend the State Opening of Parliament, he spoke angrily of a fourth enemy – corruption. Corruption is insidious. It can affect government ministers who are in the position of awarding contracts or providing other favours. It can affect hospital orderlies who demand payments from patients before they will distribute drugs, and teachers who require some financial inducement to give good marks in examinations. Corruption is not, of course, confined to developing countries. It is found whereever there is dishonesty and greed. But it thrives particularly well in countries, of which there are unfortunately many in Africa, where there is widespread poverty, where salaries are low, and where accounting and auditing procedures are lax. The greed of those at the top who become corrupt often seems to be insatiable. Not content with making one illegal fortune, they seem driven to make further millions to stash away in secret bank accounts.

In many visits to Commonwealth countries in Africa in the 1980s, it was difficult to be optimistic about the future. Economies were stagnating. Shortages of foreign exchange were making it hard to buy the raw materials which industry required or to obtain spare parts for machinery which had broken down. Currencies were being frequently devalued. Galloping inflation was commonplace. Many everyday commodities – flour, sugar, oil, soap – were in short or irregular supply.[11] The media were firmly controlled by governments who regarded criticism as subversive. In some countries, such as Malawi and Kenya, freedom of expression had been eroded to the extent that it was a serious offence even to discuss who would succeed the present leader. Leaders who no longer had any useful contribution to make to the development of their countries were clinging to power. Each country had its political prisoners, many of whom languished in detention for years without trial. In many capitals, it was no longer safe to walk in the streets after dark. Crimes of violence had become part of the urban way of life. In Lusaka and elsewhere, many residents had surrounded their houses with high wire fences and employed armed guards to patrol their property. It is a sad, depressing litany.

Looking at their countries in 1987, many African freedom-fighters of the 1950s and 1960s must have found it hard to believe that this was what 'the struggle' had been about. What had gone wrong? Why had so many of the hopes and aspirations of those earlier years been dashed? Historians of the future will analyse these questions carefully. We can look only briefly at some of the reasons, economic, political and social, for Africa's malaise.

Economically, the developing countries, including Africa, had a poor deal from the rich, industrialized countries of the so-called North. As exporters of raw materials, countries in Africa were unable to set the price of their commodities. These were determined, and kept low, by the exchanges and other market mechanisms in London, Europe, North America and the Far East. It was often buyers for the big multinational companies who determined whether a farmer prospered or was forced to default on the repayment of a loan. Julius Nyerere, for many years President of Tanzania, a country endowed with few natural resources, was fond of pointing out that the terms of trade were constantly moving against the primary producers. In the 1960s, it took x tonnes of sisal, Tanzania's main export, to purchase a tractor from Britain, the USA or Japan. By the 1980s, the cost had risen to the equivalent of 4x tonnes. The South had no influence over the cost of goods bought from the North which were driven up by high salaries and other inflationary factors. In order to protect their industries and their agricultural interests from competition from the South, the richer countries set quotas for the quantities of goods which the developing countries could export to them. Clearly, this made it difficult for the developing countries to increase their earnings, to expand their industrial bases or to find markets overseas for their cash crops, textiles and other manufactured goods.

Many countries borrowed heavily in order to get the funds which were required for national development projects. The task of servicing these debts became an intolerable burden; a high percentage of foreign exchange earnings was taken up simply in paying the interest on loans received many years earlier. When it became apparent that there was little likelihood that the debts would ever be repaid, some lending countries agreed to cancel some of the debts, to reduce rates of interest and to reschedule payments of both interest and capital over a longer period. Colleagues in the Commonwealth Secretariat specialized in helping Commonwealth developing countries in their negotiations with their creditors in the North. Not unnaturally, their fingers having been badly burned, banks in the North were unwilling to make further investments in countries which could not meet the interest charges on earlier loans. When they sought assistance from the World Bank and the International Monetary Fund, governments were faced with demands for what were euphemistically termed 'structural adjustment measures'. The conditions set by the IMF were usually very difficult: devaluation of the currency (making exports more competitive but imports more expensive); the elimination or reduction of government subsidies on items such as flour, bread, sugar and oil (forcing up prices and creating the danger of food riots); reductions in the number of public servants (leading to higher unemployment); privatization of nationally run enterprises (a move likely to lead to higher prices in the short term) and reduced expenditure on education, health and other social services.

Many countries attempted to solve their economic difficulties by setting up a network of parastatal organizations to run the industrial sector of the economy. This, it was thought, would ensure that industry would be responsive to the needs of the country, that foreign exchange and other scarce resources would be allocated to maximum advantage and that profits would be utilized for the national good. But the managerial expertise to run these parastatal organizations was usually lacking. People with no industrial experience, little knowledge of financial management, and without entrepreneurial flair were put in charge of undertakings which they did not understand and which they were quite incapable of running successfully. The inevitable result, all too often, was that the industrial sector operated at a low level of efficiency, was stifled by bureaucratic controls, lost money and contributed little to the national economy; rather, many parastatals required regular subsidies from government in order to keep afloat.

A bad mistake made by many African governments was to neglect agriculture and to allow their rural areas to become run down. Governments preferred to give priority to schemes for industrial development, prestige projects, improved housing, water

320

supplies, roads, schools, hospitals and other amenities in the towns. Not surprisingly, the post-independence years witnessed a mass migration of people from the rural areas to the towns where, it was thought, often mistakenly, living conditions were better and employment opportunities were brighter. In several countries food production declined in the years following independence. Zambia, for instance, which had been self-supporting in maize before 1964, for several years found itself in the humiliating position of having to purchase hundreds of thousands of bags of maize from South Africa. In those countries, such as Tanzania, where the Government endeavoured to control planting, cultivation and harvesting, and fixed the prices paid to farmers for their produce, the dead hand of an inefficient bureaucracy took its toll. Timing is of the essence in crop production. Seeds must be available for planting when the rains begin; fertilizers and insecticides are required at precise times; sacks must be distributed before the harvest is due; transport must be available to take the full sacks to safe storage before the harvest is spoiled by the weather or by pests. All too often, cumbersome and inefficient bureaucracies contrived to ensure that something was missing or not ready at a critical stage in the growing process, resulting in smaller quantities of foodstuffs being harvested than there should have been. A further disincentive to farmers was the low prices they often received for their produce. Governments fixed prices as low as possible in order to keep down the cost of the food bought by urban consumers. It is small wonder that many farmers gave up and joined the drift from the rural areas to the shanty towns that grew up around all the main cities in Africa. Belatedly, some countries are now reversing the trend of earlier years and are giving an increased share of national resources to their rural areas. This is an overdue development which must be welcomed.

Politically, the African experience has fallen far short of the hopes of those who took part in the campaigns for independence. Then, whether it was in Lagos or Lusaka, Accra or Kampala, the demand was for 'Freedom'. And the cornerstone of that freedom was to be universal suffrage: 'one man, or woman, one vote'. Men campaigned for the vote, fought for it, went to prison for it; some even died for it. Thirty years on, the outstanding characteristic of the African political scene is disillusionment – disillusionment with the political system, disillusionment with the political leaders, disillusionment with the fruits of independence.

In some Commonwealth countries, of which Nigeria and Ghana are tragic examples, there has been little opportunity for the electorate to exercise their votes because military regimes have taken over the government of the countries from the politicians for varying periods. In several others, where military coups have been avoided, single party systems of government have been developed. Theoretically, a respectable case can be made for permitting only one party to operate in a country. The fostering of national unity is a priority need. It is difficult to encourage such unity if the electorate is divided into several parties which are based primarily on tribal loyalties, rather than on differences in political philosophy. In theory, the single-party system allows for freedom of discussion within the party and gives the voters in each constituency the opportunity to choose between several candidates, albeit all from the same single party. In practice, however, discussion is apt to be stifled in favour of the wishes of the leader and a small group of his henchmen; candidates for election have to be 'vetted' by the leadership before they are permitted to stand; the leadership becomes self-perpetuating; persistent opponents of the leadership are expelled from the party and are likely to find themselves detained without trial 'in the interests of national security'. The leader becomes increasingly dictatorial.

African countries have a tradition of strong leadership by tribal chiefs whose authority could not be challenged. The western model of parliamentary democracy is not one which flourishes naturally in African soil. There is a case to be made for benevolent dictatorships to cope with Africa's ills. The difficulty, of course, is that benevolent dictatorships nearly always degenerate into self-seeking tyrannies. 'Power corrupts; absolute power corrupts absolutely.' The developing countries, especially those in Africa, provide far too many examples of the truth of Lord Acton's dictum. Sometimes the dictator becomes a monster, such as an Amin, a Bokassa or a Mengistu. In other instances the leader clings to power, refusing to accept that the time has come to make way for new people with fresh ideas and more relevant policies.

Archbishop Desmond Tutu, urging a second liberation for Africa commented sadly in 1991, 'Africa is bleeding. The most awful truth is that there has often been far greater personal freedom in the much-maligned colonial days than now. All that has changed for the ordinary people is the complexion of the oppressor.'

Kenneth Kaunda of Zambia never became a dictator and he was too humane a man to oppress his people. But he certainly stayed in office for far too long. The verdict of future historians on him is likely to be: he led his country to political independence and then to economic ruin. His presidency, which began in such high hopes in 1964, ended in ignominy. For 20 years after independence, hardly a voice in Zambia was raised in serious opposition to Kaunda and to UNIP. The media led and encouraged the development of a personality cult around Kaunda. No-one dared to suggest in public that the deterioration of the economy – which was plain for all to see – was due to the misguided policies pursued by the President. No-one was brave enough to say that the President had feet of clay and should be replaced.

It was not until quite late in the 1980s, when economic collapse stared the country in the face and people could see no hope of improvement while Kaunda and UNIP remained in power, that a bold and articulate opposition emerged. Criticism was directed not so much against the President as against the Party and the one-party system. Among the critics who belatedly spoke up were those who had earlier been very close to Kaunda. One late convert to multi-party democracy was Humphrey Mulemba, former Secretary-General, no less, of UNIP, who claimed: 'I have always opposed the one-party state. It leads to inertia, corruption and lack of competition.'[13] His views were echoed by Vernon Mwaanga, former Foreign Minister in President Kaunda's Government: 'The problem with the one-party system is that it monopolizes the process of finding solutions. Our best brains have fled Africa for America or Britain. Because when they came up with honest opinions and realistic solutions, they were hounded out.'[14]

Kaunda portrayed Zambia as a participatory democracy which practised the philosophy of humanism. He genuinely believed that the one-party system ensured stability in the country; to permit other parties to operate would simply divide the people on tribal lines. When a country is prospering, food is plentiful, prices are stable and services are operating efficiently, people are not unduly concerned about who governs them. But when the economy has broken down, the people are hungry, the schools and hospitals are in a poor state and the future is bleak, in a one-party state the cry of 'Out, out, out' is raised not only against the government but also against the system which keeps the government in power. In 1991, in response to public pressure, Kaunda agreed to end the one-party system. He remained confident, however, that he and UNIP would triumph when the people went to the polls. The result of the elections held towards the end of 1991 was a shattering blow to him and to the Party. Frederick Chiluba, a trade union official, swept into power as the new president. Kenneth Kaunda, President for 27 years, was humiliated. The new Movement for Multi-party Democracy won a similarly overwhelming victory in the contest for seats in the National Assembly; UNIP was reduced to a parliamentary rump. It is to Zambia's great credit that the change from a single-party government to a multi-party democracy took place in orderly fashion after an election judged by international observers (including a Commonwealth group) to have been free and fair.

It would be wrong, of course, to assume that all Commonwealth electorates in one-party states would want to change their leaders if they had a fair chance of doing so. In the early 1980s, the economy of Tanzania, where Julius Nyerere had been President for 20 years, was in an appalling state. I told a Tanzanian colleague, 'In Britain anyone with a record like his would have been voted out of office years ago.'

'Ah,' he replied, 'we look at things differently. It was he who got us into this mess. Now it's up to him to get us out of it.'

If bad government has bedevilled the fortunes of many countries in Africa, rapid population growth has been another major constraint on their development. Population policy is, of course, a subject of extreme sensitivity. Few governments have had both the will and the courage to make sustained and whole-hearted efforts to persuade couples to have fewer children. Where they have been bold enough to launch family planning programmes, even to the extent of providing free contraceptives, the results have been generally disappointing.

Educated parents usually need no convincing that large families are expensive to feed, clothe and educate; they are happy to limit their families to two or three children. Among the poorer, less-educated majority, however, the desire to have large families remains strong. Children are needed to help with growing food, herding livestock and, later, to look after their parents in old age. Since it must be assumed that some children will die, it is thought prudent to keep on having children while the mother is capable of bearing them. Poor parents who wish to keep their families small frequently fail to do so, either out of ignorance or because they do not have access to reliable and cheap methods of contraception.

The statistics of Africa's population explosion are staggering. In 1900, there were about 100 million inhabitants in the tropical area of Africa (excluding the Mahgreb, Egypt and South Africa). Since then, the population has increased fivefold to 500 million, a rate of growth without parallel in the history of mankind. At the current rate of increase, black Africa's population will double again in a little over 20 years.

Food production in the continent cannot keep pace with the burgeoning population. There is scope to increase crop yields in some countries, and tremendous advantages could be obtained by reducing post-harvest losses due to pests and poor storage arrangements. But in other countries, yields are falling as the soil becomes exhausted. Because there are more mouths to be fed, land which used periodically to be left fallow has now to be cultivated every year. As a result, because no manure, green fertilizers or composts are added, soils have become depleted. To make good the shortfall, more and more marginal land is now being cultivated. Since such land is often arid, and therefore more fragile, cultivation has the effect of destroying the plant cover of areas which were previously used for grazing animals. In an attempt to survive, many farmers try to keep bigger herds. When the scant grazing is exhausted, the animals turn to edible shrubs, which soon die. At the same time, in their search for fuel for cooking, villagers have to go farther and farther looking for trees and shrubs. The end result is desertification. Each year, millions of acres of African land which were once used for growing crops or for grazing are lost to the desert.

Persistent drought in some countries, particularly Somalia, Ethiopa and Sudan, and more recently in southern Africa, has wiped out whole crops and has brought millions to the verge of starvation, and beyond. To make matters worse, civil wars, sometimes lasting for more than a decade, have forced millions to leave their homes and fields and to become refugees. They have no option but to become dependent on the goodwill of the international community for food and shelter. Their lives are in ruins; leaders of the factions fighting for political supremacy display a cynical indifference towards their sufferings. There are ominous signs that the affluent West is becoming weary of the warnings of humanitarian and relief organizations that 10, 20 or 30 million people are likely to die of starvation. There is a growing fear that we shall witness an apocalyptic disaster in Africa, when millions will perish from starvation while countries in Europe and North America debate how they should deal with their mountains of surplus food and lakes of wine. Already the bureaucrats have coined an expression to describe the growing indifference of the richer countries towards the plight of the poor and starving in the South: compassion fatigue. Eastern Europe and the Republics of the former USSR may be given priority in the allocation of relief and development assistance funds.

Even in countries where food security is assured, the galloping population growth poses serious problems. The resources available for education, for instance, simply cannot cope with the number of new primary, secondary and technical schools, and university places which the larger population demands. Health services, housing, water supplies, sewage disposal, transport services, not to mention recreational facilities, all almost certainly deteriorate as population pressures escalate. Water and sanitation are particularly serious problems. The goals set for the International Drinking Water Supply and Sanitation Decade (1981–90) were not achieved. Some 1.2 billion people, or 31 per cent of the population in developing countries, are still without access to safe, clean water, and 1.8 billion, or 43 per cent of the population, do not have access to adequate sanitary facilities. Faecal contamination of water supplies is a common prblem throughout all continents and contributes to the high disease and death rates of infants in large areas of Asia and Africa. The Executive Director of UNEP, in his report on the State of the World Environment, 1991, warned:

Environmental degradation and population growth, with consequent increase in demand for water, have contributed to a shortage of good quality fresh water. By the year 2000, many countries will have about half as much water per capita as they had in 1985 and yet will experience much greater demand for water for agricultural, industrial and domestic use.[15]

The case for drastically reducing population growth seems unanswerable. A terrible fatalism, however, seems to have Africa in its grip. Children are regarded by parents as gifts from God, which, of course, they are. But God has given couples intelligence and self-restraint as well as the means of procreation. Surely He expects men and women to use their intelligence and to limit the number of children they bring into a continent which is basically poor and which, it is clear, cannot cope with the doubling of its population every 25 years. 'It is the will of God,' says the Christian father as the eight, ninth or tenth child is born. 'Insh 'allah,' replies the Moslem mother who is asked if she will have any more children. While such attitudes prevail, while women lack the knowledge or means to prevent pregnancies, and while governments refuse to grasp the nettle, many countries, in Africa and elsewhere, are on course for a crisis which can only result in tragedy. Let one statistic, from a recent World Bank Development Report, drive home the seriousness of the situation. The current annual gap between Africa's appetite and its agricultural production is approximately 15 million tonnes of maize. If existing trends in fertility and farming continue unchanged, the gap will grow to 200 million tonnes by the year 2020. This is roughly equivalent to the whole of America's annual cereal harvest.[16]

Beset by severe economic difficulties, an apathetic but increasingly hostile political climate, and trying to cope with a population explosion which was out of control, the developing countries in 1987 seemed to face a grim future. Of course, not all was gloom and doom. Of course there were successful development programmes; of course the living standards of many people had been raised and some had become very prosperous; of course opportunities were open then that had been denied in the past. Of course there were more roads, more schools, more hospitals, more libraries, better housing and communications. Of course, too, there were political leaders who were good, honest men and women, who were genuinely concerned for the welfare of their people. But when due allowance had been made for these achievements, and due credit given to those responsible for them, the fact remained that the quality of life for the majority of Commonwealth citizens was poor. For many, the very expression, 'quality of life', had no meaning. Survival was all that mattered.

To make matters worse, hard-pressed governments throughout the Commonwealth were – and still are – having to contend with a range of problems which did not exist, or which certainly had not been recognized, in pre-independence days. One such problem was the spread of Acquired Immunity Deficiency Syndrome (AIDS). Accurate statistics are not available but there is no doubt that large numbers of people in some countries are HIV positive. Unless medical research can quickly produce a cure for AIDS, or unless people are prepared to change their sexual practices, millions of people, particularly in Africa, are doomed to die from the AIDS virus. No less ominously, drugs and pesticides used to combat mosquitoes and the malaria parasites they transmit are proving increasingly ineffective against resistant strains. As a result, the incidence of malaria, in new and highly lethal forms, is growing rapidly.

The international traffic in drugs is another scourge with which developing countries, as well as the more industrialized countries, have to contend. For some, terrorism, practised by political and religious extremists, poses serious security problems.

Then there is the problem of rapidly changing technologies. Between bewildering varieties of technology, difficult choices have to be made, often without the benefit of expert and impartial advice. Even the growth of tourism brings its own difficulties. While the dollars, pounds, marks and yen of the tourists are welcome, the effects of tourism on the local culture and lifestyle can be devastating.

Soil and land degradation has reached crisis point in many countries. Worldwide, some 20 million hectares of land lose their productivity capacity every year. There is no lack of technical solutions to halt soil and land degradation. The benefits of soil and water conservation, reforestation, carefully planned irrigation, and integrated pest control outweigh their cost many times over. But the political will and the financial resources to tackle the urgent issue of land degradation are often lacking. Similarly, the means of protecting the marine environment from pollution and over-fishing, and of coastal areas against erosion, are well-known. But governments must co-operate and take action if the programmes developed by the UN Environment Programme to deal with these and other environmental issues are to have any chance of success. Moreover, the international community will have to help the developing countries to meet their share of the costs and provide the necessary technological transfer.

A further cluster of environment-related problems, many caused by the bad practices of the industrialized nations of the North, demands the attention of all governments. The release into the atmosphere of billions of tons of carbon dioxide and other so-called greenhouse gases, mainly caused by the burning of fossil fuels, is leading to global warming and climatic changes in the next century which are likely to have catastrophic effects. Unless the warming of the globe can be checked, it is well within the bounds of possibility that the icecaps will begin to melt, the levels of the seas will rise and large areas of land will be inundated. Tens, perhaps hundreds, of millions of people will become environmental refugees.

The depletion of the ozone layer, which protects planet Earth from the harmful rays of the sun, is another source of danger for the entire globe. The chlorine concentration in the atmosphere, derived mostly from the use of chlorofluorocarbons and other industrial chemicals, is already sufficient to open a hole in the ozone layer over the Antarctic each spring. A third danger concerns biological diversity. Experts tell us that 25 per cent of the world's plant and animal species, of which the highest concentrations are found in the forests, savannah and drylands of the tropical areas of the developing countries, are at risk of extinction during the next 20–30 years. The implications for agriculture, medicine and industry are extremely serious. As air and water are polluted, forests are cleared, wetlands are drained, dams and roads are built, so habitats are transformed and are effectively lost for certain species. The rate of extinction of species is currently estimated at between 15,000 and 50,000 annually.[17] In this context, tropical forests are particularly important. They provide the habitat for many thousands of species. Half the world's tropical rain forests have already been felled in order to provide timber for export and land for agriculture. The current rate of deforestation is estimated at 170,000 square kilometres a year. If developing countries are to stop felling their rain forests, as the North is demanding, they require massive compensation for forgoing the right to develop their natural resources and for programmes of reforestation.

These issues were among those discussed at the UN Conference on the Environment and Development held in Brazil in June 1992. Leaders of 180 countries gathered in Rio de Janeiro to consider the future of the planet and to attempt to reach agreement on ways of promoting sustainable development which are compatible with the conservation of the environment. The immediate outcomes of the conference, measured in terms of the commitments accepted by governments to reduce the emission of greenhouse gases, to protect biodiversity, and to halt the destruction of tropical forests, were very disappointing. It seemed that the world's leaders, at this greatest ever gathering of presidents and prime ministers, lacked both the vision and the political will to take the steps – unpopular though they would be with many of their constituents – that are necessary if further irreversible damage to the planet is to be avoided.

Nevertheless, the long-term effects of the Earth Summit, as it was called, are almost certain to be positive. The conference left the world much better informed on the measures which must be adopted, by both the prosperous North and the poverty-ridden South, to achieve sustainable development. It enshrined the principle that, in meeting today's needs, nations should not so degrade the environment and squander natural resources as to compromise the ability of future generations to meet their needs.

Commonwealth countries played an important part in the preparations for the Earth Summit in Rio and in the deliberations of the conference. This was consistent with the mounting concern over the environment which has emerged as the central focus of recent heads of government meetings. The Commonwealth's geographical and ecological diversity, together with its experience of dealing co-operatively with developmental problems, equips the Commonwealth to make a distinctive contribution towards the preservation of the environment. An example of what the Commonwealth can do in a low-cost, practical way to tackle deep-seated environmental issues is to be found in the Iwokrama Rain Forest Programme. In 1989, President Hoyte of Guyana offered nearly 1 million acres of his country's tropical rain forest for use in a Commonwealth–Guyana Programme for Sustainable Tropical Forestry. Part of this huge area will be used to demonstrate sustainable forestry, agricultural and mining practices. The remainder will be zoned as wilderness for observation of the flora, fauna, water, soils and biological interactions in the pristine forests. Foresters and scientists from several Commonwealth countries are co-operating with Guyanese colleagues in planning and executing the project. Amerindians living in the area will be involved at all stages; their traditional hunting and modern intellectual property rights will be specifically respected. As an important adjunct to the project, an International Centre for Research and Training in the Sustainable Management of Rainforests is being established on the University of Guyana campus at Georgetown.

The Commonwealth cannot generate the large sums of money which the world's environment problems require. But it can provide, after the disappointment of the Earth Summit, a continuing forum for informed discussion of environmental issues and of inter-governmental co-operation in tackling these issues. It can initiate model programmes, such as the Rain Forest Programme in Guyana and can develop and demonstrate best practices from which others may learn. It can continue to bring together groups of experts to consider specific problems and to make their reports available to the wider international community. The Rio Conference was the start of a process rather than its culmination. It put sustainable development on the world's political agenda. The Commonwealth is one of the organizations which can help keep it there and give it urgency.

It would hardly be surprising if Commonwealth developing countries felt overwhelmed by the number, complexity and seriousness of the difficulties confronting them. Are there any grounds for optimism? Can we distinguish some hopeful signs for the future?

Some commentators would have us believe that there is little likelihood of significant material improvement in the lot of the peoples of the developing countries of the Commonwealth, or of the Third World generally, in the foreseeable future. There are those who envisage a lengthy period of economic stagnation, the marginalization of the developing countries by the North, political instability, increasing social unrest and a slide into violence. These dangers certainly exist but I prefer to take a more optimistic view. The Cold War has ended and this must have important repercussions. As heads of government noted at Harare, it has provided

> new opportunities and greatly improved prospects for inter-national peace, security and economic development. The end of ideological confrontation has made possible more effective international co-operation in addressing the many problems, old and new, facing humanity. Foremost among these are poverty, hunger, disease and environmental degradation.

Heads of government also stated that they were 'particularly encouraged by the resurgence of democratic ideals throughout the world'. There are clear signs that a new wind of change is blowing through the world. It began in Eastern Europe where, following the fall of the Berlin Wall in the autumn of 1989, authoritarian communist regimes collapsed like a pack of cards. It reached the Third World where it is no less challenging to Third World rulers than was Harold Macmillan's speech to his white colonial audience in 1960. In Africa and elsewhere, people are again demanding freedom. This time they want freedom from inefficient, often oppressive, often corrupt regimes which replaced the colonial governments. The demand for multi-party, free and fair elections is gathering strength and is likely to become overwhelming, as it did in Zambia. It gains impetus from the insistence of Western aid donors that the provision of new aid programmes is conditional on progress being made on both political freedom and human rights issues. Some of those who proclaim the virtues of multi-party democracy are opportunists and tribalists. No-one is so naive as to suppose that the emergence of democratically elected governments will resolve all the problems of the developing countries. Indeed, there are countries with seemingly insurmountable problems which have maintained impeccable democratic credentials. The lesson is that exhortation towards democracy must be accompanied by generous assistance in addressing the problems of under-development. Unless democratization leads to some improvement in the lot of the masses, disillusionment with the democratic process will quickly set in and the way will be clear for the return of authoritarian regimes.

Another refreshing and welcome product of the wind of change is the voice of self-criticism which is increasingly making itself heard. Ever since independence, it has been the practice to attribute many of the ills of the developing countries to the allegedly selfish or foolish policies of the former colonial regimes. If the education system produed too many white-collar workers, the colonialists were blamed. If people flocked from the villages to the towns, it must be because the pre-independence governments neglected the rural areas. Now, realism and honesty are starting to take over as it is acknowledged that post-independence governments have had ample opportunity to replace any of the colonial policies which they inherited and did not like. Ten years ago it would have been heretical for an African journalist publicly to question the anti-colonial rhetoric of his political masters. It was refreshing to find Wahome Mutahi writing bravely in Kenya's *Daily Nation* in 1990 of the 'monster of African leadership'.

> That leadership blamed colonialism for all the ills afflicting African countries. Leaders led their citizens in the song of saying that we would have been materially and morally better off had the colonialists not invaded the continent. So long as there was someone else to blame, all was all right. The result is the present Africa where malnutrition, sectarian violence, plunder, environmental rape, poor health facilities and illiteracy abound.[18]

As the press becomes more free, the wind of change will gather strength.

There are some grounds for optimism, too, in the gradual return of confidence in multilateralism as the most effective means of dealing with major world issues. It was concerted international action, orchestrated by the World Health Organization, that rid the world of smallpox. It was pressure from the international community, exerted through the United Nations and the Common-wealth, that induced the Government of South Africa to renounce apartheid. It was the machinery of the United Nations that was used to respond to Iraq's invasion of Kuwait in August 1990, first by imposing sanctions and then by authorizing the use of force to drive out the invaders. Efforts to work through multilateral organizations and mechanisms in order to reconcile conflicting interests and philosophies deserve full support.

We began with David Livingstone, missionary, explorer and physician. As he journeyed, Livingstone was often moved to pity and anger by the suffering and misery he observed. This resulted partly from the slave trade and partly from the people's poverty, ignorance and disease. Were Livingstone to revisit central Africa today, he would surely be amazed at the evidence of economic and social development that has taken place since his time – the roads, bridges, dams and railways, the schools, libraries, universities and hospitals, the mines and factories, the farms and ranches, the shopping complexes and the recreational facilities. He would also rejoice to find that Christianity was widespread and that the indigenous churches were well-established.

But Livingstone would be shocked to learn of the deplorable economic and social conditions of large numbers of the population, not just in central Africa but in other developing countries, too, in Africa, Asia, South America, the Middle East. He would find that millions are victims of a new form of slavery; their chains are those of crippling poverty and almost unimaginable wretchedness. In the mid-nineteenth century, it was Livingston who shocked the British public and the Western world with his first-hand accounts of the tragic circumstances in which many people in Africa eked out a precarious and miserable existence. The response then, springing from the human heart as well as from political and commercial considerations, was immediate and substantial.

Today, we do not need another Livingstone to alert us to the needs of the developing world. The evidence is constantly before us in our newspapers and on our television screens. Our methods of responding are different from those of Livingstone's day. We have learned to be less paternalistic, less arrogant. We have developed the concepts of partnership and co-operation, of working together with peoples of developing countries, of sharing our skills and experience in order to achieve mutually agreed objectives. Although our response is different, it is, and will continue to be, I am sure, no less generous than that of Livingstone's generation.

In the final analysis, my hope for the future lies in the faith I have in the resilience of the human spirit. 'In the face of great adversity,' said Martin Luther King, 'faith can hew out of a mountain of despair a stone of hope.' Divine Providence has so arranged matters that the human spirit flourishes when it is most sorely troubled; it is seen to greatest advantage when it is threatened with extinction. When a quarter of a million Bangladeshis die in a devastating cyclone, it is the resilient human spirit that leads the survivors, when they have buried those of their dead who can be found, to rebuild their houses, to clear their fields and to plant another crop.

When the point is reached that a populace will no longer put up with the lies, the brutality, the privileges, the hypocrisy and the sheer incompetence of their rulers, an unarmed crowd will storm a presidential palace, drive out the leader and will insist that free elections are held to choose a government which will be accountable to them.

When initiative is stifled by a bumbling and corrupt bureaucracy, the inventiveness and perseverance of the human spirit will break through and will succeed in setting up new business enterprises responsive to market forces.

When the rains fail and the millet and maize wither in the soil that has turned to dust, it is the indomitable human spirit that endures the long trek to the relief camp, the indignity of having to queue for food, the anguish of watching loved ones reduced to skin and bones, and then finds the strength to return to the family lands, to try again.

For as long as the human spirit remains undaunted, we can be sure, with the Psalmist, that 'when the righteous call, the Lord listens and rescues them from all their troubles. He raises the poor from the dust and lifts the needy from their misery.' Believers of all faiths can join in praying that these promises will quickly be fulfilled. They ask that governments of all persuasions, international bodies, aid agencies, non-governmental organisations, business corporations, men and women of good will everywhere, will work together to make that prayer a reality.

Notes

1 Commonwealth Secretariat, *Declaration of Commonwealth principles* (London: Commonwealth Secretariat, 1971).
2 Address given at the Commonwealth Trust, *Fulfilling the promise of Commonwealth declarations* (London, 5 September 1991).
3 *Commonwealth Heads of Government Communiqué* (1991).
4 *Ibid.*
5 *Ibid.*
6 The Queen's support of the Secretary-General and the Secretariat, and her role as Head of the Commonwealth are well described in Smith with Sanger, *Stitches*, pp. 266–76.
7 *Report of the Commonwealth Secretary-General* (1991), p. 6.
8 *Ibid.*, pp. 1–2.
9 South Africa was also a member in 1954, of course, but withdrew under pressure in 1961. Pakistan withdrew in 1972 and rejoined in 1989. Namibia became the 50th member in 1990.
10 *Commonwealth Heads of Government Communiqué* (1987), p. 11.
11 World Bank, *Sub-Saharan Africa: from crisis to sustainable growth* (Washington, D.C.: World Bank, 1989).
12 Message to conference on African development, London, quoted in *The Independent* (8 July 1991).
13 *Times of Zambia* (3 September 1990), quoted in *News from Zambia*, no. 554 (September 1990).
14 Quoted in Andrew Rawnsley, *The new wind of change* (London: Guardian Weekly, 23 September 1990).
15 UNEP, *State of the world environment, 1991* (Nairobi: UNEP, 1991).
16 World Bank, *Development Report, 1990* (Washington, D.C: World Bank, 1990).
17 UNEP, *State of the world.*
18 Quoted in Rawnsley, *The new wind.*
19 Psalm 34, verse 17; Psalm 113, verse 7 (*Good News Bible*, London: Collins/Fontana, 1976).

Index

Index

Chilangwa, Wilfred 167
Chinsali administrative district and *boma* 67, 89–138 *passim*, 152–8
Chinyanja, language (also known as Chichewa) 55, 57, 77, 87
Chirau, Chief 260, 264
Chitambo village 67
Chitimukulu, Paramount Chief 94, 106, 112, 115
Chiwale school 83
Chorlton, Alan 174–5, 176–7
Christian Fellowship 224–5
Church of Scotland 64, 66–8, 71, 96–8, 100
Churchill, John, Duke of Marlborough 191–2
Clark, George Kitson 34, 37–8
Coillard, François 63
Colonial Office 5, 17–8, 50–1, 120–2
Colour discrimination *see* apartheid; racism
Commonwealth, the 188–335 *passim*, especially 193–6, 204, 216, 234–7, 251–3, 258, 264, 302–3, 306–12
Commonwealth Agricultural Bureaux 248
Commonwealth Committee on Southern Africa 254–5, 265, 266, 297, 298
Commonwealth Education Conferences 198–202
Commonwealth Education Liaison Committee 198
Commonwealth Foundation 234, 237
Commonwealth Fund for Technical Co-operation 204, 214–5, 220, 221, 245, 292, 314
  Commonwealth Industrial Training and Experience Programme 226–7
  Education and Training Programme 205–9, 210–15, 218, 220–7, 235, 244
  Export Market Development Programme 214
  Fellowships and Training Programme 244–9
  General Technical Assistance Programme 214, 221
  Industrial Development Unit 227
Commonwealth Monitoring Force 273–4
Commonwealth Nassau Fellowships 298–9
Commonwealth Observer Group, 1980 266–86
Commonwealth Parliamentary Association 227–8
Commonwealth Scholarship and Fellowship Programme 198, 207
Commonwealth Secretariat 188–209 *passim*, 217, 222, 229, 235, 244, 267, 287, 295, 300, 311–4
  Economic Affairs Division 227
  Education Division/Programme 197–9, 244, 255, 299
  Human Resource Development Group 244–6
  Management Development Programme 245
  Medical Programme 245
  Women and Development Programme 245

Commonwealth Youth Programme 245
Commonwealth Secretary-General 196–7, 310–11; *see also* Smith, Arnold; Ramphal, Shridath; Anyaoku, Emeka
Commonwealth Telecommunications Bureau 248
Commonwealth Volunteer Service 227–30
Commonwealth Zimbabwe Scholarship Programme 255–9, 287–8
Coombs, Philip 177
Correspondence education for refugees 258, 297
Corruption 317–8
Costa, Carole 272
Cottrell, John A. 16, 20, 87–8, 93–4, 103–4
Crabbe, Judge 272
Craft, Hugh 275
Cumber, John 269, 281
Cyprus Forestry College 220

Dayal, Rajeswar 272, 275, 277, 280, 281, 283, 286
Declaration of Commonwealth Principles 306–7
de Klerk, F. W. 301
Desegregation of Schools 89–91, 137, 142–8
de Souza, Ivo 304
Dickson, Alec 228
Distance education 292–3, 295–7
Dodds, Tony 292, 296
Dormer, Terry 256, 288, 293, 298
Duff, Sir Antony 268, 304
Dunne, Peter 268
Dutch Reformed Church Mission 59, 64–5, 72

Earth Summit 330–1
Education, European, in Northern Rhodesia 140–1
Education of girls 101–3
Education, primary 15–16, 59, 70–1, 79, 83, 100–3, 118–9, 140, 148–9, 167, 171, 176; *see also* Desegregation of Schools
Education, secondary 15–20, 59, 119, 129, 144, 171–7; *see also* Desegregation of Schools
Elections in Rhodesia 266–86
Eminent Persons Group 299–301
Environmental issues 328–31

Fairweather, Gordon 272, 283
Faletau, In'oke 237
Farwell, Philip 68–9, 73–4, 87, 273
Federation of Rhodesia and Nyasaland *see* Central African Federation
Fidelia, Sister 99
Fielder, the Rev Hugh 168
Fiji 316
Fisher, Dr Charles 46
Fisher, Dr Monica 46, 145–6

338

Index

Index

Lundazi administrative district and *boma* 54, 60–2, 66, 67–9, 94, 113, 157–9
Lundu, Chief 79–80, 159
Lusaka Accord 264–6
Macdonald, Ian 273
Machel, Samora 265
Macleod, Iain 122–6, 131
Macmillan, Harold 119–20, 332
Macpherson, the Rev Fergus 111–2, 114
Macpherson, John 275
Mahendra, Sabanayagam 213
Makasa, Robert 105
Makerere University, Uganda 207, 247
Malaria 328
Malaysia 316
Malhoutra, Moni 245–6, 272, 273, 275, 277, 281
Malvern, Lord 104
Mananga Agricultural Management Centre, Swaziland 220
Mandela, Nelson 301
Manley, Michael 264
Maraj, James 218–9
Marlborough House 188–93, 213, 244, 254, 267, 309
Matsie, Wesley 4
Maudling, Reginald 130
Mau Mau emergency 3, 126
Mayne, Arthur 30–1, 33, 34
McKenzie, the Rev William 127
McLaren, Robert 245–6
McMinn, the Rev R. D. 97–8
Menzies, Bob 274
Micallef, Dr 228–9
Miles, Muriel 167
Milne, Garry 213
Missionary Societies 59–60, 62–8, 180–1; *see also under individual societies*
Mitchison, Robin 270–1
Mittelholzer, Anne 268
Mobile Unit, Northern Rhodesia Police 116–7, 130, 154–5
Moffat, Robert 6
Monckton Commission 119, 122, 123–4
Moore, Barbara 167
Morgan, Steve 273
Mousley, John 281–2
Mpuku, Yonam 100, 167
Mpyanakunda village 75–7
Msuzi school 87
Mthoko, November 292
Mtoko District, Rhodesia 271–2, 283
Mudenda, Elijah, 181
Mudford, Father Cyril 66
Mufulira town 141, 146–7, 164
Mugabe, Robert 237, 258, 259, 260, 264–7, 270, 275, 279, 283–6, 304–5
Mukupa, Dason 100, 103

Mulaisho , Dominic 135
Mulanga mission station and school 99, 100
Mulemba, Humphrey 323
Mulenga, Petros (husband of Alice Lenshina) 111, 115
Mulikita, Fwanyanga 168, 182
Mulilo school 69, 71, 84
Mulumika village 80
Mumba, Michael 124
Munali Secondary School 1–4, 16, 20–4, 52, 70, 98, 101
Mundia, Nalumino 92–3, 137
Mushindo, the Rev Paul 127
Musumbulwa, Gabriel 109, 119
Musunsu school 119
Mutambara, Moreblessing 257–8
Mutemba, Andrew 164
Muyombe school 101
Muzorewa, Bishop Abel 260–4, 267, 274, 283, 285
Mwaanga, Vernon 323
Mwakana village 78–9
Mwalule village 94–5
Mwanakatwe, John 4, 131, 137, 143, 150, 164, 166, 174–5, 177–81
Mwase-Lundazi, Senior Chief 72–3
Mwemba, Joseph 4, 169
Mwenso village 81
Mwenzo mission station and school 67, 98, 101, 124
Mwila, Unia 136

Nagarajan, Raj 227
Namibia 288–95
Namibian Extension Unit 292–5
Namibian refugees 289–95
Nassau Fellowships 298–9
National anthem, Zambian 179–80
National flag, Zambian 161, 179–80
Native Authorities 60, 72, 79, 110, 115–6, 128–9, 152–3
Ndlovu, Laban 68, 72–85
Ndola town and provincial headquarters 137, 140–1, 161, 168
Nelson, John 98
Nganjo village 81
Ngebe, Edward Cresta 23–4
Nicholas, John (author's grandfather) 28
Nkolemfumu school 131–2, 284
Nkomo, Joshua 259–62, 264–6, 269, 275, 283, 285, 286
Nkrumah, Kwame 3, 188
Nkula, Senior Chief 95, 110, 115–6
Nkumbula, Harry 104–6, 119, 122, 133, 147, 153
Non-governmental organizations 234–7, 310
North, Mike 273
Nujoma, Sam 289, 292, 295

340

Index

Index